WAR AND GENOCIDE IN SOUTH SUDAN

WAR AND GENOCIDE IN SOUTH SUDAN

Clémence Pinaud

CORNELL UNIVERSITY PRESS   ITHACA AND LONDON

This work was partially funded by the Office of the Vice Provost of Research and the IU Libraries.

Publication of this open monograph was the result of Indiana University's participation in TOME (Toward an Open Monograph Ecosystem), a collaboration of the Association of American Universities, the Association of University Presses, and the Association of Research Libraries. TOME aims to expand the reach of long-form humanities and social science scholarship including digital scholarship. Additionally, the program looks to ensure the sustainability of university press monograph publishing by supporting the highest-quality scholarship and promoting a new ecology of scholarly publishing in which the authors' institutions bear the publication costs.

Funding from Indiana University made it possible to open this publication to the world.

First published 2021 by Cornell University Press

Library of Congress Cataloging-in-Publication Data

Names: Pinaud, Clémence, 1985– author.
Title: War and genocide in South Sudan / Clémence Pinaud.
Description: Ithaca [New York] : Cornell University Press, 2021. | Includes bibliographical references and index.
Identifiers: LCCN 2020012518 (print) | LCCN 2020012519 (ebook) | ISBN 9781501753008 (paperback) | ISBN 9781501753022 (pdf) | ISBN 9781501753015 (epub)
Subjects: LCSH: Sudan People's Liberation Army. | Genocide—South Sudan—History—21st century. | Civil war—South Sudan. | Ethnic conflict—South Sudan. | Civilians—Violence against—South Sudan. | Minorities—Abuse of—South Sudan. | Political violence—South Sudan. | South Sudan—Politics and government—2005–2011. | South Sudan—Politics and government—2011– | Sudan—History—Civil War, 1983–2005.
Classification: LCC DT159.9295 .P56 2021 (print) | LCC DT159.9295 (ebook) | DDC 962.9/04—dc23
LC record available at https://lccn.loc.gov/2020012518
LC ebook record available at https://lccn.loc.gov/2020012519

Contents

Acknowledgments

I am indebted to the many South Sudanese who shared with me very personal and difficult stories. I hope I did them justice. My South Sudanese friends encouraged me throughout. They shall remain nameless for their safety. I owe another debt to my international friends who supported my work in multiple ways, from South Sudan, Kenya, Uganda, and Ethiopia to the U.S., Switzerland, the Netherlands, and France. Most of them shall also remain nameless for their safety.

I wish to thank Roger Haydon, my editor, for supporting this project, trusting me, and offering sharp, invaluable feedback from the start. I also am very grateful to the anonymous reviewers and to William Reno and Geoffrey Robinson, who commented on a first draft during a book conference organized and funded by Indiana University in 2017. At Indiana University, a team of wonderfully engaging colleagues and friends supported this project: Purnima Bose, Gardner Bovingdon, Emma Gilligan, Michelle Moyd, John Hanson, Mike McGinnis, Jessica O'Reilly, David Bosco, Padraic Kenney, Jessica Steinberg, Amali Ibrahim, Keera Allendorf, Mark Roseman, and Barbara Breitung. Jordan Blekking patiently worked with me to create maps. I also benefited from Indiana University's funding for field work in 2017, through an Emerging Areas of Research grant directed by P.I. Elizabeth Dunn, and through a Research Travel Grant from the College of Arts and Humanities Institute.

Outside Bloomington, I am indebted to Gérard Prunier, whose intellectual mentoring helped me to develop as an independent scholar. At UC Berkeley, where I was a Fulbright fellow, Martha Saavedra, Leo Arriola, John and Peggy Cummins, and Robert Price also provided invaluable support. Nic Cheeseman and Pierre Englebert played a key role in introducing me to new scholarship. Douglas H. Johnson, Cherry Leonardi, Maria Eriksson Baaz, Henri Médard, and Marc Lavergne offered critical feedback I used throughout this book.

From Shanghai to Princeton, Nicola Di Cosmo offered me his advice, mentoring, and friendship. I am grateful to Jeffrey Lehman and NYU Shanghai for funding my fieldwork in 2014. I thank Zachariah Mampilly, Catharine MacKinnon, and Thomas Kühne for their comments on earlier drafts, and Scott Straus for his suggestions on the final manuscript. Gratitude also goes to Dirk Moses for introducing me to a new field of social inquiry, and to Christopher Cramer and Maayan Armelin for discussions on ethnic supremacy, command, and control.

Brian Da Silva, Kate Almquist, Payton Knopf, Alex De Waal, Lotje De Vries, and Rens Twijnstra also helped me throughout the years in multiple ways. I found comfort and useful feedback in the network formed with Kerry Crawford, Nicole Gerring, and Chloe Lewis on sexual violence in armed conflict. Sareta Ashraph also answered my questions on international criminal law.

This book would not have been possible without the support of my longtime friends. I am beholden to Jennifer and the Brownings for making me an honorary member of their family, to V. for the safe havens, kindness, stimulation, and entertainment across the world, to S. for always helping me out. Bloomington friends made life better while writing: Susan and Catherine Seizer, Taha Hameduddin, Seema Golestaneh, Margaret Graves, Tracy Templeton, and Amanda Vredenburgh. I found a second family in the Adolphe-Estrades of Paris, and I thank Akil, Angeline, the B. Team, Noémie, Anne-Claire and Angelica for their kindness and humor. Finally, I credit my parents for bearing with me through the hardships. Dr. Marie Jaspard, the team from the Croix Rousse hospital, Marcy l'Etoile, and Dr Kristin Sheikh also kept me alive and sane to write this book.

I dedicate this book to my father, to the victims of these wars, to my South Sudanese friends and their children, and to Adam.

Abbreviations

ARCSS	Agreement on the Resolution of the Conflict in South Sudan
CPA	Comprehensive Peace Agreement
DDR	Disarmament, demobilization, and reintegration
HEC	High Executive Council
ICC	International Criminal Court
ICTR	International Criminal Tribunal for Rwanda
IDP	Internally displaced person
IO	In-Opposition (refers to the SPLA-In-Opposition, Riek Machar's rebel group)
JCE	Jieng Council of Elders
JEM	Justice and Equality Movement
MI	Military intelligence
NCP	National Congress Party
NLC	National Liberation Council
NSS	National Security Services
SAF	Sudanese Armed Forces
SANU	Sudan African Nationalist Union
SPLA	Sudan People's Liberation Army
SPLM	Sudan People's Liberation Movement
SRRA	Sudan Relief and Rehabilitation Association
SSDF	South Sudanese Defense Forces
UN	United Nations
UNMISS	United Nations Mission in South Sudan
UNOCHA	United Nations Office for the Coordination of Humanitarian Affairs
UN POC	Protection of civilian (refers to the UN protection of civilians camps at UNMISS bases)
UPDF	Uganda's Popular Defense Forces

WAR AND GENOCIDE IN SOUTH SUDAN

FROM PREDATION TO GENOCIDE

In December 2013 . . . In Juba alone I lost ten relatives . . . They
were killed in the same house . . . There were others who were
suffocated in a container where they locked them in.

The SPLA said it wanted to kill all the people so that only birds
remain in South Sudan. They did not want to see any human
being . . . They were talking about the entire country, not just Central
Equatoria.

South Sudan became independent in 2011. Prior to this, the world's newest country had experienced two civil wars. The first conflict had peaked in the 1960s and
ended in 1972, but the second one, which began in 1983, had lasted for twenty-
two years. A peace agreement in 2005 between the Sudan People's Liberation
Army (SPLA) and the government of Sudan had terminated one of Africa's longest civil wars. It kicked off an interim period of six years marked by large-scale
corruption, culminating in the country's independence.

Three years later, the new country descended into yet another civil war in
December 2013, following a political crisis in its capital of Juba within the political branch of the SPLA and the dominant party: the Sudan People's Liberation Movement (SPLM). War quickly spread from the capital to other areas of
the country, with its cortege of violence against civilians. At first limited to the
greater Upper Nile region (Jonglei, Upper Nile, and Unity states), war engulfed
Western and Central Equatoria, and Western Bahr El Ghazal in 2015.

Due to the ethnic identities of the leaders of the two warring parties—the
Dinka president Salva Kiir and the Nuer former vice-president Riek Machar—
from the onset the media portrayed the war as a conflict between the Dinka
and the Nuer.[1] The academic community quickly mobilized against what was
considered a misrepresentation and oversimplification and argued that this
war should not be depicted as ethnic. Too much emphasis on ethnicity would
make us miss the root causes of the conflict, some argued, and might instead
risk increasing ethnic violence on the ground. Consequently, the elephant in the

1

room—ethnicity—and its role in the very root causes of the war and perpetration of violence have never really been addressed since. Most talk of "Dinka domination" was brushed off by some international observers as anti-Dinka racism and mere propaganda.

Even as the African Union and the United Nations have documented part of the violence in South Sudan and labeled it as "ethnic cleansing," no academic work has dealt with the ethnic dimension: its roots, its scale, and its meaning.[2] There exists no international legal definition or convention about what constitutes "ethnic cleansing," but it is widely understood as the forced removal of a specific group from a particular territory in order to make it ethnically homogeneous. Although there are overlapping elements between genocide and ethnic cleansing and ethnic cleansing can be part of genocide, the term "ethnic cleansing" by itself is usually used when referring to geographic areas that have historically been ethnically mixed.[3] The international community did not escalate its rhetoric to describe the violence in South Sudan as genocidal. This was at odds with the interpretation of most South Sudanese I interviewed about the violence: "If the government knows civilians are fleeing, they chase them," pointed out a civil society member from Central Equatoria.[4] They often drew parallels between violence against non-Dinka people in different parts of the country: "Whether you are a civilian, a woman, a child, they will do the same to you: they will clear you. In Shilluk land they did the same than in Unity and Equatoria," explained a Shilluk woman who lived in Central Equatoria.[5]

Genocide, as defined by Article II of the 1948 Convention for the Prevention and Punishment of the Crime of Genocide (and as replicated in Article 6 of the Rome Statute), "means any of the following acts committed with intent to destroy, in whole or in part, a national, ethnical, racial or religious group, as such:

    a. Killing members of the group;
    b. Causing serious bodily or mental harm to members of the group;
    c. Deliberately inflicting on the group conditions of life calculated to bring about its physical destruction in whole or in part;
    d. Imposing measures intended to prevent births within the group;
    e. Forcibly transferring children of the group to another group."[6]

The UN has so far considered South Sudan on the "verge" of a genocide that it warns could be like Rwanda's, the archetype of genocide in Africa.[7] This book addresses the processes that led, among other things, to the formation of an exclusionary Dinka nationalism, and argues that South Sudan's case *is* a genocide, not just ethnic cleansing—but a much different one than that of Rwanda.

Argument

The book explains how a predatory rebel state was born in civil war, reached independence, and then waged genocide. It especially investigates the links between predation and ideology. It explores the relationship between predatory wealth accumulation, state formation, and a form of racism—extreme ethnic group entitlement—with genocidal potential.

I argue that ethnically exclusive and predatory wealth accumulation was key in fostering ethnic group entitlement that became extreme. Violent ethnicized wealth accumulation was one of the engines of extreme ethnic group entitlement, until it also became a symptom. The other engines of group entitlement were group legitimacy and group worth, emerging out of ethnic ranking and past humiliations (or accomplishments). I address both throughout the book. Ethnic group entitlement eventually grew into an ideology of ethnic supremacy. Throughout the second civil war (1983–2005) and after, the international community supported the rise of a predatory ethnic state, which turned into an ethnocracy that eventually perpetrated genocide. In sum, the more wealth an ethnic faction of the elite accumulated, especially under favorable international auspices, the more entitled it felt and the more intolerant it became toward ethnic competitors. Emboldened but also threatened in its control of politics, people, and resources, it found no reason to accommodate ethnic competitors and decided to eventually annihilate them.

I contend that the genesis of ethnic ranking and ethnic supremacy must be found in the legacy of slavery and colonialism. They provided the basis for ethnic stereotypes upon which the SPLA practiced ethnic ranking in favor of the Dinka since 1983. Slavery also laid the foundation for the SPLA's exclusionary predation in areas under its control. Indeed, the very mode of production through which the SPLA elite accumulated wealth was rooted in the Sudanese history of slavery: in a mode of production that was inherently racist. In SPLA areas during the second civil war, ethnic ranking and dominant class formation resting on predation thus converged. On the whole, this dominant class had very few ethnic outsiders.

As the SPLA became even more Dinka in the 1990s, by supporting it the international community fostered a state-building process that routinized predation. Back then, the SPLA protostate, akin to a mafia state, was almost exclusively focused on extraction.[8] State-building institutionalized the Dinka SPLA's predatory mode of production. The SPLA's extractive, exploitative, and ethnically exclusive mode of production combined both material and reproductive wealth accumulation incurring real demographic and territorial gains in favor of the Dinka and to the detriment of non-Dinka groups. This started a three-pronged territorial conquest, begun during the second civil war, consolidated in the inter-war period, and expanded in the current conflict.

Through ethnically exclusive wealth accumulation and violence against non-Dinka civilians, the SPLA reinforced Dinka group ownership and groupness. This cloaked in-group competition and divisions between its two main eastern and western Dinka constituencies. The international community also contributed to mask SPLA divisions and validate the SPLA political myth of national liberation through the signing of the 2005 Comprehensive Peace Agreement (CPA) leading up to independence. The CPA strengthened Dinka group legitimacy and ownership, and eventually group entitlement. This entitlement manifested in the return of ethnic ranking and the making of a violent predatory Dinka ethnocracy in the postwar years (2005–13). Ethnic competition among the Dinka and with other groups (especially Nuer and "Equatorian") accelerated the process of ethnic ranking within the postwar state.[9] As ethnically exclusive and violent predation extended through the new state, it steered group entitlement, making it more exclusionary and extreme.

The international community also continued, as in the last civil war, to aggravate group entitlement by triggering past feelings of humiliations from slavery and the colonial period in the 2005–13 period through condescending stereotypes and perceived threats to southern sovereignty. As group entitlement intensified, the state and its Dinka followers grew more and more violent toward non-Dinka, Dinka dissidents, and foreigners. Symptomatically, Dinka hardliners close to the president organized the recruitment of parallel western Dinka militias when political competition increased. December 2013 marked the beginning of the third civil war and the start of a multiethnic genocide against nearly all non-Dinka ethnic groups.

I explore three of this genocide's phases—in Juba, Unity, and Central Equatoria—and the links between these phases. In all these phases, the state coordinated and ordered attacks against non-Dinka civilians. It used different perpetrators depending on the wartime legacy of ethnic ranking and social class formation. Across all locations, the state security apparatus and militias implemented the same ideology of Dinka supremacy that equated Dinka ethnic membership with the right to live. This ideology was at its core an ideology of extreme group entitlement: the result of decades of unrestrained predation and comforted group legitimacy. The perpetrators considered that they "owned" the country and were merely recuperating what had always been theirs.

Extreme ethnic group entitlement thus exploded into genocidal violence and predation in the third civil war. It culminated in the idea of group expansion through land-grabbing, which on a large scale amounted to a conquest. Dinka in-group competition fueled this "inner colonization" of the country.[10] This sent us back to the colonialist, expansionist, and imperialist origins of modern genocides.[11]

Theoretical Contribution

Since my objective is to offer a new historical account of the country, I remain focused on South Sudan and I avoid delving into comparisons. Yet I hope this account provides a few general insights into the relationship between predation, ethnic violence, and state-making in war.

My analysis of this relationship pivots on Donald Horowitz's notions of ethnic group legitimacy, relative group worth, and group ownership, which "merge into a politics of ethnic entitlement."[12] I pay special attention to the history of ethnic ranking and to the humiliations and trauma of slavery that are at the root of ideas of relative group worth.[13] Horowitz defined group ownership in relation to group legitimacy: "To understand the concept of group legitimacy, it is necessary to link it to ownership. Legitimacy goes to one's rightful place in the country. To be legitimate is therefore to be identified with the territory. . . . Group legitimacy provides a foundation for the recurrent psychological denial that another group owns an equal share in the land."[14]

I seek to further our understanding of how ethnic group "ownership" is made. Like ethnic groupness, it is not fixed in time: it varies throughout history.[15] I introduce a broad materialist angle to group ownership, incorporating the idea of "wealth in people" to account for the role of bridewealth exchange in the economy and politics.[16] I highlight the importance of the SPLA's mode of production in building up that sense of group ownership. I take inspiration from Paul E. Lovejoy's use of the concept of mode of production in his history of indigenous slavery in Africa.[17] Like him, I consider it an instrument of historical analysis to highlight the relationship between social organization and production and how this relationship is maintained. I do not seek to theorize the concept of mode of production. I use it rather to describe a process of wealth accumulation with political implications. I find the history of slavery particularly relevant to uncovering the historical connections of the SPLA's mode of production.[18] In referring to it as a "mode of (re)production," I mean to highlight its gendered social implications, which go beyond reproducing social relations and concern the exchange of women's reproductive capacities and the integration of the marriage market into the war economy.

The SPLA's mode of (re)production consists of ethnically differentiated socioeconomic and sexual predation; forced labor; and the ethnically exclusionary control of the war economy. It does more than just make the dominant social class that controls it and the predatory state that administers it.[19] It steers ethnic group ownership and entitlement. It generates group "ownership" via the possession of things and resources, people (women), and ultimately land. This, together with group legitimacy endorsed by the international community and in which group ownership also participates, contributes to build up group entitlement.

In its extreme version, group entitlement is the legitimate right to own (territory, land) to the exclusion of other groups, and it becomes ethnic supremacy. In a genocidal context, the legitimate right to have turns into the legitimate right to live. If you are not allowed to have land because someone else should have it, then you are not allowed to exist on it, and you are disappeared from it by whatever means necessary. I connect ethnicity and economics (class) within an exploitative and ethnically exclusive economic system (or mode of production) to explain ethnic conflict. As such, I hopefully contribute to address a gap in the literature on ethnonationalism. This literature has emphasized class conflict at times, ethnic conflict at others, but often failed to show how both "infuse" each other.[20]

In highlighting the importance of the mode of production to understanding the making of an ideology of group entitlement, I illustrate that violence is related to the organizational culture of the armed group. But I also introduce historical drivers behind this organizational culture that complexify the picture presented by some of the scholarship. It has been argued that armed groups relying on their base instead of exploiting natural resources or being supported by foreign backers typically victimize civilians less, and when they do victimize them, they do so more strategically.[21] There was little chance, however, that in relying on civilians the SPLA would not reproduce past violent and extractive behaviors like many other rebel groups have done. Its dependence on its civilian base made it violent all the same—perhaps even more so, because violence crystallizes groups—and it contributed to build an ideology of extreme group entitlement that eventually turned genocidal. This story thus confirms other recent political ethnographies on African warscapes, in that violence is "the product of a specific mode of government and a specific economy."[22] Rebel governance is indeed rooted in past patterns of social and economic relations, and this pattern must be historically contextualized.[23]

This also echoes other studies that link different events of violence and note how intimate or "privatized" violent politics are.[24] South Sudan's different wartime patterns of violence are connected, between the mostly coercive, exploitative, and extractive violence of the second civil war and the mostly discriminatory, annihilating, and systematic violence of the current conflict.[25] Analyzing these patterns may also expand our understanding of sexual violence, a field of inquiry that has changed over the past three decades.[26] There are differences in the pattern of sexual violence in both civil wars, but just as with violence as a whole, there are connections too. Indeed, genocidal rape also participates in violent processes of ethnic group ascension, ethnic group ranking, and ethnicized social class consolidation in the third civil war.

Finally, the case of South Sudan may seem puzzling to policy-makers. Its scenario contradicts studies that posit that a large international constituency would contribute to restrain violence.[27] Indeed, one would think that heavy and long-term Western involvement could yield results to stop violence against civilians. But it is this very investment by the West in South Sudan over the past few decades that has contributed to shape the ideology of ethnic supremacy.[28] After independence, the new sovereign country became very embedded in the international system, which defused means of Western pressure.[29] The interests of states, firms, and individual war profiteers in South Sudan meant that its elite considered it had nothing to lose and everything to gain in securing oil and mineral-rich areas through genocidal violence in an international context of diminishing human rights standards. South Sudan increased the number of its foreign backers, the West exerted no effective pressure, and violence continued.

Methodology

This book is mostly based on a total of 550 interviews and relies when possible on secondary sources. Archives concerning the SPLA were inaccessible.[30] I carried out interviews in various locations across South Sudan during two consecutive years (2009 and 2010) and over a span of seven months from 2014 to 2017, as well as in northern Uganda's refugee camps in 2017. Throughout these years, I conducted other interviews to a lesser extent in Addis Ababa, New York, Washington, D.C., and Nairobi. I provide the full list of the locations in the appendix.

I anonymized my respondents' identities for their protection. I decided not to include a table of interviews either for that reason. I use the term "civil society" very broadly to protect the anonymity of local nonstate and unarmed organized actors I interviewed. The term "observer" refers to respondents with deep, long-term knowledge of political events. In some instances, I purposefully indicate my respondents' ethnicity to analyze the uses of ethnicity and the ethnicization of violence. I also mean to highlight the fact that the Dinka are not a homogeneous group: they are not all on board with their government's policy, and as such they also fall victim to in-group policing.

Some readers may warn me against writing about the ethnicized nature of violence in such a way, arguing that the book could incite ethnic violence. The concern is laudable, but this warning has veered into intellectual censorship in South Sudan's academic scene and resulted in its own kind of academic in-group policing. The most damaging consequence is that it ultimately prevents us from writing about social processes that deserve and need analysis.

In this book, the argument for not identifying perpetrators and victims by their ethnicity in order to do no harm fails the test of chronology and causality. First, extreme ethnic violence is no fiction and it occurred before I wrote about it—and eventually published about it. Second, denying extreme ethnic violence does not make it disappear, as demonstrated by the processes of escalation I describe—quite the opposite. Third, this violence needs to be recorded and my primary objective is to create a historical record (I return to the choice of focusing primarily on non-Dinka victims later). Fourth, it is highly unlikely that the perpetrators, who are vastly illiterate, even at the highest level of the chain of command, would take inspiration from such academic work. Fifth, even if perpetrators read this book, the historicity, deep-rootedness, and intensity of their own ideology of ethnic supremacy imply that they do not need me to embolden or anger them. As for the victims, they already know what happened to them. Of course, victims may turn into perpetrators and victims may instrumentalize memory to generate genocidal ideologies.[31] But this still does not justify not recording and analyzing genocidal violence against them.

Selection of Respondents

Not all 550 interviews are cited in this book, but they provide the very backbone of my argument. From the beginning, I interviewed mostly civilians—men and women who were not in a position of power and not from the elite. Some had served in the SPLA, and the majority of my respondents were women. Out of them, twenty-eight were survivors of sexual violence, mostly interviewed in Uganda's refugee camps in 2017, but also in South Sudan's Unity state. I did not select them randomly, since I benefited from the cooperation of an international organization that told them about me (and not the other way around). As such, this number (twenty-eight) should not be taken as an indication of the prevalence of sexual violence in the current conflict. Besides, many other respondents whom I selected randomly turned out to be victims or witnesses of other types of violence; some had lost relatives to such violence or had escaped violence (sometimes death) themselves. Therefore, despite the number of interviews used for this book, the use of mixed methods to recruit respondents means that this is by no means a quantitative survey of violence.

The selection of my respondents was a mix of long-term relationships developed in 2009 and 2010, 2014, and 2015–17 and of more random selection and snowballing especially in that last 2015–17 period. The average ratio between a more classic ethnographic approach and random selection with snowballing was 50/50 overall.[32] In 2015–16, I selected households randomly when walking through the UN protection of civilian (POC) camp in Unity state and adopted the same approach in 2017 in the refugee camps in northern Uganda. I also spent time at these camps' entry points to interview people who had just escaped their home areas and were willing to talk to me. In addition, I selected areas of these camps where communities associated with the perpetrators lived. I sought out Dinka and Bul Nuer civilians who had just arrived to hear their side of the story. In those areas, I also randomly selected my respondents. I interviewed as many people as I could. My questions led my respondents to point me to other people, or other locations, where they knew I could find answers to my questions. Friendships from my previous two years of research in the country, also led to more snowballing. Finally, I was fortunate to benefit from the collaboration of some international organizations who told their "beneficiaries" about me: this researcher who would be more than happy to hear their stories, should they want to share them.

The result was overwhelming. For example, in July 2017 women lined up under a tree in one of the Ugandan refugee camps I visited, waiting all afternoon to tell me about how they had been raped. Some waited five hours in the blazing sun to tell their stories. People wanted to share their ordeal, even if it meant crying during the interviews. They were in shock, but displayed an impressive capacity to analyze what was happening to them: who chased and tried to kill them (and often succeeded in killing their relatives), how and why. Medical research shows that most people affected by trauma are able to remember precisely what happened to them, and this memory does not change. But memory loss can occur for war trauma victims, and traumatic memories are fundamentally different from other types of memories.[33] So I interviewed as many people as I could to recoup facts.[34]

My approach—focusing mostly on the experiences of those at the bottom of the social order—is consistent with other qualitative academic works that have defied the common assumption that only an elitist approach concentrating on the architects can account for genocidal violence.[35] Besides, not every genocide needs planning, and genocides are often not fully conceived strategies. Scott Straus writes that "leaders typically do not sit down and map out extermination as the best way to retain power. Rather, they say, in effect: 'We face a major threat from some malicious group, and we have to do whatever it takes to defeat them.' . . . the end goal may be vague even for those who unleash the violence."[36]

Finally, I should clarify that I am not trying to make a legal claim. My point is to elucidate, through empirical research, the sociopolitical processes culminating into genocidal violence. The work of a court of law and the criteria for legal analysis are different. Legal conclusions are not the only type of possible analysis, and neither are they the only ones we should rely on.

When it came to assessing the veracity of my respondents' claims, I abided to the following rule of thumb: if three people who did not know one another told me the same thing, I started to bring some credence to it and sought as much corroboration as I could with other interviews. Therefore, whenever I cite one respondent (or several in a group discussion) in this book, it implies that at least two other testimonies (but often many more) have brought credence to this version of facts. But I try to quote only one respondent so that the source is not diluted, especially when it comes to individual quotes.

Interviews

My interviews lasted from twenty minutes to three hours. They were mostly individual. When the respondent did not speak English, either someone with the respondent would translate or I used my own translator (most often a woman—always for survivors of sexual violence). I followed a semistructured interview questionnaire from memory (for safety reasons), prefaced by an introduction of who I was, what I was after, and why. I always made clear to my respondents that they could refuse the interview and leave at any moment. By 2015–16, I sometimes found myself hoping that they would refuse to speak with me, so horrendous were their testimonies. But they never did.

I was very clear on the absence of payment, advantage, or sanction of any kind resulting from the interview. Out of the four hundred interviews carried out during the ongoing conflict (2013–), only one woman, a gang-rape survivor who was interviewed in a Ugandan refugee camp, asked for money at the end of the interview. It pains me to say that I refused, explaining that this would taint the data.

Some things cannot be expressed in writing: the particular smell of fear in a woman who narrowly escaped death and hid in the bush for days with her children, the loud screams of a man receiving news that his family was killed and burned in his house, and the cries, lowered looks, and beaten down posture of gang-rape survivors. Good research without empathy is impossible, and so one does not come out unscathed from such field research. Grave illness in the summer of 2017 following field research in Uganda sent me to a prolonged hospital stay and postponed the publication of this book.

Limitations

A few limitations mark this book: first, I did not carry out field research in Upper Nile after 2013, which is where violence against the Shilluk was mostly perpetrated. Since I had to rely on secondary sources to address the case of the Shilluk,

I focus mostly on the cases of violence in Unity state and Central Equatoria state.[37] This book cannot do justice to every area of South Sudan (a country as large as France) and to the history of every armed group, or every ethnic group. It is not an anthropology book, even if it explores topics such as kinship and ethnicity. I had to pick what I deemed most important and most urgent in the public domain—mostly what was not said, and what needed to be redressed in my view. In this vein, I address the 1991 Bor massacre by Riek Machar's Nuer troops against the Dinka only because President Salva Kiir invoked it in December 2013 to justify a much different massacre on Nuer civilians in Juba. This book, as every history, is a selective history. It is written to fill specific gaps and focuses on governmental violence. This does not mean that rebel groups such as Riek Machar's SPLA-In-Opposition and the White Army militia did not commit war crimes and crimes against humanity. But the government committed human rights violations on a much larger scale, following an ideology of Dinka supremacy, and this is the focus of this book. The book ends in 2017, at the end of my field research. It does not mean that genocidal violence stopped afterwards, or that it continued at the same rhythm in the same places. Genocide, as Straus writes, is "usually a phase within a longer, broader pattern of conflict."[38]

It is very difficult (if not impossible) to completely avoid reifying ethnic groups, especially in a context where war contributes to reification—the "Equatorians" are for example a myriad of different ethnic groups.[39] I do not wish either for this book to be an accusation toward the Dinka as a people. An ethnic group should not be understood as inherently coherent and following the same objectives.[40] This book hopefully shows the many tensions traversing the various Dinka communities and their competition since the second civil war (1983–2005) and since genocide unfolded from 2013 onwards. The book shows that in-group policing has been going on since the very formation of the SPLA. The current government has continued to practice it to silence dissidents within its own ethnic community while attempting to foster Dinka group identity. Yet this approach should not obscure the fact that ethnic identities can be so entrenched that they become structural, and this book does argue that South Sudan became an ethnocracy.[41]

There is nothing "necessary" about a genocide against non-Dinka civilians in South Sudan.[42] My goal is not to blame an entire group for the misdeeds of an elite. The perpetrators happen to be *some* Dinka (and *some* sub-contracted Nuer), and the victims are mostly not Dinka (for now). Neither does this mean that an evil Dinka elite masterminded everything against the will of ignorant masses. This book addresses the ties between the elite and its executants on the ground (including non-Dinka perpetrators) and describes the historical roots and development of what is, on the ground, a genocidal Dinka conquest.

"Proving" Genocide

Of course, there is a wealth of academic literature that provides multiple definitions of genocide and acknowledges the political processes behind the passing of
the UN convention on genocide and its exclusion of political groups from the list
of protected groups.[43] I do not wish to create a new definition, and I do not fully
disagree with the UN definition of genocide either.[44] At the same time, since this
book is not a legal document but a sociopolitical study, a nonlegal definition is
necessary. Following Straus, I understand genocide as "sustained large-scale violence against a social category that aims at that group's destruction."[45] The state
and a broad coalition of actors, typically including local collaborators, civilian
officials, and national security agencies (including paramilitaries), are the ones
with the most capacity to wage this group-selective and sustained mass violence.
The execution of this violence can be centralized or decentralized through coali-
tions usually coordinated by the center. This particular type of discriminatory
violence is designed to destroy the group, including its ability to survive, and to
prevent its regeneration (including through attacks on its reproductive capacity)
in a given territory. The "group" is a social construct that the perpetrators use to
inflict violence on the perceived threat.[46] When I use the term "genocidal," I simply mean violence as a part of, and furthering, what I just defined as "genocide."
In other words, I do not use "genocidal" as a euphemism for "genocide."

The Burden of Proof

From an international legal perspective, genocide must demonstrate the perpetrator's intent to destroying a group in part or in whole.[47] The infliction of violence on particular individuals must be part of a higher goal to destroy a group.
But no written document or video that is authenticated as from the government
of South Sudan has proven that intent so far.[48] Yet it is as if one expected the
government of South Sudan, which is regularly advised by a myriad of foreign
consultants and legal advisers, to make it easy to produce that evidence by ratify-
ing documents exposing its genocidal plans. Even in the case of the Holocaust,
documents showing authorization of the 1941 Final Solution have remained elusive to historians.[49]

Unfortunately, no member of the government of South Sudan or of the Jieng
Council of Elders (JCE)—an organization of powerful Dinka figures—writes a
journal like Joseph Goebbels did. We live in an interconnected world where, if
progress has been made on accountability through the establishment of various
international tribunals and international and hybrid courts, perpetrators and
architects of genocide are wary of making public speeches that are recorded or

of writing policy documents that can tie them to genocidal violence. As Mark Levene notes, "On paper the committing of genocide is as morally unacceptable as it is internationally illegal—whatever the circumstances—and so the modern protagonists of exterminatory power have indeed been forced into entirely new modes of behavior."[50] They adapt their political strategies to international politics to blur the picture of genocide and scape-goat rivals for genocidal violence— like Salva Kiir did when he dismissed then SPLA Chief of Staff Paul Malong in May 2017.

"Genocide is always presented to the world as something other than what it is," Levene writes.[51] Besides, as far as written documents would be necessary to prove a genocide in South Sudan, the vast majority of the SPLA is illiterate (including at the highest levels), which means issuing such directives would be of little use on the ground. Finally, executants on the ground may be of a different ethnicity than the architects, and have different stakes in the violence and different immediate interests. This is one of the issues this book explores in the case of Unity state.[52] What this means is that issuing genocidal directives through such documents might not be all that necessary, so long as the government is able to manipulate fears and competition between different groups on the ground through its chosen intermediaries, as it did among the Nuer sections of Unity state.

The multitude of ethnic identities and kinds of perpetrators, added to the multiplicity of sites of violence, may be part of the reason why the South Sudanese genocide has been intractable for the few international investigators who have tried to intervene. Indeed, the government has made use of a variety of executants in its violence, including Nuer groups (referred to as different "sections" of the over-arching Nuer group) such as the Bul Nuer or Jagei Nuer, to victimize others such as the Dok Nuer (Riek Machar's section). South Sudan does not fit the (comparatively simple) genocidal archetype that Rwanda has become in Africa, where one ethnic group (Hutu) massacres another (Tutsi). But ethnicity can be used by both perpetrators and victims and should be understood as a "social radar" to navigate through war.[53] Therefore having Nuer perpetrators of genocide on Nuer victims does not mean, as I will show, that Nuer perpetrators were not defending a Dinka supremacist agenda while pursuing their own goals. An analysis of the pursuit of various motives on the ground (especially in the case of ethnic defection) confirms that the vision of a supremacist elite is never totally "hegemonic" in its very execution.[54]

This book illustrates that the genocide in South Sudan has been waged in an ad hoc manner, adapting to local contexts but always following the same rationale. Where the government could co-opt local militias, and even armed groups from neighboring countries, it did. Where destroying opposition was more urgent in the face of a dire military situation, and where local groups could not be subcontracted to perpetrate violence, the government sent its own Dinka militias. This complicates the picture of ethnic violence and of genocide. In this way, the South Sudanese genocide is much less straightforward than Rwanda's efficient hundred-day genocide and much closer to the Armenian genocide, where a variety of actors were used to wage violence and create mass exodus. It is also different from violence in Darfur for a few reasons, though it shares connections.[55] The South Sudanese state most likely learned from the international criminal court (ICC) experience in Sudan and has been careful not to get on the record like the Sudanese officials had.

But the absence of written documents proving genocidal intent does not mean that speeches were not made. As one of my respondents asserts, speeches were delivered, for example in Wau in the summer of 2016, where President Salva Kiir declared in the midst of the violence that "if he were the commander of the SPLA in Wau, he would kill all the people for it to be empty, because the place of Wau is for the Dinka." My respondent continued, "He spoke Arabic when he said this. This was not on TV but he spoke in public at a rally in freedom square. Everyone in Wau heard about this. But this was not recorded because all the world would know."[56]

This testimony is illustrative of our dilemma. We are faced with a moral choice: who do we listen to? This book provides an oral history of war: a "history from below," told mostly by ordinary people, a lot of them women. This is particularly evident when I focus on intent as expressed by the perpetrators to their victims rather than on a chain of command coming from the top, even if my book shows that there evidently is one. Interestingly, in the trial of Sylvestre Gacumbitsi at the international criminal tribunal for Rwanda (ICTR), international jurisprudence recognized that genocidal intent could be deduced from the perpetrator's "deeds and utterances considered together, as well as from the general context of the perpetration of other culpable acts systematically directed against the same group."[57] In other words, from an international legal perspective, speech matters, not just actions. My work has partly consisted in tracking back what the perpetrators' ideology entails. But my conclusions are just the tip of the iceberg. A lot more research is needed on Dinka supremacist ideology.

Indeed, if ideology matters, it has largely been abandoned as an analytical category in the context of South Sudan in favor of a focus on "greed." Because the South Sudanese military elite has displayed predatory and corrupt political behavior, analysts from the political economy camp (largely still favoring "greed") have mostly won over those of the "grievances" one. This book is therefore also about bringing ideology back. Here I am inspired by Straus's idea that an exclusionary ideology—a "founding narrative"—is one of the conditions for a genocide to occur and a defining feature across the board.[58] Yet I do not choose between predation and ideology: I explain how their combination, rooted in the *longue durée* of centuries of extractive and racist relations with Sudan, resulted in violence.

Genocide or "Ethnic Cleansing"?

A common idea that surrounds the "meta-conflict" on South Sudan and whether violence in the current conflict is genocidal or not is that of its scale and modus operandi.[59] "In Equatoria, killing all the men and raping the women is probably below the threshold of genocide," an international human rights investigator once told me. "If they're driving everyone out and if that's just to drive people out, then it falls short of genocide."[60] But systematic killing and raping is what a genocide looks like. Rape has been recognized as a tool for genocide by the international criminal tribunals for Rwanda and the former Yugoslavia, and this book explores its function in South Sudan's third civil war.[61]

Besides, the SPLA did not mean to just forcibly displace people. "If it was just ethnic cleansing, the government would just let them flee," commented the South Sudanese civil society member from Equatoria quoted earlier.[62] He was referring to the regular labeling by international agencies of violence as "ethnic cleansing," always "on the verge" of genocide. In fact, as I noted earlier, ethnic cleansing is not defined under any international legal convention and it is often used as a euphemism for genocide.[63] It is generally understood as mass violence meant to "push" civilians of a different ethnic group out of a given confined geographical zone, not to annihilate them.[64] If mass killings take place, they are understood as some sort of "side effect" of the main goal—which is to push out, not to exterminate. That is what supposedly makes ethnic cleansing different from genocide in its goals.

The reality is of course different: if there is a difference in scale, ultimately what matters is the perpetrators' definition of the territory they intend to "cleanse," which can expand. Though there may be a difference in intent between genocide and ethnic cleansing, not only does one not exclude the other, but they often go together. For example, the Armenian genocide was what is understood as an "ethnic cleansing," but above all it was a genocide. To want to "get rid of" an ethnic population inherently means that this population should be destroyed within the boundaries of a given territory—it should leave or face destruction. A woman gang-raped recalled what her perpetrators said to her: "They said: 'you should move away from South Sudan, and if you don't, we'll kill you.'"[65]

The bottom line is that the target group is not allowed to "exist" within a given territory, and it is up to the perpetrators to determine the boundaries of that territory. In South Sudan, this territory turned out to be the entire country.

This merely made the so-called ethnic cleansing exercises different phases of one genocide. A member of a civil society organization in Yei summarized this genocidal strategy best: "They want to kill us, disorganize us, and come with their cattle . . . Their plan is to drive us out and take our land . . . It's a properly organized killing by the regime to eliminate certain groups of people so they don't exist in the map of South Sudan now."[66]

Death Toll and Accountability

No exact death toll has been calculated in South Sudan, but total group annihilation is not legally required for genocide.[67] Some humanitarian organizations took on the burden of estimating mortality in Unity state and Equatoria. In 2016, the Office of the Deputy Humanitarian Coordinator for South Sudan found a crude death rate that exceeded the emergency threshold of 1 death/10,000 people/day in Unity state.[68] In 2017, Médecins Sans Frontières (MSF) found in the Equatoria region—mostly Central Equatoria state—that most deaths occurred in the village of origin rather than during the journey.[69] But even on the journey, according to one of their staff who participated to the survey, "most people fleeing Equatoria are not successful. Out of a family of 15 people, 8 are killed on the way."[70]

In 2018, the London School of Hygiene and Tropical Medicine estimated that since December 2013, this war had likely led to the violent death of roughly two hundred thousand people.[71] No investigation into the crime of genocide has been launched at the time of writing. Long-time observers noted the reluctance of the UN Mission in South Sudan to gather fresh forensic evidence and death toll estimates right after dust settled from the Juba massacre in December 2013.[72] Evidence disappeared, while the perpetrators also deliberately tried to destroy it.[73] The turnover of investigators, the lack of strategic thinking in data collection, and the shadow of the failed ICC adventure in Darfur did not help either.[74]

In this context, the publication of this book continues to show how political the decisions behind starting these international legal processes are, not to mention their implementation. After all, the international community supported the Khmer Rouge for a long time, well after their fall.[75]

FROM THE TURKIYYA TO THE SECOND CIVIL WAR

1820–1983

Economic and political marginalization, and a pattern of extractive relationships imposed by the north, have marked the history of South Sudan. Early states along the Nile and across the east-west Sudanic belt built their power on the hinterlands, which provided them with manpower, slaves, wealth, and food supplies.[1] Muhammad Ali, Egypt's ruler, invaded Sudan in 1820 with the objective of supporting his power and military build-up by grabbing gold and slave soldiers. By 1850, the Turco-Egyptian regime in the Sudan (the Turkiyya) had reached into the very south of Sudan, into what is now the northwestern part of Uganda, and raided Kakwa, Kuku, and Madi villages.[2]

South Sudan: A Reservoir for Plunder and Slaves

Slavery structured the relationship between the center of power and its peripheries—the Nuba hills, the Ethiopian borderlands, and South Sudan—where civilians tried (and failed) to escape slave raids.[3] In the Turkiyya, the Dinka were the most prized slaves, which meant that slave raids into northwestern Dinka land were constant, particularly on the southern lands beyond the Kir/Bahr el-Arab border.[4] "Black" became synonymous with "slave."[5] Slavery differentiated people according to their Islamic or non-Islamic pedigree, their brown or black skin color, and their Arab (meaning those who are Muslims, who *think* of themselves as "Arab," and who keep slaves) or non-Arab descent. While the Arabs identified as Muslim freemen, they considered the equally imagined community of black pagan Africans as enslaveable, without any history or religion, and not human—in sum, as mere commodities with the same legal status as livestock. Arabization of the slaves, while leading to some advancement of their status, could never lead to equality with their masters, given the immutability of skin color and descent.[6] No matter how important the position of a southern Sudanese, he or she was stigmatized by presumed slave origins.[7]

Merchant companies in military-commercial expeditions, including Nubian slave soldiers recruited in Khartoum, first entered Bahr El Ghazal in the 1850s. They expanded southwest into what is now Western Bahr El Ghazal and Western Equatoria.[8] Locally captured southern slaves were turned into soldiers and were preferred to the Nubians since they knew the countryside best. Military slavery was key in crafting the state in Sudan.[9] Even after the official abolition of the slave trade in 1854, slave raids continued well into the 1860s and prospered in the 1870s.[10] Effectively, private slave armies ruled Bahr El Ghazal in the 1850s, and in later decades, the southwestern country was described as "zariba country."[11] The Ethiopian borderlands, the Nuba hills, and the Bahr El Ghazal region provided the bulk of the slaves for the army. The army considered these areas to be ideal suppliers of "martial races." They were especially at risk because they were both dependent on the center (thus marginal) and held in contempt by the state elite and by other ethnic groups. Successive states would hold up the idea of "martial races."[12]

From the late 1850s onward, European and Arab traders also pushed south from Dinka land into Azande land (from western Bahr El Ghazal to what is now Western Equatoria). The European explorers and ivory traders entered the region during this period of the Turkiyya, and their narratives became the basis of future colonial manuals.[13] German explorer Georg August Schweinfurth's description of the Dinka was telling of the racist undertones of those future manuals, comparing them to "swamp-men," "the darkest of races," with "hideous contortions" and "an expression scarcely better than a baboon's."[14]

Explorers also described the Nuer as aggressive toward foreigners and toward their Dinka neighbors—an oversimplification appealing to the future generation of colonial administrators. Ethnic stereotypes were alternatively used by both locals and outsiders. For example, some groups (such as the Dinka) reinforced and manipulated ethnic stereotypes to inflict revenge from previous raids by the Nuer, and the Egyptians were drawn into local quarrels.[15] Meanwhile, European traders such as Alphonse de Malzac also manipulated ethnic rivalries in Bahr El Ghazal in order to acquire cattle and exchange it for slaves and ivory.[16]

The Mahdist state (1883–98) overthrew the Turkiyya, but its power still relied on slave armies coming from the south and the west. Slave soldiers fought on both sides.[17] The jihad state's incursions in the south were only to plunder it for food and slaves at critical times, and its rule was even weaker than its predecessor.[18]

All in all, in both the Turkiyya and the Mahdist regimes the hinterlands were exploited, the army exerted coercive power in the economic and political spheres, and the state separated those belonging to the central heritage who had legal rights from those who did not.[19] Neither states deployed an administration in the south, which was simply considered a reservoir for human and material resources.[20]

In 1882, the British army invaded Egypt and in 1889 occupied the country permanently. From there, the Anglo-Egyptian reconquest of the Sudan started in the 1890s. It culminated with the fall of the Mahdi in the Battle of Omdurman on September 2, 1898. The main worry of the British was to suppress any dissent to protect the Nile waters against other foreign interests and ensure Egypt's stability.[21] Although the colonial government did not capture people to enslave them, it was probably more effective in raiding the south than the Turkiyya and the Mahdiyya had been.[22] Militias were used during "pacification" patrols to harass civilians, force them to pay taxes, and bring them under control.[23] But the British only had mild success, and the south remained again at the periphery of government central thinking for the period of the Anglo-Egyptian Condominium.[24]

Colonialism and the Reinforcement of Ethnic Identities

The North/South Divide

The British practice of colonial administration, called "Indirect Rule" in other countries, was referred to as "Devolution" or "Native Administration" in Sudan, and further distinguished the south from the north. The government barely intervened in the south, administered through a system of government chiefs.[25] The 1920 Closed District Ordinance, and the "Southern Policy," passed in 1930, further divided northern and southern Sudan.[26] It paved the way for a growing southern identity, in opposition to the Arab-Islamic nationalism of the northern elite, and articulated around Christianity, English, and the notion of a southern territorial entity.[27]

The administration continued to maintain its power through coercion. The south was still viewed above all as a "reservoir" to form the Egyptian army's battalions, and the origin of the conscripts matched the old slave-raiding areas. Since conscription was forced, it continued (on a smaller scale) the exploitative pattern of the nineteenth century and entrenched racism.[28] Besides, the British were careful not to upset too abruptly a social system based on slavery. The British only gradually abolished slavery for fear of rebellion in slave-holding communities. This meant that negative attitudes of dominant northern Sudanese toward slaves and their descendants prevailed.[29] The British still considered the Nuba hills and southern Sudan to be the main reservoirs of soldiers for the army and encouraged the sons of slave soldiers to enroll.[30] Descendants of slave soldiers still regarded the army as their chosen profession well after the abolition of military slavery. The system of military slavery infused society.[31]

Other patterns of exploitation continued. By the time of independence, inequalities between north and south were even greater than what they had been at the time of the Mahdiyya.[32]

The Making of Ethnic Divisions in the South

There were no clear ethnic boundaries in the south, to the surprise of the British officers who came in 1898. Trained with the *Handbook of the Sudan*, which was compiled in the Intelligence Division of the British War Office from the accounts of travelers to facilitate conquest and administration, these officers used interchangeably the terms "nation," "race," "tribe," and "class." The *Handbook* categorized different groups according to the color of their skin, which was thought to be related to the color of the soil.[33] The *Handbook* was largely based on previous explorers' narratives about the south, such as those of Schweinfurth.[34] Racism infused the highest levels of the British administration, who, much like the explorers before them, continued to compare Nilotes to "monkeys."[35] The British, like those before them, also continued to consider the Sudanese the ultimate "fighting" race.[36] The Dinka were described as a "race of cattle-breeders," "pitiless and unrelenting in war," since their martial qualities were developed in military slavery. The Nuer were a "warlike tribe somewhat formidable to the Dinka."[37] The anthropologist Sir Edward Evan Evans-Pritchard, who started a study of the Nuer to inform the British government in 1930, also relied on former explorers and administrators' narratives, and described the Nuer as a society organized and relying on a constant state of warfare. The bias against the Nuer, inherited from the narratives of previous explorers, continued in the colonial administration for the first two decades (1898–1920). The Nuer were considered low on the evolutionary scale: they were "fierce" and "intractable" despoilers of the country, their aggressiveness was what sustained their political system, and they were resistant to change. Again, the ethnic stereotypes of the British were manipulated by the local Anuak and Dinka, much like those of the Egyptians some sixty years earlier. Fed by non-Nuer informants, the British perceived the Nuer as "usurpers" of the land, cattle-raiders, enslavers, and destroyers of neighboring tribes.[38] Those ethnic stereotypes would be reenacted in the country's successive civil wars as well, and particularly in the violence of the third civil war—most disturbingly in the idea that the Nuer and other non-Dinka groups are usurpers of the land.

The fact that the British's own stereotypes were partly fed by all ethnic groups does raise the question of the exact share of responsibility on the part of the colonial administration in starting these stereotypes. At any rate, whoever started it, the colonial administration reinforced it.

In search of leaders to co-opt who could guarantee the submission of various intermixed groups in Nuer territories, the colonial administrators sought to recreate—and in fact, to a certain extent create from scratch—"tribal" structures. This meant separating the Dinka from the Nuer and having the Dinka report to newly appointed chiefs. The separation and definition of tribes went hand in hand with the 1920s Native Administration system and with the advancement of the colonial state's taxation system. Interethnic mixing reduced as the administration hampered interethnic support networks.[39] Nuer and Dinka groups were to be purged of one another's influence to recover tribal organization supposedly lost to slave raids. Ethnic separation was enforced in the most ethnically mixed areas, and interethnic marriages, settlements, and religious practices came under administrative attack. The administration pursued "Dinka integrity" to advance government control. It adjusted provincial boundaries to separate Nuer from Dinka to preempt tax evasion.[40] The fact that it extirpated Dinka members from Nuer communities and told them to return to their supposed homeland, says that ethnic "integrity" amounted to a policy of "ethnic purity."[41] The Nuer were also sorted out and repatriated to what was considered their original settlements.[42]

The colonial administration impacted the ethnic partition of what would later become South Sudan. It also organized population movements from the north to the south. Colonial administrators worried the Dinka were becoming "infected with northern influence" and negotiated moving Dinka populations from Kordofan to Bahr El Ghazal and Upper Nile.[43] Therefore, not only is there a strong colonial legacy of forcibly relocating people to their "home" in South Sudan, but also going back to colonial times and even further back, this home is always imagined—no one is actually "from" there, including the Dinka. This is important to remember when understanding denationalizing discourses of Dinka perpetrators to non-Dinka victims in the third civil war, telling non-Dinka people that they are not "from" South Sudan. In this respect, Stephanie Beswick highlights that originally "the geographic cradleland of East Africa's Nilotic peoples is the central rather than Southern Sudan; that this Nilotic frontier has been shifting southwards for centuries; and that the Western Nilotic Dinka were the last of the Nilotes to migrate out of the central Sudan into Southern Sudan. . . . In time, they (the Dinka) underwent massive ethnic expansion (by marriage), coming to geographically dominate much of the central Southern region."[44] If anything, the second and third civil wars as well as the two interwar periods (1972–83, 2005–13) considerably accelerated the Dinka's expansion in South Sudan.

Despite their best attempts, the British were unsuccessful in fully segregating the Nuer from the Dinka because the narratives of explorers never matched the reality on the ground. The floods and civil war of the 1940s and 1960s increased interethnic cooperation and integration.[45] The British administration of the Nuer became more humane after the 1930s, but the administrators still considered that if the Nuer were not as hostile as they expected, it was thanks to the civilizing nature of the administration and its positive effect on the supposedly aggressive Nuer character.[46] Besides, the British, when investing (little) in education, aimed to avoid "detribalizing" pupils at all cost, and instead reinforced ethnic identities.[47]

The reinforcement of ethnic identities was compounded by the differences in administrating pastoralist versus sedentary communities, which formed the bases of the disparities between the Equatoria and the Bahr El Ghazal and Upper Nile provinces and of future resentment. The British developed two different patterns of administration in the south: between the pastoralists of the Upper Nile clay plains and Bahr El Ghazal, and the agriculturalists from Equatoria and the Ironstone Plateau of Bahr El Ghazal. The southernmost regions became much more integrated in the Native Administration for the sole reason that their chiefs and courts were more sedentary than those of the clay plains. Parts of Equatoria thus developed a stronger bureaucratic culture, in addition to benefiting from the largest agricultural development project (the Zande scheme) and being well connected to the neighboring countries' economies. The administration also considered that pastoralist areas were not worth the investment in terms of education. Until the 1940s, to preserve their potential for tribal leadership, very few sons of chiefs in pastoralist areas were educated in the few existing mission schools. This was not the case in more sedentary areas such as parts of Western Bahr El Ghazal and Equatoria. In Equatoria, sons of chiefs had more opportunity to go to school than in any other part of the region. This changed only in 1946, ten years before independence, when all chiefs—including in pastoralist areas—had to send a quota of boys to school. Inequalities in development and in the integration of southerners into the Native Administration were the result of decisions taken by the British. Yet they were explained by the British in terms of cultural differences between southern people: between the conservative and "backward" Nuer and Dinka (underrepresented in schools and the administration) and the progressive people of western Equatoria (particularly the Azande and the people of Yei).[48] These potent ethnic stereotypes resulted in ethnic stratification, as explained by a former Dinka government official: "The Equatorians before the first war were treated the best and the most developed. Then the Dinka were treated better than the Nuer. *Dinka jenge* meant 'naked Dinka.' They were stigmatized by the Arabs.

'Brutal,' 'less cultured' were the stereotypes of the Dinka, and they've been passed from generation to generation."[49]

The differences in administrating pastoralist and sedentary communities formed the bases of disparities that would continue to affect southern Sudanese politics even today. Indeed, in its last few years, the Anglo-Egyptian administration recruited southerners mostly from those regions most integrated into the Native Administration (Equatoria and Western Bahr El Ghazal). The sons of the chiefs in Equatoria also crowded the civil service, the police, and the army. Most of the Equatorial Corps and the police were populated by ethnic groups from Equatoria, such as the Azande, Moru, Madi, and Lotuko; and from Western Bahr El Ghazal, such as the Jur. They would be the ones to "pacify" the reluctant Dinka and Nuer areas, as they were stationed throughout the country. In the civil service, there were very few Dinka, due to the inequalities in access to education. The few Dinka present were from Bor, since a mission school was established there in Malek in 1905. In the 1970s, these Dinka would occupy positions in Juba and would be accused of "Dinka domination."[50]

Unequal access to education dating back to the colonial period would be used to mobilize Dinka support in the third civil war. Indeed, the informal rhetoric would pit the Dinka groups who did not benefit from any investment in education during the colonial period against those who did—from the Bor Dinka to the Nuer and Shilluk, arguing that these groups were favored by the British over the Dinka and that they also had migrated to northern Sudan or Ethiopia to access education.[51] In the third civil war, "lack of education" would thus ironically become equated with being a "real South Sudanese"—a Dinka.

All in all, the southern Sudanese who were part of the government and formed the southern political leadership were not representative of the whole of the region when forming a response to independence.[52]

Independence

The Sudan was the first African British colony to be granted independence after the Second World War. But this independence was more the product of diplomatic competition between Egypt and Great Britain and of Britain's abandonment of its empire after both World Wars than of genuine nationalist aspirations.[53] As both countries courted the northern Sudanese nationalists, they felt under no pressure to reach an agreement with the southern Sudanese.[54] The future of southern Sudan ended up being determined without the southerners, and as noted by Gérard Prunier, "Sudan's independence process was mainly an Arab affair."[55]

The "Sudanization" process of the administration meant the beginning of the internal colonization process of the south by the north as northerners were appointed to all senior positions in the south.[56] No strong southern Sudanese opposition could emerge at the time, which was marked by personal and ethnic rivalries.[57] Independence would merely signify the transfer of authority into the hands of the Arab Sudanese elite, from the same constituency that had been engaged sixty years earlier in the slave trade.[58]

In the summer of 1955, a few months before the country's independence from British rule on January 1, 1956, and after weeks of growing tensions marked by violent clashes in Juba and Western Equatoria in July and August 1955, a mutiny broke out in the garrison of the town of Torit following an attempt by the government to disarm and relocate the Equatoria Corps to the north.[59] The mutiny was launched by soldiers from the Equatoria region and mostly had an impact there. While northerners were killed, very few southerners died at the time. Most of the mutineers and their families fled to Uganda as order was restored by the Sudanese government and the army, helped by British officials.[60] Although southern Sudan vacillated between states of war and peace at the time, the Torit mutiny was presented as the official start of the first civil war.[61]

Britain was anxious to separate itself from Sudan, and the date of independence was brought forward before the final constitutional arrangements were finalized, to January 1, 1956. At the time, there was not yet much inclination for southern independence; rather, southerners supported a form of federalism that would respect the religious and cultural integrity of the south.[62] In the end, the British colonial structure was just transferred to the northern Sudanese nationalists.[63] In 1958, the Umma Party's government handed over the power to the army, and the military coup of General Ibrahim Abbud marked the end of civilian rule and electoral politics, as well as the end of the constitutional debate.[64]

The First Civil War

The military government of General Abbud built national unity around the principles of Arabism and Islam.[65] The government sought to reverse the policy implemented by the British and did not consider the south worth developing.[66] The southerners understood that they were going to be marginalized, and the south stagnated economically and socially.[67] This favored the consolidation of a southern identity against the legacy of slavery, Arabization, and Islamization. Yet it was still confined to a small elite and originated more in the feeling of marginalization than in any sense of "southernness."[68]

By suppressing dissent, the government reinforced the divide between the northern administrators and the southerners, who continued to be perceived as "primitive" and incapable of governing themselves. In the years following the 1955 Torit mutiny, the south experienced increasing violence.[69] In the late 1950s, Abbud's government started burning villages and torturing and arresting civilians in the south.[70] This steered further southern opposition. In 1960–62, southern politicians, mostly from Equatoria, joined the 1955 mutineers and created an opposition party called the Sudan African Nationalist Union (SANU).[71] In 1963 they mounted a southern guerrilla army, the Anyanya (vernacular name of a snake's poison).[72] This—rather than the 1955 Torit mutiny—is what really marked the beginning of the Sudan's first civil war. The Torit mutiny mostly had an impact on the region of Equatoria and failed to mobilize the Nilotic Dinka and Nuer from the Upper Nile and Bahr El Ghazal regions, who perceived Equatorians as part of the colonial apparatus.[73] There were very few Dinka involved in the opposition movement. With most of the SANU and Anyanya leaders and later Joseph Lagu's Southern Sudan Liberation Movement (SSLM) being Equatorian, the Torit mutiny and by extension the first civil war crystallized differences between Equatorians and Nilotic people.[74]

Government troops destroyed half the churches in the south by 1965 and targeted priests.[75] The first substantial massacres of southerners also happened in 1965, which ended the prospect of a political solution.[76] This intensified the war, which destroyed what little infrastructure existed in the south.[77] Government violence affected the Equatoria region most, where the rebels were only able to hold territory in the countryside.[78] While the rebels limited their retribution most often to individuals, the government punished the southerners collectively.[79]

It was not until the late 1960s that the name "Anyanya" was accepted as the brand of all guerrilla groups scattered in the bush.[80] But the Anyanya was poorly equipped and organized, and the southern leadership was divided. Members of SANU split over how to respond to the fall of General Abbud in October 1964 and the return of civilian rule in Khartoum.[81] SANU became divided between William Deng, one of the only Dinka in the movement who stayed in Khartoum (SANU "Inside"), and those who retreated again to Uganda (SANU "Outside"). A southern party also formed in Khartoum, the Southern Front.[82] It is during those years that some of the most prominent Dinka ideologues of the third civil war cut their teeth.

While factions multiplied, fighting in the south intensified from 1965 to 1969. Politics were radicalized, and governments kept on changing in Khartoum.[83] The 1965 elections did not include the south, and the region was absent from the new parliament.[84] Following the assassination of Deng in 1968, SANU and the Southern Front both allied with other independents (including representatives of the Nuba Mountains and the Beja) in a coalition led by the Dinka politician Abel Alier. Shortly after this, on May 25, 1969, Colonel Jaafar Nimeiri came to power through a bloodless coup supported by free officers in the army, Communists, and Socialists. The new government included a few southerners, such as Abel Alier from the Southern Front.[85]

The Anyanya counted at its peak fifteen to twenty thousand recruits.[86] For a few years, the rebel movement was fragmented, and guerrilla activities even decreased in 1968 due to splintering.[87] The guerrilla group started to emancipate itself from the divided southern politicians and to enter the stages of guerrilla warfare, acquiring more recruits and weapons.[88] In 1969, Colonel Joseph Lagu, who had formed his own Anyanya National Organization, announced that he was forming the Southern Sudan Liberation Front, a united military command with other provincial military leaders that also had a political wing.[89]

The unstable coalition of radical factions behind Nimeiri adopted a new stand toward war in the south, declaring that the solution would be political and not military. It officially supported regional self-government and included a few southerners within its government.[90] The situation was also favorable for the southern guerrillas that now spoke with one voice under Lagu's leadership. Supported by Israel through Uganda, he was able to supply and train the guerrillas on a whole new scale and finally unite them in the expanded Anyanya Armed Forces.[91] Lagu's Southern Sudan Liberation Front, later renamed the Southern Sudan Liberation Movement (SSLM) in the 1970s, was recognized an equal partner to the government in negotiations in Ethiopia.[92]

The Addis Ababa Agreement and the Regional Governments: 1972–83

Lack of Implementation and Uneven Development

In February 1972, Nimeiri's government and the Southern Sudan Liberation Movement (SSLM) of Lagu signed the Addis Ababa Agreement.[93] The SSLM had to give up on the idea of independence. It wanted a federation with an autonomous status for the south, but obtained far less in the new Southern Regional Government, with its own High Executive Council (HEC) and Regional Assembly. The regional government had limited economic power, and there was no clear understanding of how the security arrangement would be implemented.[94] The implementation of the ceasefire and the absorption of the Anyanya guerrillas into various security branches were the most delicate tasks for the national and regional governments.[95]

Insecurity continued to affect the southern Sudanese for many years after the Addis Ababa Agreement.[96] Military technology and access to weapons increased, while development in the south was at a standstill.[97] The new Southern Region had no autonomy in terms of economic planning and education, and the north failed to fulfill its financial obligations toward the south.[98] Most southerners remained uneducated because of almost nonexistent school facilities.[99] The little development that occurred was uneven, especially between the Bahr El Ghazal and Upper Nile provinces and the Western and Eastern Equatoria provinces, which were more developed.[100]

Nimeiri, under pressure from the radical and fundamentalist elements, had to organize a "national reconciliation" in 1977 with his Islamist opponents: the Umma and the Muslim Brothers.[101] Oil, the main asset of the Southern Region, had been discovered only after the signing of the Addis Ababa Agreement, in 1978, by the US oil company Chevron.[102] The Umma, the Muslim Brothers, and Nimeiri decided to exclude the regional government from petroleum affairs after disputes about where to place Chevron's oil refineries. The oil companies Total and Chevron were granted concessions without the regional government's consultation.[103]

Lieutenant General Lagu, the former Anyanya leader, was elected president of the Southern Region in 1978. After two years of controversies, he was replaced by Abel Alier (a Bor Dinka), who was appointed by Nimeiri as interim president and then elected in 1980 to a new term as president of the HEC. Alier had to face a lot of obstacles in forming his new government. Those obstacles included ethnic divisions and the competition between the "insiders" who remained in Sudan during the war and the "outsiders" who had fought in the bush and been exiled, the reward for their participation in the war, as well as corruption and the frustration of the southerners.[104]

Ethnic Tensions, Anti-Dinka Racism, and Redivision

The issue of the reinstatement of the three colonial provinces (Upper Nile, Bahr El Ghazal and Equatoria), presented as "decentralization" by its advocates from Equatoria—or, by its mostly Dinka opponents, as the "redivision" of the southern region—was intertwined with ethnic tensions dividing the southerners. Indeed, once the first civil war was officially over, one of the contentious issues that remained unresolved was the growing confrontation between the Nilotes (mainly the Dinka) and the Equatorians.[105]

Most of the literature so far has presented hostility toward the Dinka in this period under the broad umbrella of "anti-Nilotic racism." But it would be much more accurate to call it "anti-Dinka racism." Indeed, this racism did it not affect the Nilotic Mundari who inhabited the Equatoria region. Besides, many fewer Nuer and Shilluk (other Nilotes from Upper Nile) than Dinka people migrated to the new capital of the southern government, Juba, in 1972 and even earlier.[106] There had also been more Nuer recruits in the overwhelmingly Equatorian Anyanya than Dinka, which may have contributed to better relations between people from Equatoria and the Nuer.[107] In any case, animosity was directed first and foremost at the Dinka. Yet the perception of a "Dinka domination" was not irrational (as implied by some academic accounts), and the attempt to upset power dynamics inherited from colonial times not unreal.

The first reason for interethnic hostility was that confrontation between the Dinka and the Equatorian groups increased following the Addis Ababa Agreement through the creation of new government positions for the small southern elite. One Kakwa respondent (an Equatorian) recalled, "We Equatorians had never had interactions with the Dinka. That became an eye opener for the southerners."[108] The second reason was that these positions and the potential for patronage they offered became the object of competition.[109] When a financial crisis hit the country in 1977–78, this competition became even more rife.[110] The explosive combination of postwar competition over shrinking resources available for patronage and rising ethnic patronage and ethnic hostility would resurface in the second interwar period the country would experience (2005–13).[111]

Coming out of the first civil war in 1972, there were also several competing discourses of group legitimacy that contributed to interethnic hostility (just like, again, after 2005). Equatorians believed that because of the overwhelmingly Equatorian composition of the 1955 Torit mutiny, they had launched the start of the southern nationalist movement. The government of Sudan also made sure to present the guerrilla group as exclusively supported by a small number of Equatorian groups and not by the Dinka, Nuer, and Shilluk.[112] Equatorians resented those who were "insiders" and happened to be mostly Dinka. These "insiders" were considered backward and were suspected of collaboration with the north.[113] Such beliefs would have a startlingly long legacy, since in 2017 some Equatorians still thought of Abel Alier (a Dinka) as a collaborator, owing also to his relationship with the Sudanese president Omar El Bashir.[114] They considered his coalition heading the SANU and Southern Front in Khartoum with Nuba and Beja groups in 1968 enough proof. "The Arabs didn't honor what they had said they would do. But the Dinka were not part of the struggle. Dinka and Nuba were married to Arabs to fight the Equatorians," explained a Kakwa (Equatorian).[115] Interestingly, Alier brought a few Dinka from the Southern Front into his government; they would later become prominent figures of the Jieng Council of Elders (JCE) in the post-2005 years (Bona Malual and Ambrose Riiny Thiik, both of whom, like the current president, Salva Kiir, are from Warrap in Bahr El Ghazal).[116] This group of Dinka interests would continue to be associated with Khartoum.

Those who defended the "division" of the south (*kokora* in the local Bari language) argued that "insiders"—above all the Dinka—had taken over regional government positions. They were hoping that a "division" of the Southern Region into the three smaller former regions of Equatoria, Bahr El Ghazal, and Upper Nile would divide resources equally and send the non-Equatorian newcomers to Juba (that is, the Dinka) back to their region.[117] Pamphlets went around, including one written by Joseph Lagu detailing the share of Dinka versus non-Dinka people occupying senior government positions. Edward Thomas writes, "In a thoughtful response to Lagu's pamphlet, a group of national parliamentarians calling themselves the Solidarity Committee of the Southern Members of the Fourth People's National Assembly acknowledged that non-Dinka perceptions about Dinka overrepresentation might have some basis, but stressed that economics, not tribal, differences, were at the root of the South's problem."[118] The rhetoric took off especially after Joseph Lagu, representing the "outsiders," lost his Dinka supporters in the Legislative Assembly. Appealing only to his Equatorian constituency, Lagu was dismissed by Nimeiri and replaced in 1980 by Alier, who represented the "insiders."[119] In Uganda, the fall of Idi Amin, famous for his anti-Nilotic rhetoric, also precipitated the influx of northern Ugandan refugees. Lagu welcomed Amin's supporters, which brought more supporters to anti-Nilotic racism. Lagu's reputation was tarnished by rumors of corruption. But he also accused Alier's group of the same.[120] Once back in office, Alier appointed Dinka to half the ministerial posts to win over his former opponents. This only confirmed the fear of a Dinka domination and justified the agenda for a separate Equatoria region.[121]

According to Douglas Johnson, it was impossible to conclude that an intra-Dinka coalition existed back then. He noted, "They have shown no tendency in the past to unite either politically or militarily. In national and regional politics, Dinka have been found on virtually every side."[122] It was true of the 1970s to a certain extent, since Alier, a Bor Dinka, appointed mostly Bor Dinka peers to regional government positions and not Dinka from other regions. This owed to local patronage ties and to the fact that few Dinka were educated. At the time, there was as yet little intra-Dinka mixing in comparison to future wars, as one Dinka Padang respondent from Upper Nile explained: "The Dinka are the Dinka. But many of us don't know the other Dinka . . . we in Upper Nile don't (normally) know the Dinka from Bahr El Ghazal. The Dinka in Ruweng (Unity state) we know, and the Dinka from Jonglei. But the Dinka from Bahr El Ghazal, we didn't know. Along the Nile, we've been marrying ourselves. But these people of Bahr El Ghazal, we don't (traditionally) know."[123]

Yet two elements sit uneasily with the allegation that there was no intra-Dinka coalition back in the 1970s and therefore no attempt to dominate as a (united) people back then. First, there was a Dinka political coalition: all Dinka banded together behind Alier's reappointment to the HEC in 1980. This, according to a Dinka politician, could be compared to the Dinka banding together behind Salva Kiir during the third civil war.[124] Then, a proto pan-Dinka ideology emerged in the 1970s. This revanchist discourse of Dinka group legitimacy and entitlement competed with that of the Equatorians and was rooted in frustrations from the colonial era and its uneven distribution of power and development. To the Dinka, the Equatoria province had always benefited from more resources than the Upper Nile and Bahr El Ghazal provinces had, and people from Equatoria had been more represented in the government and armed forces until the Addis Ababa Agreement. Johnson argued that even if the Addis Ababa Agreement reintegrated Nilotic Anyanya fighters (Nuer, Dinka, Anuak, and Shilluk) from the Upper Nile and Bahr El Ghazal into the armed forces, this still did not outweigh the prevalence of Equatorians in clerical positions and the police. The impression of a "Dinka domination" was, according to him, due to the sudden surge of Dinka in government positions in which they had previously been underrepresented.[125]

But was the domination just an impression? Did the reintegration of Anyanya Nilotic fighters (though more Nuer than Dinka) and the appointment of Dinka to various positions not largely tip the balance in favor of the Dinka? Did the attempt to fix past inequalities turn into a resolution to dominate? As noted earlier, a group of parliamentarians opposed to the "redivision" acknowledged that "non-Dinka perceptions about Dinka over-representation *might have some basis*."[126] Who occupies civil service positions is an important indicator of who "owns" the country—in this case, the region.[127] Elements of speech/discourse during that period indicate that this translated into group entitlement. Several respondents have dated back the emergence of a "born to rule" ideology to these years. To some respondents, the Bor Dinka domination was very real and more than just an impression, as a Lango from Ikotos (Eastern Equatoria) remembers: "In 1977, the Dinka started saying that they were 'born to rule,' when I was in intermediate school (before being a senior)—I was 23 years old then. Abel Alier, when he was in power, he recruited all Bor Dinka—and few Dinka from Bahr El Ghazal—in the police, the wildlife, fire brigade and army—all these organized forces. They started applying that rule 'born to rule' then. I heard the term *moinjur* in Kapoeta, roughly in 1979. The Dinka population was really high in Juba. The Bor Dinka were dominant—more than those of Bahr El Ghazal."[128]

Other respondents dated the "born to rule" protoideology to even earlier and explained how this was spread during the 1970s: "The 'Dinka born to rule' thing started in 1972. Martin Majier, from Bor, a lawyer and at some point a judge in Bor, served the regional government under Abel Alier. During his administration, he was one of his ministers. He did articulate the myth of Dinka born to rule. And two other Dinka politicians and intellectuals, Dr. Justin Yac Arop from Bahr El Ghazal, a medical doctor by training from the University of Khartoum . . . The second politician from Bahr El Ghazal was Bona Malual. He made similar statements about the Dinka being there to rule. Barnaba Wani Dumo, a Kuku from Kajo Keji, was minister of housing under Abel Alier's regional government, and heard a statement in the parliament in Juba by Justin Yac about the Dinka being there to rule people in Equatoria. So these voices have been there before—the Dinka claiming they're the men of the men (the same than the Nuer) . . . From the regional government time, tribalism under Abel Alier, led to animosity against the Dinka and then the Nuer."[129]

According to Beswick, the term *moinjiang*, which the reader will see appear throughout this book, is the Dinka equivalent to the Nuer's *naath*. *Moinjiang* is what the Dinka called themselves before the foreign name "Dinka" was applied to them by non-Dinka neighboring groups in Gezira or by a stranger who approached the Dinka Padang. The name "Dinka," originally *Dengkak*, referred to a chief called Deng and to his people, and meant "Deng over there." It was popularized before the eighteenth century and was largely cemented during colonial times, when Dinka themselves began identifying with this name. Interestingly, *zanj* (which evolved into *jiang* or *jieng*) was a term in the central Sudanic literature of the nineteenth century that referred to Dinka people and other southerners as "non-Islamic Africans"—and therefore up for grabs as slaves. *Jur*, on the other hand, designates non-Dinka people as "aliens."[130] Another Kakwa respondent explained:

> *Moinjiang* means the "man of man," the "ruler of the man," it's a belief that no one is stronger than them (the Dinka). It's a legend that they're born to rule. It's a Dinka word: it's always been there. When they're seated, they call themselves *moinjiang*. When they see the Equatorians, they call them *moinjur*: the "ruled."[131]

Dinka society is ranked, or hierarchical, socially stratified by wealth and status. Much like that of the Nuer, it is far from egalitarian and classless. Yet the Dinka are more hierarchical than the Nuer, and the only way to "belong" to them and acquire Dinka citizenship is by marriage. The Dinka incorporated elements of the Nilotic kingdoms of Meroe and Alwa, distinguishing "aristocrats" from "commoners." Not all Dinka clans are equal, and they have historically been competing for the most arable land. Therefore the Dinka also differentiated between "commoners" and "chiefly" clans.[132] In other words, non-Dinka people were not equal to Dinka people, Dinka society itself was hierarchical, and different clans were not equal among Dinka either.

The Dinka accused of domination were above all Bor Dinka from Malek mission school, even if there were also a smaller number of Dinka from Bahr El Ghazal in prominent positions.[133] This is an important fact to remember to understand intra-Dinka competition in the next decades; indeed, the Equatorians were not the only ones to resent the Bor Dinka—so did the many other Dinka groups from Bahr El Ghazal who still did not have access to those positions because they had even less access to education to begin with.[134] Equatorian groups were against upsetting the status quo of the ethnic distribution of power in South Sudan. They wanted to keep the system ranked and remain at the top of the hierarchy. Meanwhile, the Bor Dinka who finally had access to various positions of power were trying to upset the ethnic division of labor that is typically inherited from colonial periods.[135] As a matter of fact, they already exhibited traits of class consciousness. They defended class interests by blocking access to non-Dinka men to institutions such as the police. A testimony from an Equatorian, cited in a report on *kokora* (division), is quite illustrative:

> Ethnic favoritism was not only perceived to occur at the senior levels. As testified by a respondent in a focus group discussion, it also affected people looking for jobs in the civil service:
>
> > "I wanted to become a police officer. [But] because the person responsible there was a Dinka, [and] most of the people who were in the police were Dinkas, [this was not possible for me]. That's why I had to find my way to community development. Because somebody in community development, who comes from my place, was able to employ me and train me to become a community development worker."[136]

According to Øystein H. Rolandsen and M. W. Daly, during that period petty politicians reached for the "ethnic card" to mobilize their constituencies by intensifying the "Dinka domination" discourse. Their conclusions are interesting because they imply that this discourse had little echo within southern society: "Politicians increasingly mobilized along ethnic lines by intensifying the discourse of Dinka dominance. Despite their divisions, Southern politicians anyway belonged to a tiny segment or society . . . they had more in common with their northern Sudanese former colleagues than with the masses and, in most cases, had fallen out of touch through long absence from their purported constituencies."[137]

In fact, the theme of Dinka domination gathered much momentum on the ground. Conflict erupted in schools in various parts of the south in the late 1970s between the Dinka and the Shilluk in Upper Nile, or between Nilotic and Equatorian groups in Equatoria, over power-sharing.[138] Tensions rose over land-sharing as well, tied to the issue of marriage. People from Equatoria perceived that the Dinka used marriage as a gateway to land, which they used for cattle grazing. To them, the acquisition of both women (through bridewealth paid in cattle) and land served Dinka demographic and territorial expansion.

The Dinka had brought their cattle to graze on Equatorian pastures starting in the 1960s, destroying crops.[139] This movement increased after 1972, when large numbers of Bor Dinka brought their cattle and referred to Juba as "New Bor," which considerably angered the Bari.[140] Still, even if according to the Dinka themselves the elite already had a lot of cattle in the 1970s, it was still less than what the SPLA would accumulate in the second civil war (1983–2005) and its aftermath.[141] But Dinka newcomers already expropriated land, built houses, and opened shops.[142] The fear of various Equatorian groups that the Dinka were after their land to graze their cattle may seem irrational, but Equatorian groups understood the coming of the Dinka as a snapshot of a larger and more permanent Dinka settlement.[143] Many Equatorian groups worried that the Dinka newcomers were using intermarriage as a gateway to settle on their land. They were anxious to protect the territorial and political integrity of the region.[144] Dinka SPLA soldiers themselves outlined a logic that would fully unfold during the second civil war: "You have to marry more, so that you can have money, you have more land, and you can protect your cattle."[145] Not just that—the Dinka were agropastoralists and they needed land to cultivate grain (*dhurra*).[146] Therefore, to counter what they considered to be a first attempt at inner colonization by the Dinka after independence, the Bari instructed their youth to marry among themselves in the early 1980s and not with the Dinka.[147] They were not the only Equatorian groups to explicitly avoid intermarriage with the Dinka—so did the Acholi and most likely others.[148]

In seeking to defend themselves against Dinka expansion, these groups ended up defending ethnic integrity and purity. One Didinga respondent argued that mixed marriages tended to dilute physical features and endanger languages with a small number of native speakers.[149] In other words, Equatorian groups were preoccupied with protecting their "race" against marriages they saw as mostly extractive because some of the children born out of these marriages would leave the region with their Dinka father. It is accurate to describe the mounting hostility against the Dinka as "anti-Dinka racism." But this does not mean that the perception of a "Dinka domination" was irrational, particularly in light of Dinka expansion through intermarriages in past centuries. From a group that arrived in the fourteenth century and settled in Western Bahr El Ghazal circa 1650–1700, the Dinka had become the majority by "massive ethnic absorption of non-Dinka people" through marriage with peripheral Nilotic and non-Nilotic neighbors with cheaper bridewealth prices. Beswick wrote that "by the twentieth century Dinka ethnic expansion was such in Southern Sudan that their ethnic circumference was one thousand miles."[150] Equatorians were well aware of the Dinka's history in the *longue durée* of the south and of the demographic fate of non-Dinka groups who had intermarried with them.

Equatorian supporters of the administrative division of the south, presented as decentralization, aimed to fend off what they saw as Dinka inner colonization. Those (largely Dinka) who opposed it saw it as a "redivision." To them, it meant that the Southern Region's nascent public opinion would no longer be able to stand as united against the encroachment of the central government. Opponents doubted the northerners' assurance that real decentralization was what was being offered. During these years, all the most prominent opponents to regionalization were arrested and the recalcitrant ex-Anyanya garrison in Bor attacked. When Nimeiri announced by decree the division of the south into three regions, there was no one left to organize constitutional opposition. In the end, the powers of each of the three southern regions (Bahr El Ghazal, Upper Nile, and Equatoria) were much less than what had been granted to the Southern Region in the Addis Ababa Agreement. They could no longer elect the president of the HEC and their governors, who were appointed by the president. They had no control over their own taxes, collected by Khartoum and redistributed by the president.[151] In the end, to its Dinka opponents, supporters of the "redivision" were "unpatriotic" and had let themselves be manipulated by Khartoum in dismantling the Addis Ababa Agreement.[152] This bolstered their discourse of group legitimacy—the Dinka were the true patriots.

To compound this, the announcement of the division of the south into three regions had real consequences for the Dinka in Juba. What followed was the forcible relocation of Dinka workers. Ironically, the tables would turn in the third civil war, when Dinka troops would tell the Equatorians (and others) to "return to where they come from." Yet the comparison between the two periods can only go so far, as explained in the next chapters. The parallel merely shows that from the colonial administration to the current government, the forced removal or relocation of populations has been used to impact (maintain or avoid upsetting) the order of power.

The forced relocations of the early 1980s constituted an important historical precedent because it was engineered and carried out by southerners onto other southerners, as a Dinka from Bahr El Ghazal recounts:

[It was a] very harsh implementation. People were chased out of homes, and imagine that was about June and July, rains were falling. So this is my experience of the *kokora* because I was in it. I had to leave because even my employees were not looking at me, in a friendly way. And some of the workers whom I left in Mangala, . . . they were actually removed physically by people of the area.[153]

But this process of forced relocation, which one might have supposed would appease the fears of the Equatorians, also further catalyzed their hostility. Some Equatorian women married to Dinka men left with them, as a Didinga woman remembers: "The Dinka were dominating everything. And the Equatorian girls were educated and worked in the ministries and were married by the Dinka. The Equatorian girls married to the Dinka were taken by them at the time of the *kokora*. Communities were angry."[154] The perceived uprooting of Equatorian women further antagonized the Equatorian communities for decades to come. The same respondent compared this early 1980s period, to the post-2005 era carrying into the third civil war. She expressed the anxiety felt by many non-Dinka and Equatorian groups faced with what they considered a Dinka domination in both government and army positions as well as on the marriage market. Both were related: unequal access to government positions created wealth inequalities, compounded by the fact there were already rumors of corruption at the time. Wealth inequalities played out on the marriage market, which had demographic implications: higher Dinka bridewealth prices disqualified Equatorian men from marrying Dinka women.[155] It allowed Dinka men to marry "cheaper" non-Dinka/Equatorian women, which furthered Dinka expansion. The political-economic-demographic pattern of domination was expressed by this respondent when she asked, "In a hundred years, will the minorities of South Sudan all be finished?"[156] Meanwhile, the demeaning depiction of Dinka women as less domestically skilled than Equatorian women and therefore less apt to shoulder the political duties of representation participated in Equatorian discourses of group legitimacy and entitlement.[157]

Thus the 1970s–early 1980s postwar era, instead of pacifying relations, reinforced ethnic stereotypes and ethnic competition for newly available (and then shrinking) resources. Unequal access to government positions augmented resentment, fears, and discourses of group legitimacy and entitlement.

The Beginning of the Second Civil War: 1975–83

The 1973 constitution had established the Sudan as a secular state. But any change in the law would affect the rights of all non-Muslims in Sudan. Nimeiri had moved toward Islam to survive his Islamic opponents. To please the majority, in September 1983 Nimeiri imposed shari'a law (the "September Laws") soon after the dissolution of the Southern Regional Government. The division of the south into three regions in June 1983 now made the creation of an Islamic state easier, since the south no longer controlled a Southern Regional Assembly.[158] In parallel, the reinforcement of the ties between the Sudan and other Arabic countries worried more and more southerners, who felt the state was getting closer to be an Arab Islamic state.[159] As noted by Peter Woodward, "Nimairi [sic] did not unite Southerners, but he did make many of them feel that the Addis Ababa Agreement was no longer the basis of a relationship."[160] With the "September laws" and the division of the south into three regions, he had alienated most of the southerners and prepared fertile grounds for a rebellion. Different segments of the society joined in to complete what was left unfinished by the Anyanya and the South Sudan Liberation Movement—the independence of South Sudan.[161]

But the few remaining ex-Anyanya fighters in Ethiopia were not a significant military or political force.[162] "Anya-Nya II" was a generic term for bands operating in the south, not all of whom had contacts in Ethiopia. The military successes of the various Anya-Nya II groups were meager, but the more it became apparent that Khartoum was abrogating the Addis Ababa Agreement, the more popular the groups became among civilians and soldiers in the south. They started proliferating in the Upper Nile, Jonglei, Bahr El Ghazal and Lakes provinces. Most armed groups were not connected to one another. It was difficult to distinguish whether or not, in the beginning of the 1980s, they were sharing common grievances or were just opportunistic. Indeed, in the context of an economic no-man's-land, these ex-fighters found that taking back arms and raiding cattle would provide an easy source of income.[163] While only a few received support from Ethiopia, the fall of Idi Amin in Uganda in 1979 brought new weapons in the south.[164]

From 1980 to 1983, the Anya-Nya II attracted deserters not only from the army and the police but also from secondary school students and other civilians who were trained in Ethiopia.[165] By 1982, more southern army officers were in contact with the guerrillas. Throughout April and May 1983, more and more police and military officers joined them.[166] By 1983, these groups were active in Nasir and Bentiu; along the Jonglei Canal line; and in Aweil, Tonj, and Rumbek districts.[167] The army's response in tackling the ambushes of these groups on trucks and attacks on rural police posts was to retaliate with helicopter gunships. The US had alerted Nimeiri about the consequences of abolishing the Southern Region and imposing Islamic law. But since Sudan had become a counterweight in the region against communist Ethiopia, Nimeiri had already acquired weapons. He could afford to ignore the American concerns and knew that the American administration would continue supporting him militarily against Russia's allied Ethiopia and Libya (who both gave weapons to the Anya-Nya II), no matter what he did in his own country.[168]

In January 1983, the army battalion 105, with garrisons in Bor, Pibor, and Pochalla and under the command of ex-Anyanya officers, refused the order coming from Khartoum of moving to the north based on their interpretation of the Addis Ababa Agreement that they would only serve the south. Dhol Acuil, then vice president of the HEC, tried to mediate, and so, it would seem, did John Garang, at the time head of the Staff College in Omdurman, by coming to Bor. But it turned out that Garang had been involved in the planning of the defection of battalion 105 with some other Southern Command officers. The Bor garrison repulsed the attack by the Sudanese army, and Garang joined them in Ethiopia.[169] Combined with the abolition of the Southern Region, the Bor mutiny triggered other mutinies and desertions in garrison towns across the south.

The Sudan's People Liberation Movement/Army (SPLM/A) was founded in July 1983 in Ethiopia out of the amalgamation of veterans of the ex-Anyanya, the Anya Nya II, and the new mutineers of Bor. But there was immediately a struggle over its leadership, between the senior ex-Anyanya officers who pursued southern independence and the younger Anyanya veterans who advocated for a more revolutionary transformation of the entire country.[170] By the end of July 1983, Garang took the command of both military and political wings of the Ethiopia-backed movement.[171] Despite the tensions, this new movement was clearly more coordinated, sophisticated, and apparently clearer in its aims than the Anyanya rebels had been, and posed a greater military threat to the government.[172]

Thus started the second civil war. In contrast to the Torit mutiny of 1955, it started officially with the Bor mutiny of 1983 and was organized by Nilotic officers in the Upper Nile region. The SPLA recruited first in Bahr El Ghazal and Upper Nile and was depicted as a Dinka army. The Equatorian leadership (including Lagu and Tembura) was still motivated by its aversion to the Dinka. It supported government assaults and ethnic opposition against the mutiny, which started in the rural areas within the first months of the civil war.[173]

Legacies of Slavery and the Ethnicization of Identities

A few deep trends from this sweeping pre–second civil war history continue to impact the politics of South Sudan to the present day. They concern the legacy of military slavery, the making of ethnic identities, and how this set of hierarchical relations conditioned group attitudes, especially for the Dinka.

Slavery was not only the ultimate ranked relationship, but it persisted even after the abolition of the slave trade, well into the 1950s and beyond.[174] In South Sudan, it was deeply connected to the military. The military is the institution closest to slavery in modern nations, and Johnson noted how military slavery had been an institution in Sudan in which "the slave soldier became a slave by being a soldier." Ethnic ranking was also key to understanding military slavery and its choice of "martial races," which particularly affected Dinka areas.[175] The descendants of slave soldiers would serve in both the colonial and post-colonial Sudanese army.[176] The British had fostered a culture of militarized masculinity in their soldiers, which, according to Decker, "produced fierce warriors who did not question authority and were not afraid to use violence."[177] By the time the second civil war exploded in 1983, some families of professional soldiers were still the descendants of Sudanese slave soldiers.[178] The experience of slavery—and military slavery in particular—remain key to understanding the SPLA, an army dominated by those most affected by this form of degradation, the Dinka. Besides, the Sudanese army also continued to forcibly conscript South Sudanese people throughout the second civil war.[179] The use of camp followers and child soldiers in the SPLA would echo that of the gun boys, female agricultural slaves, and female concubine slaves during the Turkiyya and the Anglo-Egyptian Condominium, while military patronage evoked the central role of the patron in slave soldiers' units.[180]

Military slavery would also tie the destinies of Uganda and South Sudan forever, as the British incorporated the Sudanese slave soldiers into what would become Uganda's army. During South Sudan's first civil war, Idi Amin, a Kakwa (which in South Sudan amounted to an Equatorian), incorporated southern Sudanese refugees into Uganda's army.[181] After Amin's fall in 1979, some of these recruits returned to South Sudan, bringing along their Ugandan comrades.[182] These comrades from ethnic groups overlapping the Sudan-Uganda borders, such as the Kakwa, the Madi, or the Lugbara, were considered foreigners; labeled "Nubians," "Sudanese," or "Anyanya" in Uganda; and had to flee to South Sudan to avoid retribution.[183] In the third civil war, these very same groups and others on the South Sudan-Uganda border would be told, this time by the SPLA, to leave South Sudan and "return" to their country—this time supposedly Uganda.

Colonial rule in Sudan was brief, and its imprint was even shorter in the south than in the north, since territory in the south had only effectively been under control since 1920, with a very small British presence.[184] But about thirty years of increasingly effective colonial administration still reinforced—or even sometimes created—tribal structures and divisions. Most important, it consolidated the legacy of ranked relations within the south, from military slavery to the ranking of ethnic groups. Colonial attempts to sort out "pure" ethnic groups and send them back to their areas also formed a precedent for future episodes throughout the history of South Sudan, such as the violent forced relocation of Dinka surrounding the *kokora* in 1980. The Equatorian victims who fled government attacks in the third civil war would make a direct link between the *kokora* years and the "payback" inflicted by their Dinka perpetrators[185]

Historical memory and tradition were adapted to fit new wars. The first civil war and the Addis Ababa agreement reinforced ethnic divisions by providing legitimacy to groups who claimed ownership over the national project and by creating competition and tensions over the allocation of resources. Just as Equatorians felt that they led the struggle for national representation in 1972 and had little tolerance for other groups benefiting from shrinking resources, so did the Dinka in the 2005–13 period. The third civil war (2013–), because of its genocidal violence, would antagonize ethnic identities even further. The process of war and violence would considerably bolster, deepen, and develop ethnic identities and stereotypes.

Slavery and the colonial ranking of group worth impacted group attitudes. Dinka expansion, although achieved through material and human capital accumulation, was also driven by motives such as domination, autonomy, legitimacy, or prestige, all of which may take precedence over rational economic interests.[186] Dinka myths retell how they started to flee the Gezira area to escape drought and slave raids by the "Arabs" in the "north" centuries ago. Over time, slavery went on intermittently, from the sixteenth century to the second civil war. During the second civil war, militias comprising Baggara Arabs from the north would raid those areas for slaves again. There was and would be little intermarriage between Islamic northerners and non-Islamic southerners—the northerners would not want a "slave" in the family, and the Dinka would not marry a "slave trader" who would consider them as second-class citizens.[187]

The violent and traumatic legacy of this abusive relationship with the north cannot be overstated. Ethnic groups are typically driven by the goal to improve their social identity in competition and comparison with other groups.[188] This drive and the constantly reopened wound of slavery would continue to impact Dinka attitudes toward the north. Fights over defining the north-south border— the former slaving frontier—would stir a predominantly Dinka nationalism after 2005.[189] Most Dinka hardliners and architects of genocidal violence would come from these border areas most vulnerable to slave raids.

The trauma and humiliation associated with being considered "primitive" in comparison to other more "advanced" groups during colonial times, combined with other factors such as shrinking available resources, become explosive. Donald Horowitz's conclusions are particularly illuminating:

> For certain groups, the discovery that ethnic strangers had mastered the modern skills associated with the colonial rulers more completely

than they themselves had, compounded and perpetuated the humiliation of the colonial experience.... There is much evidence that so-called backward groups are more frequent initiators of ethnic violence and advanced groups more frequent victims.[190]

As many groups who have been considered "backward" and instructed to "catch up" with their competitors have done, the Dinka would seek group legitimacy in the political system. This translated into an influx of Dinka into government positions after 1972 in what was perceived as a "Dinka domination." Overall, being considered mere "animals" by both the northern Sudanese and the colonial administration—and to a certain extent by their ethnic competitors who internalized these categories—the Dinka would exhibit the same behavioral traits as many other "backward" groups before them. First, they displayed a fear of extinction, which participated in their drive to "catch up" with other groups "before it is too late." This would impact the Dinka's attitude toward state-building during and after the second civil war. Second, they exhibited severe anxiety about threats from other groups, which included both northerners and other ethnic competitors.[191]

Interestingly, fear of extinction typically reflects demographic insecurity. A fear of extinction and a real demographic superiority, as contradictory as they seem, often go hand in hand.[192] This demographic insecurity underlined many Dinka cultural principles meant to guarantee their demographic strength. Accordingly, they effectively gained and maintained numerical superiority over other groups for centuries. The Dinka fear of extinction as a group would continue to impact the decisions of its elite, with grave consequences right before and during the third civil war. Most important, because the British left the south to Khartoum and a new wave of Arab inner colonization ensued, the decolonization of the south only came into full effect in 2011. Only independence freed the southerners, which is typically a moment where fears of being subordinated by other ethnic competitors resurface. The anxiety of being "dominated" again persisted in all group attitudes after 2011, both those toward one another and those toward Khartoum.

The Nilotic frontier continually shifted southward from central Sudan through the large-scale absorption of other ethnic groups, to coincide with the north-south frontier.[193] In 2011, South Sudan became independent, and even though several border points with Sudan remained contentious, South Sudan officially had a border and a defined territory. The SPLM/A lost the battle with Sudan to incorporate its neighbors to the north and had to give up the Nuba Mountains and Abyei.[194] Thus the north-south Nilotic frontier was confined.

So, within South Sudan, the Dinka tried to push further south and east. They had to contend with laxer rules of incest, which meant they increasingly practiced endogamy, limiting their expansion.[195] They also had to cope with non-Dinka groups actively resisting their expansion through the prohibition of intermarriages with the Dinka in interwar periods (that is, in times of peace, when they could). This made Dinka expansion by other nonpeaceful means the only other option. Dinka expansion still relied partly on marriage but was increasingly coerced and achieved through violent capital accumulation accelerated by war. The second civil war would herald an often violent Dinka inroad into non-Dinka territories (particularly Equatoria), while the third civil war presaged an even more violent conquest.

Ethnic competition in the south and the legacy of the Dinka demographic expansionism were never lost on the Sudanese government. Khartoum instrumentalized fears of Dinka domination and built on the legacy of ethnic stereotypes. Non-Dinka groups were perfect candidates to be armed and formed into militias to fight the new SPLA in 1983 and throughout the second civil war.[196]

THE SPLA AND THE MAKING OF AN ETHNIC DINKA ARMY

1983–2005

In its first year, the SPLA looked like an activist rebellion: a national liberation movement with a Marxist rhetoric, constrained by scarce resources and therefore entertaining better relations with civilians it had to rely on.[1] But the SPLA's ideology was highly contextual and short lived. Regional politics explain why the SPLA formulated a Marxist project in the first place. Sudan and Ethiopia each sponsored rebel groups in one another's territory, and the SPLM/A ended up depending on Ethiopia's support. This was used by some officials in Washington to justify continued American military support to Khartoum. In reality, the SPLM/A had few options other than relying on regimes disapproved of by the West (such as that of Mengistu).[2] The SPLM/A's main and immediate goal was to overthrow Sudan's President Nimairi, who was backed by the West. But it was not the only anti-Nimairi group and it needed to ally with the national opposition. Ethiopia was fighting its own separatists as well, and a "national liberation movement" was expected to attract more sympathy.[3] Besides, without clear borders, implementing separation from the north of Sudan posed many problems. The north and the south could not exclude each other physically or economically. The last decade following the Addis Ababa Agreement had proved that establishing a first front in Juba instead of Khartoum was already admitting defeat.[4] Former SPLA members explained, "Garang thought that for us to get what we wanted, we needed to go to the head of the snake in Khartoum, and the tail was in the south. He thought we needed to go to Khartoum."[5]

As a result, "revolution" and not "separation" became the official motto of the SPLM/A.[6] The problem was that this decision was mainly taken by the leadership

FIGURE 2.1.   John Garang, leader of the SPLA, speaks to journalists on June 11, 2002, in Kapoeta, then southern Sudan. Photo by Simon Maina/AFP via Getty Images.

to attract national and external support but did not reflect the aspirations of the SPLA's (increasingly Dinka) constituency. According to the same former SPLA members,

> Garang came up with his agenda of unity, but the songs of his soldiers were all about separation. So there was a division between the political and the military. In 1986, it was still not even clear that Garang was so pro-unity. He would openly declare that getting the Nuba Mountains on his side was meant to neutralize the Anya Nya II. Garang was struggling with his Arabic. He never lived in Khartoum much. When he addressed these constituencies, he called it a tactic ... Garang's problem was his constituency. He had a message for his constituency in the south, another for the north, and another for the international community.[7]

The SPLM/A exposed its ideology in its July 1983 manifesto, which focused on the specific grievances of the south.[8] Through language focusing on underdevelopment, religion, and nationality, this manifesto was designed to win broader support by appealing to other regions and sectors of Sudanese society. The SPLA's project of a "New Sudan," a secular state, enabled it to forge political and military alliances with other neglected regions of Sudan. It purported that the central government's attempts at creating a Sudanese national identity based on Islam and the Arabic language and culture had obscured the common grievances the south shared with other neglected regions of Sudan (especially the west and the east). It built on the failure of the 1972 Addis Ababa Peace Agreement implementation and on the central government's intent of undermining it.[9]

With this rhetoric, the SPLA gained popularity in both the south and the north. Even though the US government and opponents to Mengistu dismissed the SPLM/A on account of its Marxist rhetoric, John Garang started to address a wider audience over Radio SPLA broadcast from Ethiopia and to talk about the real experiences of Sudanese without the communist jargon. He mentioned social and economic problems that were common to all Sudanese, and although he admitted that the south's grievances were a more intense form of these issues in Sudan, he dismissed the idea of separation as a solution to it.[10] On the contrary, Garang proposed a true autonomy of the regions of Sudan, the restructuring of the central government, and the fight against racism and tribalism as the foundations of a "New Sudan."[11]

The SPLM/A purported to fight against imperialism and reactionaries in general but identified its enemies as religious fundamentalists and members of the elite—both northern and southern Sudanese—preoccupied with their own jobs. This was a clear reference to non-Dinka southerners (mostly Equatorians) who had supported the redivision (the *korora*) of the south into three regions and were considered unpatriotic. Other southern Sudanese enemies included Anya Nya II warlords (often Nuer) who were reluctant to ally themselves with the SPLA and who, along with ex-Anyanya (mostly from Equatoria), were dedicated to a separatist agenda. In other words, political enemies were mostly non-Dinka. Different ethnic constituencies competed for different political projects (revolution/unity, separation, redivision). Yet even within the SPLA ranks, the question of revolution/unity versus separation was never solved, and competition also divided different Dinka constituencies. Such unresolved dilemmas gave room for future dissension within the movement.[12]

It is not surprising then that the SPLM/A's military machine was a strategic means for winning military support and impressing colleagues, not an engine meant for radical Marxist-inspired social transformation.[13] By 1991, at the time of the SPLA's split, no one was talking of socialism anymore and the 1983 manifesto had been forgotten.[14] Did it matter? After all, even Stalin had a very primitive reading of Marx, and the overthrow of old regimes by revolutionary vanguards often has little to do with ideology.[15] In the case of the SPLA, the mostly pastoralist recruits loathed Marxism and harbored conservative views of society.

Inside the SPLA: Recruitment, Brutality, and Ethnic Discrimination

Recruitment and Organization of the Guerrilla Group

The SPLA drew most of its recruits from the Upper Nile and Bahr el Ghazal regions. The thousands of soldiers and refugees fleeing South Sudan in the beginning of the war were the first source of manpower for the SPLA.[16] The guerrilla army organized their movement into Ethiopian refugee camps where they could access food and medical supplies.[17] The first wave of recruits was mostly composed of secondary school and university students as well as office workers, all of whom were trained and incorporated into the *Jamus* (Buffalo) battalion in 1983.[18]

But the SPLA still had to organize recruiting campaigns by sending officers into Bahr El Ghazal.[19] These campaigns seem to have been quite successful, since thousands of recruits quickly crossed the Nile River into Ethiopia. Most recruits were Dinka.[20] Soon the SPLA rank and file was composed of poorly educated and ill-trained recruits.[21] Mostly illiterate, they made foreign and national observers compare the SPLA to a peasant army of volunteers.[22]

The recruits, despite some ethnic differences, shared nationalist and patriotic sentiments. The leadership initially thought that, socialism being the ideology of the poor, more people would rush to join the struggle. But it soon found out that very few of the southerners who joined were socialists. Anger and frustration at Khartoum's regime, especially after the division of the southern region and the imposition of shari'a law in September 1983, were what drove recruitment into the SPLA, combined with an economic crisis and the paralysis of state institutions.[23] Dinka communities also feared that ethnic rivalries and animosities would be instrumentalized and magnified by Khartoum. This was quite useful to the SPLA, who tapped right into the Dinka cattle-keepers' anxiety of losing their herds to raiding by other groups supported by Khartoum, such as the Murle. A Bor Dinka remembered, "The people who joined the SPLA and had cattle didn't really know what they were fighting for. But the SPLA sent in mobilizers to tell them they had a training center: 'You better come and train so you can protect your cattle from the Murle,' they told the Dinka. So basically, 80 percent of the able male population in 1985–86, joined the movement. Very few were politicized. Most just wanted to protect their cattle."[24]

Meanwhile, a clear divide emerged between the military officers, the politicians, and the intellectuals. "Bourgeoisie," "reactionary," "revolutionary," and "comrade" were common terms in the vocabulary of the SPLA and of some civilians behind the SPLA frontlines. The SPLA ostracized, marginalized, and imprisoned intellectuals and politicians. This Marxist political game (especially practiced by young officers) did not reflect the reality of South Sudan. Many members of the SPLM/A were not socialist, even at the highest levels. They did not read the war in terms of conflict between capitalism and socialism. And as for the "peasants," most of them were hostile to it. The very harsh and dehumanizing training conditions of new recruits and the techniques used within the movement to control the potential for dissent created mistrust and frustration at the improvised Marxist cadres. Those who had gone through the school of political training were the most assiduous reactionaries against the "revolution."[25]

Aversion for the movement's revolutionary ideology contributed to inhibit the formation of a strong link between the national liberation movement's soldiers and the very people they were supposed to fight for.[26] Some commanders also appealed to the soldiers with the lure of gain or invoked fear or hatred for different ethnic groups to motivate them to fight.[27] Aversion to Marxism only strengthened the conservative reactions of many recruits, who felt that the Marxist ideology advertised in these SPLA camps threatened traditional social structures and practices. As a matter of fact, most men in the SPLA, from high-ranking officers to the lowest rank, felt a strong repulsion at the idea of women's participation in direct combat and believed that the traditional social order should be protected.[28]

By 1984, the mostly illiterate Nilotic men, many of them cattle herders, farmers, and other poor workers from the towns, were given weapons by the SPLA. In 1984, the Jarad division graduated, followed by the Mour Mour (1985), Kazuk (1986), Zalzal (1987), Intifada (1988), and Intisar divisions (1989)—all in Ethiopia's Bonga training camp. They numbered over fifteen thousand troops. Understandably, the guerrilla army had not exerted any social, political, or economic criteria to select its recruits. The SPLA had welcomed people from all walks of life, including fugitives from the Sudanese justice system who took refuge in the new rebel group. Some people lied about their occupation prior to their joining to obtain higher ranks, thinking they could start a new life at a higher social level and with a clean slate. An insider, Peter Adwok Nyaba, attributed to these "rogue" recruits many of the human rights abuses and wastes of resources that occurred during SPLA advances.[29] But this is very unlikely: most of the SPLA recruits were fathers, brothers, uncles, and cousins belonging to the same set of families, not to mention their female relatives who also contributed to the struggle.[30] They and a new generation of men born just prior to and during the war—not lone delinquents—made up the bulk of the troops. They were the ones more likely to be involved in human rights abuses than this minority of outlaws first recruited, especially considering the length of that civil war (twenty-two years).

Violence

Nyaba also traced back the origin of some SPLA soldiers' violent behavior toward civilians to a particularly brutal training.[31] But violence went back even earlier:

the recruits had already experienced violence prior to joining the SPLA. In the early years of the war, they had suffered through the arduous journey to Ethiopia's training camps and were sometimes met by either hostile SPLA troops or by other armed groups.[32]

This triggered a cycle of SPLA retaliation, which had serious repercussions on Nuer civilians and lasted until 1988.[33] It also formed the backdrop of the 1991 massacre, as a Bor Dinka explained: "The SPLA soldiers passed through Nuer Gajaak land and were commanded by Kerubino and William Nyuon, who were both horrible guys. They made reprisals on the Nuer Gajaak. From 1985, the Dinka from Bahr El Ghazal trying to join Ethiopia were killed on the way . . . Bad blood between the Dinka and the Nuer goes back to the years between 1984 and 1986, when Dinka recruits from Bahr El Ghazal crossed to go into Ethiopia for training—the Dinka Agar, Dinka Malual. The Gajaak Nuer were particularly targeted in reprisals."[34] Decades later, while the Dinka remembered the 1991 Bor massacre, the Nuer remembered the massacres of 1987–88: "When the SPLA troops came to the area of Lankien, in 1988, Kerubino was killing cattle for meat, and you just kept quiet, otherwise you'll be harmed. They just raped and left, forbidden by commanders from taking the women with them."[35]

Once they reached Ethiopia, the new SPLA recruits, who were both survivors and perpetrators of violence, were brutalized by their future brothers-in-arms. Training was very harsh, often involving menial tasks for months on end, especially in the early days.[36] SPLA training camps, even if rather typical of military training camps, were described as spaces of dehumanization. Insiders linked the soldiers' internalization of oppression there to the violence they perpetrated later, characterizing it as a way to regain their manhood.[37]

But more important, violence acted as a group crystallizer.[38] And the new guerrilla army was desperate for internal cohesion: struggles over leadership had not fostered unity. Besides, even the Dinka were far from being a homogeneous "group." So violence acted as a glue between the new recruits: escaping attacks from the Anya Nya II on the way to Ethiopia, surviving brutality in the training camp, and afterwards fighting both the government and its militias. Research shows that "primary group relations, i.e. solidarity and cohesion in the small, face-to-face units of an army, based fighting morale, not the soldiers' identification with anonymous, imagined 'secondary' groups such as the entire army or their country."[39] Decades later, the Dinka recruits drawn from Lakes state were still friends with each other—they behaved as members of the SPLA "big family." Paternalistic ties and comradeship typically ensure combat effectiveness, and the sponsoring of soldiers' marriages by commanders and their own contributions to their comrades' marriages did just that: they successfully reinforced those patrimonial ties and became part of the military strategy of the SPLA.[40] The perpetration of violence against civilians—particularly sexual violence and the forceful accumulation of women—would also foster groupness.

But first, within the SPLA training camps, violence against other peers from different ethnicities within the SPLA promoted a sense of exclusive groupness—a groupness that was ethnically differentiated, Dinka, and variable in scale following political events. That groupness between comrades from the same constituencies went hand-in-hand with ethnic discrimination is no surprise. Indeed, comradeship has been constituted through othering and both inclusion and exclusion in armies throughout the world, including the Wehrmacht army.[41]

Ethnic Discrimination in the SPLA

Power struggles over the SPLA leadership from the onset of the war greatly contributed to violence within the guerrilla army and against new recruits. The split between the Anya Nya II and Garang's faction was as much ideological as personal. Garang had only served eight months in the Anyanya during the first civil war when he was made a captain, and he was often perceived as arrogant. Although a colonel by the beginning of the second civil war, he relied on more experienced Anyanya veterans for advice on how to conduct the war. His lack of military experience caused tension with some more senior experienced elements.[42] Ethiopian interference into the struggles for the SPLA leadership created further dissension in Itang.[43] Two factions emerged: one, under Samuel Gai Tut, represented the unfulfilled goals of secession of the Anyanya (with Akuot Atem and William Abdallah Cuol); the other, under Garang, expanded the political aspirations to a new national dimension (with William Nyuon Bany and Kerubino Kuanyin Bol).[44]

Meanwhile, there were also tensions from the onset between Garang and the Malual Dinka from Bahr El Ghazal. It was estimated that the Malual Dinka made up about 45 percent of the SPLA ranks once they arrived in Ethiopia, and their percentage would only grow throughout the years. But some of them also joined the Anya Nya II. The Malual leader Kawac Makuei was made lieutenant colonel and appointed fifth in line in the SPLA leadership. He commanded the Jamus battalion in Bahr El Ghazal. Garang arrested Makuei after he refused to turn on his own community, and Makuei would remain one of the longest-held prisoners of war in SPLA camps. His imprisonment would strain the relationship between the Malual and Bor Dinka troops up to the end of the war.[45]

As a result, by 1988 and the neutralization of the Anya Nya II, there were three factions in the SPLA: the Dinka of Bahr El Ghazal, the Bor Dinka (in fact from around Twic East and Bor), and some Nuer. There were some representatives of other ethnicities, but they mattered little at the highest leadership level.[46] All in all, about 80 percent of the SPLA was Dinka.[47]

Ethnic discrimination was key in the process of "ethnicizing" further the Dinka-dominated SPLA. The SPLA's ethnicization was also the result of the past century's legacy of ethnic ranking. By promoting ethnic homogeneity through discrimination, the SPLA removed what Donald Horowitz calls the "irritating comparison" with other ethnic groups inherited from colonial times.[48] The ethnicization of the SPLA effectively removed non-Dinka recruits who had been, in the eyes of Dinka recruits, favored by the colonial administration and were once at the top of the ranking system. Since the Dinka were not a coherent group, ethnic discrimination against other non-Dinka recruits increased their "groupness." This groupness was driven by the Bor Dinka, led by Garang, and culminated in the 1991 split, when Garang openly played the "ethnic card" against his Nuer rival Riek Machar, a popular commander in northern Upper Nile who had called for his removal and displayed the attributes of an ethnopolitical entrepreneur (much like Garang) to mask governance issues and contain intragroup issues within the SPLA.[49]

Ethnic Discrimination against the Nuer

Nuer recruits were the first victims of racism in the SPLA. They had been considered suspicious especially following the SPLA assassination of Samuel Gai Tut (a Nuer) in 1984 over leadership struggles and over debates on what exactly the SPLA should "liberate" (the south or the entire country). Access to training was ethnically discriminatory: Dinka recruits from Bor and from Bahr El Ghazal were given privileged access to military training. One former SPLA soldier, a Nuer trained in Itang, remembered, "The majority of the people in senior military positions, and those military officers who had been sent to military school, were Dinka, most of them from Bahr El Ghazal and Bor. During training, the Nuer felt the difference between Dinka and Nuer due to the suspicion against Nuer soldiers following the rift between Gai Tut and Garang. You remained an NCO when your other colleagues went for training. There was racism in SPLA troops against Nuer recruits during the training."[50] SPLA soldiers used derogatory terms and insults against the Nuer, including the term *nyagat*, which meant "looter" or "rebel"—a direct reference to how the SPLA viewed the predominantly Nuer Anya Nya II, and a reminder of colonial stereotypes of the Nuer as "usurpers."[51]

Discrimination against the Nuer by the Dinka also concerned child recruits, and ethnic ranking imbued society in SPLA-controlled areas. For example, a Nuer man remembered joining the SPLA as a boy and being merely used as a domestic slave by a Dinka family: "In 1991, the Bor Dinka would keep Nuer children as house boys while they sent their own Dinka boys to school. I was used as a house boy by a Dinka family, a foster family. In 1987–91 and then onwards, John Garang would tell children that they would go to school and in fact I could not."[52] Discrimination against Nuer recruits would continue impacting the composition of the SPLA for decades: most of its trained senior military officers would be Dinka, and the Nuer recruits would never be trained to handle heavy artillery, which would leave them at a disadvantage in the third civil war (2013–).[53]

The wound left by Gai Tut's assassination and the discrimination against Nuer recruits would also fester and become a recurrent grievance of the Nuer, who felt robbed of the liberation movement's leadership by a treacherous Dinka-led SPLA. The Nuer did have a role in the start of second civil war, marked by the defection of army battalion 105 with garrisons in Bor, Pibor, and Pochalla in January 1983. A former Dinka commander acknowledged the part played by these garrisons: "Jamus, following the 104–5 battalions, was a battalion that moved to Aweil and recruited in Bahr El Ghazal into Mourmour division in 1984–85. Timsa battalion remained in Jonglei and attacked Pibor. Timsa was mostly Nuer . . . Jamus was three-quarters Nuer. Koryom had mostly recruits from Jonglei and Upper Nile. Battalions 104 and 105 were mostly Nuer recruits. Battalion 104 was headed by Kerubino (a Dinka), and battalion 105 by William Nyuon Bany (a Nuer). The Dinka came after the formation of Koryom division . . . Therefore the movement was started by the Nuer. Anya Nya II was started by Bol Kuany (a Nuer) in 1975."[54]

The assassination of Gai Tut and the SPLA massacre of Nuer civilians in 1986–88 in Upper Nile would serve in 1991 to justify to the Nuer troops their massacre of Dinka in Bor.[55] The Nuer political elite would also use Gai Tut's assassination to gain political capital and motivate its constituency around the prospect of the assassination of another Nuer leader, Riek Machar, in the third civil war.[56] Ultimately, as one Nuer respondent explained, "the Nuer feel they've been spoiled of their military leadership since 1955. Garang took over after the assassination of Gai Tut."[57] All in all, Nuer "groupness" varied just as much as that of the Dinka and other ethnic groups. Violence acted as a catalyst of group crystallization, and so violence against Nuer recruits of various places contributed to group-making there as well.

Ethnic Discrimination against Others

But the Nuer were not the only ones to be discriminated against within the predominantly Dinka SPLA. A former Equatorian (Lango) SPLA first lieutenant recounted, "I joined the SPLA in 1989. I was trained in Kapoeta . . . a Dinka was the commander . . . There was unity among the South Sudanese to win independence, but most officers were Dinka. So by the time of independence, most high ranking officers were Dinka. The Equatorians were voiceless. If you raised your voice, they killed you ... When Dinka people mistreated other tribes, before 1991, they were united. Most of the high-ranking officers were Dinka and they gave ranks to Dinka only. It was not only the Equatorians (who were discriminated), the Shilluk too—the Nuer were a bit better off—the Balanda people had no people in high ranking positions—neither did the Murle."[58]

Ethnic discrimination against non-Dinka recruits extended across all ages and genders and culminated with the creation and promotion of a female Dinka elite matching the Dinka SPLA cadres.[59] The promotion of Dinka recruits to positions of power to the detriment of others raised the question of the leadership's responsibility. A long-time Western observer of the country argued that "the initial formulation of SPLA was very much Dinka. (But) Garang was against others when it came to tribalism ... Garang was trying to build a national movement and the role of Yusif Kuwa (a Nuba), Malik Agar (from Blue Nile) and the National Democratic Alliance and the Eastern Front were big."[60] Yet this observer also admitted that it took until the 2004 Rumbek conference, on the eve of signing the 2005 peace agreement and amid an internal political crisis, for the SPLA leadership to advocate publicly for broader ethnic representation in the SPLA. Not much would change afterwards. A Kuku civilian had a much soberer diagnosis of Garang's nationalist appeals, which echoed the statements of earlier Nuer SPLA recruits about the vacuity of the SPLA's communist project and its appeal to the non-Dinka and non-southerners: "Garang wanted to 'liberate' Equatoria. He used that language because it was the expectation and it made the people join."[61]

Under Mengistu's patronage until 1991, Garang concentrated both the political and military leadership from the start. No SPLM/A convention would be held for another ten years after the founding meeting of the movement in 1983. Civilian figures had no role or say in the making of policy, which was telling of how much the SPLA privileged its military organization over its civilian base.[62] For the troops, this also meant that force was used instead of persuasion to maintain cohesion, thus suppressing the dissenters but not the causes of dissent.[63] The SPLA had the same military structure as the Sudanese army, with an internal security branch, and mimicked its relationship to its own soldiers and to civilians.[64] After 1984 and the escalation of the war with Anya Nya II, the SPLA purged suspected government agents within its own ranks.[65] Garang's inner circle was instrumental in organizing those purges over the years. That included his wife, Rebecca, and Salva Kiir, the future president of South Sudan, as former government officials remember: "Salva was the first military intelligence chief in the SPLA. He was trained as a first lieutenant by the SAF in military intelligence ... One unique skill he has is that he remembers faces, remembers the names, even the rifle numbers. He's good at it. He's an introvert. He's discreetly intelligent in blackmailing people. He knows how to manage people ... Salva was the right hand of Garang to eliminate all his colleagues—so he didn't have to do it himself."[66] All in all, the SPLA employed ruthless methods to enforce discipline and obedience to the leadership, demoralizing soldiers and making them feel indifferent, apathetic, fearful, and distrustful.

Despite the SPLA's savagery against certain ethnic groups and ethnic discrimination and violence within its own ranks, the SPLA still grew rapidly in numerical strength, attracting more Dinka recruits.[67] Within a couple of years, the SPLA turned from a hit-and-run guerrilla into a rebel group capable of fighting using conventional warfare.[68] By 1991, it totaled between 100,000 and 120,000 troops: nearly the size of the Sudanese army, minus the air force and navy.[69] The SPLA had a much stronger command than its predecessor, the Anyanya, but its reliance on Ethiopia and the fact it sent its "national" force wherever needed created further frustration among its recruits—especially those of Bahr El Ghazal, who could not protect their home areas from raids by government militias.[70]

The 1991 Split and the Dinka SPLA

In 1991, the movement split. The split was rooted in the SPLA leadership style and ethnic discrimination of the past decade. On August 28, 1991, two senior SPLA commanders from Upper Nile, Riek Machar (a Nuer) and Lam Akol (a Shilluk), declared the "overthrow" of Garang via the SPLA two-way radio network and repeated it in a BBC interview. Since they were politically and militarily marginalized, they decided to attract Khartoum's military support. This event signified the beginning of the split of the SPLA into two factions, and paved the way for the multiplication of armed groups throughout the rest of the war.[71] What it also did was to considerably increase the Dinka composition of the SPLA, which ultimately left room for tensions between Dinka constituencies spearheaded by Garang and his deputy Kiir.

Further Ethnic Discrimination after 1991

The increasing ethnicization of the SPLA during the post-1991 period was the result of both ethnic discrimination and defections. Such defections increased suspicion and reinforced ethnic discrimination against non-Dinka recruits still in the SPLA, perceived as potential traitors.[72] This in turn increased defections in a self-sustaining cycle of disintegration and further ethnicization. A former Equatorian SPLA first lieutenant remembered the rise of degrading insults against Equatorians after the split and their demoralizing effects: "They [SPLA] called us *niam-niam*, us Equatorians: 'people who eat people.' They called people of Equatoria like this, from 1991 onwards. That was when we didn't want to be with them. There was no *niam-niam* before 1991."[73]

Discrimination also extended to other areas beyond military promotions and was meant to create long-term structural inequalities to the advantage of Garang's inner circle. This included access to education, a valuable commodity in the south. An Equatorian (Kuku) respondent evoked how "the Bor Dinka were sent abroad to get an education and rule over the country should they win the war."[74] In the end, discrimination against non-Dinka groups further coalesced anti-Dinka sentiments born out of the interwar period.[75] The creation of the South Sudan Defense Forces (SSDF) under Khartoum's auspices in 1997 not only allied all the non-SPLA militias—it "made" this group (composed mostly Nuer and Equatorian, but also Murle, Fertit, etc.) and formalized the rift between this new group and the Dinka.[76] The SPLA leadership and rank and file—and, by extension, the Dinka, depending on the varying levels of Dinka groupness fostered by the leadership—would also build their own perceptions of the SSDF group (encompassing in fact a myriad of non-Dinka ethnicities): they saw them mostly as funded by Khartoum and therefore as traitors and enemies.

Dinka Tensions within the SPLA

Ethnic discrimination against non-Dinka recruits, the 1991 split, and the trauma of the Bor massacre had contributed to increase the level of groupness of the Dinka, coalescing around the person of Garang, a Bor Dinka.[77] The instigation, provocation, and dramatization of violence with ethnic outsiders can be used to define ethnicity.[78] The 1991 Bor massacre contributed to defining the Dinka as the Bor constituency. But more important here, the provocation and dramatization of violence also worked to deflect challenges within the group. The ethnicized split and violence, the Bor massacre, and intragroup policing within the SPLA all worked to deflect challenges against Garang.

But this was not enough. Within a few years, emotions around the Bor massacre subsided as the war continued, and the ethnicized and ethnicizing SPLA was left to deal with its own ethnic demons and its own dwindling groupness. The leadership was very much identified with the Bor Dinka. Not only was the SPLA leader a Bor Dinka, but most of the early recruits in 1984 were from the Upper Nile region, especially from Bor and Baliet. Back then, these early recruits faced a much stronger Sudanese army, and the SPLA suffered a lot of casualties between 1983 and 1985. Dinka recruits from Bahr El Ghazal came in 1985.[79] Bahr El Ghazal had suffered especially from the legacy of unequal access to education.

Therefore, the most educated officers in the SPLA were from Jonglei, in the Bor region. Garang reinforced this trend by fostering the education of Bor Dinka recruits, especially after the 1991 Bor massacre: he sent Bor Dinka officers abroad for training and Bor Dinka youth who had been separated from their families (called "lost boys") were provided education in the West. Meanwhile, officers sent their relatives abroad.

The promotion of Bor Dinka recruits over others nurtured frustration that dated back to the 1970s, when the Bor Dinka were especially accused of domination. One of those Bor Dinka "lost boys" explained: "In 1972, a lot of civil servants were from Bor. That was a problem for the Equatorians and the Dinka from Bahr El Ghazal. In 1983, the SPLA promoted people often based on education. In 1991, the Bor massacre led to displacement . . . The 'lost boys' proximity to Ethiopia meant that they were educated in Kenya, Ethiopia and then the USA, Canada."[80] A further aggravation was that the Dinka recruits from Jonglei, although less and less numerous throughout the years than their Dinka peers from Bahr El Ghazal in the SPLA, were perceived as contemptuous of them.[81]

The Bor Dinka also acquired a reputation for focusing on "business," both inside the south and in neighboring countries. Meanwhile, the Dinka recruits from Bahr El Ghazal, the bulk of the troops, thought of themselves as doing most of the fighting. Their families were the victims of Arab militias raiding for slaves in the northern areas of Bahr El Ghazal. They thought the Bor Dinka were profiting from the war without fighting it anymore. Tensions mounted between these two competing Dinka constituencies, especially after 1991, when fewer non-Dinka recruits acted as a "buffer" between them: "There was tension between the people of Bor and of Bahr El Ghazal: most of those in the frontlines were of Bahr El Ghazal and the leader [Garang] was from Bor, but his people didn't participate in the war. Most of the people of Garang were in the refugee camps."[82]

Tensions combined with increasing political competition between, on the one hand, Garang, followed by his constituency and officers he favored (the future "Garang boys"); and on the other, his second-in-command Kiir, perceived as the representative and spokesperson of the Bahr El Ghazal faction.[83] This competition occurred in the context of a growing SPLA administration marred by corruption, which fostered ethnic patronage that contributed to group-making.[84] Tensions and competition between those two Dinka constituencies were reflected in the evolution of military kinship ties. After 1991, not only did such interethnic military ties and interethnic marriages decrease, but these ties were organized more and more at the Dinka section and clan level. Relations between soldiers and commanders became much more based on ethnicity and nepotism than before, including among the various Dinka sections.[85]

The allegiance of troops was ever more important, given the post-1991 wave of desertions. Commanders who dominated the war economy and turned into warlords posed political threats. But Garang had difficulty removing individuals like Paul Malong, an increasingly powerful Dinka commander from Northern Bahr El Ghazal who would become the SPLA chief of staff in the third civil war, from these positions. This meant that Malong continued to amass wealth, to sponsor his soldiers' marriages, and to marry from different clans locally. Effectively, he was, in the words of a respondent, building a local "empire": "Malong has 86 wives. Where does he get the cattle? From the people. His close family is made of 400 people."[86]

The post-1991 era was especially favorable to the rise of the Dinka Bahr El Ghazal constituency within the SPLA. This was illustrated in the rise of Malong and in his association with the likes of Bona Malual, a long-time Dinka politician from Bahr El Ghazal (Warrap) and one of the future architects of the postwar version of the Jieng Council of Elders (JCE), the group of Dinka interests associated with genocidal violence from 2013 onwards. The political faction of the Dinka from (northern) Bahr El Ghazal formed by Malong and other prominent members of the diaspora aggregated around Kiir. As a former Bor Dinka SPLA commander explained, "Salva was chief of staff and vice-chairman—the next most powerful. Bona Malual and Justin Yach wanted to use him as a steel point to help them break through leadership . . . Garang favored Salva a lot. Salva was just a Sudanese Armed Forces captain when he went to the bush. Garang promoted him as major and member of the High Command. He'd keep him close to him. Garang was always happy with people not challenging him. He took him as a loyalist . . . But over time, it cracked, because of pressures of Salva's constituency."[87] As the relationship between Kiir and Garang deteriorated and Kiir mobilized his troops in Yei in November 2004, Malong saw the opportunity to step in and offer him military and financial backing.[88]

A few different interpretations exist of the reasons for the rift between Garang and Kiir, but they center around the very issues of ethnic representation and leadership, tribalism, and money. The rift followed rumors in November 2004 that Garang intended to arrest and replace Kiir as his deputy with Nhial Deng, another Dinka from Bahr El Ghazal (also from Warrap).[89] At the time, peace negotiations had already started and Garang and Kiir did not see eye to eye on the issue of self-determination or on the issue of the other southern militias grouped in the SSDF. Kiir, a known separatist, supported negotiating with the SSDF and had pushed for the self-determination clause in the 2002 Machakos Protocol, which was a roadmap for the future secession of the south. This completely caught Garang off guard. Garang was a secular unionist and did not support negotiations with the SSDF, in his eyes Khartoum's agents. Garang's reaction had been to remove Kiir from the negotiations and replace him with Nhial Deng. Kiir then felt largely excluded from decisions taken by Garang, who was surrounded by his close circle of allies, the "Garang boys." Without strong personal constituencies, they were the exact opposite of Kiir—educated and considered loyal—and they included Nhial Deng, Kiir's competitor.[90]

Another interpretation of the rift was that it was the result of the growing influence of the emerging faction around Kiir (what would become the JCE) who, paid by Khartoum, sought to postpone the signing of the peace agreement to delay sharing oil revenues with the south. Garang explicitly referred to how much Khartoum would gain from this strategy (US$2.5 billion).[91] To him and his loyalists (one is quoted below), Khartoum sought to split again the SPLA just as it had in 1991, by sponsoring the future JCE faction and by bolstering the SSDF to question the SPLA's legitimacy as an equal partner at the negotiations' table:

> In Yei in 2004, there were tensions between Salva and Garang. One layer was the problems between Garang and Bona Malual, who was very close to Salva. And Bona tried to mount pressure on Salva: Bona Malual wanted to lead but he didn't have any direct link with the SPLM . . . This was one of the factors behind the tensions with Garang . . . Khartoum saw an opportunity to divide the SPLM and to scatter the peace process . . . They promised Salva they'd conclude a peace agreement with him, just like Riek Machar in 1991. If the SPLM split, they would buy time . . . In 2004, Khartoum paid a lot of money to Salva's group to achieve this strategy of splitting the SPLA. They were ready to bring all militias on board. Negotiations with Matiep (the SSDF leader) started then, to make the split of the SPLA bigger and undermine the signing of the CPA and question who was legitimate to signing the CPA and buy time regarding the oil money flowing.[92]

Surely Khartoum's financial gains from a split between the predominantly Bor Dinka leadership and Kiir's constituency do not automatically mean that it engineered it. Garang's appeal to the elusive prospect of power-sharing could very well have been meant to sweep under the rug issues of governance and ethnic favoritism within the SPLA. But Kiir and Garang were certainly at loggerheads when it came to negotiating with the SSDF, and because of Garang's resistance, the Comprehensive Peace Agreement (CPA) would ultimately be signed without incorporating the rest of the south's plethora of armed groups. Only after Garang's death—in 2006, when Kiir was in charge—would the Juba Declaration be signed with the SSDF, formalizing their integration into the SPLA. It is also true that after the 1991 split, this group of Dinka interests—composed of seasoned South Sudanese politicians from the period of the Addis Ababa Agreement and since exiled to London, who had been accused of Dinka domination and were known as anti-Garang—would eventually make their comeback through Malong and Kiir.

Interestingly, Equatorian SPLA soldiers in Yei still considered Garang less tribalistic than Kiir, even though they were no longer enticed by the SPLA's nationalist rhetoric. To them, Kiir's tribalist inclinations were even part of his rift with Garang, and it was clear he had the upper hand: "When Salva came to address the crowd [in Yei], he said 'you people have issues with the Dinka? The Dinka can stay anywhere and nobody can talk.' When the people of Yei heard this speech, people were annoyed . . . That's what brought the tension. Salva saw that the soldiers from Bor were few—the Dinka from Bahr El Ghazal were more, so he had power there . . . he was trying to overcome Garang because he had that manpower with many people from Bahr El Ghazal."[93]

So, was Kiir's mobilization of troops in Yei mostly about a struggle over leadership, resource allocation, and ethnic representation between, on the one hand, Garang, his "boys," and Bor Dinka constituency; and on the other, the Bahr El Ghazal constituency and those dissatisfied with Garang, spearheaded by Kiir? Or was the rift engineered by Khartoum through the group of Bona Malual for financial gains? Or was it a testimony of the tensions between unionists and separatists who undermined the SPLA's nationalist rhetoric, by their manipulation of peace negotiations and their tribalism? It was probably all those things at the same time.

The SPLM Rumbek conference, organized between November 29 and December 1, 2004, right after this military build-up in Yei, became a forum for voicing many grievances. Discussions concerned the corruption of the movement leaders and Garang's personal control over the movement. They also featured the issue of negotiations with the other southern militias (especially SSDF) and the tensions between the unionists and the separatists. It was openly said that the rift between Garang and Kiir dated back ten years, to 1994, when Khartoum had refused to sign the Declaration of Principles (DoP) that first acknowledged the right to self-determination.[94] The minutes of the Rumbek meeting were a testimony to how much contestation there was against Garang then and to how vocal Kiir was about it. The meeting turned into a trial of Garang's leadership. It also featured clear references to the London-based group of interests coalescing around Malual. It revealed the constitution of a clear coalition from Bahr El Ghazal around Kiir. This block included Malong but also other commanders from Bahr El Ghazal and non-Dinka commanders dissatisfied with Garang (such as the Equatorians Mamur Obote and James Wani Igga), who would all stick with Kiir in the third civil war.[95] The SPLA was then a pressure cooker. Yet after Rumbek much of the same autocratic structure remained, and Garang continued to favor Bor Dinka officers over others.[96]

The SPLA's Political Myth of Liberation, Dinka Group Ownership, and the Seeds of Exclusionary Ideology

Ethnic Ranking within the SPLA

Social groups are only evaluated comparatively, and ethnic comparisons are especially potent because, as Horowitz writes, "to lose out in competition and comparison to others who are differentiated on a birth basis is to be afflicted with an apparently permanent disability." Of course, the colonial era had already compared groups and grouped them into the categories of "advanced" and "backward," a language so internalized that it appeared in the SPLA manifesto (the south was part of the "Backward Areas"). Groups labeled as "backward" are generally more intent on securing their place in the political system to confirm their group worth. Especially when a country becomes independent, the greatest anxiety of a "backward" group is a renewed ranking system reminiscent of colonial times, where it is again at the bottom. As struggles over relative group worth transferred to the political system, the SPLA acted as exactly that: a political system.[97] It imported ethnic and social tensions from the Addis Ababa Agreement period.

Ranking permeated the SPLA, where appointment of non-Dinka to high-ranking positions merely amounted to ethnic window-dressing. It also pervaded society in areas it controlled, since most of the administrators were Dinka, even in non-Dinka areas such as Equatoria. I next illustrate how the predominantly Dinka SPLA came to amass and monopolize resources in such areas and eventually created a new dominant Dinka class, the ultimate form of ranking. The SPLA was not just ethnically but also socially ranked—a system that patrimonial ties between commanders and soldiers meant to soothe, ethnicized violence and rhetoric against outside groups meant to hide, and the postwar nationalist discourse meant to mask.[98]

The post-1991 period continued to validate the myth rooted in the past century of military slavery that the Dinka were a "martial race," as the SPLA became further ethnicized. The peace negotiations, culminating in the signing of the CPA, endorsed the ethnicized SPLA as the sole representative of all southerners, including those non-Dinka that it had discriminated against, and the SPLA's political myth of liberation. Promoted to the position of the only southern counterpart of the government in the CPA, the Dinka as a "group" had "liberated" and therefore officially "owned" the south. Yet tensions broiled in the predominantly Dinka SPLA.

Power Dynamics in the SPLA: The Pressure Cooker

The SPLA and the government of Sudan signed the Comprehensive Peace Agreement on January 9, 2005, and Garang became first vice-president of the Sudan. On July 30, 2005, just six months later and less than a year after the Rumbek meeting where he was put on trial by his peers, Garang died in a helicopter crash. He had lost considerable authority among other high-ranking officers who criticized him for his authoritarian leadership style and ethnic favoritism. He had contended with a mounting faction coalescing around Kiir. Kiir was the only other surviving officer of the original members of the High Command. Once reputed to be Garang's hitman, he was immediately nominated as his replacement upon his death.[99]

Garang's few long-time soldiers who had weathered the splits and the rise of the Northern Bahr El Ghazal's constituency left the SPLA. Their decision to leave was related to Kiir being in charge, which spoke volumes about the rift and the changing dynamics within the SPLA by the time of Garang's death. Kiir, who was perceived as "meek-mannered," "in the shadow of John Garang," and "uninspiring," was in every way less charismatic than Garang.[100] He was said not to have "demonstrated any interest in or capacity for politicking or visionary leadership."[101] He was much less known to the international community and had always been vastly underestimated. Over the next decade, he would radically change the demography of the SPLA to retain its control.

Group Legitimacy and Group Entitlement: Toward Exclusionary Ethnic Nationalism

Different discourses of group legitimacy, inherently tied to one's place in the country, were born out of the second civil war. They did not dissipate with time.[102] With the endorsement of SPLA claims by the international community with the CPA, the Bor Dinka SPLA leader Garang was catapulted into the status of "national hero" (especially after his death). The Dinka felt they owned the national liberation project and the south's new equal footing with the north.

But the Dinka were divided in competing constituencies with their own discourses of Dinka group legitimacy. The Dinka from Northern Bahr El Ghazal felt that they were the ones who fought the war—not the Bor Dinka—and suffered the most from northern slave-raids. The discourse of group legitimacy of the Dinka from Northern Bahr El Ghazal, coalescing around the figure of Kiir, would eventually prove lethal. What made this group within the SPLA different was that it was the one to most openly embrace separatism, which opened the question of who "owned" the south—not the vast multiethnic Sudan that the SPLA never in the end "liberated." This paved the way for ethnic and therefore exclusionary nationalism. The Bahr El Ghazal Dinka discourse of group legitimacy held that they had fought the government when others had not. This was only made worse by the constitution of the SSDF, which clearly identified in one block—one "group"—those who had not and who were of different ethnicities. After the CPA, this nationalism would translate into a more and more aggressive discourse of group entitlement and an uncompromising style of governance.

There are probably as many discourses of group legitimacy as there are ethnic groups in South Sudan. The Nuer also had their own. It included the role of the Nuer in Anya Nya II and in the Bor mutiny of January 1983. The Nuer felt they had launched the (separatist) national struggle that culminated in independence. But their discourse, because it was never endorsed by the international community as was the Dinka's through the signing of the CPA, would never prove as potent and therefore as lethal.

From discourses of group legitimacy derived discourses of group entitlement.[103] Because the Nuer thought they had launched the struggle for national liberation (culminating in independence) and because they had lost the battle over SPLA leadership, they felt robbed from their leadership and from "owning" the country. So did the Equatorians, who would consistently bring up the 1955 Torit mutiny and their role in the first civil war as proof and justification of their own "ownership" of the country. In the third civil war, the anti-Dinka sentiments expressed in Nuer and Equatorian discourses of group entitlement would also form the basis of their alliance in opposition groups.

These two discourses of group entitlement, because they expressed frustration with the Bor Dinka and their domination of first the Southern Regional Government and then the SPLA, intersected at the time with the interests and discourses of group entitlement of the Dinka from Northern Bahr El Ghazal. Their own discourse of group entitlement was that they deserved more representation in the predominantly Bor Dinka leadership of the SPLA since they had done most of the fighting. After the war, Malong would tap more openly into the deteriorating intra-Dinka dynamics in the SPLA. Group entitlement discourse would permeate the Dinka militias he recruited, especially in Bahr El Ghazal, under the auspices of the future president Salva Kiir. It would foster group-making by resorting not only to what Brubaker has called a type of "middle-range" historical legacy—like the SPLA struggle—but also to elements of the *longue durée*, such as slavery.[104]

Past and Future Ideology

Yet the SPLA ideology in the second civil war was not anything like the ideology deployed in the third civil war. Even if the SPLA's ideology was as versatile as Garang himself, there is no doubt that Garang was a unionist nationalist. As mentioned earlier, Garang's goal was the "head of the snake"—Khartoum—and he could not afford openly to promote his own constituency, unlike Kiir, who seemed quite open about it both in Yei and in Rumbek in 2004.[105] Garang's newly gained popularity with the West, which propelled the SPLA to an equal footing with Khartoum at the negotiation table, acted as a form of moral restraint on the process of inner colonization. If Dinka expansion was violent on the ground, it was not genocidal. As a matter of fact, the Dinka SPLA soldiers came to settle in Equatoria through (often forceful) intermarriage—meaning they absorbed other groups.[106] This was nothing like the annihilating campaign of the third civil war meant to get rid of the local population and replace it. An Equatorian (Kuku) explained, "In the last war, SPLA soldiers did not settle with the wives and children in Equatoria."[107]

But there was a relationship between the second civil war and the third, because the third war's ideology made use of the political myth of national liberation promoted during the second civil war. The SPLA's leadership—in the person of John Garang—had built a political myth of national liberation meant to attract foreign support and mask the ethnicization and tensions within the SPLA. The CPA, signed under international auspices, legitimized and endorsed this myth. It gave the SPLA legitimacy to rule over the region and the future country in 2005. It disregarded the other southern armed groups drawn from different (above all non-Dinka) ethnic constituencies and grouped under the SSDF and it thereby excluded them from the political community of the future country.

This was particularly hazardous because the danger of revolutionary—and in this case, violently ethnicized—movements is that once in power, they can seek to transform society in their image. Once in power, they "reconstruct the system of legitimacy and the political myth."[108] The ethnicization of the SPLA served the consolidation of this myth: what mattered was not if the Dinka had effectively liberated the south. What mattered was that the myth resonated with the "born-to rule" protoideology of the interwar period and that the predominantly Dinka SPLA rank-and-file believed that they—the Dinka as a "group"—had liberated the country. Symptomatically, as one of the few non-Dinka high-ranking officers

(James Wani Igga) complained, none of the non-Dinka signed important peace negotiation documents in the SPLA's name.[109] This was merely a reflection of who the leadership thought "owned" and propelled the movement.

In the third civil war, what was, in an Equatorian (Kuku) civilian's words, a "new legitimizing myth of Dinka supremacy" made use of this older political myth that had emerged out of the second civil war. Perpetrators' "utterances" to their victims showed that Kiir's regime used the overwhelmingly Dinka composition of the SPLA in the second civil war as the backbone of its annihilating ideology. What was puzzling but consistent with both the resignation of Garang's followers in 2005 and the contradictions inherent to myths was that neither the ideologues nor the perpetrators were the old fighters.[110] In fact, the perpetrators didn't even need to be in the SPLA anymore, as a Balanda victim from Wau noted, which illustrated the spread of this new ideology: "Now the Dinka come and take the land and say: 'you've not been in the SPLA to the bush to fight, so we're taking the land.' Most of them came when they're soldiers after 2013. They don't wear uniforms when they come, but they come wearing weapons—guns."[111] Thus the ideology exceeded the confines of Dinka political and military circles.

All in all, Garang had managed to avert a coup and keep the lid on ethnic supremacist impulses until his death in 2005 through a mix of pan-ethnic Marxist ideology and autocratic rule. But his leadership could not prevent colonial and interwar legacies from combining with wartime violence and ethnic competition to further ethnic groupness on all sides. The groupness of the Dinka constituency from Bahr El Ghazal was arguably the strongest as they made the bulk of the SPLA troops. Yet this did not fully explain why violence in the context of a civil war would become genocidal. The post-2005 period would provide the triggers.

WAR ECONOMY AND STATE-MAKING IN SPLA AREAS

1983–2005

War economies are "system(s) of producing, mobilizing and allocating resources to sustain violence."[1] While war economies are meant to produce and sustain violence, they also produce social reordering and new forms of governance through the accumulation and control of capital. Charles Tilly's famous words—"war made states, and vice versa"—are especially applicable to the SPLA.[2] Its war economy was supposed to sustain its war-making capacity, and in a drive reminiscent of what Tilly observed in sixteenth- and seventeenth-century Europe, war-making fostered the organization of taxes, police forces, and courts and ultimately led to state-making.[3] The SPLA's state-making also came together with the formation of a dominant social class. In this sense, the war economy actually created different groups, with different types of group legitimacy and entitlement. South Sudan's war economy was indicative of what kind of state would emerge after the war once these different military elites fused together. Postwar predation networks would expand on wartime networks in South Sudan.[4]

Looting, Taxation, and the SPLA Administration

Looting

The SPLA's war economy was multifaceted. The first aspect of the SPLA's war economy that I examine is its looting, in what seems to be the most "disorganized" aspect of its resource extraction.

The SPLA consistently plundered civilians for various reasons. It often pillaged out of necessity to survive and continue military operations.[5] Just like civilians, the SPLA was sometimes famine-stricken.[6] Lack of international aid in rebel areas meant there were no relief supplies to be taxed, looted, or hijacked. This pushed the various militias (on both the government and SPLA sides) and marauding bandits to pillage civilians to sustain themselves—at least at first, before trade networks expanded after 1991.

Whatever the motives (need or opportunism), the SPLA troops often moved into civilians' houses, confiscated and ate their food, and robbed them of clothes, kitchenware, and livestock.[7] When humanitarian aid effectively reached SPLA-held areas, troops appropriated relief supplies while brutalizing civilians.[8] Whatever they looted, the SPLA forced the communities to carry.[9] SPLA troops behaved in the same fashion in many parts of the country—especially those they were not from.[10] Yet the looting prompted some civilians to flee with their resources.[11] This was exactly what the SPLA wanted to avert through its administration's taxes. Thus the "roving" bandits described by Mancur Olson had to become more stationary in order to control looting, protect production by civilians, and maintain a steady influx of resources.[12]

Taxes and Administration

The SPLA's rudimentary administration played a key role in sustaining military campaigns with resources it extracted off civilians. It was essential in making the areas under SPLA control at least sustainable economically. Based almost entirely on the old structures of the Native Administration and the provincial governments of the old Southern Region, the SPLA administration was officially meant to restore law and order. But much more important, its purpose was to support the troops and serve military operations.[13] The efficiency of this strategy was demonstrated in the SPLA's rolling back of government advances at the end of 1995, which would have been impossible without civilian support provided through the civil administration.[14] In this sense, war-making steered the development of the civil administration.

Yet the SPLA administration did not amount, according to Øystein H. Rolandsen, to a "well-oiled government machinery."[15] The SPLA administration was rudimentary before the 1990s, although this varied by area. It partly relied on the rural population's payment of taxes in kind. The SPLA taxes consisted of cattle, milk, sorghum (dura), and anything else that could be eaten or traded by the troops.[16] According to Johnson, the SPLA extracted a rough 20 percent tax on items supplied for civilian use.[17] But it is truly impossible to know the exact percentage. Taxes were collected through a chain of intermediaries. The SPLA used colonial structures to coerce civilians into paying tribute and chiefs to assemble it.[18] Violence was the glue that held the system of taxation and forced labor together, and the SPLA sometimes did not even have the monopoly of theft until it asserted control over its territories. Civilians were often forced to feed alternately the army, militiamen, and the SPLA.[19]

The struggling population—especially in areas soldiers did not originate from—often only paid these taxes out of fear of being further robbed. Non-Dinka communities perceived the SPLA as a hostile "Dinka army" who forced food contributions that were merely "organized" looting.[20] The situation looked at first sight different in Dinka areas. In Lakes state in Bahr El Ghazal, a former child soldier recalled that "it was very different: everyone knew what his contribution to the movement was as a Dinka: it was a moral obligation."[21] Households took turns in contributing cattle, but food contributions were supposed to be presented by every family each year.[22]

Yet not all Dinka civilians felt the moral obligation to contribute to the Dinka army. They felt pressured too. A Bor Dinka civilian recounted how people in his community often did not have enough food to feed themselves after the SPLA passed through: "The SPLA taxes consisted of cows, milk, sorghum (dura), and pretty much anything that could be eaten. The joke among locals was that whenever the SPLA was approaching, instead of keeping things in their houses, people would keep their belongings in the bush, and sometimes bury them. The SPLA found out and went outside villages to dig for dura. An old man asked them what they were looking for. Were they looking for *rap* (dura in Dinka)? The old man told them: 'My friends, Garang sent you to fight the enemy, the Arabs, not *rap*.' That's the joke. The SPLA was taking a lot of food . . . The SPLA would leave marks on the ground to tell absentees that when they came back they needed to prepare food for them. Even bulls in cattle camps were to be milked."[23]

Thus, even in Bor Dinka areas, civilians saw the SPLA as busier accumulating resources than fighting against its sworn-enemy. South Sudan was not that different from other African civil wars more famous for their war economies, such as Sierra Leone, where there was also, as David Keen described, "space for a wide variety of parties to engage in their own exploitative 'games' under the cover of a righteous civil war." Soon, the SPLA similarly emerged as a "twin threat" with government forces and other armed groups, including in its home areas.[24] Non-Dinka civilians were not alone in feeling that taxation amounted to extortion. Some Bor Dinka felt this way too, probably aggravated by the fact that troops were by then mostly Dinka from Bahr El Ghazal, the competing constituency.

Rolandsen highlights two competing interpretations regarding how sophisticated or rudimentary the SPLA administration was before 1994. The first, by Alex De Waal, argues that the SPLA administration was mostly very minimal because leadership devoid of democratic inclinations and the availability of food aid meant that the armed group did not need to rely on civilians as much. The second, by Douglas Johnson, posits that the administration was well-structured and developed, but undocumented and too authoritarian, which the 1994 convention was meant to address. This is also the SPLA's own interpretation. According to this view, Rolandsen writes, "the role of the chiefs and their courts should be studied more closely." The chiefships, under the supervision of the civil/military administrators (CMAs), were heavily militarized and instrumental in gathering taxes and manpower for the troops.[25] Chiefs were either intimidated or coopted, and the rulings of customary courts were also used by all armed groups to procure more resources. Therefore, the two interpretations are not incompatible. Instead, they complement each other: the SPLA administration was indeed minimal. It relied on chiefs and courts whose (arguably main, in the case of the chiefs) purpose was to gather resources. If there was anything "civil" about this administration, it was militarized to serve the SPLA's war-making and personal enrichment machine.

SPLA Forced Labor

Looting and taxes were inextricably linked with forced labor. Civilians were forced to transform goods stolen or extorted from them, into support for the troops.[26] Women were at the forefront of food production. Typically, in Dinka areas such as Lakes in Bahr El Ghazal, women mostly willingly supported the SPLA troops through women's organizations.[27] But in Equatoria, other women, mostly from ethnic groups less represented among troops, were forced to cook food and brew beer for the troops. They also cultivated tobacco, sunflowers (for oil production), and honey. The SPLA took at least half of what they cultivated in collective crops (in Lobone camp in eastern Equatoria, for example) or of what they picked up in the bush.[28]

Support was especially coerced when the SPLA was in a fragile military position. For example, women from Nimule remembered being forced to support SPLA troops when the government tried to retake the town from 1994 to 1998. In those days, one of them recalled being forced to grind sorghum and to brew over twenty barrels of alcohol a day to be taken to the frontlines.[29] Other women remembered that the only way to escape cooking day and night for the SPLA troops was to run away and hide in the bush.[30] Women recalled that if they refused to cook, they were beaten and/or raped, or threatened to be. They were also beaten or raped if they refused to welcome and feed soldiers who came to their houses, sometimes in large numbers. Most SPLA soldiers were from Dinka or Nuer groups—and increasingly Dinka.[31] They did not speak the same language as these women. This fostered misunderstandings and further beating.[32] Once they had been coerced, it was common for these women to walk and carry food for several days for the SPLA.[33] Some of them ended up being forced to join and assist the troops on a more permanent basis, being turned into de facto camp followers.[34] Others were reportedly traded by commanders.[35]

Back during slavery, the accumulation of women through polygamy and trade was a way to obtain labor.[36] In fact, most slaves in Africa were women.[37] Slavery and particular modes of production interacted. Citing Emmanuel Terray and his study of the Asante people, Paul E. Lovejoy noted that according to Terray, the Abron society's mode of production was based on slavery, with three economic sectors: agriculture, gold mining, and transport (portage). The SPLA replicated exactly these economic sectors in the areas under its control. It forced civilians to work on mines and farms and to carry all sorts of goods for its troops (i.e., portage). Lovejoy noted that "slave owners may have many sources of income, but a substantial portion must derive from activities related to enslavement, trade in slaves, and the appropriation of the product of slave labour."[38] The next chapter of this book continues to show how women, at the forefront of food production, were also reproductive capital in themselves and were exchanged.

The SPLA's mode of production thus resulted in the accumulation of both material wealth and wealth in people through the acquisition of women. This accumulation of wealth, even if especially concentrated in the dominant class, trickled down to the lower strata via the expansion of military kinship networks and increased group ownership.[39] Group ownership, in turn, contributed to build up group entitlement. Because it was reminiscent of slavery, a system of economic exploitation rooted in racism, this mode of production was prone to foster extreme and exclusionary ethnic group entitlement.

Men also participated in war-related activities.[40] In SPLA-captured towns and settlements, they were forced to support the troops as well. Some of those who had initially joined the SPLA freely, like the Lotuko who rallied out of disappointment with the Equatorian regional government of Tembura, were confined to the roles of porters.[41] Such examples of ethnic discrimination against non-Dinka recruits are reminiscent of the colonial division of labor and of military slavery. Overall, a lot of men, women, and children across all ethnic groups carried food, soldiers' belongings, and ammunition, sometimes for long distances.[42] Yet many men—especially in Equatoria—fled to the bush to escape the SPLA and often never came back to their families during the war, leaving women vulnerable to attacks as single heads of households.[43] SPLA soldiers especially pressured single women to support the troops, visiting them at night and inquiring about where their husband was, particularly in the wake of desertions after the 1991 split. A Madi woman remembered, "If after three times they've come to your house and you cannot prove you've got a husband, they torture you and then they force you to grind sorghum and bring it to the frontline."[44]

As mentioned earlier, the SPLA also organized farming throughout the areas it controlled to increase food supplies for both its troops and trading activities. A Kakwa (Equatorian) man remembered that in Lobone, eastern Equatoria, "the SPLA forced people to cultivate for them. They caught you and forced you."[45] But Lobone was not just a farm: it was also a mine, where the SPLA forced civilians to dig.[46] In other locations, such as Lobonok in central Equatoria, the SPLA also had the local chief provide one bucket of gold per month, and each member of the community work one day a week in the mine.[47]

Even if forced labor in SPLA-held areas was not slavery, it certainly was reminiscent of its economy. The SPLA also used its court system to force civilians with a prison sentence to work in its farms/mines and earmarked some of the production for the division commanders, much like it used court fines to collect cattle.[48] This was again a remnant of the organization of slavery.[49] SPLA-run farms were reminiscent of the system of the *zarai'b*—especially prevalent in Bahr El Ghazal during the nineteenth century. There, female slaves were forced to cultivate too.

The slaving frontier between the "free north" and the "slave south" had continued to move south in the *longue durée*.[50] To a certain extent, the SPLA, in its expansion to the far south, the Equatorian region, and its practice of forced labor continued to move this frontier further south. Forced labor was essential to the development of the three economic sectors outlined earlier (agriculture, mining, portage), and their profits, added to those derived from the capture of cattle, also contributed to the development of a dominant class.

Cattle Raiding and Cattle Looting by the SPLA

Indeed, in addition to looting, taxation, and forced labor, the SPLA raided cattle in both the communities it administered and in those it considered enemies.[51] Cattle was a much sought-after economic and social resource—not only did it sustain the troops but it was also sold and used to cement kinship ties with military implications, as I further explore in the next chapter.[52] In raiding cattle, the SPLA acted much like other parties to the conflict who raided cattle on a large scale. Whoever (factions or SPLA) defeated the enemy effectively took all its cattle.[53] Unfortunately, no reliable and precise estimates exist to determine the scale of such raiding, given the absence of a southern cattle population census before, during, and after the war. Yet the SPLA's cattle raiding affected virtually every ethnic group.[54] Throughout the 1980s, the guerrilla group expanded its cattle raiding into Ethiopia when its presence grew in the southwestern part of the country, just like other groups sponsored by the Sudanese army or its militia allies.[55]

Within the territories under its control, the SPLA also used various punitive measures to appropriate cattle. The fact that the SPLA itself raided cattle did not prevent it from also acting as local police, supposed to prevent raiding. If the owner was found guilty of raiding, the SPLA confiscated cattle, always seizing more than what was originally raided.[56] In addition, the SPLA used the court system to collect cattle from civilians. The heavily militarized nature of the SPLA administration meant that commanders without any judicial training were appointed as judges. A former Dinka SPLA child soldier explained how this worked: "Cattle could be gotten through looting (since there was no real judge, a commander could be a judge), and by using civil-related cases and imposing a fine, or through collecting cattle to feed the soldiers and giving a percentage to the commanders."[57]

But the SPLA was not an isolated case. Its expropriation of cattle was mirrored in government-affiliated militias areas. Paulino Matiep and Riek Machar traded with the Sudanese army using looted relief supplies, sorghum, cattle, and weapons in the Upper Nile region.[58] Matiep's South Sudan Defense Forces (SSDF) also employed the customary court system to amass cattle in Unity state. His officers used the administration system they had set up (the counterpart of the SPLA administration) to threaten the chiefs. A Nuer civilian from Unity state elaborated on how this system worked: "Paulino Matiep had a lot of cows: if civilians made some mistakes (according to the bosses), they had to give to the boss. For offenses like elopement, you had to pay a 5 cows fine. Only one cow would go to the father of the girl, the rest was for the boss. Matiep's people, the SSDF, worked with the chiefs. The chiefs were threatened."[59]

Racketeering was also profitable. A racketeer is, according to Tilly, "someone who produces both the danger and, at a price, the shield against it."[60] In the early 1990s, SPLA commanders demonstrated the full extent of this definition. First, they forcibly mobilized Dinka communities into militias called *gelueng* in reaction to cattle raids by various enemies. *Gelueng* militias would protect cattle but also raid cattle in neighboring Nuer areas of Unity state. Thus, after producing the "shield" against threats of cattle raiding by neighbors, they also produced the "danger" to civilians living in SPLA areas.[61] As a former child soldier from the area recounted, "Daniel Awet, the former Governor of Lakes, decreed all young men should be armed and be stationed in cattle-camps. This SPLA-created militia meant civilians had to pay for protection in cattle."[62]

Historically, what mattered in state-making was the effort, the movement to build infrastructures to collect protection rents—not whether that protection worked. And in this movement, "war making, extraction, state making, and protection were interdependent."[63] As such, the SPLA's racketeering was an inherent part of its process of proto–state-making.

The SPLA also wove together the threats of both economic and sexual predation, because women were capital. The threat of sexual violence was meant to foster men's enrollment in the SPLA to protect their properties and female relatives, a Dinka respondent claimed: "The SPLA took cows to feed itself, to frighten people, to force them to join the troops: 'If there's a son in your village in the SPLA, then he will protect the daughters, the sisters, the wives, the properties,' it said."[64]

After 1991: Increased Resource Capture

The 1991 SPLA split intensified predation by all armed groups, while trade networks involving the looted material expanded.[65] The multiplication of armed groups, the removal of a single SPLA administration, and the loss of the SPLA's bases in Ethiopia (and its fragile position), meant that resource capture was no longer centralized.[66]

But if resource capture increased in 1991, it did not mean that the SPLA became "richer"—at least not for a few years. Indeed, tensions around access to resources ultimately created further splintering within armed groups—therefore generating more competition for these resources.[67] Interfactional fighting and government advances on the ground made relief operations extremely difficult yet easily manipulated by warring parties—which would soon make the SPLA richer. The concentration of displaced persons renewed the demand for the delivery of large quantities of aid while amplifying the diversion of these relief supplies for military use. Relief supplies and the sympathy of relief agencies became objects to be won by competing SPLA factions.[68]

Ultimately, the 1991 split would prompt the SPLA to further build the institutions of its rudimentary administration, which as the next pages show, went hand in hand with predation. The SPLA developed its administration for various reasons—first out of competition with its splintering factions.[69] Then, Sudan increasingly became a pariah state in the eyes of the U.S. for its sponsoring of terrorism. The SPLA leader tapped right into these international developments. In the eyes of his southern competitors, "Garang projected Khartoum as Islamist, racist and terrorist on Capitol Hill."[70]

By 1993, the U.S. and European states considered Sudan a "rogue state."[71] But the SPLA also needed to gain popularity, and improving its human right record was one way to boost its image to foreigners and expatriates. Shortly after the split in 1991, the SPLA's Political Military High Command had agreed on the

Torit Resolutions, which paved the way for a transformation of the civil adminis-tration.[72] In April 1994, the SPLA organized its first National Convention, eleven years after its creation.[73]

The convention was supposed to signal the movement's democratization, and the SPLA put much effort into being seen to strengthen the features of its pro-tostate. This first meant practicing "reform rhetoric." The convention itself was described in academic accounts as a "show for external consumption." In this the-atrical act, the Dinka were overrepresented, and elections that reelected the lead-ership were far from being free and fair.[74] If one of the main achievements of the convention was to separate the civil from the military administration and subor-dinate it to a new national executive, a South Sudanese intellectual compared this institutional exercise to "window-dressing."[75] In fact, "the military administra-tion was disguised as civil administration until the signing of the CPA."[76]

Expansion of the SPLA Administration and Predation

After 1994, the administration remained heavily militarized and the protostate violent and extractive. The SPLA used its expanding civil administration to maxi-mize its predation.[77] The Sudan Relief and Rehabilitation Association (SRRA), the relief wing of the SPLA since 1986, had already been accused of diverting money meant to alleviate famine in Northern Bahr El Ghazal back in 1988 and of divert-ing food aid in Ethiopia's refugee camps to support SPLA military operations in the South.[78] After 1994, the SRRA was still tied to the SPLA despite claims of sepa-ration.[79] It became more central in the system of predation as more international relief supplies arrived in the years following the 1994 convention.[80] In 1996, the SPLA movement created the Civil Authorities of New Sudan (CANS), but much like the SRRA, all decision-making staff from the CANS were military officers.[81]

Observers had criticized the 1994 convention for overrepresenting the Dinka.[82] After 1994, access to resources remained with the leadership, and due to the effects of the 1991 split and the ethnicization of the movement, resources also stayed firmly in the grip of the Dinka. The SPLA's number three, James Wani Igga, who was from Equatoria (a Bari) and the secretary for finance and eco-nomic planning, had no financial resources to dispense. The only money was reportedly either in the office of the chairman (Garang) or with the SRRA.[83] The heads of the SRRA remained Dinka—from Justin Yac and Elijah Majok to Benjamin Majak and Mario Muor Muor. Thus state-making maximized preda-tion and mostly benefited a new dominant Dinka class, who controlled modes of production and resources.

The SPLA was not necessarily more corrupt than before; rather, its increasing popularity with relief agencies, which prompted observers to nickname the south "NGO-istan," augmented the influx of resources (aid) into its protostate.[84]After the 1991 split, the UN and other agencies within Operation Lifeline Sudan (OLS) Southern Sector had entered a dialogue with the southern movements to redefine the humanitarian principles underlying relief.[85] By 2001, South Sudan was the world's largest humanitarian operation.[86]

More resources flowing into the SPLA went hand in hand with institutional development, in a typical state-making movement. OLS pushed for the development of institutions within the SPLA, to move from relief to development, in the context of a wider intellectual debate about how neutral positioning avoided addressing the roots of the conflict. It did so hoping to democratize the movement, even if it was clear, four years after the 1994 convention, that the SPLA's promises, made mostly for the benefit of foreign spectators, had not come to fruition.[87] The aid community accepted that predation over relief aid was a given, to the extent that it allowed the SPLM/A, in the 1995 Ground Rules, to tax anyone— Sudanese or foreigner—working for foreign agencies.[88] This trend continued for years, with aid workers complaining that the SRRA was trying "increasingly to identify new opportunities to enrich themselves by milking the NGOs as they have done already successfully with UN/OLS."[89]

What mattered for the SPLA was giving the international community the impression of trying to build a democratic state.[90] SPLA complaints were consistently voiced during conferences attended by international donors, and meant to justify (not account for) the lack of development at the local level.[91] At the local level, few resources fed anything other than what was related to military operations and/or personal enrichment.[92]

A former Dinka SPLA child soldier summarized the movement that combined institutional growth and predation: "The 1994 civilian administration was a good way for the SPLA to continue these practices on a larger scale: that's when the system of rationed contribution was set up and looting increased, becoming systematized . . . The 1994 convention in Chukudum involved the same soldiers: the commissioners, payam administrators, judges, were all army officers. Although people with civilian skills were assigned civilian positions, the military orientation of the movement remained much stronger. There were more contributions to the SPLA after 1991 because the SPLA relied more on them. After 1994, it became more systematized with the regional governor, the payam administrator, the county administrator."[93]

Civilian contributions increased as the guerrilla group relied ever more on them. A former Dinka SPLA battalion commander from Bahr El Ghazal (Lakes) explained, "The civilian administration was created in 1996 and was tasked to mobilize resources, and then only to administer civilians which included coordinating between civilians, SPLA and NGOs, and resettlement and protection of IDPs, refugees, returnees."[94] He continued to explain how when managing resources, the SPLA seized about 60 percent out of any civilian contribution or NGO donation and supposedly gave the remaining 40 percent to the civilian administration. To funnel the 60 percent, the division commander formed a resource committee headed by three people of his choosing. This resource committee was the top institution, composed of loyalists to the division commander— usually his relatives. The committee reported back to the division commander so he could decide what he kept for himself and reinvested in other ventures, and what he gave his soldiers to sustain his authority and the running of his troops.

The division commander and his resource committee were key spots for resource accumulation. They decided what amount of cattle and what portion of the salaries looted from SAF convoys were to be distributed to soldiers. They also decided what community contributions were to be traded and sold, and what amount of trucks or cars (or other hard items) captured and cattle looted were to be reinvested or traded and sold, including in neighboring countries such as Uganda. SPLA division commanders held a privileged position in the circuit of predation, and as the former commander put it, "they enriched themselves to death."[95]

But most of what was earmarked for the civil administration went right back into the SPLA's war-making and self-enrichment machine. Indeed, out of the 40 percent assigned to the civil administration, at least 60 percent (some even said 90 percent) was given back to the SPLA as community contributions in the form of cattle, relief items, etc. collected by the chiefs.[96]

In this circuit of predation, the richest people at the top of the civil administration and the SPLA and its relief wing (SRRA) all got a share of the 40 percent earmarked for the administration. Position in this circuit mattered much more in accessing resources than rank. The battalion commanders, finance officers, and logistics officers held key spots since they had a commission on every resource and contract they brought in and administered.[97] The civil/military administrators also held privileged spots as they were the ones to collect the SPLA taxes off the chiefs.[98] Positions such as regional governor, payam administrator, and county administrator were also key nodes in this circuit of predation.[99] The graph below illustrates the circuit of predation.

When OLS officials estimated that up to 50 percent of the aid was diverted, they probably just scratched the surface of it: even the remainder (the other 50 percent) of what they assumed was given to civil administration was mostly not.[100] Yet USAID was adamant about making NGOs understand that they had to accept the SRRA's siphoning of aid. Zachariah Cherian Mampilly writes,

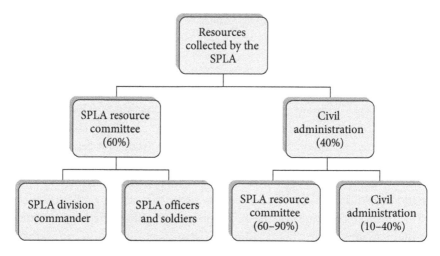

FIGURE 3.1. The circuit of predation.

"The SRRA could also rely on its close relationship with USAID, the source of much aid into the region . . . USAID made it clear to NGOs that sought its support that they would have to go through SRRA structures."[101] The World Food Program (WFP) also made its peace with aid diversion, assuming that this relieved some of the pressure on civilians to produce food themselves.[102] But this was most likely not true. WFP also built road infrastructure that facilitated SPLA-run trades. Meanwhile, SPLA commanders created companies such as Lou Co. Ltd (James Hoth's company), Imatong Co Ltd (Oyii Deng Ajak), and Ghazal Co. Ltd.[103] Aid agencies employed logistical services offered by these companies and those of other wealthy SPLA commanders to deliver aid to areas afflicted by man-made famine, and bought food supplies from SPLA-run farms relying on forced labor.[104]

International politics also combined with aid delivery to foster predation and the rise of globalizing military entrepreneurs in South Sudan. As the SPLA gained popularity in the U.S., especially in view of Khartoum's harboring of Bin Laden, high-ranking officers in both the SPLA and government-affiliated militias started signing business deals with U.S. companies interested in operating in the country safely, continuing to "globalize" the country's war economy.[105]

At the same time, the SPLA already felt threatened in its legitimacy and claims of sovereignty by aid agencies. Aid workers back then admitted that "many NGOs wanted to run the country themselves." The SPLA aimed to coerce NGOs into obeying its rules, its program, and its diversion of aid through threats of expulsion meant to reassert the sovereignty of the SPLA's protostate.[106] The hostility against aid agencies back then is particularly relevant to understanding the postwar (2005–) and post-independence (2011–) anxiety at losing sovereignty to aid agencies, whose presence only continued to grow. Research shows that feelings of shame play a decisive role in driving the perpetration of violence. In Sierra Leone, the presence of wealthy aid workers working for relief agencies meant to "develop" the population made the Sierra Leoneans feel that they were "illiterate," "poor," "useless," and "behaving like animals." This participated in their grievances, which war only fed.[107] In South Sudan, international aid agencies during the war promoted the discourse that the "traditional" society was "breaking down."[108] Meanwhile, the Dinka from Northern Bahr El Ghazal, displaced to the north by Khartoum's militias, were expected to abandon, under the influence of international aid agencies in displacement camps, their "backward" cultural practices and finally be "developed."[109]

Aid agencies thus reenacted colonial discourses and contributed to strengthen the shame and humiliation inherited from centuries of slavery and colonialism. This feeling of humiliation, fueled by neocolonial aid agencies (rulers of the "NGO-istan"), would easily fester into an entitlement ideology.[110] It would play an essential role in making the ideology of the future génocidaires after the war and in sustaining the violence of the third civil war—a point I later return to.

States inherit the features of their making in the *longue durée*.[111] So the logic of maximizing profits off of people and things, a mode of production inherited from slavery, would root the military elite's understanding of the functions of a postwar and independent state. The SPLA dominant class's hijacking of the wartime proto–state-building exercise was a blueprint for how to divert state resources after the war while consolidating class ascendency with increased international support.

Trade and the Rise of Military Entrepreneurs

Ultimately, wartime predation resulted in a process of social class formation dominated by the military elite.[112] To a certain extent, the transformation of SPLA commanders into a dominant class was a necessary feature of war-making that culminated in state-making. Yet the trade that sustained the incoming flow of resources within and outside the country also eventually threatened the protostate through the rise of warlords, "businessmen of war."[113]

The SPLA's trade monopolies demonstrated its attempts at defending nascent class interests and the fact that it was developing a class of its own. From the inception of its armed struggle in Ethiopia, the SPLA and the officers controlling the trade of relief goods out of Itang refugee camp established a monopoly on this trade to prevent the rise of a competing bourgeoisie.[114] The SPLA enforced violent monopoly strategies in Equatoria's various trades as well.[115] By using collusion and intimidation, the SPLA behaved in all its trade endeavors in a similar fashion to the government, in the "forced" markets of its garrison towns.[116]

Such trade monopolies were typical of state-building projects.[117] Already in Ethiopia, trade went hand-in-hand with state-making, since the SRRA was involved in accumulating and distributing the loot. At the time, a human rights report described that "in Itang, the main beneficiaries remained those who controlled the allocations of relief. The SPLA was acquiring some of the characteristics of a centralized state, allocating the resources it controlled for its own policy ends, while certain individuals extracted benefits from their positions."[118]

Both Khartoum and the SPLA profiteered off civilians, sometimes in strikingly similar fashion. Once the SPLA controlled areas in the south, trading opportunities expanded along looting avenues. SPLA soldiers traded the clothes they stole from civilians and the food civilians received from relief agencies (mostly cooking oil and lentils) into Uganda and Kenya's markets.[119] Much like the Sudanese government, the SPLA was implicated in creating the conditions for famine, and its trade followed a similar pattern to trade in government-controlled areas.[120]

The SPLA's presence increased in eastern Equatoria after its ousting of Ethiopia in 1991 and the Bor massacre, which pushed Dinka civilians south and precipitated their migration into areas such as Narus, New Kush, New Site, Natinga, Kapoeta, or Chukudum. These areas were not just connected to neighboring markets but also served as transit points to the Kakuma refugee camp in Kenya. Over the years, both combatants and civilians were joined by relatives and settled in the region. There emerged a local "military-commercial network."[121] Anne Walraet noted that "while this network cannot be equalised with the Dinka migrant community as a whole, it was perceived as such by many interviewees."[122] Members of the Dinka diaspora also sent remittances during the war, which played a role in the emergence of a rising class of Dinka businessmen associated with the SPLA in both Kenya and eastern Equatoria.[123]

The commerce in eastern Equatoria was multifaceted. The Bor Dinka commanders prominent in the region after 1991 generally controlled these trades with Uganda and ran them through their Dinka soldiers. This reinforced the locals' view of an army of occupation at the service of wealth extortion and accumulation.[124] The SPLA "big men" collaborated with local chiefs to contribute to their own economic interests and military power.[125] They controlled both cattle raiding and cross-border cattle trade in eastern Equatoria (Budi county) after 1991, while involved in the Ugandan markets.[126] They brutally seized local crops, such as the tobacco of the local Didinga, to trade in exchange for more cattle from the Toposa or in markets such as Agoro's in Uganda's Acholi corridor.[127]

They also enforced a monopoly over the Didinga's cattle and tobacco, when not confiscating, by forcing them to sell at a disadvantageous price—just like they did to the Toposa for gold.[128]

The cross-border trade itself generated income, as SPLA commanders issued departure orders and money was collected at border points and redistributed back to them.[129] A former SPLA soldier from Ikotos (eastern Equatoria) who worked in the finance department described the system of cross-border cattle trade: "I was in Kapoeta county. I worked most in the payam, in the finance department, in Narus. The resources were: they (SPLA) taxed those who brought cattle to Narus and taxed goods from Kenya and Kapoeta. From the SPLA, they distributed money to those on the frontlines and these high-ranking officers. Cattle taxed was brought from Kapoeta to Narus and then from Kapoeta to Ikotos to Agoro—to be auctioned. That was the cattle of the Toposa. Agoro was a big market where Ugandan and South Sudanese exchanged goods and cattle . . . Cattle was sold. High-ranking officers would get the money . . . money was made on cattle taxes and Kenyan goods taxed."[130]

But money was also made on the backs of laborers on the SPLA farms. A Kakwa civilian recalled of Lobone's farm in Magwi county, "Big people used the farm for their interests, getting their food from there . . . They sold the food for their own interests—it transited in Nimule and they also sold it for themselves in Uganda."[131] The SPLA also sold agricultural products from its farms in Yambio to international organizations.[132] Thus aid organizations "fed" the war economy. The SPLA logged the teak forests too in the entire Equatoria region—in Yambio, Maridi, Yei, Nimule, Chukudum, and Narus (all SPLA bases)—to sell to Uganda, and beyond: "Logs from Yei were taken to India, China, the USA. Money was taken by big commanders."[133]

The SPLA commanders also got involved in the drug trade. In fact, they competed with Khartoum.[134] Khartoum wanted to control the marijuana trade in western and central Equatoria (in Tambura, Ezo, and Yei)—not only for northern consumption but also to profit from trade spilling over to the DRC. Yei was the commercial hub for products from the Congo and Uganda, including marijuana and ivory. SPLA commanders controlling areas of passage taxed the marijuana entering the DRC and sold in Aba.[135] A Dinka former SPLA child soldier recalled that "marijuana was traded to DRC with the knowledge of the SPLA, from Kalgulu to Aba in the DRC. Commanders in control of areas of passage taxed any trade, including marijuana. The Government of Sudan was involved too, but less than the SPLA, since the SPLA controlled the areas outside of Yei."[136] Some commanders like Kuol Manyang also organized the farming of opium in eastern Equatoria to sustain the troops on the frontlines. Yet he was more notorious for his involvement in gold mining.[137]

Gold was a key component of the SPLA's war economy in greater Equatoria, and beyond. For example, in Blue Nile in 1998, "according to the SPLA Governor of Kurmuk, Malik Agar, records seized at the mine showed an annual net production of US $11 million a figure that has not been independently confirmed."[138] Though Agar may have been exaggerating, the SPLA was certainly already exploiting the belt from Kurmuk to Kapoeta. The guerrilla group dominated the gold trade in eastern (Kapoeta) and central Equatoria (Yei).[139]

The gold trade had been historically much more developed in eastern Equatoria. There, in Kapoeta, gold, cattle, and guns had been traded even before the start of the second civil war (1983).[140] Once the SPLA controlled this area, it took an interest in this trade. The SPLA leadership partnered with foreign companies to mine the area without involving the local population in decisions. It tried to control the gold trade by preventing local inhabitants from continuing to mine on their own from the rivers. But local mining continued, on a small scale. Gold was bought in Chukudum (Eastern Equatoria) in Lauro/Nyaguro (in Budi county), to be sold in Kenya.[141]

Garang and members of his inner circle, such as the SPLA commander Kuol Manyang (who controlled Kapoeta), reaped the benefits of this trade.[142] Other individuals, such as Luis Lobong, the postwar governor of the area, also made a profit. A former SPLA soldier who was working for the finance department in Kapoeta explained, "Luis Lobong was the chief commander and commissioner in Kapoeta and he was the only high-ranking officer there so he made a lot of money. He's a son of the soil (land)—a Toposa. During the war, he sold relief food and used that money to buy gold and resell it in Uganda and Kenya . . . He would not take it directly from relief agencies, he would tax it from the people and said it was for the SPLA, but it was for his own use. That's how he became rich. One gram of gold was cheap. It was being sold for ten times more in Uganda."[143] A Kakwa civilian from Kaya also remembered that in Kapoeta and Lobone, "relatives of SPLA big people managed the extraction of the gold. Junior officers got gold and gave it to big officers and got their share. The gold was sold to Kenya and even outside Africa. They traded it for luxurious goods—hummers and cars and houses in Nairobi [and] Uganda. They bought new houses. It was coming out through Kaya, and when they pushed the Arabs out of Yei (1997) and through Nimule."[144]

The SPLA extended its search for gold to central Equatoria, between the border and Kajo Keji, and the western part of the state (Tombura), where it also found diamonds (around Ezo and Ibamdu).[145] There, the SPLA governor for Equatoria, the Zande Samuel Abu-John, was also personally involved in various trades, from looted aid relief supplies in western Equatoria to timber in Yei and gold, and diamonds in Ezo. His accomplices included Pascal Bandindi, the first SRRA secretary in Yambio and then secretary for agriculture and animal resources.[146] The National Economic Commission was also instrumental in forcing communities to sell resources at a reduced rate and at facilitating trade throughout the Equatoria region.[147]

The case of Samuel Abu-John, the Zande SPLA governor of Equatoria, demonstrated that some non-Dinka commanders were just as predatory (including sexually) as Dinka commanders, and remained in place for a long time (eleven years in his case), though Abu-John's constituents considered his appointment mere "ethnic window-dressing" and accused him of reinforcing anti-Dinka sentiments.[148] The fact remains that predation was practiced by all, no matter what their ethnicity was. The SPLA "big men" were not the only ones to benefit from trading looted resources in Equatoria. Local militia men, local cattle raiders, and chiefs consenting to it also benefited from it.[149]

Yet Dinka officers particularly benefited from the war economy because of ethnic discrimination in military promotions. In other words, structural inequalities based on ethnic ranking were such that they conditioned the accumulation of capital, which in turn reinforced these structural inequalities. In this movement, capital was patrimonial and marriages key in social climbing.[150]

The leadership actively promoted the rise of the dominant class. For example, in 2002, when the SPLA took Kapoeta's old town, Garang himself distributed the few brick buildings left by Arab traders and others to his commanders. After the war, these buildings housed companies that SPLA commanders were involved in, thanks to capital they accumulated through the trans-border economy. This culminated in 2005, when the war ended, with the creation of the Jonglei Trade Association in Kapoeta town—of which Garang's wife, Rebecca Nyandeng, was an active member.[151]

But the Bor Dinka monopoly on trade eventually contributed to tensions within the SPLA. The Dinka from Bahr El Ghazal, who by now made up the bulk of the troops, came to see the Bor Dinka as mostly traders merely leeching off the movement that they (those from Bahr El Ghazal) really supported. High-ranking Dinka officials from Bahr El Ghazal were equally skilled at running trade, however. Indeed, a well-oiled system of intermediaries also operated the trade from cattle paid in taxes by civilians in the Bahr El Ghazal region. Similarly, cattle from Dinka civilians were sold in Uganda to buy ammunitions and fuel.[152] But there was also a major SPLA-controlled cattle trade with the northern markets. In Northern Bahr El Ghazal and Warrap, the SPLA commander Paul Malong ran a trade tied with northern Sudan so efficiently that it bore long-term political implications. The trade he ran irrigated the entire region, as a Dinka civilian from the area noted: "Malong opened a market in Warawar in 1991 to bring the Misseryia and that's why he refused to be redeployed (by Garang). Traders from

Meiram, Muglad, in south Kordofan, were coming using camels, horses to carry goods to the market of Warawar, the main market of Northern Bahr El Ghazal and the closest to the border. Malong's followers brought goods from Warawar market to sell in other markets of Malualkon, Malith Aladiai, and Akuem markets. Malong made profits and used them to finance Salva Kiir. It was difficult to get financial support at that time."[153]

Malong made such profits that he impacted SPLA politics. He provided financial support to his former boss, Salva Kiir, who used to be the greater's Bahr El Ghazal zonal commander back in Yei and New Site. Kiir had been promoted to deputy in command, but tensions had grown with Garang, as detailed in the last chapter. Malong's support to Kiir, originating in his grip over Northern Bahr El Ghazal's war economy, was key in creating a long-lasting debt from Kiir, who would eventually become president of South Sudan.

Besides, Malong's local prominence through his control of the war economy also enabled him to challenge Garang's authority. He refused Garang's order to be rotated in 2004 after the Rumbek conference. Garang's policy of rotating commanders before they established a local fiefdom had sought to contain the rise of warlords. The rebel leader was a state-builder, an exercise that consisted in "eliminating, subjugating, dividing, conquering, cajoling, buying as the occasions presented themselves."[154] But Garang failed with Malong, whose control over the local war economy went unchecked long enough that it could no longer be contained.[155]

Malong also participated with others in his area in a scam that would fester tensions with Garang and the Bor constituency. The scam dated back, according to SPLA officials who denounced it, to at least 1994, right around when the guerrilla group sought to improve its image and boosted its protostate institutions.[156] In fact, the head of the SRRA was involved in the scam as well.[157] A former SPLA commander from Bor explained how the scam—a slave buy-back program—worked: "Malong collected children in villages. Those redeemed were not actual slaves. Malong collected women and children and called his Messiriya friends—and sometimes he called Akech Tong Aleu, dressed him with a *jalabiya* (traditional dress typically associated with Arab traders) and he (Aleu) would act as a go-between, freeing the slaves. They (led by John Eibner) would come with a camera from the Christian organizations . . . Eibner would come with a quarter million US dollars in one trip. And this money would be given to the Misseryia, and then Malong, who divided it, and Salva was a beneficiary . . . Bona Malual came with those of John Eibner so every time he would travel with them, and they used Christian Solidarity International [CSI] to mobilize planes and installations . . . It continued until 2003."[158]

Here again, successfully extracting resources (through whatever means) was supposed to neutralize and co-opt what Tilly refers to as the "great lord's rivals," which typically led to state-making.[159] For Garang, this type of co-optation may have worked for several years in Northern Bahr El Ghazal. But soon (circa 1994), through this scam, a rival coalition reemerged around Bona Malual. Paul Malong, Bona Malual, Justin Yac Arop, and Akech Tong Aleu were those most notably involved. They were all from Bahr El Ghazal, some from Warrap, Kiir's home area. And they did not seem particularly sorry to be caught with their hands in the cookie jar when foreign journalists uncovered the scandal, as a *Washington Post* article citing Justin Yac suggested:

> "There was a lot that has been done with the money, with the profits from the currency exchange," said Yaac. He listed rebel officials' purchases in just two of three affected counties: 26 Toyota Land Cruisers, more than 7,000 uniforms, plus fuel—all purchased for the war effort, Yaac emphasized, brushing aside allegations of personal enrichment . . . "It is none of the business of CSI," Yaac said, "because if I exchange money with you, it is none of your business to know what I am going to do with it."[160]

Such remarks were quite telling of the feelings of group entitlement in this coalition.[161] It is not surprising then that the slave-redemption scam became the subject of arguments within the SPLA. In December 1999, during a National Liberation Council (NLC) meeting, Bona Malual and Justin Yac's names surfaced.[162] According to the same former Bor Dinka SPLA commander cited above, the scam became part of the problem between Kiir and Garang: "Then came the issue of the slave redemption—Bona, Salva, and Malong were big beneficiaries in Bahr El Ghazal . . . There was tension between Garang and this group—because it became obvious it was a scam and he wanted it to stop. This escalated the situation . . . When Garang started to express some harsh views on this, the relationship became lukewarm . . . This was one of the factors behind the tensions with Garang. Salva was Chief of Staff and vice-chairman—the next most powerful. Bona and Justin Yac wanted to use him as a steel point to help them break through leadership."[163]

And break through the leadership they did. At the time, if the SPLA spokesperson—Samson Kwaje—admitted that the racket came "right from the top," he also pointed out that Garang had limited power to do anything about it, fearing to further antagonize those commanders.[164] After the December 1999 NLC meeting, Garang reportedly forbade the escorts involved in the scam from travelling with CSI director John Eibner to Northern Bahr El Ghazal. He instructed the chief of the SRRA to escort him instead.[165] But since the chief of the SRRA was reportedly one of the original escorts of Eibner to the slave-redemption sites, Kwaje was quoted as saying, "You may be changing one mafia for another."[166]

Control over the war economy related to military power in multiple ways. This scam spoke volumes about Garang's loss of control over commanders like Malong. Malong was already posing a real threat to Garang and his constituency, and the SPLA was a pressure cooker by the late 1990s. Malong reinvested money obtained from the scam into the expansion of his military kinship network.[167] At that time, he already had about forty wives.[168] Kwaje called Malong a "warlord" outright and admitted, "There are some commanders who you, more or less, call them warlords." He continued, "They can more or less do things without accountability.""[169]

On all sides, South Sudan's military elite had bewildering skills at amassing wealth. It practiced two types of reinvestment, a former Dinka SPLA battalion commander recounted:

> Garang had companies. So did Riek Machar and Paulino Matiep in Khartoum. They had a share in the oil companies. . . . The smart commanders reinvested their wealth in companies and buildings and got rid of the cattle. Oyii or Hoth or Manyang didn't keep the cattle, Malong did. Smart commanders distributed cows to their soldiers to sustain themselves or marry. They kept the hard items like cars or trucks to sell to Uganda or to invest in companies. Visible and captured wealth was redistributed to soldiers by the commanders. Invisible money, such as donation by NGOs, international community, Diaspora, gifts from the leadership, were invisible and were invested in bank accounts in Kenya, Uganda and Ethiopia. Bank accounts were opened under wives or children's names for discretion.[170]

Material "gift giving" to soldiers was key in creating and retaining military allegiance. So the commanders (like Malong or Matiep) who retained more material wealth than others and reinvested it into expanding their kinship networks, could still be considered great military strategists.[171]

The enrichment of the elite destroyed the SPLA's legitimacy in several ways. The lure of gain attracted soldiers to join the struggle and try to become officers, but it created tensions too.[172] A lot of soldiers thought that commanders kept too large a chunk of civilian contributions in bulls and heifers or food rations to themselves.[173] A former Dinka SPLA child soldier commented, "Certain people became rich, in gold, teak, cattle. The commanders in Bahr El Ghazal had a lot of cattle. Some of the cattle (maybe a quarter or more) could stay in the hands of the commanders and not ever reach the movement or soldiers. The same went for what was collected as rations."[174]

A lot of commanders did not redistribute nearly as much to their soldiers as they did to their immediate kinship networks. Soldiers saw commanders send their riches out of the country to relatives.[175] Commanders were especially under pressure to redistribute to their relatives when they had built large kinship networks through large-scale polygamy.[176] There was no distinction between the funds meant for the SPLA and those sent to relatives or used for their own personal wealth. Some of the lieutenants in Garang's inner circle kept the funds of the movement in their personal accounts.[177]

Some commanders lived, as Julia Aker Duany noted, "removed from the field of battle . . . in luxury homes in the suburbs of Nairobi and Kampala."[178] The perception that the commanders spent too much time outside taking care of their own ventures resulted into a crisis of confidence in the SPLA leadership.[179] Khartoum also exploited some commanders' thirst for (or anxiety about) economic gains by encouraging them to split through bribery, corruption, or blackmail. This impacted allegiances and alliances and ultimately eroded any southern nationalist project in favor of the commanders' small economic gains.[180]

By the end of the war, the enrichment and subsequent exile of many SPLA commanders had resulted in desertions and a general loss of political legitimacy that would never be recovered—if it was ever strong to begin with. A Dinka civilian from Aweil shared the view of many other civilians, considering most of the SPLA's cadres to be thieves at best, if not criminals: "Most SPLA commanders had gone out to Australia and other places. They were gone out of the frontlines. Very few people in the SPLA were there for political reasons. Most of them were criminals. The end of the war was not in sight so a lot of people left the SPLA and went out. Soldiers were not paid."[181]

State-Making, Social Class Formation, and Group Ownership

The Making of the Protostate and Dominant Class

Looking back, the war economy in SPLA areas triggered long-term sociopolitical processes: it created both the state and various other groups. Reminiscent of other processes of state-formation in Europe's *longue durée*, war-making, resource extraction, and organization contributed to build the protostate in SPLA areas.[182]The SPLA needed to strengthen its military machine to become a serious contender against Khartoum, have a seat at the negotiations, and eventually rule the future independent country. This required military force, which demanded organizing the war economy to support it, and started the process of creating the SPLA state. The international community, by looking more favorably at the guerrilla group in the mid-1990s, flushing the south with quickly diverted aid, and pushing for the movement's institutionalization, participated to state-making. Already, it started to "swell" the state—which contributed to the process of class formation.[183]

State-formation went hand in hand with dominant class formation.[184] This dominant class owned the guerrilla group and turned it into an engine for social class formation and ethnic domination. Despite tensions between the leadership and warlords, monopolies on coercion and trade demonstrated shared class interests. Monopolies and the practice of kinship expansion also illustrated class consciousness and coherence. The dominant class used the accumulation of things and people to consolidate and transmit class status through generations, thus enlarging itself.

The wartime SPLA protostate was so ethnically ranked that it borrowed elements from both the feudal and slavery systems.[185] Warlords presided over local war economies functioning on the back of forced laborers. The legacy of war impacts the shape of states: according to Tilly, "Relative balance among war making, protection, extraction, and state making significantly affected the organization of the states that emerged from the four activities."[186] Faced with poorly disciplined foes confined to garrison towns and government-controlled areas, the SPLA engaged into fewer battles as war went on. It did what many other governments and armed groups did in other countries, from Sierra Leone to Vietnam to Afghanistan: while publicly expressing its intention to defeat its enemy, using cheap propaganda, the SPLA leadership also took advantage of the lengthy war to engage in lucrative abuse, which attracted only little international criticism.[187]

As the war went on, the SPLA concentrated more on extraction, mafia-like protection, and state-making rather than on war-making and service-provision. Wartime predation forecasted postwar endemic state corruption. Because the SPLA leadership was involved in a "war system," it needed its foes to function, and the same was true of them.[188]Similar processes of class formation and state-making occurred in SSDF areas, and different dominant classes came together into a temporary "fusion of elites" in the capital of Juba after the war.

Group-Making and Group Ownership

The war economy did not just foster social class formation—it also reinforced ethnic group-making. Much like slavery reinforced groups, so did forced labor, violent expropriations and resource extraction.[189] The SPLA accumulated resources to the detriment of other ethnic groups. Because the SPLA was mostly Dinka but controlled non-Dinka areas (such as Equatoria) that were key to its war economy, forced labor became ethnically ranked in those areas as well. Forced labor, ethnic ranking in access to military training, and ethnic discrimination in access to positions of resource control against the few non-Dinka officers reinforced anti-Dinka sentiments and bolstered the coalescing Equatorians and Nuer groups who opposed the SPLA.

The SPLA's war economy also reinforced the Dinka's own group-making and group legitimacy: not only did the Dinka fight for the liberation of the country, but they literally came to "own" it. As such, the socioeconomic transformations springing from the organization of the SPLA's war economy, an ethnically differentiated mode of production rooted in the *longue durée* of racism and slavery, impacted the development of an ideology of group entitlement too.

By contributing to the literal sense of "ownership," the war economy reinforced Dinka group legitimacy and ultimately entitlement.[190] The slave-redemption scam in Northern Bahr El Ghazal from the mid-1990s to the early 2000s also demonstrated how the local Dinka "military-commercial network" itself felt an increased sense of group entitlement, thus contributing to reinforce the groupness of the two competing Dinka constituencies.[191]

SPLA VIOLENCE, GROUP-MAKING, AND EXPANSION

1983–2005

The perpetration of violence against civilians—particularly sexual violence and the accumulation of women—fostered groupness and perennial discourses of ethnic group legitimacy and entitlement. It also became an expression of ethnic group legitimacy and entitlement. It was no surprise, since violence was an inherent part of the ethnicized mode of (re)production in SPLA-controlled areas. Through the often violent accumulation of women and through the performance of forced labor mostly by women, this mode of (re)production continued to evoke the legacy of slavery.

Although focusing on the predominantly Dinka SPLA, this chapter provides elements pointing to similar patterns in other armed groups' areas of control, especially those of the Nuer. It gives an overview of pre-1991 violence by the SPLA and then addresses the 1991 Bor massacre before turning to the SPLA's practice of sexual violence and its far-reaching implications regarding social class formation and state-expansion.

SPLA Violence

Violence against Civilians

The SPLA was involved in a cycle of conflict with the (mostly Nuer) Anya Nya II from the beginning of the war. Since the SPLA was better organized, SPLA retaliation was always more ruthless. Each massacre triggered more hostility, ethnic hatred, and unrestrained revenge.[1] This formed the background of the 1991 Bor

massacre, popularly considered the peak of Nuer-Dinka ethnic violence during the second civil war.[2] The general environment of fighting in South Sudan
did not help restrain SPLA troops: they operated in a context where all militias
instrumentalized civilians equally. Johnson and Prunier noted that "the pattern
of fighting between the SPLA and local Southern militias involved attacks on
civilian populations by both sides, entailing the wholesale destruction of villages
and farms. This affected the SPLA's reception in areas outside of the main Nilotic
recruiting grounds (Dinka, Nuer and Shilluk)."[3]

The guerrilla army resorted to more violence in areas that were not typical
recruiting grounds, such as in the Equatoria region, where civilian support was
harder to obtain and more often coerced.[4] It was particularly harsh on civilians living in areas where government-sponsored militias roamed, such as eastern Equatoria and Upper Nile, where it targeted the Murle, the Toposa, some
Mundari, and the Gajaak Nuer.[5] The list of ethnic groups victimized by SPLA
troops goes on. Massacres by the troops also expanded across boundaries, and
the SPLA manipulated local conflicts to consolidate its grasp over the south, just
like the British and the Sudanese government had done in the late nineteenth and
early twentieth centuries.[6]

The SPLA's treatment of civilians in non-Dinka areas followed a drive to expand
the Dinka's reach to new territories—a protoconquest.[7] The fact that the victimized communities were not grounds for SPLA recruitment contributed to SPLA
violence but did not drive it. Indeed, the SPLA was never genuinely interested in
promoting ethnic groups other than the Dinka within its movement. Ethnic discrimination against non-Dinka recruits were a key factor behind the 1991 split, and
its uncompromising leadership transformed the SPLA into an ever more Dinka
army, where the presence of a few non-Dinka leaders amounted to ethnic window
dressing. Therefore, discourses of group legitimacy of the Dinka as national liberators were intended to mask the fact that this was in fact a self-fulfilling prophecy.

Indeed, not only did SPLA soldiers often look down on unarmed people as
conquered and at their mercy. In many parts of the country, civilians migrated
en masse to escape the advance of the SPLA, struggling to survive attacks by wild
animals as well as landmines on the roads to garrison towns.[8] The men who
stayed behind were faced with forced conscription—or forced labor—serving
the SPLA commanders' capital accumulation. Women were also forced to labor
for the troops. But they fell victim to another form of predation: sexual violence.

Sexual Violence

Rapes occurred throughout the entire Equatoria region, day and night, both in
houses and outside, without any seeming pattern.[9] In Nimule, eastern Equatoria,

women insisted that rapes were so frequent that whenever mothers left their daughters alone in the house, soldiers raped them.[10] Gang-rapes were common and pushed some women to flee the town in 1989, only returning about ten years later.[11] A woman from Yei, central Equatoria, confided, "Sometimes I was hiding in the forest because I heard the news that the SPLA was taking girls."[12] In western Equatoria, sexual violence was endemic as well.[13] At night, the SPLA especially searched the houses for men running from forced conscription and considered deserters. Women were more likely to be raped when the soldiers did not find any men inside and became frustrated. Women were left alone with their rapists, a woman in Nimule remembered, because "no one would come rescue, everyone was too afraid to come rescue at night."[14]

Because the SPLA relied even more on forced conscription after its 1991 split, entire communities were emptied of men, replaced with increasingly Dinka SPLA troops and displaced Bor Dinka who relocated from Ethiopia and Bor to (eastern) Equatoria.[15] There was little mystery as to the perpetrators' identity, as women in Morobo, central Equatoria, lamented: "So many girls have been raped by those Dinka."[16] This did not mean that the Dinka wives of SPLA soldiers were not affected by sexual violence, but Dinka soldiers behaved even worse with women of different ethnic groups.[17]

Sexual violence is typically "easier" on the perpetrator and as such more likely if the victim is from a different community, seen as "racially and culturally foreign and inferior," notes Joanna Bourke of contexts of interethnic violence.[18] The SPLA rapists thought of themselves as superior: they were the true nationalists (not the traitors supporting the *kokora*), the "liberators"—and on top of that, the men of the men, above all other "slaves," if we go back to the roots of the term *moinjiang* (Dinka). Gang-rapes, as a form of group violence, reinforced Dinka group cohesion.[19]

Sexual violence thus also became an expression of group legitimacy and entitlement. It was not about opportunism. The presence of local men did not discourage the rapists; quite the opposite. Even when the local men stuck around in the villages, rapes still occurred. Soldiers sometimes raped and gang-raped married women in the presence of their husbands; the husband was tied to a tree by the soldiers who lined up to rape his wife.[20] Alternatively, women in Morobo related, "the husband lay down and became the mattress of his wife being raped."[21] One such husband, a Kakwa, talked about how his wife contracted gonorrhea and eventually died from it: "She was raped in 1987 by SPLA soldiers in Yei. They (the soldiers) went to the bush and raped women. They could do whatever they wanted."[22]

As such, rape was an act committed not just against women but also against men. Rape was, to use Catharine MacKinnon's words, "a way men communicate with one another."[23] SPLA commanders especially—but regular soldiers too—appropriated married and unmarried women and forced them to become their concubines: they made what "belonged" to other men theirs. Here again the parallels with slavery were striking.[24]

Rape was only the beginning: forced marriage (or forced concubinage) often followed, without bridewealth exchanged or with very little bridewealth paid, and sometimes even without the parents' knowledge.[25] A Moro man from Mundri in western Equatoria remembered how threatening the SPLA soldiers were to the parents of women they forcefully married: "The SPLA soldiers had promised dowry to the Moro girls' parents. But they told them, 'If you want dowry, you come to Bor to pick it up.' But the parents were afraid to come to Bor."[26] In eastern Equatoria, a woman raped and forced to marry her rapist insisted, "Whether you liked it or not, the SPLA raped you and forcefully married you."[27]

Women as Capital

The capture of women did not just amount to sexual predation; it followed the rationale of capital accumulation because women were seen as capital. Soldiers took women and girls as they moved from house to house collecting food, kitchen utensils, clothes, etc.[28] Women were considered resources to be looted. But they were different: even if they were commodified in the process, they were also extremely valuable capital to acquire. They generated wealth in cattle, they were a gateway to settling on new land, and they could be exchanged or distributed on the political market for military allegiance.

Women (including the SPLA female elite) treated as capital were instrumentalized in the process of social class formation serving the interests of that male dominant class. This does not mean that women were a class either, since not all women were equal and therefore women didn't all experience war in the same fashion.[29] The SPLA dominant class, for instance, also created its own female elite, whose status was mediated through that class.[30] Women across all classes were conceived of as both political and economic capital because of certain social relations.[31] Both forms of capital had military benefits. I use Thomas Piketty's definition of capital: "all forms of wealth that individuals (or groups of individuals) can own and that can be transferred or traded through the market on a permanent basis."[32] In Piketty's definition, only in slavery can people be considered "capital." Slavery is exceptional in the sense that it is tied both to labor and to the absolute lack of choice on the slave's part.[33]

Production in non-Dinka SPLA areas—and to a certain extent in Dinka areas too—was accomplished through forced labor, a mode of production sharing similarities with slavery and performed mostly by women, just like in slavery in sub-Saharan Africa. Women had no choice in the matter, faced with beatings and sexual violence.[34] As the war went on, SPLA commanders concentrated wealth and monopolized violence. Thus marriages, whether sealed through bridewealth exchange or not, were irrevocable.[35] Marriages were integrated into the SPLA's circuit of predation from the onset of the war, while violence and heightened inequalities skewed the initial equilibrium of bridewealth exchange and prices. The marriage market itself became a "forced market."[36]

In this context, women were capital as much as slaves were. Their offspring were equally a source of future wealth and as such they were controlled and taken, as an Acholi (Equatorian) civilian recalled: "They collected even the past children of the women—and the [new] children she bears—and abandon her."[37] Thinking of women as capital also allows us to think of capital as akin to wealth and to analyze the institution of bridewealth in this context as the exchange of women-as-capital.[38] Again, context matters, especially how women were turned into capital in this social landscape.

The women who were raped and forcibly married (with bridewealth exchanged or not) were especially entrapped in slavery-like conditions. They were either forced to or resigned themselves to be with the troops. Those who did willingly follow the troops made the same "choiceless decision" as other women in similar conundrums.[39] They became concubines, workers without wage, cooking and washing the clothes of their abductors, thus performing labor essential to the running of the SPLA.[40] The banality of concubines in SPLA troops was such that they went by the nickname of "outpost women."[41] Once following the troops, they were still subjected to sexual violence by the soldiers. By performing labor without wage and being forced into sexual labor, they became akin to sex slaves for the troops. The root of sexual violence was neither unmet needs nor opportunism. As capital, these "outpost women" were the objects of competition between soldiers. This could cause death by execution, since SPLA commanders saw these women as a threat to troops' cohesion.[42] But as capital, these women were also exchanged, accumulated, and invested.

SPLA Rhetoric versus Reality

Officially, the SPLA looked like it cared about limiting human rights abuses. This was part of its rhetoric and of its legitimacy to outsiders. From the beginning of the war, in 1983, it enacted its own disciplinary law, ratified in 1984, along with a penal code and a code of procedures.[43] The disciplinary law described a number of crimes by military personnel, including rape and looting, that were punishable by the death penalty.[44] Yet this structure was more theoretical than practical, with a lack of trained magistrates and of copies of legal texts in the SPLA areas.[45]

Garang never held any of the high-ranking officers whose troops were known for their atrocities accountable, and executions were mostly carried out to sideline rivals.[46]

The organization of the SPLA's headquarters and its field bases was reminiscent of a feudal system ruled by warlords answering to a king (Garang). In this system, apart from combat activities, the leadership could barely weigh in on the relationship between its soldiers and civilians.[47] The soldiers accused of crimes against civilians were mostly tried according to customary laws. In many cases, the soldiers coerced or co-opted the chiefs and were subjected to a series of fines, typically used by commanders to amass wealth.[48]Appointments of commanders in their home areas sometimes limited human rights abuses there (as in the case of Yusif Kuwa in the Nuba mountains), but sometimes not (as in the case of Samuel Abu-John in western Equatoria).[49]

The 1991 SPLA split led to new factions and multiplied rape, killing, and looting.[50] What the Bor Dinka considered "good commanders" (like Kuol Manyang) were in fact "butchers" to the eastern Equatorians who lived under their reign. After 1994 and its National Convention, the SPLA postured at improving its human rights record in several conferences that had no real impact. This culminated with the 1997 SPLM-Church Dialogue, the last attempt to redress fourteen years of a poor human rights record.[51] Human rights abuses continued, since there was, at the SPLA's highest level, never any will to redress them.[52] Garang was even more on his guard since his authority had diminished in the eyes of the SPLA's rank and file.[53] Soldiers were demoralized, a typical sign of a breakdown of the chain of command.[54] Symptomatically, they were less inclined to listen to orders.

As desertions increased after 1991, securing troops' cohesion was more important than ever.[55] So commanders allowed their soldiers to take more "booty" in women in a bid to retain authority, foster allegiance, and create new military kinship ties.[56] In doing so, they hijacked the disciplinary system. It was easy: the SPLA had not even defined legally and culturally what constituted rape.[57] The soldiers, less and less trained and increasingly forcibly recruited, understood disciplinary measures as mere warnings and reinterpreted them as threats forcing them to "legalize" the rape post-facto by marrying their victims to cover it up.[58] They did so under the watch of "benevolent" commanders who had supplied them with alcohol. A Nuer civilian described the ambiance in those groups: "*Suksuk* is the alcohol given by SPLA commanders to their soldiers . . . used during fighting. Whatever needs to get done, will get done. And they don't feel guilty about what they're doing."[59] This was typical of armed groups with low cohesion and forced recruitment, where rape was a "bonding experience" replacing other exercises in boot camps meant to increase cohesion.[60]

This practice facilitated rape and forced marriages, which fostered group cohesion. A female Bor Dinka SPLA soldier recounted how the soldiers hijacked the disciplinary rules: "Soldiers that kidnapped girls from their own places and they brought them as their wives . . . they married sometimes. Because there was a time when the SPLA put a rule to these people. 'You rape somebody, you will be shot.' At least, you want to marry. So, some of these cases (of rape) they come in a legal way . . . most of these commanders had to pay dowry for their soldiers."[61] The hijacking of disciplinary rules was not exclusively practiced in the Equatorian region, since Nuer respondents corroborated this trend in the Upper Nile region too: "In Nuer areas, rape was not [punishable by] fire-squad either, just like in Equatoria—as long as you married the victim."[62]

SPLA Groupness through Violence

The Bor Massacre

SPLA groupness, fostered by the othering of non-Dinka (including through sexual violence), was exclusive but still variable in scale following political events. Dinka SPLA groupness was especially strong after the 1991 split and the Bor massacre, when Garang and Machar acted as ethnopolitical entrepreneurs.[63] They both had large-group wounds to capitalize on—including feelings of humiliation from slavery, colonialism, and northern racism and struggles over the SPLA leadership and associated massacres. These feelings had already played a role in the formation of group entitlement ideology and discourses before the 1991 split. The 1991 split accentuated both Nuer and Dinka group entitlement ideologies and antagonism, which facilitated their manipulation by both Garang and Machar.[64]

Ethnopolitical entrepreneurs or ethnonationalist leaders frame their arguments in resonance with narratives defining and praising their group and its heroes while blaming group enemies. These narratives shape ethnic, racial, or national identities. This framing of their arguments in resonance with these narratives and prejudices has an influence on how their organizations develop—in the case of the SPLA, a more and more ethnic Dinka army after 1991. But these leaders also frame their arguments referring to these narratives because they need to—their organizations' needs influence this framing.[65]

In other words, both Garang and Machar needed to reach for the "ethnic card" after the 1991 split if they wanted to have enough recruits.[66] Machar capitalized on anti-Garang and anti-Dinka feelings to win more support. The massacres by Dinka SPLA troops between 1984 and 1988 were sufficient for the Nuer to consider the Bor massacre a retaliation. As for Garang, he rallied support among the Dinka of Bahr El Ghazal who were otherwise disappointed with the SPLA's neglect of their region.[67] This allowed him to contain this competing Dinka constituency while losing other ethnic "buffers" in the SPLA, whose humiliation and discrimination had helped coalesce Dinka groupness and mask tensions between the two Dinka constituencies.

The Bor massacre proved that the Nuer were "looters," "thieves without honor" who supposedly committed a "genocide" against the Dinka in Bor. Each side would, in the decades leading up to the third civil war, capitalize on macabre events before, during, and after the Bor massacre to gain political legitimacy and military manpower. Of course, negative stereotypes and discrimination against non-Dinka groups already existed prior to the 1991 split and the Bor massacre. In other words, what Stuart J. Kaufman calls "symbolic predispositions" (ideology and prejudice) against the Nuer already prevailed and had real consequences.[68] What the Bor massacre did was to materialize the perception of a Nuer threat: not only were the Nuer rebels, looters, and traitors to the national cause, but after killing some Dinka recruits from Bahr El Ghazal on their way to the refugee camps back in the 1980s they were now the killers of the Bor Dinka, Garang's home constituency.

The Bor massacre would become what Vamık D. Volkan and J. Christopher Fowler call a "chosen trauma" for the Dinka, united as a group in its remembrance and transmission passed from generation to generation: a symbol for decades in the Dinka leadership's nationalist exclusionary and war-mongering discourse.[69] Its perception was not rational, but it did not need to be.[70] As Volkan and Fowler intimate, "the historical truth about the event is no longer a psychologically key element for the large group; what is important is the sense of being linked together."[71]

Indeed, the idea of the "Bor massacre" would become different from the massacre itself. The 1991 massacre occurred in the context of past massacres and fighting. In the short run, the November 1991 massacre in Bor was the culmination of a series of interfactional fights after the SPLA split of August 1991. In September–October 1991, the Nasir faction under Riek Machar, reinforced by the Anya Nya II and armed civilians referred to as the "White Army," fought with Garang's SPLA around Ayod, in Jonglei.[72] Both factions attacked civilians on both sides of the Nuer-Bor Dinka border. Machar's troops counterattacked deep into Dinka territory around the district of Kongor, situated less than a hundred miles away, north of Bor. In November 1991, Machar's troops and Anya Nya II troops, along with armed Nuer civilians, launched another attack against Garang's troops in Kongor and Bor: these attacks, although they also affected Kongor and Duk county, are what are known as the "Bor massacre." They were initiated by the Fangak Anya Nya II and the Mor Lou Nuer from Akobo, Nasir, and Ayod counties—communities affected by SPLA killings in the 1980s.[73]

Both Nuer and Dinka soldiers and civilians interviewed for this book felt that the Bor massacre was retaliation for past SPLA violence against Nuer civilians. The massacre was designed to target Garang's homeland in Twic East and Bor. Both Nuer and Dinka respondents (some of them personally involved in the fighting in Bor at the time) stressed that the massacre was not about ethnicity but about politics and payback.[74] In the end, none of these were mutually exclusive: they all combined in violent politics, ethnicized from the beginning of the SPLA's formation.

Comparing the 1991 Bor massacre to the 2013 Juba massacre of Nuer civilians—which was also payback—a Dinka SPLA officer who fought in Bor during the 1991 massacre recalled, "The massacre in Juba in December 2013 was worse than the Bor massacre of 1991. The massacre of 1991, it was not Riek who started it, it was the SPLA. The SPLA killed the Nuer in Akobo, Nasir, Maiwut. This started in 1983 until 1991, to curb the Anya Nya II and it resulted into looting and killings. That's what angered Riek Machar and led to the retaliation in Bor 1991. In 1991, Riek wanted to capture Garang's home."[75]

Interethnic fighting had indeed already started before 1991 between multiple groups, and it continued afterwards.[76] Immediately after the Bor massacre, the SPLA burned down Nuer villages, and retributions against the Nuer continued well into 1993.[77] Violence against civilians continued to occur throughout 1993 and 1994, in Equatoria, Upper Nile, and Bahr El Ghazal, although on a lesser scale.[78] Civilians were generally dragged into the fighting by both SPLA factions.[79]

The exact casualties of the Bor massacre are still unknown, but the distinction between civilians and soldiers was problematic throughout the conflict.[80] Dinka SPLA soldiers who fought Machar's troops under the command of Kuol Manyang in Bor in 1991 insisted that both soldiers (SPLA and those under Machar) and armed civilians were killed. One of them gave a much more nuanced picture than the common depiction of the massacre of defenseless Dinka civilians:

> The SPLA used the Bor massacre for propaganda to ethnicize the war. Both Riek's and SPLA soldiers killed people in Bor in 1991. The Bor massacre was not only against the Dinka. It was against both (Nuer and Dinka). But the SPLA used it for propaganda. Bodies were in decay so they could not be identified . . . And the SPLA told the UN it was just Dinka civilians. The Nuer who died in Bor were soldiers but also civilians who came to loot the cattle. Civilians were on both sides. But "civilians" and "soldiers" were categories used by both sides. The SPLA said "civilians," Machar said "soldiers."[81]

Machar resorted to arming civilians because he did not have enough men, and he allied with the Anya Nya II at the outset of the fighting.[82] Another Dinka SPLA soldier who fought against Machar's troops in Bor recounted, "Machar's forces crossed the whole Bor land from Bor North to Bor South and to Mangala. Riek's intention was not to kill ethnic Dinka. They looted cattle and killed people. It was opportunism. They had their own agenda, which was to raid others. Cattle was taken. Civilians were killed in cross-shooting and in looting . . . The majority of Riek's troops were not officers, they were cattle-keepers . . . Most of the White Army was cattle-keepers. The cattle they looted, they kept for themselves."[83] A soldier from Machar's troops who descended on Bor in 1991 offered a similar account: "The civilians fighting for the White Army took the cattle. Whenever there's a military defeat, be it between the Dinka and the Nuer or the Murle and the Nuer, whoever wins always collects the cattle . . . Cattle taken by Lou Nuer was distributed among soldiers."[84] Just like Garang, Machar—and the rest of the splintering commanders—had no genuine interest in disciplining their troops.[85] Lack of discipline and proper command, looting in the absence of wages, and grievances for past massacres of the Nuer all played a role in large-scale violence against the Dinka.[86]

But did the Bor massacre amount to a genocide, as it has been portrayed by some Dinka activists since then? Sharon Hutchinson and Jok Madut Jok noted a more primordialist and racialist understanding of "ethnicity" by Nuer soldiers after the split versus before. They argued that before the SPLA split, the definition of "ethnicity" was more fluid, and that women were considered "illegitimate" targets in the context of Dinka and Nuer ethical codes of warfare.[87] Hutchinson also argued that the SPLA did not take captives and that women were annihilated: "Women and children were gradually recast by rival Southern military factions as legitimate targets of ethnic annihilation."[88]

Peter Adwok Nyaba's account of the "massacre" indicates that the aggressors' motivations were economic and related to kinship expansion. Their goal was not to decimate the "Dinka race" through the killing of women and their children or through the impregnation of Dinka women with Nuer children.[89] Nyaba's account was corroborated by that of John Young, who wrote that usually in attacks, there was a "willingness to assimilate . . . the conquered people."[90] Women and men from Bor and from Garang's SPLA interviewed for this book denied that women were specifically targeted during the massacre. One of the Dinka SPLA soldiers who fought Machar's troops in Bor in 1991 stressed that even though a lot of people had died in Bor, including women, the majority of them (including women) were killed in crossfire and that some women had been killed when they attempted to protect cattle from looters.[91] One female Dinka SPLA soldier from Bor corroborated Nyaba's analysis: "No, they were not targeted as women. But you know, the moment people fight, and you are defeated, women are taken . . . Because in our culture when they get women, they take them and they marry them."[92]

Other interviewees, both Dinka and Nuer, confirmed that the Lou Nuer inter-married with the Bor Dinka women they captured following the Bor massacre. But these marriages were forced and did not involve the payment of bridewealth. A Dinka man from Bor recounted how in 2008 (seventeen years after the mas-sacre), one of these women who had birthed four children to her Nuer abduc-tor finally escaped from Nasir.[93] This woman's escape resonated with how other women from Equatoria also tried to break free from their Dinka (or Nuba) SPLA abductors. There too the SPLA often absorbed the women that its soldiers raped.[94] Thus predation strategies, more than ethnicity, ultimately drove both Machar's faction and the SPLA's treatment of most civilians and especially women.[95] This was a marked difference with the nature of the sexual violence of the third civil war.

Violence, Predation and Cohesion

After 1991, the perpetration of sexual violence and the accumulation of women-as-capital came in handy to the disintegrating SPLA: it fostered groupness and perennial discourses of Dinka group legitimacy. In other conflicts such as Sierra Leone (1991–2002), rape and especially gang-rape socialized combatants and reinforced group cohesion. It was used when soldiers were coerced into joining armed factions with little internal cohesion. Rape—especially gang-rape—can create bonds of trust more rapidly among strangers, in part because it is risky due to STIs. The perpetration of high levels of violence such as gang-rape can thus increase group identification and ensure group longevity.[96]

In the SPLA, sexual violence also reinforced groupness because marriage fre-quently followed rape. This was the opportunity to create new exchange con-tracts.[97] The patronage of marriage by commanders created new ties of obliga-tion between commanders and soldiers and reinforced troops' cohesion. Com-manders substituted themselves for the fathers of their soldiers by either paying the bridewealth or witnessing the agreement between them and the bride's fam-ily, thus guaranteeing the future payment of the bridewealth.[98] A former Dinka SPLA soldier illustrated how the patronage of marriages created feelings that reinforced loyalty to commanders:

> The problem of postponement of dowry, it's because there was no resources (to pay it). Some commanders and soldiers who did it, they were telling me that commander x, y, z, was the one who paid dowry for my wife, proudly. And you know, to do that, it's somebody that really loves you, it has to be a member of the family, and even sometimes in a real family, they don't do it. Not everyone will give dowry for you, it

has to be the closest, your best friend, that will pay dowry for you. And so, some say that, proudly, that commander x, y, z paid dowry for the wife . . . or do negotiations, with the chiefs and the relatives.[99]

Feelings of pride illustrated the soldiers' sense of place—their own perceptions of their place in the social order, under their commanders.[100] The payment of the bridewealth by their commanders or their role as guarantors did not represent just a "courtesy" or a "favor," nor could it be summed up as material assistance. The "gifts" made by the SPLA commanders to their soldiers constituted ways to retain their authority.[101] Other examples of voluntary participation in bridewealth payments by nonrelatives to retain political allegiance also existed prior to the war, not just among Dinka but also among the Nuer.[102] Therefore the SPLA commanders' "gifts" dressed their military power with the traditional attire that resonated through the communities of their soldiers, solidifying their power as patrimonial rulers.[103] These commanders and soldiers, along with the bride's kin, became part of the same social contract bound by obligations.

The patronage of marriages became part of the SPLA's military strategy early on: without it, its soldiers might have contested the authority of polygamous commanders or deserted. In Dinka culture, where procreation affords immortality, poor men without sufficient cattle for bridewealth often feared they (in fact, their line) would "perish."[104] War magnified such a threat, and the fact that these soldiers were far from their home areas and without their cattle augmented the risk of dying without an heir. Most soldiers were poor, but answered to the orders of wealthier polygamous SPLA commanders. These commanders rarely granted them the luxury of a permission to return to the village and marry.[105] From the soldiers' point of view, "if you got a small chance to marry, you took it!."[106] For the SPLA leadership, if not handled, the soldiers' celibacy was a ticking bomb. A former Dinka SPLA platoon commander who contributed to pay his own officers' bridewealth confirmed this: "If I solve this problem—marriage—soldiers will remain with me. The SPLA has become a big family."[107]

Garang facilitated the patronage of these marriages: he instructed that following the centralization of captured resources at the SPLA headquarters, the zonal commander would dispatch the resources earmarked for bridewealth (cattle or money) to the platoon commander who would then pass it on to his officers.[108] Commanders and officers paid some of the installment or at least signed a letter of guarantee of payment in presence of the paramount chief, in order to secure their soldiers' kinship expansion—sealing their acquisition of women-as-capital.[109]

In the SPLA "family," commanders acted as fathers, and the brothers-in-arms as the traditional uncles and other relatives.[110] No one else had the temerity to "bid" for the bride.[111] Decades later, those brothers-in-arms who contributed to one another's bridewealth were still friends with each other—they behaved like family and they referred to the SPLA as a "big family." The wartime postponement of bridewealth payments to a peaceful future contributed to the longevity of those social contracts between commanders and soldiers, which multiplied when soldiers practiced polygamy.[112] By the end of the war, many soldiers in the SPLA had more than one wife, most between two and four.[113] One SPLA soldier remembered, "They married, they married from each location! They had so many wives! . . . If you had an opportunity, you just married! Wherever they go, they get married!."[114] Yet in this patrimonial capitalist economy, the SPLA (and factions) commanders always remained on top.

SPLA Social Class Formation

Large-Scale Polygamy by the Dominant Class

Thanks to their control over the war economy, commanders acquired women-as-capital through large-scale polygamy. Combined with their patronage of their soldiers' marriages, this consolidated their ascendency as the dominant class. This was not unusual: throughout the lineage slavery systems in west-central Africa in the seventeenth to nineteenth centuries, the uneven distribution of women also enforced social control and socioeconomic domination. Important polygamous men in Nigeria's Biafra region even became a class distinguished by the size of its polygamous families and number of slaves and clients.[115] Similarly, the acquisition of women contributed to building the power of SPLA commanders like Paul Malong.

Polygamy, afforded through the reinvestment of looted cattle, provided the SPLA commanders (and commanders from other armed groups) with the perfect avenue for wealth display.[116] New wives served as a testimony of a man's military exploits, as one former SPLA battalion commander put it, "You get new wealth, new wives. If you defeat your enemies, you keep their wealth! If not, they take yours!."[117] Capturing resources were key to sustaining the acquisition of these new wives.[118] Commanders like Malong used relief money diverted from the slave buy-back programs in the 1990s to marry more wives.[119]

In fact, marriage was the best way to immediately "invest" into valuable long-term capital sowing strategies, explained a Nuer civilian: "They marry and [thus] use the loot to reinvest and get rid of the cattle as soon as possible before it gets looted."[120] Large-scale polygamy—or the large-scale acquisition of women-as-capital—was meant to generate long-term wealth, a former Dinka SPLA soldier attested: "War wealth is associated with big families. You have more money or you have more cattle, you want to have more wives . . . And then you have more wives, you have a lot of children, most of them girls, who will be married. This is the whole mentality."[121] In extending their lineages, commanders increased their political power. These powerful men were generally not subjected to customary bridewealth prices and often paid them later. There was no competition for the women they coveted and sometimes eloped with, which meant they could pay as little twenty cattle for bridewealth.[122]

The SPLA's dominant class was mostly Dinka, especially after 1991. Intermarriage between non-Dinka commanders and Dinka women was rare given that the Dinka monopolized most SPLA positions granting access to resources. But promotion to the same status of a Dinka could happen for a few non-Dinka men, similar to in Rwanda where before the genocide a Hutu man could experience upward social mobility through access to cattle and in the process be "tutsified."[123] This demonstrated that ethnicity could be more or less primordialized depending on the parties' interests.[124] Yet the Toposa (Equatorian) wife of a polygamous Kakwa SPLA colonel who also married a Dinka woman explained, "He was recognized in the community and with resources, and he attracted Dinka women too," but "the Dinka family was not happy about their daughter's marriage to a non-Dinka."[125] All in all, ethnic absorption was mostly one-sided, and the alien ethnic identity of men intermarried with Dinka women endured in the eyes of the Dinka beholder.[126]

SPLA commanders used the taxes collected from civilians while pulling the strings of the war economy to acquire more women-as-capital. For the Dinka, no limit except age and wealth restricted how many women one could marry, and their practices echoed those of other powerful Dinka men before them, such as chief Deng Majok who married around 250 wives in the 1940s–60s.[127] Parents volunteered their daughter for marriage to the powerful SPLA (and factions) commanders.[128] Some of the less prominent commanders did not bother to pay any bridewealth, or paid very little.[129] Polygamy was reputed to be most practiced in the Dinka areas of the Bahr El Ghazal region, but it also prevailed in Equatoria and in Nuer areas.[130] There, lower bridewealth prices facilitated even more the accumulation of women-as-capital, as Nuer men explained: "Eastern Equatoria was 'free of charge.' There was no bridewealth paid sometimes, and besides the bride prices were cheaper."[131]

The demographic bias in the marriage market—with men dead, on the frontline, or fleeing as refugees while commanders preyed over single (or sometimes married) women—made it easier for the commanders to acquire new wives.[132] Many of Garang's commanders had multiple wives and monogamy was the exception.[133] These commanders were reputed to marry tens of women and did so more easily in the countryside than in the scrutiny of the towns.

Respondents remembered commanders who married fifteen, twenty, forty, even fifty-one wives.[134]

Paul Malong, running the war economy of Northern Bahr El Ghazal, "built a wide network of connections" through large-scale polygamy.[135] He already had about forty wives in 2001.[136] He sent out his soldiers to collect them from different communities in his home state (from Aweil North, Aweil Center, Aweil East, and so on) and bring them to him, a Dinka civilian from his home state remembered: "Malong married in four different communities—all of them from Northern Bahr El Ghazal. This is a very strategic plan! Because you can't fight with the husband of your sister. And he used to pay so many cows!"[137] By 2015, when Malong had become the SPLA chief of staff, a Nuer civilian compared this wide network to an "empire," adding, "Malong has eighty-six wives. Where does he get the cattle? From the people. His close family is made of four hundred people."[138] In oil-rich Unity state, Nuer commanders did exactly as Dinka commanders.[139] For example, Peter Gadet "always married on the way, wherever he passed."[140] Bridewealth payment was key to legitimizing kinship expansion, and was understood as a long-term investment.[141]

Signifying their ascendency, commanders used bridewealth payment and price as a marker of social distinction meant to convey their command over others: "Gadet paid for the dowry of his wives—some parents even offered their girl but he wanted to pay . . . Parents are very proud, so they don't demand dowry. But high-ranking officers use it to demonstrate they can afford it. They're proud to pay."[142] For parents, marrying their daughter to a commander meant protection. But commanders also expected it in return: "Parents gave their daughter for promotion. If your daughter has been married by a big person, you can do whatever you want, you can be protected. Also if someone mistreats Peter Gadet, you have to go and defend him."[143] This exchange revealed a codependency that was typical of a patrimonial relationship.[144]

Large-scale polygamy was key to building and sustaining political and military power, and it is no coincidence that some of these (very) polygamous wartime commanders—from Malong to Matiep, Gadet and Gatluak Gai—proved to be forces of disturbance during the war and long after.[145] Their own large-scale polygamy extended social contracts beyond even the kin of their brides. Indeed, other men were involved in tending to the reproductive potential of the women-as-capital, as former Nuer SPLA soldiers explained: "[Military] leaders marry with many wives and have them stay with somebody. When you marry twenty wives, thirty wives, you marry and look for another one once the marriage is completed and you can have other children."[146]

Paul Malong reportedly had his relatives and followers, whose bridewealth he paid, impregnate his more than forty wives for him, much like the Nuer prophet

Deng Laka in the nineteenth century.[147] The Nuer commander Peter Gadet also paid for his followers' bridewealth, or accumulation of women-as-capital, and also had them impregnate his wives, a respondent explained: "Gadet has about eighty wives. He doesn't know who impregnated which one. He just birthed the first boy, the rest doesn't matter. Even his soldiers can impregnate them, so long as the child is named after him, he doesn't care. He paid for the dowry of the wives."[148]

The Creation of a Dependent Middle-Class

SPLA soldiers thus tended to their commanders' own women-as-capital when necessary, and they could only marry because their commanders allowed them to. In this manner, the SPLA dominant class evidently created for itself a lower stratum. First, it was guaranteed followers by crafting new military kinship ties through "gifts" of bridewealth. That reinforced cohesion, permitted the acquisition of women-as-capital, and reinforced and mitigated risks for class conflict between the dominant class and its followers. It also demonstrated to the followers their "place" in the social order, under their commanders.[149]

Secondly, the elite ramified its lower base through the elevation of SPLA soldiers to an economic status superior to that of the local population.[150] This new stratum became the intermediaries between the "rulers," and the "ruled."[151] By enabling its lower stratum to marry so many wives, the elite allowed these men to taste the privileges it enjoyed, thus fostering the illusion of a commonality between the rulers and its intermediaries, which typically paves the way for future collaboration.[152]

Without the creation of this military middle class, the SPLA would have collapsed. The dominant class could not have sustained its accumulation of capital—including women-as-capital—and its tending to it. Instead, the middle class helped the dominant class accumulate capital to the detriment of the masses of ordinary civilians. This codependency was typical of patrimonial systems of domination.[153] The system, of course, remained stratified. Capitalism in SPLA areas was decidedly patrimonial. Upward social mobility was only afforded through marriage.[154] This middle class could only climb the social ladder by marrying the daughter of a commander, which was the passport to a promotion and to more capital accumulation.

Symptomatically, not all soldiers were allowed the opportunity to commit rape, marry, and accumulate women as they travelled, as Dinka SPLA wives explained: "Not all the soldiers have married a lot. Because there are others who have no power."[155] As a result, inequality increased greatly during the war as the dominant class concentrated its wealth. This explains why polygamy still generally decreased during the war, due to the depletion of resources and their concentration in the hands of a few.

Expansion and Protoconquest

Equatorian groups such as the Bari and the Acholi had explicitly and actively avoided intermarriage with the Dinka back in the 1970s–early 1980s to counter what they considered to be a first attempt at Dinka inner colonization after independence.[156] This was against the backdrop of centuries of demographic expansion by the Dinka that turned it into the majority group.[157]

The second civil war considerably accelerated Dinka expansion through the violent ethnic absorption of non-Dinka groups. Non-Dinka groups in Equatoria were worried about their demographic future, and with good reason: Jok noted of the Dinka troops, "Undeclared roles, at least for the rank-and-file, included viewing reproduction as a national obligation, not as an individual one."[158] The Equatorians could no longer refuse intermarriage once the predominantly Dinka SPLA violently conquered them.[159]

Sexual violence was deeply connected to territorial and demographic expansion, because as MacKinnon points out, "violating other men's women is planting a flag; it is a way some men say to other men, 'What was yours is now mine.' . . . As often happens when men plant flags, someone was already living there."[160] The SPLA's territorial and demographic expansion was tantamount to a protoconquest. SPLA military advances came with sexual violence, forced marriages, and land-grabbing, which all followed a logic of capital accumulation rooted in a mode of production inherited from slavery.

The accumulation of women-as-capital went hand in hand with the SPLA's "occupation." In Equatoria, communities associated sexual violence with plunder, conquest, and domination by the SPLA.[161] A former female Kakwa (Equatorian) SPLA soldier explained her comrades' brutality by their predatory drive: "Many of them were illiterate. The vision of the SPLA was that they were not oriented at all about the future. They were oriented that: 'when we capture a place, the houses, we take them! We take the houses, we take everybody, the women there, we take!' This is *what* they were orientated *on*!"[162]

Sexual violence was thus not opportunistic, and the risks associated with it were well worth the benefits.[163] A former Dinka SPLA battalion commander explained the capitalist logic: "You have to marry more, so that you can have money, you have more land, and you can protect your cattle."[164] The protoconquest expanded south into Equatoria with the 1991 split, the Bor massacre, and the need for new pastures. A Moro civilian from western Equatoria confirmed that the SPLA's logic of capital accumulation culminated in land grabs: "The SPLA was all over Mundri before 2005. . . They want our land! During the SPLA time [second civil war], they took their cattle there on Moro land, and their cattle are doing well there!"[165]

The logic applied from west to east in the southern region. In central Equatoria (Yei), a Kakwa (Equatorian) husband whose wife was raped by soldiers in 1987 recalled, "The SPLA did not want to see any other tribe in Yei . . . The SPLA was now in Yei, the Dinka. My house was occupied by the SPLA, my food taken away."[166] In eastern Equatoria (Nimule), the SPLA used rape to terrorize and displace people so they could settle on the land—in the words of one woman, "They grab your wife, they grab your land, and then they settle."[167] The same trend was depicted in western Equatoria (Mundri), as a Muru civilian explained: "Muru girls were raped and the marriages between Muru girls and Dinka were forced, leading to Dinka settling on the land during the second civil war. Similarly to what happened in eastern Equatoria, the Dinka stayed."[168]

The SPLA's multifaceted predation—its mode of production—thus resulted in Dinka expansionism. After 2005, Dinka settlers would consolidate this inner colonization in the interwar period. Finally, in 2013 a new war would start the third, and this time annihilating, phase of conquest.

Predation, Social Class Formation, and Dinka Nationalism

Looking back, the ascension of the dominant class-in-formation largely relied on the reinvestment of its economic predation into the acquisition of women-as-capital. This dominant class thought of itself as "the best" and as such became a military aristocracy.[169] It partially distributed women-as-capital to a predominantly Dinka group that had become violent and exclusionary. To many non-Dinka civilians, the power of the SPLA was like "the power of the rapist over the raped."[170] An Acholi (Equatorian) man explained, "If you want to have a scar that will never heal, you'll come mess with our wives."[171]

The SPLA's ethnicized mode of (re)production, resting on predation and culminating in a protoconquest, thus fostered feelings of group ownership over the country and therefore Dinka group legitimacy.[172] These feelings initially originated in the SPLA myth of national liberation, created in 1983. This myth, conveyed through propaganda and acted out in international political arenas by Garang, gained traction mostly among the Dinka. It could not have been otherwise, given the progressive Dinka-ization of the SPLA and the violence the SPLA committed against non-Dinka civilians.

The SPLA myth of national liberation evolved with the fluctuation of Dinka groupness following political events and the way in which Garang handled them. Garang was not a proactive ethnopolitical entrepreneur throughout the twenty-two-year-long war. His actions were dictated rather by the pressures he felt within the SPLA. But the "founding narrative" of SPLA nationalism became increasingly Dinka and exclusionary. This was partly Garang's responsibility because the SPLA leadership was not genuinely interested in fostering ethnic diversity in its ranks. If it had been, it would have curbed ethnic discriminations in its ranks, promoted other ethnicities to real positions of power, and actively combated human rights violations, especially against other ethnic groups. But it did none of these things, while capturing enough international leverage to be considered the representative of the southerners at peace negotiations with Khartoum. As a result, what emerged in 2005 when the peace agreement (CPA) was signed was an SPLA nationalism mostly identified with the Dinka. This implied that other ethnic groups, associated with other armed groups formed in protection from and retaliation against the SPLA, were conceived of as "traitors" to the national cause championed by the SPLA.

Stereotypical Dinka symbolic predispositions (ideology and prejudice) about the Nuer and the Equatorians shared similarities, especially to the extent that they were all lumped into a "non-Dinka group" of traitors and rebels, people who could not be trusted (just like the Northerners), had no "vision" (something Garang prided himself on), and would squander the SPLA's national project. Because the Equatorians had not contested the SPLA leadership early in the war and because their women were consistently considered "cheap" by Dinka soldiers and raped and appropriated, Equatorian men were emasculated and as such they were considered "cowards" in Dinka symbolic predispositions. The Nuer were stereotyped as "fighters" from colonial times. They had contested power within the SPLA, which, when compounded with the 1991 Bor massacre, made them a real threat, a perception that extended to groups allying with them.

By 2005, there was already more than the embryo of an idea that non-Dinka groups had been undermining the southern "nation" throughout the war of "national liberation," which is a key ingredient in genocides. After all, the Germans also thought of the Jews as undermining their nationality before the Holocaust.[173] The third civil war would intensify this exclusionary nationalism following a political crisis that reactivated prejudices against the Nuer.

NATIONALISM, PREDATION, AND ETHNIC RANKING

2005–13

Postwar nationalism, promoted by Garang's followers and indirectly encouraged by the international community, provided the roots of the exclusionary ideology deployed in the third civil war by perpetrators. After Garang's death, Salva Kiir's faction hijacked this nationalist rhetoric to infiltrate and control the state. Different ethnic dominant classes that had come to coexist in the capital of Juba during the CPA period continued to compete, yet the SPLA Dinka dominant class won this competition. Salva Kiir's faction sidelined other Dinka competitors from Garang's faction and other ethnic competitors. This propelled ethnic ranking within the state. Nationalism, a new security landscape, and widespread violence were instrumental in making the start of the third civil war in December 2013 genocidal.

Nationalism, Group Legitimacy, and Sovereignty

The Impact of the CPA on Group Legitimacy

Peace was not the result of a military victory. The government had control of the towns and oil fields and most of the Upper Nile region through the SSDF.[1] The 2005 Comprehensive Peace Agreement was rather the result of both external and internal threats on both signatories and the culmination of years of negotiations under international aegis.[2] The step-by-step nature of the CPA agreement (made up of different agreements) was an indication of the parties' reluctance to settle,

FIGURE 5.1.   South Sudan's president Salva Kiir (right) with the rebel leader and then first vice president Riek Machar (left) in Juba on April 29, 2016, after the first cabinet meeting of the Transitional Government of National Unity. Photo by Jason Patinkin.

and Garang admitted that the agreements were only reached because of external pressures.[3] This fooled no one on the ground: "No one was sincere about the peace," corroborated an Acholi (Equatorian) man. "The CPA was imposed from outside."[4]

The CPA provided for a six-and-a-half-year interim period in which the SPLM/A and Khartoum's National Congress Party (NCP) would rule in a Government of National Unity, implementing the agreement's provisions. It would culminate, six years later, in a referendum for the south's self-determination in January 2011. These negotiations provided for the SPLA to not be absorbed into the SAF but instead to control the entire south.[5] The negotiations had denied participation to the SPLA's competitor, the predominantly Nuer and Equatorian South Sudan Defense Force (SSDF), tied to Khartoum, whose size was comparable to that of the SPLA.[6] A lot of South Sudanese at the time believed that this exclusion would eventually lead to a renewed civil war in South Sudan among southerners.[7] They were correct.

In the end, the CPA excluded more than half of South Sudan's armed groups who were not Dinka. In other words, it denied the existence of armed groups other than the predominantly Dinka SPLA. In doing so, it built the foundations of what international norms dictated would be a new "nation-state" on exclusion.

The CPA was just another deal between the southern and northern bourgeoisies.[8] Precisely because it endorsed the SPLA and because its design was mostly technical, the CPA was perfectly fitted to "swell" the state through international state-building assistance and consolidate the position of this predominantly Dinka dominant class.[9] This was a continuation of the "NGO-istan." Endorsement of the SPLA and the development of the "nation-state" blended with the nationalism of the predominantly Dinka SPLA. This, especially under the control of Salva Kiir's faction, would grow into an exclusionary ideology with genocidal potential.

The SPLA Elite's Insecurity

The SPLA's claims to ownership would not have been successful without the support of the United States, Norway, and the United Kingdom, both during the CPA negotiations and after.[10] The SPLA elite knew how much it owed to U.S. advocates, who had improved Garang's image to the point that the entire U.S. policy had come to rely on him (and therefore collapsed after his death).[11] Norway had supported the SPLA directly through its aid agencies and through the diplomat Hilde F. Johnson, the head of the UN peacekeeping mission supporting the semi-autonomous state who was personally involved in the CPA negotiations.[12] The signal was clear: the SPLA was still surrounded by friends, but it was also closely watched and under Western supervision.

Garang's death meant that the movement lost its popular face abroad and as such part of its international social capital. Salva Kiir, Garang's deputy and since the 2004 Rumbek conference his official competitor, took his place. The international community did not take him seriously—they considered him to be a shy, barely articulate professional military man in Garang's shadow. As noted earlier, this was a grave misconception. There was a good reason why Salva Kiir was the only one of the original founding officers to survive the twenty-two-year-long war. He looked unassuming because he was discreet. But he was savvy, incredibly patient, and a skilled ethnopolitical entrepreneur.

By the time Kiir took over the SPLA, it was already a pressure cooker. Other groups with their own discourses of group legitimacy and entitlement—especially the SSDF—were integrated into the SPLA through a separate south-south agreement: the 2006 Juba Declaration.[13] Yet their integration did not work, and the original SPLA elite still perceived them as a threat. The SPLA elite was of course aware of its own lack of broad legitimacy in the south and of the divisions in its Dinka cadres and recruits. Insecurity in ownership claims and control thus manifested in an attempt to usurp collective memory.

Postwar Nationalism

POSTWAR NATIONALIST SYMBOLISM

Overcompensating for the SPLA's lack of broad interethnic popularity, the new statesmen promoted the political myth of SPLA national liberation to garner popularity among the Dinka, foster Dinka groupness, and secure their hold over society. In doing so, the statesmen reinforced a "founding narrative." Such a narrative typically defines the primary community of the state by telling, as Scott Straus argues, "a story about the state and nation—what it is, where it comes from, what it stands for, what it should achieve, who should captain it, and whom it serves."[14]

Advertised myths and official state history reflect the dominant group's ideology and therefore play a crucial role in the creation of a political myth.[15] This is particularly important because the act of making a political myth is essential to the creation of a founding narrative, which in turn can easily become an exclusionary ideology.[16] In other words, there can be no exclusionary ideology without a founding narrative based on a political myth.

The new state's selective memory demonstrated that not only did it valorize its own version of history, it also devalued and silenced the wartime experiences of an entire segment of the population. This was typical of revolutionary wars, which often create legitimate and illegitimate communities.[17] It was a logical evolution of the internal dynamics of the SPLA during the second civil war and of Garang's creation of a political myth of national liberation meant to attract foreign support and mask the ethnicization and tensions within the SPLA. The overwhelmingly Dinka recruits believed that they—the Dinka as a "group"—had "liberated" the country. Even if many non-Dinka civilians felt occupied rather than liberated, what mattered was that the Dinka believed it.

The CPA promoted the idea of Dinka group legitimacy, which reinforced the making of ethnic categories and ethnic prejudices, as I have argued in previous chapters.[18] The Nuer were seen as traitors to the cause of national liberation for their role in the 1991 SPLA split and their alliance with Khartoum. By extension, they were traitors to the nation.[19] The Equatorians and by extension the smaller groups were also viewed as traitors who had allied with Khartoum and defended the kokora, or as cowardly bystanders. Therefore they could not be trusted either. Only the Dinka were the true national liberators who could be trusted to defend the interests of South Sudan. This ranking between legitimate and illegitimate ethnic categories had genocidal potential because it reinforced the distinctness of groups. Most important, it provided a justification for excluding non-Dinka from holding the reins of power: as Straus writes, "the idea that the state belongs to a category of people helps convince others that challengers who do not belong to the in-group do not have a right to control the state."[20]

The international community unwillingly helped the SPLA in building up its founding narrative by funding demilitarization programs it knew were largely a scam, thus promoting the pro-Dinka SPLA's picture of the second civil war. In the words of a former Nuer SPLA officer, "we [the SPLA] sacrificed the truth."[21] This sacrifice of "truth"—whoever's truth it was—essentially meant there was no counternarrative that could have deescalated the genocidal potency of the SPLA's founding narrative.[22] The state thus advertised the history of the Dinka elite, which did not correspond to the experiences of many non-Dinka civilians, including women. It was in total contradiction to the experiences of ordinary South Sudanese people.[23] But it was the reflection of the image the state wanted to project: that of a proud society able to defend itself thanks to Dinka SPLA patriots, not to be toyed with, and not to be raped.

Examples abound to show how the state celebrated the predominantly Dinka SPLA as the genesis of South Sudan's nationhood. South Sudan never changed the name of its army (SPLA), even after the 2011 independence. The 2006 Juba Declaration, the south-south peace agreement bringing in the SSDF, was never to be celebrated—contrary to the CPA, which was meant to convey the SPLA's successful claims of legitimacy over the future independent country.[24] Apart from peace agreement day, national holidays included an SPLA day (no SSDF there) and a martyr's day that started taking place in 2007 at John Garang Mausoleum on the anniversary of Garang's death. All these national holidays were attended by foreign diplomats. Of course, the most famous one was the celebration of South Sudan's independence on July 9, 2011. This first celebration of independence provided the opportunity to showcase new national symbols, designed in a hurry. The idea that South Sudan automatically became a "nation" with independence was incredibly pervasive, from the media to academic writing on the country.[25]

Throughout all these national celebrations, little room was left for other armed groups from the first civil war and other key political events that had promoted self-rule. This particularly frustrated the Equatorians, who felt violated in their own group legitimacy and whose discourse relied on their political activism during colonial times and their role in the first civil war.[26] The South Sudanese national anthem mentioned the "patriots" and "martyrs," and it was clear that the patriots were from the SPLA. John Garang's face was on all the bills—which showcased whose constituency truly "owned" the country.[27] Symbols of Garang that spoke to the Dinka constituency, whether obvious or not, proliferated in many different places. All in all, postwar symbolism mainly catered to the Dinka.[28]

John Garang's mausoleum, which always featured in national processions, manifested his status as founding father of the new "nation," further validated by international diplomatic visits. With all his sins silenced, he was elevated to the status of a secular saint. The mausoleum helped mass mobilization, and the architectural site of Garang's personality cult also served in-group policing by invoking his figure.[29] The mausoleum's location in Juba, which was both the national capital and the state capital of Central Equatoria, also cemented the Dinka protoconquest of the region.[30] This political myth of national liberation mostly appealed to SPLA supporters and to the Dinka population in general. Official promotion of this political myth reflected who was excluded, denied, and neglected by the state.

DDR PROGRAMS: A CORRUPT MEMORIALIZATION OF THE WAR

Demilitarization programs, by offering a symbolic picture of the war, contributed to the SPLA's political myth of national liberation. They did so especially because the demilitarization process, started in 2005, was highly political and characterized by scores of issues.[31] One of these issues was that the lists the SPLA gave the international agencies in charge of these programs were based largely on personal networks.[32]

These Disarmament, Demobilization and Reintegration (DDR) programs frustrated those who had supported the troops but were not rewarded for it. They considered themselves forgotten—in other words, excluded from history and from the nation.[33] A Kakwa (Equatorian) man relayed the general sentiment of the Equatorians: "The SPLA was always dominated by the Dinka. The recruitment of SPLA was segregative and discriminatory . . . Benefits of DDR for Equatorians were not as much as for the Dinka and Nuer. The veterans had their assembly points in their own homelands. The Dinka joined in their homelands but also in Equatoria . . . Some Dinka became rich because of that money. That created very much frustration for the Equatorians. What you were expecting to get, you were getting one quarter or nothing. Yet you fought the same war, but now you're considered a second-class citizen."[34]

The DDR programs thus usurped the individual and collective memories of the war. The international community once again allowed the usurpation. "The UN turned a blind eye to the SPLA's corruption," an Acholi (Equatorian) UN DDR worker lamented.[35] And since the nationalist "founding narrative" equated citizenship with membership to the SPLA, being excluded from DDR packages or from their full benefit amounted to being excluded from the nation. The corrupt DDR programs contributed both to realizing the SPLA's "founding narrative" and to excluding groups that were not Dinka or lucky enough to be coopted, thus relegated to the category of "second-class citizen."[36]

Sovereignty and Anxiety

JUBA'S RELATIONS WITH KHARTOUM

This exclusion was the reflection of how unsettled South Sudan's national identity really was. Its mostly derivative national symbols and its blatant war-mongering showed how much the relationship with Khartoum deeply influenced the new country's identity.[37] Centuries of northern violent exploitation and racist humiliation, including through slavery, resulted in the southern elite's decisions being partly dictated by its fear of losing sovereignty and its desire to improve its group worth.[38]

Mutual suspicion between the SPLM/A and the NCP continued, with good reason. The CPA implementation was rocky at best, and mostly a failure.[39] Yet the SPLM's relationship with the NCP was related to its own divisions between the unionists of Garang and the separatists of Kiir.[40] The result of such drawbacks in CPA implementation was to further convince the southerners that independence was their only option. The January 2011 referendum was prepared in a hurry in the context of a tug-of-war between Khartoum and the SPLM, and won the independence of South Sudan with nearly 99 percent voting in favor.[41] By independence, John Young noted, "none of the post-referendum issues—including borders, treaties, citizenship, oil revenues, and the fate of Blue Nile and Southern Kordofan—was resolved."[42]

Tensions with Khartoum did not just stem from political disagreements; they had military implications. Khartoum continued to sponsor militias to destabilize the south.[43] Proxy wars between Sudan and South Sudan maintained a very volatile military environment in and between both countries, especially in 2010 and 2011.[44] The CPA was initially conceived of as a first step to negotiations about other war-torn areas in Sudan such as Darfur and East Sudan.[45] But war continued in Darfur, and resumed in Blue Nile and the Nuba Mountains in 2011.

Since both Khartoum and the SPLA had been involved in "war systems" they both benefited from, neither could function without the other.[46] Hence the necessity of continually producing an enemy and of abetting violence that was in fact politically useful, at least to South Sudan's leaders.[47] Indeed, tensions with Khartoum gave license to the SPLA to engage in an arms race.[48] This had two advantages for the SPLA: first, the SPLA signaled its readiness to protect the south's sovereignty against the militarily superior north; and second, the SPLM/A also gained the advantage over other potential competitors in the south. Arms acquisition combined with continuing ethnic discrimination within the SPLA favoring especially the Dinka from Bahr El Ghazal.

Tensions between SPLM/A factions continued throughout the entire CPA period and impacted relations with Khartoum. On the one hand, Garang's followers vied for power at the center, in Khartoum. On the other, Kiir's faction was much more willing to collaborate with the NCP.[49] Even though Garang's faction was progressively marginalized, it still was behind some of the most daring moves against Khartoum. The SPLA was obsessed with catching up with Khartoum's war capability to safeguard hard-won sovereignty and affirm itself as a worthy opponent. This behavior was justified and reinforced by the absence of a well-defined border.

Six border points neither party agreed on were essential to the country's growing nationalism.[50] Oil-rich Abyei, southern Blue Nile, and the Nuba Mountains were border territories on the frontline of the second civil war. But the SPLM/A had to give up on their inclusion in the CPA early in the negotiations, which nearly caused the party to split.[51] The fate of these territories would be sealed through other separate agreements, which would lead to their eventual sellout.[52]

A turning point came in 2012: in April 2012, fighting between the SPLA and SAF in Heglig/Panthou, the oil-rich eastern part of Abyei, provided the perfect avenue for Salva Kiir to stir up nationalism when his authoritarian rule was being increasingly contested at home.[53] The increasingly Dinka elite needed to divert public attention from the fact it had embezzled at least a third of the state's resources and had mortgaged half of the state's budget. It adopted a war-mongering posture. But not everyone was on board: "The few of us who were against going into fighting were seen as traitors," remembered some of the Nuer government officials present at the SPLM's National Liberation Council meeting on Heglig. "The SAF was not actually attacking. It was bogus . . . The SPLA-North (the SPLA comrades in the Nuba Mountains and Blue Nile) was seriously mobilizing the South to fight the North."[54] Upon deciding to engage militarily in Heglig, "Salva was celebrating," remembered a puzzled Dinka member of the Garang faction, and "emotions were high."[55] "Salva got up and declared war, and everybody applauded and got up . . . Singing went on for a good five minutes," the Nuer officials recalled.[56] Yet the elite had focused so much on amassing wealth and weapons that it had completely neglected building real war-making capacity.[57] It became clear throughout this episode just how "uncontrolled" and "chaotic" the SPLA was when confronted with the SAF.[58] Paul Malong, then governor of Northern Bahr El Ghazal state, still capitalized on the fighting to recruit more Dinka militias in his and Salva Kiir's home states.

Three months later, following a disagreement with Khartoum over oil trans-port fees, the south decided to shut down oil production in August 2012. This was another grave miscalculation by the SPLM elite, who wanted to signify the south's sovereignty and its own newfound ascendency. Salva Kiir had reportedly pushed for the chaotic military adventure in Heglig with the support of the Garang fac-tion, still tied to its former comrades of the SPLA-North across the border.[59] This time, the Garang faction took the lead even more on the bold economic move, conceived as economic warfare.[60] This decision illustrated the elite's own anxiety at "lacking" resources it considered it was entitled to. Yet the bold move of closing the oil tap did exactly the opposite of what was expected: it eventually led to a less favorable price-per-barrel.[61] It created more tensions within the SPLM, while Khartoum's air strikes increased in Unity and Western Bahr El Ghazal states, known to harbor rebel groups from Darfur and the Nuba Mountains.[62]

If the SPLM elite acted besieged, in fact the NCP was already "inside" the party. Its intermediaries had joined the SPLM after the CPA and infiltrated Salva Kiir's faction. The SPLM was more unstable than ever and it had more to lose after it secured independence and access to oil revenues. Tensions continued to rise until relations with Khartoum improved in 2013, when Kiir's faction won over Garang's.[63]

JUBA'S RELATIONS WITH THE INTERNATIONAL COMMUNITY

The relationship with the international community also impacted the elite's sense of group worth and sovereignty. Indeed, the international community played a prom-inent role in peace-making and peace-building.[64] The "aid rush" to South Sudan meant that South Sudan became not only an El Dorado for imperialist countries (especially China and the U.S.) but also a profitable haven for shady contractors.[65]

The elite took advantage of these international interests. The government paid lobby firms and individuals within the country and in the U.S. to maintain its image as liberator and continued to invoke the Sudanese terrorist threat in meet-ings with U.S. diplomats.[66] It leased land to international firms to the detriment of local communities.[67] On the surface, this partnership benefited all—diplomatic missions, aid agencies, international firms, and the governing SPLM/A elite—to the detriment of ordinary civilians.

Yet neocolonial attitudes were never lost on the governing elite. As a result, it continued to portray the state as a "baby nation" to attract international sympa-thies and funding instead of opprobrium for its serious shortcoming.[68] In doing so, it played right into condescending stereotypes reminiscent of colonial times that were carved into the collective memory on both sides. This was mostly lost on the international community, who continued to grossly underestimate the southern elite and obliviously offend the South Sudanese. A condescending and ultimately racist attitude was prevalent in the UN, where it was advertised at the highest levels.[69] This negatively impacted group worth. Racist neocolonial stereotypes reminded the South Sudanese elite—and more ordinary citizens—of their perceived inferiority and by extension of the humiliations of slavery and colonialism. This contributed to stir the elite's besieged mentality and feed its fear of losing sovereignty not just to Khartoum but also to aid agencies—especially to the very large UN peacekeeping mission, UNMISS.

Yet the elite—and especially Kiir—were patient. Despite its concern for what it perceived as an encroachment on its sovereignty by the international community, the elite capitalized on its instrumentalization by the U.S. and other powers in the region, and strategically chose not to express its distaste for neocolonial attitudes before the referendum.[70] As soon as South Sudan became independent in July 2011, the elite became much less submissive and conciliatory, which left diplomats and aid workers dumbfounded. This corresponded with a radicalization of the regime under Salva Kiir's faction. These feelings of animosity towards the international community in the south had always been there. But they had been aggravated and repressed, and xenophobia could finally be expressed only now that sovereignty was secured.

Thus, both Khartoum's NCP and SPLM elite competition contributed to stir an increasingly war-mongering and exclusionary brand of nationalism, centered on the predominantly wartime Dinka SPLA. But so did the international community—from its support of the SPLA in the last war and its endorsement of the SPLA's founding narrative to its sponsoring of exclusive DDR programs and its stirring up of deep feelings of humiliation.

State-Building and Predation

The Elite's Capture of the State-Building Exercise

Initially, the UN peacekeeping mission in Sudan (UNMIS) was supposed to safeguard the CPA's implementation, which it was assumed would develop an inherently peaceful democracy.[71] There was a neocolonial element to state-building, and even its proponents admitted that it was akin to "social engineering." One implication of this sociopolitical engineering was to make the state more vulnerable to ethnonationalism.[72] Indeed, the future South Sudanese nation-state would now have to participate in the international system of other nation-states driven by concepts of unity and homogeneity—a system associated with the globalization of genocide.[73]

Over the six-and-a-half-year CPA period, state-building incurred massive spending devoted to new institutions, service delivery, equipment, and trainings.[74]

The U.S. was the largest donor in South Sudan.[75] Between 2005 and 2016, the U.S. would spend US$11 billion in humanitarian, peacekeeping/security sector, and transition and reconstruction assistance.[76] The UK and Norway followed. Together with the U.S., this "Troika" funded half of South Sudan's aid for that period.[77]

Aid was not the only or main source of income for the new state, even if it was essential.[78] Through the CPA, South Sudan finally accessed 50 percent of its own oil.[79] The flipside was that 98 percent of its own revenues now came from oil.[80] Meanwhile, participation in state administration had long been equated with membership in the SPLM, directly funded by the U.S. since at least 2006.[81] "It's a rent-seeking economy," observed a European diplomat. "Everyone wants to be in the government . . . And it's a one-party state: if you control the party, you control the state and then the oil money."[82]

Despite the leadership's attempts to cloth the SPLM in the attire of democracy, there still was no real difference between the army (SPLA) and the political party (SPLM). An Ethiopian general who knew the guerilla group since its early days noted, "The SPLM is not really a political party, and the SPLA is not really an army. They influence and reinforce each other. The SPLM is a political arena in which these military leaders interact."[83] Accordingly, much like the state and the SPLA, the SPLM—the party-state—swelled and became more and more a politically empty shell marked by complacency, lack of internal debate, and competition between factions.[84]

Through access to oil revenues and aid, the state became the prime vehicle of resource accumulation and the instrument of social differentiation leading to social class consolidation.[85] Therefore state-building and social class formation continued to go together as kinship networks expanded.[86] For example, Paul Malong acquired many new wives (from ten to forty) during the CPA period as a notoriously corrupt governor of Northern Bahr El Ghazal state. Polygamous SPLA and militia leaders who had many children and relatives typically placed them at all echelons of the government and the army once the new institutions were created. For instance, the sixty children of one of the founders of the SPLA were placed in the Office of the Vice-President; in the Southern Sudan Centre for Census, Statistics, and Evaluation; in other government institutions; and in the SPLA itself.

Commanders controlled the state and security institutions through kinship networks. The military elite also used the affirmative action criteria of the constitution, which stated that at least 25 percent of the organization must be female, to appoint the wives of commanders and of lower-stratum intermediaries to important army, police, and government positions.[87] Demilitarization followed by reintegration into government jobs was, in the words of a Nuer nurse, "like a pension fund. Although it's only people of the circle who benefit from it."[88]

Corruption thus became the cement of the entire system of political and class domination in South Sudan.[89] As a result, the acronym GOSS (Government of

South Sudan) took on a new meaning in social media: the "Government of Self-Service." The state expanded, mostly in the capital Juba, which retained the most resources, and then in the capitals of the other nine states. It was a centralizing clientelist state with decentralized ethnic patrimonial networks.[90]

Neither forms of spending (on governance or security) resulted in real capacity-building. The state and the army were merely vehicles of wealth accumulation and they remained geared towards predation rather than effective control of South Sudan's large territory. This would not have worked without the international community—spearheaded by the U.S.—who had endorsed the SPLA and was now supporting the whole edifice. Indeed, much like in the last war, the state invested so little in social service delivery that the international community ended up shouldering most of the burden.[91] The international community's complicity became even more blatant when the elite invested in the security sector rather than in governance institutions.[92]

The international community thus practiced the same "functional ignorance" that it had in the last war.[93] It continued to be told—and was willing to believe—that the state needed help "developing." Only three months before independence, donors limply increased pressure for the state to address corruption.[94] But the judicial anticorruption institutions had resembled what Jean-François Bayart calls a "décor of *trompe-l'oeil*" since 2005.[95]

Political tensions were broiling between SPLM factions, and accusations of corruption were thrown to sideline opponents or coerce bystanders into actively supporting Kiir's faction.[96] In possession of a letter accusing seventy-five officials of stealing US$4 billion from the state, President Kiir postured as a reconciliatory figure by granting them amnesty (through anonymity). In fact, the political temperature was rising and this move corresponded with in-group policing.[97]

By 2012, a year before the third civil war, the elite had essentially embezzled a third of the state's revenues and mortgaged over half the state's budget already: over half the state did not belong to South Sudan anymore.[98]

A Temporary Fusion of Elites

The elite was corrupt across the ethnic board.[99] In the last war, processes of dominant and middle class formation had been very similar in the SPLA and in the SSDF. In 2005, therefore, the CPA brought these dominant and middle classes from different ethnic groups to Juba to coexist. A Juba resident remembered how the middle-class/lower strata followed the upper strata consisting of former fighters turned officials: "Cousins or nephews of the ministers will bring their friends in their house . . . They sleep, they eat. It's almost a new middle class."[100]

At first, the different ethnic dominant classes had more in common with each other than with ordinary people. They shared dominant class interests and were temporarily fused in their predatory behavior. Yet such fusion was never complete because they retained their own military and financial bases upstate. They did so through patronage networks, which they maintained through the multiplying territorial administrative units and spoils from cattle raiding.[101] A Nuer member of parliament explained, "After 2005, when the commanders came to Juba, each of them had a house and a commando—especially the big bosses, like Salva Kiir, Wani Igga, Wani Konga, Ismail Kony, and Paulino Matiep. These people retained their own soldiers and supported them to get married, even after 2005. In the villages, in Bor or in Bahr El Ghazal, they have so many cattle."[102]

This meant that after the April 2010 elections, it was easy for some of those former warlords to go back to their "roving bandits" habits when they did not secure political office, and start their own rent-seeking rebellions.[103] Kiir was perceived by the international community as a somewhat boorish and pragmatic figure for his efforts to accommodate the warlords and bring them to Juba, trying to "outbid" Khartoum who often supported them.[104] In fact, he seemed overconfident and indifferent to the long-term implications of this largely unsustainable form of governance. He declared that the history of the SPLM was "full of defections like a dog [who] lives with you at home and when you beat him he will run away, but still will come back and lay down near you because he has nowhere to go and live."[105] In reality, Kiir's big tent policy was not just unsustainable: by 2013, two years after independence, there were still about eighteen militias associated with three rebel groups roving the country.[106]

This also masked a deeper trend: the coexistence of different ethnic constituencies had quickly turned into ethnic ranking favoring Kiir's constituency. Ethnic ranking was back, and ethnicity trumped class again. Still, class and ethnic identities infused one another. As Michael Mann notes, "Ethnonationalism is strongest where it can capture other senses of exploitation."[107] Feelings of humiliation rooted in centuries of racist exploitation (slavery's mode of production) merged with those of group legitimacy and entitlement. In this sense, the Dinka were not so different from Rwanda's Hutu. In-group competition among SPLM/A Dinka factions particularly fueled ethnic ranking.

Making the Ethnocracy

THE IMPACT OF GARANG'S DEATH

The signing of the CPA did not end the rivalry between Garang's and Kiir's factions within the SPLA or between their discourses of Dinka group legitimacy and entitlement. In the six months that Garang spent in Juba following the CPA's signature, his relationship with Kiir did not improve. Garang continued to rely on his close allies in the SPLM, the "Garang boys."[108] His vision was to vie for national power, which presented a real threat to Khartoum. He continued to favor his own constituency: "In 2005, the government gave positions to Bor people," one of his beneficiaries admitted.[109]

Shortly before his death on July 30, 2005, Garang embarked on restructuring the SPLM. He appointed Kiir, then SPLA chief of staff, as his new vice-president to neutralize and demote his rival. Of course, Garang did not anticipate that his death would effectively promote Kiir back to the position of chief of the SPLA and president.[110] Additionally, Garang's restructuring plans left the SPLM without structure by the time of his death. This left room for Kiir to concentrate a lot of power in his new role.[111]

Once Kiir was in position, his appointments to various positions in both the government of South Sudan in Juba and the Government of National Unity (GoNU) in Khartoum reopened his rift with Garang's followers. The separatists gained more footing in the SPLM through Kiir. They prioritized securing southern independence over regime change. They were keen to collaborate with the NCP who courted them.[112] Khartoum's influence thus grew within Kiir's inner circle and relations with Khartoum improved in 2013.[113]

Kiir's faction was mostly made up of Dinka from the Bahr El Ghazal region. It included some former SSDF, known for their separatist ideas and for their anti-Garang sentiments, but the majority was Dinka and from Bahr El Ghazal.[114]

THE RISE OF THE JCE

Members of Kiir's faction had supported him against Garang in Yei in 2004. This clique had been dissatisfied with Kiir's exclusion from the CPA negotiations by Garang after the 2002 Machakos protocol securing self-determination for the south. The faction had little buy-in in the Navaisha round of negotiations that was about making unity with Khartoum attractive. Some of Kiir's followers had been bedfellows in the SPLA's slave-redemption scandal.[115] That included Paul Malong, Kiir's staunch supporter in the last war and warlord of Northern Bahr El Ghazal, and Justin Yac, former head of the corrupt wartime SPLA relief wing (the SRRA), also known for his role in the slave-redemption scandal and for his radical views on Dinka entitlement and supremacy. Others included Alieu Ayeny Alieu, Telar Riing Deng (both from Lakes), Tor Deng Mayuen, and Arthur Akuen Chol.[116]

Some members of Kiir's clique had not even been SPLM/A members. For example, Ambrose Riiny Thiik and Bona Malual had served the Southern Regional Government during the Addis Ababa Agreement period (1972–83), which back then had been accused of "Dinka domination." They had opposed Garang's SPLM/A and had both been exiled to London. Ambrose Riiny Thiik was the chairman of the Jieng Council of Elders (JCE), initially a traditional ethnic council for the Dinka. Other groups such as the Nuer also had their own traditional ethnic council.[117] But the JCE would be implicated, as I explain later, in the recruitment of Dinka militias and government policies during the third civil war.

So was the JCE just an ethnic council? A Kuku intellectual compared the JCE to a "kitchen cabinet," meaning an informal inner circle of advisors: "It's the 'kitchen cabinet' story: Salva Kiir was surrounded by people of his own tribe—from Warrap and close relatives who were his advisors, including illiterate village elders."[118] But the JCE was more than just a "kitchen cabinet" because its membership was broader and would expand over time, in an attempt to get rid of its persistent Bahr El Ghazal brand and foster Dinka "groupness." Besides, Kiir would play catch-up with the JCE in the third civil war.

The phrase "ethnonationalist and Dinka supremacist organization" more accurately describes the rather secretive JCE.[119] The JCE became influential once it was back in South Sudan after the signing of the CPA, and especially after Garang's death, under the leadership of Thiik and Malual. Bona Malual had been involved in the slave-redemption scandal and, more important, in efforts to undermine Garang in the SPLA throughout the 1990s and more recently in Rumbek in 2004.[120]

A Bor Dinka member of the Garang faction explained the roots of the JCE: "The JCE was created in the early 1990s, in London. It was rooted in Bahr El Ghazal, with Bona Malual and Ambrose Riiny who were active in their advocacy on Bahr El Ghazal issues, and to challenge Garang indirectly. When Salva Kiir ascended to power, it took the form of Bahr El Ghazal regional conferences . . . that was one way of promoting ethno-regional sectarianism . . . That's a basis of patrimonial power . . . and this is what they wanted to use to dominate politics."[121]

The JCE had initially been shaped by anti-Garang former Dinka politicians from the diaspora. This demonstrated just how potent ties formed abroad and communication via journals and meetings were in developing an "imagined community" essential to Dinka ethnonationalism.[122] Once back in South Sudan after 2005, the JCE continued to use the political myth of SPLM/A national liberation to its advantage. The general usurpation of collective memory described earlier was facilitated by the return of members of refugee diasporas, including JCE members. The impact of their return was reminiscent of the role played by other refugee associations' returns, such as in 1930s Germany.[123]

Back in South Sudan, the JCE quickly turned into a freeloader off of the state, as an Acholi civilian suggested: "The JCE wants to use the system to amass wealth and resources."[124] It welcomed elite Dinka members from different professional backgrounds—SPLM/A prominent members, politicians known for their anti-SPLM stance, businessmen, and traditional figures such as chiefs and their descendants. As such, it was an organization with ethnopolitical entrepreneurs defending Dinka interests, but not just any Dinka: it had the interests of Kiir's faction most at heart, and this faction's center of gravity was rooted in Warrap state.[125]

In 2005, Kiir appointed Thiik, the JCE chairman from Warrap, as the chief justice. This appointment, combined with state violence, was symbolic of who would have rights in the future country. The JCE influenced the corrupt and weak South Sudan Legislative Assembly, taking advantage of the absence of a definite constitution.[126] The parliament had no oversight over the SPLA, and the JCE was described as "the real parliament behind the scenes."[127]

The JCE went along with this political myth of national liberation despite its dislike for Garang to gain influence. It cultivated the idea of extreme group legitimacy, which translated into an ideology of Dinka supremacy or Dinka "ethnic extremism," and sent its followers abroad as representatives of the government.[128]Through the ambassadors and other members of the diaspora and assisted by foreign consultants, the JCE reached out to the international community and lobbied it: "The JCE preached more outside at first than at home," explained a Kuku (Equatorian) medical student. "Initially the JCE understood how the international community was important to gain independence."[129] Indeed, the JCE kept its eye on the ball: cementing power though independence.

"JUST" DINKA DOMINATION?

It is not quite accurate to label the government's ethnicization as a general "Dinka-ization" of the state, since Kiir did not appoint just any Dinka. He favored his own constituency of northwestern Dinka and sidelined Garang's followers and protégés.[130] He did it as soon as he came into office in 2005, instrumentalizing the swelling of the state to cement ethnopolitical control. This drive of ethnic ranking within the state was felt in the capital of Juba but also outside, for example in the state capital of Wau, as a Balanda civil society member explained: "After 2005, most of the Dinka came and had positions in the government . . . After 2005, the Dinka from only Bahr El Ghazal came."[131] Of course, both competing Dinka factions still survived through capitalizing on the same brand of anti-Khartoum SPLA nationalism. But Kiir's faction was resolutely more exclusionary than Garang's faction because it was more overtly ethnicized, allowing only a few respected members from different ethnic groups in its ranks, to undermine Garang's faction's non-Dinka members by engineering divisions in their constituencies.

In reality, the fact that Kiir's faction included western northern Dinka who had not fought in the SPLA illustrated that ethnic membership trumped SPLA membership. This explained why discourses of group entitlement related to wartime Dinka contributions would be so pervasive among Dinka SPLA troops in the third civil war. These discourses meant to obliterate the fact that this war was especially rooted in the rise of a Dinka dominant class led by individuals who had not fought the war but were Dinka from the same region as Kiir. As a matter of fact, six months after independence and less than a year before his assassination, the Bor Dinka journalist Diing Chan Awuol (alias Isaiah Abraham) called out Kiir's faction and especially Thiik, the JCE chairman, for appropriating the title of "father of the nation" (promoting Kiir instead of Garang), and for "gogrializing" the state—Gogrial being the capital of Warrap, the home state of both Kiir and the JCE chairman.[132]

What Abraham was describing was an ethnocracy: the "rule of one ethnic group over diverse populations." It catered only to the *ethnos*: the Dinka, especially from the Bahr El Ghazal region, especially those close to Kiir's home state of Warrap. And typically, the fusion of the *demos* with the *ethnos* presaged problems for other ethnic groups in the same territory.[133]

COMPETITION BETWEEN THE SPLM FACTIONS

Competition between the Kiir and Garang factions is what especially drove ethnic ranking in the state and the army. Garang's faction emerged stronger from the 2007 crisis, when the SPLM pulled out of the Government of National Unity than did Kiir's faction.[134] This threatened Kiir's faction, who was convinced by rumors that Garang's faction, coalescing around the Shilluk Pagan Amum, then SPLM secretary general, was fomenting Salva Kiir's ousting.[135]

In 2008, the second SPLM convention, held in preparation for the 2010 national elections, did nothing to solve these tensions: it left the party-state more divided and weaker than before.[136] Kiir felt threatened by both the Nuer Riek Machar, then SPLM first deputy chairman, and Amum.[137] A member of the Garang faction expounded: "In 2008, Salva didn't want Riek as his deputy in the SPLM, or Pagan Amum as his secretary general. Salva was left in his place. No elections took place . . . Issues were postponed until 2013."[138] "The status quo was maintained," a Dinka insider explained, "fighting under table was not taken to the public."[139] "The 2011 referendum was the only thing that prevented the crisis of 2008 from spilling over," said a member of Machar's entourage.[140]

While tensions boiled between Kiir's and Garang's faction, the relationship between the Bor Dinka and the Nuer elements of the SPLA gradually improved from 2008 onward. Machar became closer to the Garang faction and, after independence in August 2011, in the home of Garang's widow, Rebecca, in Juba, apologized for the 1991 Bor massacre. This was an important political gesture that contributed to increase Machar's status of dangerous political competitor to Kiir. Still, discourses of group entitlement and group wounds continued to divide

Dinka and Nuer, and the elite's reconciliation efforts were too little too late on both sides, especially given the role played by members of the diaspora, who did not always catch up with developments on the ground.[141]

Yet violence did more to bring these two sides—Garang's and Machar's—into a nascent coalition. Salva Kiir and his clique felt threatened by their reconciliation. In 2012, the assassination of the Bor Dinka journalist Abraham brought the Nuer and Bor Dinka even closer.[142] Various alleged coup attempts—of which one, in 2012, was blamed on Nuer generals—supposedly occurred before the third civil war erupted.[143] At the same time, it is also possible that the government fabricated these coup attempts to justify in-group policing.

ETHNIC RANKING

Competition between the SPLM factions thus drove state violence and ethnic ranking. Ethnic ranking relied on the SPLA "founding narrative" identifying the Dinka as the primary and most legitimate constituency that the state meant to serve, to the detriment of others, who should not rule.[144]

The process of ethnic ranking accelerated after South Sudan's independence, as an ordinary Kakwa (Equatorian) civilian described: "After 2011, and the separation, things changed quickly in South Sudan. Ranks were given in the government especially to the Dinka. The Dinka from abroad came to take the positions of the Equatorians and the Nuer who had fought in the SPLA in the last war, in the ministries, and the embassies."[145] "The fact that the minister of defense, the minister of interior, and all the high ranks in the SPLA police were Dinka was a clear sign of early warning," explained an Acholi (Equatorian) civil society member.[146]

In 2011, Peter Adwok Nyaba wrote that "it is not an exaggeration to say that certain ministries are staffed by persons hailing from the same ethnicity, or at least 80 percent hail from the same county." The president; the minister of presidential affairs; the minister of internal affairs, police and security forces; the minister of SPLA affairs; and the minister of legal and constitutional development (and others) were all Dinka, as were presidential advisors, ministers, undersecretaries, and the heads of the twenty commissions—and the majority were from Bahr El Ghazal, particularly Warrap.[147]

The Garang faction inadvertently made things worse by pushing for the decision to shut down oil production in August 2012.[148] This led to a less favorable price-per-barrel.[149] The oil shutdown affected the state-level first, where budget cuts were announced.[150] In Northern Bahr El Ghazal, Malong, Salva Kiir's longtime supporter and now the governor, stirred up exclusionary nationalism in favor of the Dinka from Bahr El Ghazal.[151] The diminution of resources available for predation and patronage made the state more ethnicized, and violent.

After the oil shutdown, a member of the Garang faction explained how "people were polarized, between the Garang boys, and the tensions between Salva and Riek from the 2008 SPLM Convention would resurface later towards the end of 2012-early 2013. 2013 was the year of the SPLM Convention when Riek started talking about his presidential ambitions."[152]

LEAD-UP TO THE THIRD CIVIL WAR

In March 2013, the SPLM started preparing for its third convention, in advance of the 2015 national elections. The Garang-Machar coalition pushed for the democratization of the SPLM. Machar, Garang's widow Rebecca, and Amum openly said that they would run in the National Liberation Council (NLC) elections for the position of SPLM chairman. Whoever was elected would run in the next national elections. Machar was certainly the most aggressive in his criticism of Kiir. This most likely convinced Kiir that Machar and his Nuer constituency were "unwinnable"—a perception typically key in building a rationale for genocide in the mind of the perpetrators.[153]

In May 2013, Kiir blocked the party's reforms while a committee unsuccessfully tried to mend his relationship with Machar.[154] Right around that time, Kiir gave several speeches outside Juba in his home state of Warrap meant to stir up uncompromising views of Dinka group entitlement and the perception of a threat.[155] In the summer of 2013, members of the Garang faction noticed that Kiir's faction was training troops from his home state. One of them explained that "Kiir felt there was a threat to his seat, if the convention took place, then his seat could be challenged."[156] The state had grown into a violent Dinka state, and yet this ethnocracy felt vulnerable to opponents. It felt a sense of "moral outrage" at competitors it despised.[157]

In July 2013, Kiir fired his rivals, including Machar, Amum, and the entire cabinet. A former minister remembered, "Over twenty ministers were relieved. No one was given an official reason . . . We were just surprised . . . The president was not happy with the desire for democratic reform. He refused the dialogue in the party. Particularly on the constitution of the party."[158] Kiir brought in newcomers who had not been in the SPLM before, fitting the profile of the JCE membership.[159] The sacking further coalesced the Garang-Machar coalition, and Machar did not back down.[160] Repression increased, including on the press.[161]

Subsequently, Kiir toured the Bahr El Ghazal region. In all three state capitals—Wau, Aweil, and Kwajok—he gave bellicose speeches against Machar and the cabinet, broadcast on national television. He waved the threat of his ousting by Machar and his coalition. He attempted to awaken the rather dormant "chosen trauma" of the 1991 Bor massacre, appropriating the Garang faction's group legitimacy. He incited his constituents (especially in Warrap) to resist any political compromise.[162]

Around that time, soldiers' presence and insecurity increased on the streets of Juba, and a few elements indicated planning for at a least military confrontation.[163] Juba residents noted before the explosion of the third civil war in December 2013 that "there was already violence in Juba . . . People would bring over dead bodies to the parliament to protest the killings by the Dinka."[164] Everyday violence in Juba itself was on the rise.

In mid-November 2013, Salva Kiir dissolved the SPLM structures.[165] On December 6, 2013, Machar and members of the Garang faction held a press conference in Juba denouncing Kiir's faction. In this press conference, they summarized the past eight years: they called out the rise of the JCE, the primacy of ethnicity over wartime membership to the SPLM/A, and the NCP's infiltration of the SPLM, the government and the parliament. They denounced Kiir for forming a "personal army, in the guise of presidential guards" on top of his dictatorial and corrupt leadership.[166]

On December 14–15, 2013, the National Liberation Council was set to meet in Juba. On December 14, Salva Kiir's rhetoric against Machar and the rest of the political contestants was particularly bellicose. He made references to Machar's splintering from the SPLA in 1991 and compared the current conflicts to those driving the 1991 SPLA split. He viewed the behavior of his opponents as amounting to "indiscipline"—which in wartime SPLA language could lead to execution. They were a threat to South Sudan's sovereignty.[167] On December 15, intimidated, Machar and the members of the Garang faction did not show.[168] Later at night, around 10:30pm, fighting broke out between the little integrated Nuer and Dinka presidential guards, following an attempt to disarm the Nuer contingent.[169] The third civil war had begun.

Appropriating the Founding Narrative

Looking back, the JCE infiltrated the SPLM/A and the state and pulled the rug out from under the Garang's faction's feet. It completely hijacked the nationalist rhetoric from Garang's faction and its founding narrative.

The JCE could not have become such a very versatile and powerful ethnonationalist and Dinka supremacist organization, branding itself as defending Dinka interests, without the structure of the CPA, which promoted the predominantly Dinka SPLM/A. The international community did not acknowledge the process of ethnic ranking or the fact that postwar nationalism only catered to what it considered the state's legitimate political constituency (the Dinka), which meant that it had genocidal potential.[170]

Kiir's behavior and that of his faction were typical of a leader's attitude when on the verge of losing power, confiscating resources and ignoring the long-term economic consequences of his actions.[171] They controlled the ethnocracy and did not tolerate any dissent. Therefore, there would be no restraint when violence turned genocidal.[172]

A civil war coded and fought along ethnic lines would mask the JCE's appropriation of the founding narrative and of Dinka group legitimacy. In the eyes of the JCE and its allies, it would hopefully stir the unity and "groupness" of the whole Dinka *ethnos*, the country's only legitimate political community.[173]

THE MAKING OF A VIOLENT ETHNOCRACY

2005–13

The 2005 Comprehensive Peace Agreement promoted the SPLA to the position of sole armed ruler of the entire south.[1] But this did not correspond to reality on the ground, which set the SPLA up for either war with its former rival, the South Sudan Defense Forces, or absorption. Upon Garang's death, Kiir decided to favor the absorption of the former foes from the SSDF. The SPLA thus followed the same trend as the SPLM and the state: it grew, thus becoming the site of struggles for its control. Throughout this interwar period, the power struggles between the SPLM factions, which drove the progressive ethnic ranking of the state, were mirrored in the SPLA.

Tensions within the ruling elite had driven ethnic ranking, ultimately forging an ethnocracy. Since ethnic ranking needed to be enforced, the ethnocracy grew more and more brutal and turned into a violent Dinka state. The elite's corruption negatively impacted civilians' security. They experienced rising violence as the dominant class consolidated power through brutal demilitarization campaigns, undemocratic elections, everyday domination, and large-scale cattle raids. Combined with exclusionary nationalism, the shadowy military landscape and widespread violence converged to make the start of the third civil war in December 2013 genocidal.

Contest over the SPLA's composition intensified with the signing of the CPA. The predominantly Nuer SSDF, the SPLA's competitor, was actually comparable in size to the SPLA but, as discussed earlier, was not included in the CPA, referred to instead as one of the "Other Armed Groups" (OAGs).[2] The Juba Declaration,

FIGURE 6.1. The Presidential Guards, commonly referred to as the "Tiger Battalion" and here deployed at a cantonment site outside Juba, chant and raise their weapons at a parade on April 14, 2016. Photo by Jason Patinkin.

signed on January 8, 2006, between the SSDF and the SPLA, finally included the SSDF in the CPA through its integration within the SPLA.[3]

This absorption transformed the SPLA. The SPLA had become more and more Dinka over the twenty-two-year-long civil war, and especially after the 1991 split and the Bor massacre, the brunt of its fighting had been borne by Dinka troops from Bahr El Ghazal. By the time the CPA was signed, the original SPLA fighters who had followed Garang into the bush were very aware of the power struggles between Garang and Kiir. They saw Kiir as a divisive figure, especially after the 2004 Rumbek conference. They interpreted Garang's death and his replacement by Kiir as their cue to decamp, especially now that SPLA "victory" against Khartoum was secured through the CPA. One of them, from Bor, explained, "I left the SPLA when Garang died. I was fighting to push the Arabs . . . A lot of soldiers from the last war in the SPLA were from Jonglei . . . When the SPLA payroll was done after Garang's death, the names of old soldiers since 1980s were not there."[4]

Six months after Garang's death and these initial departures, new men from the SSDF came into the SPLA and competed for ranks in an army that already seemed progressively more biased against Garang's followers and in favor of Kiir's constituency.[5] A former Dinka SPLA battalion commander described the absorption of the SSDF: "In 2006, the SPLA became composed of 70 percent militias, and 70 percent Nuer. 30 percent of the SPLA was Dinka and Equatorian . . . Most of the militias wanted to remain in the SPLA. They numbered about 50,000."[6] This absorption motivated even more of the original, older, more experienced, and more educated Dinka SPLA soldiers to leave. They felt threatened with marginalization following Garang's death and the Juba Declaration. "People from militias were given big ranks (generals and brigadier generals), and some Dinka with a lot of fighting experience, including against these very militias, refused to be commanded by them. Very few people had fought from 1983 to 2005. They were usually in low ranks. And they preferred to leave the army and take civilian jobs," the former Dinka SPLA battalion commander continued.[7] They left the SPLA with mainly younger, less experienced, less educated, less loyal, and less disciplined recruits.[8]

The SPLA's demography was thus radically transformed, and tensions ran high with the newly integrated and mostly Nuer SSDF fighters.[9] A high-ranking Dinka SPLA officer from Lakes (Bahr El Ghazal) illustrated the prevalent feelings in the SPLA about the newly integrated SSDF at the time: they were "99 percent illiterate, without any education: just beasts."[10] Ethnic prejudices were more alive than ever when this integration transfigured the SPLA's ethnic composition. To the Dinka in the SPLA (across various ranks), on one hand, the Nuer armed threat could not be contained: it overwhelmed the SPLA. The SPLA was no longer a largely Dinka army, and SPLA soldiers were wary of potential traitors. On the other hand, the former SSDF were resentful at the SPLA for all the abuses it had committed against the non-Dinka communities they came from.[11] These feelings of animosity, anxiety, and fear, added to the competition between factions in the SPLM, were all typical conditions for genocide.[12]

Garang had appointed the Shilluk Oyay Deng as the first postwar SPLA chief of staff. Deng was one of Garang's close officers. Unsurprisingly, Kiir did not get along well with Deng and clashed with him several times after Garang's death. After four years of trying to replace Deng with a member of his own faction most likely affiliated with the JCE (such as Dominic Diim Deng), Kiir replaced him in 2009 with the much more conciliatory Nuer James Hoth Mai instead.[13] However, neither of these non-Dinka chiefs of staff succeeded in curbing ethnic discrimination favoring the Dinka. Kiir appointed the former SSDF leader, the Nuer Paulino Matiep, as his deputy. Meanwhile, his clique recruited parallel Dinka militias in 2011 to off-balance the Nuer contingent within the SPLA. Thus the appointments of non-Dinka chiefs of staff were precisely meant to hide the fact that the SPLA was being progressively ethnically ranked again, just like in the past.[14]

Class Domination within the SPLA

Indeed, once swollen through the integration of the SSDF, the new SPLA was traversed by two types of social stratifications: class and ethnic rankings. First, the SPLA was deeply socially stratified because of the inequalities between the military aristocracy, its lower strata/middle-class, and more ordinary soldiers. Both former SSDF and SPLA commanders were in dominant class positions through which they continued to concentrate resources. As explained by a former SPLA Dinka commander, division, brigade, and company commanders on both sides made money: "They were the ones with a lot of ghost names. Many commanders pretend to have more soldiers than they have—ghost names—to have salary money."[15]

They used those riches to continue irrigating their networks, thus consolidating their power base. They trickled down just enough of the resources they amassed to their followers who depended on them. They continued to dispense favors and to expand their own lineages, cementing and creating new military kinship ties at a relatively low cost. They kept their soldiers on a short leash, which had a potentially destabilizing effect on the army but served their dominant class interests: "Soldiers have delayed salaries for two months. Commanders use [the delay] to keep soldiers' salaries [which] they use . . . to speculate on the black market, so they use it as capital on the black market and later on pay them," described a Nuer nurse with relatives in the SPLA.[16]

The SPLA dominant class thus used widespread corruption within the army to strengthen its power. Corruption permeated the SPLA in all aspects: from the distribution of salaries (80 percent of the defense budget from 2011 onwards) and the allocation of contracts to the distribution of DDR packages and positions. The lack of payroll greatly facilitated corruption.[17] An Ethiopian insider noted, "Without payroll, there's no idea of how many men are serving in the SPLA. A division can have three thousand people, but the commander will say he has ten thousand men. There's no payroll to verify. There's no accountability and there's resistance in the highest levels of the SPLA to reform."[18]

Such resistance was not surprising, since the "highest levels"—rich SPLA commanders—were in positions that afforded them privileged access to resources.[19] This was worrying because no one knew how big the SPLA really was—a point to which I return later. A former Dinka SPLA commander explained one of the multiple ways the system of corruption worked: "For example, the deputy chief of staff asks the director of procurement and finance for money to pay for a division of ghost names. The director of procurement (responsible for food, ammunition, cars/trucks, tanks/arms, planes/helicopters) will contract a company abroad and the deputy chief of staff will secure a commission, after negotiating with the company to get as much as possible on top of bribery. The money will then be distributed between the director, the deputy chief of staff, and the chief of staff, who will approve the purchase—and since he's the one who appoints key people and is accountable to the assembly, he gets the most money. These people are the same senior people as in the past war. Salva Kiir used to be chief of staff."[20]

Of course, the spoils from armament contracts off budget were especially lucrative, and the defense budget more than doubled from 2006 to 2011—from US$586 million to well over US$1 billion in 2011.[21] The amount of off-budget contracts and the spoils from commissions taken by SPLA officers most likely also doubled. Another avenue the officers used to irrigate their extended kinship networks was the Disarmament, Demobilization and Reintegration (DDR) process. South Sudan's DDR was one of the most expensive packages in the world after that of Afghanistan, and the "reintegration" into government jobs was riddled with corruption.[22] A neighbor to a former female SPLA captain from Central Equatoria recalled how "for five years, she had her name and her salary taken at the SPLA HQ by the Nuer wife of the brother of Salva Kiir, even though seven witnesses had said that this woman was not her . . . There are millions of fake names in the government . . . But the most corruption is in the SPLA."[23]

Since the military elite amassed and concentrated resources, it is no surprise that the SPLA did not downsize as agreed in the CPA—quite the opposite.[24] Donor countries were alarmed at the SPLA's inflation.[25] A former Dinka SPLA battalion commander expounded: "In 2005, the SPLA was downsized: Ten divisions with about 7,500 men each. So the SPLA numbered around 75,000 men. Before December 2013, the SPLA counted 150,000 men . . ."[26] The African Union even estimated the SPLA at 200,000.[27] Nothing could be certain given the widespread corruption around the SPLA payroll.

What seems probable is that before the conflict erupted, the SPLA had over seven hundred generals with their own escorts (about thirty-five people each) who were paid up to US$10,000 a month (without a payroll system and a fixed structure). In contrast, neighboring Ethiopia had about fifty generals, each with an escort of about three.[28] The SPLA officers were reportedly the best paid in Africa.[29] The expanded SPLA afforded the military aristocracy a larger base, which needed tending. And thus the SPLA's focus remained, more than ever, predation—not war-making. This, in itself, was a factor of instability: it magnified the perception of threats by Kiir's entourage, since the system of violent class domination created resentment within and outside the army, and it increased the likelihood that the state would have to resort to outsiders (such as Uganda) to defend itself against competitors.

Cattle Raiding

The military elite also created instability through large-scale and deadly cattle raids in multiple ways.[30] These raids undermined security and more broadly the state. They became part of the "corruption complex."[31] High-ranking members in the government and the SPLA used them to disguise their operations and their trade and reinvested gains from these raids into sustaining their own stocks and their militias—much as they had done during the previous war.[32]

Jonglei state was particularly affected. In 2009 alone, over two thousand people died during cattle raids, and eight hundred thousand cattle were looted there.[33] "People below do the cattle raiding for the bigger people . . . The generals are the ones commanding the raids," a former Nuer county commissioner explained.[34] In Lakes too high-ranking government officials themselves confirmed that "some members in the government and the SPLA are corrupt and organize cattle raids."[35] In some cases, the brother of a general himself directed the raiders as in Jonglei; in others, it was difficult to point fingers given the very large kinship networks at play.[36] Yet UN staff considered raiding to have been "master-minded" in Warrap and Unity states: "Many of the raiders are not civilians. Many of the military personal have participated . . . Cattle raiding is a venture with other people behind [i.e., backing it] at high political level . . . So the warlords continue to plunder the other warlords' base."[37]

Politicians involved in cattle raids used it to compete at the local level or with other ethnic rivals, but the constant was that through their involvement in cattle raids, they all defended and consolidated their dominant class interests to the detriment of other ordinary men.[38] In the words of a Bari (Equatorian) woman, "It's only one part of the population that gets richer and richer . . . A portion of the raided cattle will be given to the big shots. Then the cattle is sold or given to the people in rural areas to keep them (loyal)."[39]

Cattle raiding was thus the extremity of the neopatrimonial system. The elite continued to use it to expand the military kinship networks it built in the past war. A Nuer member of parliament recounted, "So many have their cattle taken care of by their soldiers. Huge camps belong to one person . . . So they give their soldiers cattle [so that they can] marry."[40] The dominant class thus sustained its control over its lower strata, who depended on it to acquire cattle and women.

This type of patrimonial relationship, based on kinship ties, was rooted in the legacy of the SPLA's and SSDF's wartime mode of production. It was extremely favorable to the creation and mobilization of large-scale ethnic militias, especially as tensions escalated within the SPLM/A.[41] Large-scale raids, through elite manipulation, festered interethnic tensions.[42] Various ethnopolitical entrepreneurs existed on different ethnic sides, manipulating ethnicity for their own gains and contributing to reify ethnic groups, just like any ethnopolitical entrepreneur.[43] A Dinka intellectual alluded to the practice of ethnic "miscuing," stating that "it's particularly easy to pretend being another group if language and marks are similar."[44] In Jonglei, a former county commissioner explained, "Generals set up platoons to raid Nuerland, and then they go back through Murle land and accuse the Murle of raiding. But the raiders . . . might come from Lakes, ordered by generals."[45]

As a result, ethnicity increasingly motivated the raiders. From 2009 onward, they started targeting entire villages and killing everyone. This departure from "traditional" raiding, that focused primarily on cattle looting, reflected the growing ethnicization of politics and contributed to future violent behavior.[46] As the predatory state and SPLA became increasingly ranked in favor of the Dinka from Bahr El Ghazal, violence increased and became more and more ethnicized, with increasingly reified ethnic categories. Thus ethnic ranking, ethnicized violence, and the reification of ethnic categories all grew together.

Ethnic Ranking

Ethnic conflicts masked class interests.[47] But class domination did not exclude ethnic domination either, and both forms of social and ethnic stratifications ultimately converged. Indeed, the SSDF integration into the SPLA created more competition for resources. Since economic rivalries within the dominant class still mostly followed ethnic lines and ethnic group competition, social class domination combined with the quick return of ethnic ranking within the SPLA, especially for ordinary soldiers.[48] This process would accelerate after 2009 and independence.

Especially after Kiir got rid of one of the "Garang boys" from the position of chief of staff in 2009, the SPLA dominant class turned increasingly Dinka, and mostly from Bahr El Ghazal. The police, crowded by the generals, was "a photocopy of the SPLA."[49] A former Kakwa SPLA soldier explained how "the boss of the police (the police commander) in Torit (Eastern Equatoria) was a Dinka, and so was the prison commander. In all organized forces, the Dinka dominated."[50] Kiir also retired six deputy chiefs of general staff and twenty-nine major generals by decree in January 2013. "They were from every tribe," recalled a Dinka political activist in Northern Bahr El Ghazal, "and the official reason was to reorganize the SPLA. In fact, this was a coup within a state. Malong and Salva were trying to create an army loyal to the both of them."[51]

On the frontline of ethnic discrimination were the recruits from the former SSDF, who unlike their promoted leaders were not absorbed in other units.[52]

They were predominantly Nuer, but also from smaller groups such as the Murle and Fertit. The Equatorian soldiers (whether former SSDF or SPLA) were considered the most "unthreatening" due to old ethnic stereotypes, discourses of Dinka group legitimacy, and wartime sexual violence that emasculated them. They were rarely in leadership positions.[53] "[A] commander from Dinka is more respected by the Dinka than if he's from Equatoria," explained a Kakwa journalist.[54] As a result, Equatorian recruits needed the least accommodation and continued to be the worst off. A former SPLA first lieutenant, a Lango (Equatorian) from Ikotos, recalled, "By the time of independence, most high ranking officers were Dinka. The Equatorians were voiceless. If you raised your voice, they killed you."[55] Another, a Kakwa (Equatorian) captain, said, "Every three years, there's a promotion, but if you're Equatorian, you won't be promoted."[56] Ethnic ranking accelerated after independence, a Pojulu (Equatorian) soldier noted: "My salary was always smaller than my Dinka colleagues'."[57] Some of the Equatorian soldiers would be sent off to fight the Sudanese troops in Abyei in 2011.[58] The SPLA would continue to rotate Equatorian troops to take them as far away from their home region as possible. Meanwhile, Dinka SPLA soldiers, traders, and government members were settling on their land.

Dinka Militias and NSS

Mathiang Anyoor

The process of ethnic ranking within the SPLA did not go unregistered or unresisted. It created tensions after Garang's death and the SSDF integration. But with the strong contingent of Nuer soldiers from the SSDF, Kiir's faction was still limited in its attempts to win the race in changing the SPLA's demography. In the mind of Kiir's faction, ethnic discrimination was second best after changing the army's ethnic composition.

Redesigning the ethnic makeup of the SPLA was the ultimate goal: only this would secure absolute loyalty. So in order to circumvent the Nuer chief of staff, the Nuer contingent of the SPLA, and outsiders who would all resist recruiting exclusively new Dinka men from the Bahr El Ghazal region, Kiir's faction went outside the SPLA. Kiir, Paul Malong, and Ambrose Riiny Thiik, the chairman of the JCE, teamed up at least as early as 2010–11 to create Dinka militias.[59]

Malong, the governor of Northern Bahr El Ghazal, was in a perfect position to steer mass mobilization for recruitment into a militia.[60] With "real" military power on the ground through his expanded kinship networks, he retained his fiefdom. He had experience raising a local militia to defend the border. He had reportedly started to recruit a local militia in his state in preparation for fighting over the issues of Mile 14 and the Abyei referendum, two of the most contested zones on the ill-defined Sudan-South Sudan border. In 2010, at a meeting in Wau with senior military officials from Bahr El Ghazal, he reportedly started to float the idea of recruiting more troops from the region to form "Mathiang Anyoor."[61] He continued to leverage the military escalation of tensions with Khartoum at the border from 2010 to 2012.[62] This was used as a "smokescreen" to instigate the recruitment and training of troops that would later be integrated into the SPLA.[63] Kiir endorsed the project and gave authority to Malong to recruit men in his state and in Kiir's home state of Warrap.

Malong held speeches reinforcing sentiments of fear, group legitimacy, and group entitlement, with clear references to how much the Dinka from Bahr El Ghazal had suffered in the last war at the hands of the northerners. Meanwhile, Kiir did exactly the same before 2011.[64] While taking an aim at Khartoum, this nationalist discourse signaled that no other group in the south should be allowed to "snatch" the rewards of independence. It was meant to dodge any accountability for corruption, now that resources were starting to dry up. Abject poverty— which, as the governor of Northern Bahr El Ghazal, Malong was largely responsible for—as well as drought made the impoverished communities more susceptible to joining the new militia.

The recruitment of a Dinka militia helped Malong position himself as the first leader from Northern Bahr El Ghazal with national stature. He frequently travelled to Juba from 2012 onwards.[65] "The longest time he spent consecutively in the state was thirty days. Otherwise, he was briefing Salva," remembered a Dinka high-ranking government official from Northern Bahr El Ghazal.[66] At this stage, Malong was more powerful than the Nuer SPLA chief of staff James Hoth Mai, who he circumvented thanks to Kiir.[67]

These troops, mostly from Northern Bahr El Ghazal under Malong's impetus, were also recruited in Warrap. A Dinka civil society member noted, "People contributed food, money, clothes, for the soldiers of Mathiang Anyoor . . . Everything (money, food, clothes) was taken to Northern Bahr El Ghazal . . . They officially were mobilized to fight northern Sudan."[68] Warrap's governor Nyandeng Malek, the only female governor of the country since 2010, organized the distribution of blankets to the troops and the collection of recruits in Western Bahr El Ghazal, Lakes, and Abyei—though these only formed a minority of Mathiang Anyoor troops. No recruits came from the eastern Dinka of Jonglei and Upper Nile, a reflection of Kiir's competition with the Garang faction.[69]

This was truly a Bahr El Ghazal project, and the first batch of these militias, called Mathiang Anyoor ("brown caterpillar" in Dinka), graduated in 2011 from the training center of Pantit in Aweil East, reportedly under the command of the SPLA lieutenant colonel Wol Anyaak, from Lakes.[70] More batches of recruits and more graduations would follow, especially after fighting in Heglig in April 2012.[71] A former Dinka National Security (NSS) officer from Northern Bahr El Ghazal illustrated the scale of Mathiang Anyoor's recruitment: "Almost each village of Aweil had two to ten people recruited."[72]

The JCE was directly implicated in the recruitment of these militias through its chairman Thiik, who helped mobilize recruits in Bahr El Ghazal alongside seventeen other elders. The JCE chairman's involvement and his friendship with controversial figures such as Bona Malual, dating back to the Southern Regional Government in the 1970s-early 1980s, raises the question of how entwined the militia project was with the Dinka intelligentsia. Financing came from the Office of the President, but as demonstrated by Paul Malong and Nyandeng Malek's personal involvement, significant logistical support was organized by state governors.[73]

Unfortunately, official documents on the planning of Mathiang Anyoor most likely do not exist; at any rate, they have not been found.[74] But changing the ethnic makeup of the SPLA served several political purposes. As the former Dinka NSS worker from Aweil admitted, "It's possible that Malong planned the recruitments of Mathiang Anyoor not to fight against the Arabs."[75] Plans for Mathiang Anyoor were conceived after the April 2010 elections. The Dinka militia may have been recruited in anticipation of the 2015 national elections, which could have triggered a civil war.[76] Kiir's faction also foresaw the impending struggle for the SPLM leadership—this time much more public than ever before—and the military contest it would lead to.

By 2012, the roughly ten to fifteen thousand men recruited into Mathiang Anyoor were deployed not to the northern border but rather in major towns throughout the country.[77] Mathiang Anyoor troops were also deployed further south, including in Juba and Yei (Central Equatoria).[78] Planting the Dinka militias in different locations throughout the country as early as 2012 pointed to a strong element of planning. But it did not mean that this planning was meant for a genocide—rather, for crushing the opposition. Symptomatically, Mathiang Anyoor was just one of the military side-projects of Kiir's faction.

Presidential Guards/Tiger/Dut Ku Beny

Indeed, Kiir, Malong, and Thiik also intended to impact the ethnic makeup of the Presidential Guard, commonly referred to as the "Tiger Battalion."[79] Tiger was composed of both Nuer (former SSDF) and Dinka troops, easily split between Machar and Kiir. But Kiir wanted a Presidential Guard loyal to him only. So he organized for the recruitment of more Dinka Presidential Guards in 2011, off the books.[80] This entailed incorporating the local Titweng and Gelueng cattle guard militias from Bahr El Ghazal. These local militias had continued to be tied to Dinka government officials after 2005 through cattle raids. This time, the new Tiger recruits were mostly drawn from both Warrap and Northern Bahr El Ghazal.[81]

Malong continued to be the executant: he reopened the training centers in Majak Tit and Aweil North (Northern Bahr El Ghazal) to continue recruiting from the local youth. He delivered speeches in Aweil meant to draw in more recruits. A Dinka political activist witnessed how in the main town's square, "[Malong] said that people from Aweil had paid a very high price by standing behind Garang . . . Lots of youth had lost their lives. He said that now they stood behind Salva Kiir. He said it was time for people from Northern Bahr El Ghazal to think that they could also have a leader. This was intended for people to perceive him as a leader to stand by."[82]

Although Mathiang Anyoor (predominantly from Northern Bahr El Ghazal) and the new elements to be integrated into Tiger (predominantly from Warrap) were two separate entities, Malong organized for the transfer of some of Mathiang Anyoor's recruits into the newly remodeled Tiger and sent them to Juba in early 2013.[83] More men were reportedly recruited from Warrap and Northern Bahr El Ghazal in May 2013.[84] The new recruits graduated from Kiir's personal cattle camp in Luri, about 16 km (about 10 miles) from Juba.[85] This explains why some Mathiang Anyoor recruits also ended up in Kiir's Luri cattle camp and became part of what would be known as *Dut Ku Beny*—meaning "defend the boss" (Kiir) in Dinka, to be integrated into Tiger.[86] Thiik especially took the lead on the Dut Ku Beny project, funded through the Office of the President.[87] Malong flew some Mathiang Anyoor recruits from Aweil to Juba, right around the time that conflicts in the SPLM were escalating.[88] Dut Ku Beny thus incorporated members of the Titweng/Gelueng militias and of Mathiang Anyoor.[89]

Civilians noticed an increase of soldiers' presence on the streets of Juba in August/September 2013. Mathiang Anyoor and the new Tiger recruits were also seen scouting Juba, masquerading as town cleaners to identify Nuer houses in November 2013. On the second week of December 2013, the SPLA started disarming Nuer elements in the SPLA, in preparation for the SPLM National Liberation Council meeting, and "security personnel were prepared and armed."[90] Ugandan troops were positioned at the border in early December 2013.[91]

The Nuer and Dinka contingents of Tiger would fire the first bullets in Juba on December 15, 2013.[92] "In the night of December 15, there was an instruction by Salva Kiir to disarm the Nuer elements of the Presidential Guards. So when the Nuer soldiers resisted, shooting started," explained a former detainee. "'Why do you disarm us? We are the same people,' they said."[93] Following the splintering of Tiger/Presidential Guards, Dut Ku Beny—including members of Mathiang Anyoor—would come in as a reinforcement to the government's side on December 16.[94] They would participate in the Juba massacre.

NSS and Military Intelligence

In addition to recruiting Mathiang Anyoor and new elements to be integrated into his Presidential Guards/Tiger, Kiir also wanted to cement his military advantage through the security services, especially as independence was approaching.

Before independence, the south shared the National Intelligence and Security Services (the NISS) with the north. In 2011, Kiir focused on shaping a powerful National Security Service (NSS) with the support of Israel, the UK, and the US.[95] One of Kiir's closest collaborators, Akol Kuur, worked directly with him to secure lightweight Israeli assault rifles that would later be used in the Juba December 2013 massacre.[96]

As the NSS quickly grew more powerful and was directly funded by the Office of the President, it became a reservoir for the few educated, literate, and loyal Dinka recruits from Bahr El Ghazal. Akol Kuur, from Warrap, was appointed as head of the NSS in 2012. Since recruits were well paid and equipped, SPLA generals quickly crowded the NSS with their relatives.[97] Meanwhile, the South Sudan National Police Service (SSNP) worked as a dumping ground for less-connected soldiers transferring from the SPLA.[98]

Kiir's faction used the NSS for in-group policing. For example, the NSS was rumored to be behind the 2012 assassination of the Bor Dinka journalist and long-time SPLM/A member Diing Chan Awuol (also called Isaiah Abraham), who had criticized Kiir.[99] The faction also resorted to the increasingly powerful Criminal Investigation Department (CID) and Military Intelligence (MI) to arrest dissenters, for example in the town of Wau (Western Bahr El Ghazal) from December 2012 onwards, following popular protests. The police also played an instrumental role in shooting the protesters.[100]

All in all, the various security organizations—NSS, police, MI, CID—were used to increase state repression. They served the interests of the violent ethnocrats who wanted to cultivate their Dinka base while policing (Dinka) dissenters within it. These security forces were consistently involved in grave human rights abuses rather than law enforcement. If anything, they were skilled at stirring chaos and at pinning it on other ethnic groups so they could start repression campaigns—as was most likely the case in Wau in 2012.[101]

Widespread and Rising Violence in Peacetime

Violent Demilitarization

Throughout the CPA period, the increasingly Dinka state demonstrated its violence. It engaged in extremely brutal demilitarization campaigns in 2007, 2008,

2009, and 2012 in the Upper Nile region to subdue non-Dinka communities who sided with Khartoum back in the war. The SPLA practiced ethnic targeting from the start. It tortured and mistreated Murle civilians in Jonglei.[102] In Upper Nile, violence reached levels that the Shilluk intellectual Peter Adwok Nyaba compared to "ethnic cleansing" against the Shilluk in 2009. Kiir carried on with CPA celebrations, endorsing both the violence and the annexation of Shilluk land by Dinka officials in a form of "pay-back" to one of his main political rivals, the Shilluk Pagan Amum.[103]

There was no restraint on state violence. The UN peacekeeping mission UNMIS was complacent with these disarmament campaigns until 2012, when it finally recognized that human rights abuses marred them.[104] It was ineffective at protecting civilians already then, when death rates in Jonglei reached wartime levels. The rate of people murdered between 2011 and 2013 in two counties there (Akobo and Pibor) was seven times the rate in the most homicidal city in the world (San Pedro Sula, Honduras).[105]

Cementing the Conquest

The rise of ethnicized violence diverted attention from a slower trend also mired in violent ethnic politics: land grabs. Both the Dinka and non-Dinka elite (including Kiir and Machar) leased land for decades without proper consultation with and consent from the communities, through local co-opted politicians.[106] From 2007 to 2010, foreign companies, governments, and individuals gradually acquired an area of land that was larger than Rwanda.[107]

On the ground, civilians felt the advance of more ordinary Dinka, often SPLA soldiers. In Equatoria, they settled on family properties and cemented their wartime protoconquest. A Latuka (Equatorian) lawyer recalled, "After the CPA in 2005, many people from Nimule who had been displaced by the war came back to their land and found their land occupied by these people from Bor . . . People settling on the land are sometimes armed and they're from the majority [the Dinka]. They're asked to compensate the owners but they don't pay."[108]

This type of settlement thus amounted to a widespread land grab rooted in the SPLA's protoconquest of Equatoria. But it was also driven by the large cattle raids the military elite was involved with.[109] The same cattle guards evoked earlier grazed the cattle essential to the elite's military power.[110] The ecological push to more southern territories needs further exploration, but since the 1970s, rainfall has decreased while temperatures and incidents of floods and droughts have increased in South Sudan.[111] The reduction of rainfall has affected particularly (but not only) the northern and western parts of Bahr El Ghazal (Northern Bahr El Ghazal and Warrap). Becoming drier and hotter, it became more susceptible to drought and food insecurity.[112] A Mundari (Equatorian) government worker affected by cattle raiding commented, "The land of the Dinka and Nuer are in real jeopardy now so they move to Magwi, Lobonok and Nimule . . . Because of generations of herding and grazing, vegetation in Upper Nile and Unity is diminished. That's why the Dinka resist driving the cattle out of Equatoria."[113]

The type of predatory mode of (re)production described earlier in the last civil war continued during the interwar period, thus expanding the conquest and as such reminiscent of the expanding slaving frontier of the past, a racist system of exploitation that laid the foundations for the SPLA's wartime mode of production. The ties between large cattle herds originating from cattle raids and territorial conquest are particularly important. Indeed, conflict between the elite's cattle herders and the local landowners would contribute to the expansion of the genocidal campaign to Equatoria in the third civil war.

The Dinka newcomers justified their settlement to the original inhabitants of the land by referencing their group legitimacy, worth, and entitlement. In Central Equatoria, a Kakwa medical student for instance described how "often in Juba, when there are issues over land when the Dinka claim Bari land, they claim 'we fought for this country,' and still they maneuver to take it over."[114] In Eastern Equatoria, a similar process occurred, with Bor Dinka settling particularly in Nimule and Ikotos. As an Acholi (Equatorian) trader from Magwi explained, "When you wanted to go back to your place in 2007, some places were taken up by Dinka—especially Nimule—Madi land. The Dinka said 'we fought for this place. So if you want it, you also have to fight for it.'"[115]

The Dinka settlers' discourse was the prelude to the denationalizing discourse of the third civil war's génocidaires. They often made references to the "blood" they had shed in the war, to convey their superior group legitimacy and their natural ownership over the territory.[116] It was meant to delegitimize the Equatorian communities much less associated with the SPLA. This proclaimed Dinka group entitlement to land emanated directly from the discourse of Dinka group legitimacy validated through the CPA. This discourse was not a form of indigenous autochthony—a primordial discourse that would have consisted in claiming an ancestral "homeland."[117] It illustrated the potency of postwar nationalism based on the SPLA founding narrative, which in turn rested on a wartime protoconquest that had most likely changed the imagined shape and boundaries of Dinka country.

The fact that some of these Dinka settlers were new confirmed the potency of the postwar discourse of group legitimacy and ownership.[118] The ability of the Dinka settlers to stay on Equatorian land demonstrated how ethnic ranking at every echelon of the local administration facilitated this land grab to consolidate conquest.[119] It was typical of an ethnocracy where the dominant *ethnos* has superior rights in comparison to the other ethnic groups and therefore can easily practice a form of settler colonialism.[120]

In other non-Dinka areas of the country, new Dinka settlers practiced the same discourse of group legitimacy and entitlement, benefiting from ethnic ranking in corrupt state institutions to make their settlement permanent.[121] For example, Balanda civilians reported a similar trend in the town of Wau, which was not traditionally Dinka either. What happened in those "peaceful" years was key: it transformed the way the Dinka viewed those territories. The Dinka did not have demographic superiority in the Equatoria region, but they were in virtually every state and county—and especially in visible locations, including border points. Whether "planned" or not, this consolidation (and in some cases expansion) of the Dinka conquest surreptitiously changed the imagined confines of Dinka land.[122]

Cementing the conquest went hand in hand with winning the demographic race. As noted earlier, the Dinka were typical of other groups considered "backward" who feared extinction but had a real demographic superiority.[123] Marriages served to catch up with the perceived demographic lag by the Dinka from Bahr El Ghazal, particularly affected by war casualties. A former Dinka Agar SPLA lieutenant colonel explained the role of ghost marriages: "My uncle died before he could produce an heir, so I married his second wife in his name in 2004. . . there was no wealth during the war, so you postpone it after the war. Many people did that, and I believe that's why there's a baby boom now among the Dinka, and that's why we're the majority. Now the Dinka marry for the lost men. My comrade from the SPLA has also married his second wife for this reason."[124] If, as this Dinka former SPLA soldier claimed, the Nuer typically "did the same," a look at the 2008 census still gave the demographic edge to the Dinka.[125]

The Dinka were winning the demographic race. This was the result of both traditional practices and the elite's predation and concentration of wealth, combined with the progressive ethnic ranking of the state and the army.[126] Of course, this territorial-demographic advance was not unprotested and could only be sustained by increasing state violence.

Political Repression

Indeed, as the state became increasingly ranked, it also turned more and more repressive and violent.[127] An important stage of state violence was the April 2010 elections, marked by extreme violence and lack of real multiparty competition.[128] For example, people in Pibor county, in the state of Jonglei, were thrown into holes with burning rubbish at their feet while women were threatened to be "raped with guns" if they did not vote for SPLM candidates.[129] In Northern

Bahr El Ghazal, a UN worker recalled how "one of the candidates against Malong was kidnapped by the SPLA and chained to a tree for fifteen days . . . All the other independent candidates were harassed. Opponents were prevented from voting."[130] When voting did occur, "the election ballots were taken by the SPLA at gun point."[131]

Still, the international community endorsed these "democratic" elections, which signaled to Kiir's faction that such violence was acceptable and marked a deterioration for the South Sudanese.[132] Quickly after, the parties mobilized for the referendum of independence. Kiir declared in September 2010 that unity with the north was no longer "attractive" because of the stalling on the part of Khartoum's National Congress Party in CPA implementation and adhering to sharia. In fact, Kiir was a known separatist from the start, and sharia had little impact in the south.[133]

On January 9, 2011, the referendum vote took place. It was anticlimactic, with 98.3 percent voting in favor of independence. International monitors considered the process "generally credible." Yet the proseparation campaign had left absolutely no space for a debate on what secession would imply in the south. The process was still marked by violence. The SPLA harassed communities it perceived as prounity and dragged prisoners and hospital patients out of prisons and hospitals to vote at the polling stations.[134]

Right after independence in 2011 and until mid-2013 when Kiir fired the entire cabinet, civil society organizations tried to steer the country back on a democratic path. But as an electoral non-SPLM candidate recounted, "After the referendum, the SPLM excluded others. If you're a good friend to the SPLM, then you're a minister. It's only been a facade of democratization . . . Political parties have been saying to the SPLM 'you need to recognize others.'"[135] But civil society organizations were brutally overpowered by the state.[136]

While frustration mounted, the state grew more violent, and the police brutally crushed popular demonstrations—for example (but not only) in Wau in December 2012.[137] Kiir's speech in Wau denied any ethnic dimension to the Wau riots and government involvement and endorsed government repression.[138] The rise of both small- and large-scale political and ethnic violence—in the case not only of protests but also of large-scale cattle raids—signaled to the state that some groups could not be subdued. This most likely influenced Kiir's faction into thinking that these populations were unwinnable and uncontrollable.

The state increasingly relied on in-group policing since frustrated citizens included the Dinka themselves from all regions, who pointed fingers at the Dinka elite from Bahr El Ghazal. The elite was suspected of carrying out assassinations of political activists. It regularly intimidated, imprisoned, and tortured journalists—including prominent Dinka journalists like Nhial Bol, who was also from Warrap—especially when they investigated the corrupt dealings of Kiir's faction in Warrap.[139] It tortured activists and political figures who dared question its corrupt rule, including in Warrap and Northern Bahr El Ghazal states, where the state governors were both regularly imprisoning parliament members while recruiting for Mathiang Anyoor.[140]

In-group policing of Dinka dissenters was key to Kiir's faction. Without it, it could not take over, control, and foster the "groupness" of its Dinka constituency, which it intended to use to further its supremacist political goals.[141] In-group policing thus turned particularly violent during those years, right when Kiir's faction was recruiting Dinka militias meant to both promote groupness and accomplish a takeover of the SPLA—and, ultimately, complete control over the state. Dissenting Dinka voices merely disrupted the narrative that the state was under attack by other ethnic competitors, especially when these dissenting voices originated from Bahr El Ghazal.

Xenophobia

State violence was not invisible to the international community. But as South Sudan was viewed as being in a perpetual state of emergency, pervasive violence was regarded as somewhat acceptable and normal, even if on the rise.[142] The idea inherited from colonial times that the South Sudanese—and especially the "backward" Dinka—were essentially violent blinded aid workers and diplomats to the increasingly exclusionary ideology and behavior of Kiir's faction. Yet as soon as the country became independent, the state expelled two UN officials in the span of six months, and threatened foreign correspondents.[143] It did not ratify any international or regional human rights treaty either.[144]

Xenophobia did not just affect aid workers, journalists, and diplomats. Foreign workers from neighboring countries had come to flock the aid and service industries of South Sudan. They were also working as construction workers and traders. They were from the start the targets of disgruntled South Sudanese who latched onto the idea that they "deserved" the work that these foreigners stole—even if they had neither the desire nor the skills to fill those positions.[145] These foreigners were particularly susceptible to being the targets of violence in Dinka areas (for example in the Lakes and Bahr El Ghazal regions) or by Dinka security officers in the capital of Juba.

This xenophobic resentment was an expression of Dinka group entitlement. As such, xenophobia did not impact areas where fewer Dinka and mostly Equatorian, Nuer, or other non-Dinka groups lived nearly as much. Indeed, these groups had strong kinship ties with communities across the borders who had welcomed them in the last war as refugees. Besides, none of those groups had discourses of group entitlement and ownership as strong as the Dinka did because their legitimacy had not been endorsed by the international community through the CPA. If anything, they were also the victims of the Dinka's sense of entitlement over the state and territory. In the third civil war, the Dinka perpetrators would make explicit references to these neighboring countries to denationalize and uproot non-Dinka ethnic groups.

The Warning Signs

By the time of the political crisis in late 2013 that would precipitate the third civil war, the SPLM was already an authoritarian party-state, similarly to other pregenocidal societies.[146] The events leading up to the December 15 crisis and the subsequent genocidal violence were evocative of those leading up to the Rwandan genocide. There, the International Criminal Tribunal for Rwanda later concluded that "preparations are completely consistent with a plan to commit genocide. However, they are also consistent with preparations for a political or military power struggle."[147] The SPLM political crisis had converged with the rise of an exclusionary Dinka nationalism.[148]

Genocide was possible because South Sudan had grown into a violent Dinka state dominated by Kiir's faction and infiltrated by the JCE's hardliners. Kiir's faction practiced an exclusionary ideology of Dinka group legitimacy and entitlement, based on the "founding narrative" at the root of the SPLM/A's warmongering nationalism. Salva Kiir's faction had transformed the state into an ethnocracy, the "rule of one ethnic group over diverse populations." Its hardliners had sidelined, imprisoned, or murdered Dinka moderates. Ethnic ranking permeated society through ethnic prejudices, xenophobia, and attempts to denationalize non-Dinka groups. The regime was "democratic only within the *ethnos*, like settler regimes."[149]

Ethnic violence, especially that inflicted directly or indirectly by the state, was escalating and went unchecked. Mounting political and economic stress affected the country and combined with military confrontation with Sudan throughout those years. Kiir's faction was typical in exhibiting "severe anxiety about threats emanating from other groups."[150] Even if it dominated both the state and the security organs, it perceived the Machar-Garang coalition as threatening. This may have been a projection, given the massacre in Juba that ensued in December 2013.[151] But due to the 1991 SPLA split and Machar's attempts to throw shade at Kiir since 2005, Kiir's faction saw the Nuer as especially unwinnable and dangerous.[152] It viewed the Nuer presence in the SPLA and other security organs as uncontainable, hence the need to recruit parallel Dinka militias.

Despite the swelling of the war-making machine, South Sudan did not have the capacity to even assert control over its own territory—much less defend itself—due to the corruption and fragmentation of the SPLA.[153] South Sudan was the typical example of a military state that had focused so much on predation instead of war-making that its army was capable of doing little else.[154] Therefore it is little surprise that Kiir called on Ugandan troops to take position at the border in early December 2013 when he felt threatened by his opposition in the SPLM.[155] After December 15, Kiir would rely on a multitude of external allies to remain in power.[156] Without them, and without the international community's apathy, Kiir's faction would not have been able to remain in power and use the state to wage genocidal violence against the Nuer.

CIVIL WAR AND THE FIRST GENOCIDAL PHASE

December 2013

On the night of December 15, the SPLA split into two. Accused by Salva Kiir of a coup attempt, Riek Machar ran for his life and headed for Bor.[1] Meanwhile, Juba woke up on December 16 to the country's largest systematic mass killing. The Juba massacre had started, and there was no stopping the third civil war. SPLA divisions split the country, soldiers turned on one another, Nuer commanders defected to join Machar, and soon the SPLA lost at least half of its troops.[2] Kiir also ordered the arrest of the eleven politicians from the Machar-Garang coalition who had participated in the December 6 press conference with Machar.[3] These events revealed to the international community what this regime had become over the past eight years: a very violent ethnocracy.

Machar had positioned himself as an opposition leader, especially after independence, and he had repeatedly angered and offended Kiir. He may have belonged to the category of politicians in opposition who could benefit from genocidal violence. Yet he may have been taken aback by the actions of former SSDF commanders like Peter Gadet, who splintered from the SPLA to join Machar's group on December 18, 2013.[4] Besides, Machar only had a few options. Not standing up for the Nuer being massacred in Juba and other locations would cause him to lose face and would mean his political death. It was not so much that he had something to gain from a rebellion; it was more that he thought he had nothing to lose and that he had little choice. The problem was that there was no chance to "win" this war: Kiir outsourced war-making to Ugandan troops already positioned at the border and to other armies and mercenary groups. This gave the SPLA the military advantage from the very beginning.

FIGURE 7.1. Remains of a house destroyed during the Juba massacre of December 2013. Photo taken by Adriane Ohanesian in the neighborhood of Munuki West on January 19, 2014.

In hindsight, this new rebellion was a political mistake for Machar. This was probably why Kiir manufactured the third civil war in the first place: military victory for Machar was impossible, and the new rebellion supported Kiir's narrative of an attempt to overthrow his regime and ultimately realized his self-fulfilling prophecy. If anything, members of the rebellion inadvertently served Kiir's goals much more than those of the Nuer. The fact that the Nuer themselves had violently retaliated after being massacred in Juba made the violence against them by the SPLA look "ethnic" but not genocidal. In other words, the civil war narrative did not leave any room for the genocide one. The question of genocide was dismissed in one paragraph by the African Union's investigative team. This chapter shows that some of the violence was genocidal. In fact, a key feature of the genocide in South Sudan was that it occurred in several phases precisely because it was not binary: the Dinka hardliners targeted first the Nuer, then the Equatorians, and then the Shilluk, in addition to other minorities already victimized by the SPLA in the past eight years. The fact it was carried out in phases was the only way that the Dinka majority group, which was still a minority against all the others aggregated, could take over. Yet it was, as in most genocides, the result of a political and military escalation rather than an earlier elite master plan.

Fostering Dinka Groupness

In-Group Policing and the "Attempted Coup" Narrative

The Juba massacre was the first phase of the genocide. It set the tone—deadly—and it was the first attack on the Nuer as a people in what became the third civil war. It started fully on the morning of December 16, as the fighting that broke out on December 15 carried over to the morning.

During the massacre, two key events fostered Dinka groupness and were as such instrumental in enabling and accelerating the killing: first, in-group policing, and second, the activation of the dormant "chosen trauma" of the 1991 Bor massacre. I first explore those before turning to the massacre itself, because they contributed to increase the massacre's magnitude.

In-group policing by the state, dominated by Kiir's faction, was key in silencing dissenting Dinka voices who could have acted to restrain the massacre. On December 16, Kiir appeared on television and announced that he had successfully quashed a coup attempt led by Machar and his accomplices. The "attempted coup" narrative was used to justify in-group policing. On the same day, the Ministry of the Interior, headed by a Kiir loyalist much like every other security institution, started arresting eleven members of the Garang faction (including Pagan Amum) under the suspicion of "coup plotting."[5] One of the "political detainees" remembered, "Around 10am that day, *one of the other future detainees* [name withheld for the protection of the former detainee] called me. He told me the Minister of Interior was in his house to ask to accompany him to the police headquarters. I was warned by my cousin in this *state agency* [name of institution withheld for the protection of the respondent and his family] that I needed to pack. I was considered a 'Garang boy.' There was a list and I was on it. Machar stayed in Juba for two days hiding until he discovered everyone was arrested."[6]

In fact, there was no coup attempt by the Machar-Garang coalition.[7] Kiir's faction had military superiority, and the Garang-Machar coalition was acutely aware of it. As a matter of fact, it had even rung the alarm bells about the presence of Dinka militias in Juba. Machar knew that if he were caught in a coup attempt, he could be killed, and he did run for his life. Twenty-seven of his relatives were killed.[8] As for his so-called accomplices (the political detainees), only strong international pressure would get them freed.

The attempted coup narrative served to cover up a military process underway for years, which had escalated in recent months and meant to violently crush any opposition. Not only did Kiir's attempted coup narrative not stand up to facts, it came after the Juba massacre had already started at dawn on December 16.

Activating the Dormant Chosen Trauma
of the Bor Massacre

Kiir articulated his attempted coup narrative in a speech on the afternoon of December 16. The fact that Kiir delivered the speech around 1pm while killings had already started early in the morning and the SPLA Nuer splinters had already been pushed out of Juba suggest that his speech was meant to legitimize the violence, galvanize perpetrators, and enroll prospective ones to accelerate the killing.[9] Effectively, this speech played a key role in legitimizing, expanding, and accelerating the Juba massacre. Kiir's speech reignited shootings in the barracks on December 16, incited violence, and motivated supporters.[10]

Kiir's appearance on national TV in military attire was meant to convey a sense of existential threat. Kiir reactivated the "chosen trauma" of the Bor massacre, largely dormant throughout the interwar years, especially after Machar's apology to the Bor Dinka community in August 2011 and his rapprochement with Garang's followers. After accusing Machar and his accomplices of an attempted coup, Kiir declared, "Let me reiterate my statement during the opening of the NLC [National Liberation Council] meeting two days ago, in which I said that my government is not, and will not allow the incidents of 1991 to repeat themselves again. This prophet of doom continues to persistently pursue his actions of the past and I have to tell you that I will not allow or tolerate such incidences once again in our nation."[11] Kiir was surrounded by his allies, including Kuol Manyang, the minister of defense and one of Garang's kinsmen, from Bor. Manyang was always known for his strong dislike of Machar, whom he never forgave for the 1991 Bor massacre. His presence served Kiir's narrative.

Coining Machar as an enemy of the Dinka served to foster Dinka groupness and mask the fact that the Bor Dinka from Garang's factions had in fact been the victims of in-group policing and ethnic ranking favoring Kiir's constituency for the past eight years. The fact that Kiir, a western Dinka from Bahr El Ghazal (Warrap), positioned himself as the defender and leader of the Dinka "group" under Nuer attack was a clear indication that the center of gravity of Dinka identity had shifted west. This was the sign of an attempted takeover of Dinka identity.

With his references to 1991, Kiir successfully merged the threat to Dinka identity and the threat to national sovereignty. In Kiir's account, Machar never changed: he was still the same treacherous man who had doomed the prospects of an SPLA victory over Khartoum and independence ten years before the CPA negotiations. The subtext was that without him, the SPLA would have secured independence for South Sudan earlier. First, this implied that the Nuer would never change, that they could never be trusted. The Dinka had to strike first. Second, references to 1991 and the use of the word "doom" implied that the nation was under attack. Since Machar had received support from Khartoum after 1991, it was not just South Sudan's stability but its very sovereign existence that was under threat of destruction.

Kiir's speech accomplished several things by tapping into the collective memory of 1991-related trauma and the feelings of humiliation from past centuries of servitude. It made Dinka supporters more likely to support a violent reaction to what Kiir depicted as an assault on their life, freedom, and sovereignty. References to the 1991 Bor massacre and its reactivation worked so well on the ground that it reached Dinka groups that were not from Bor—such as in Malakal.[12]

On the ground, another rhetorical strand meant to slow down the Nuer response. The government attempted to control the narrative in order to manage the timing of the violence. Controlling the timing would be key throughout the war. Kiir and his allies in all the security organs denied that the conflict was ethnic. Even if they defended a very predatory ethnocracy, they still painted their adversaries as petty politicians motivated by greed. This was the message they sent to the international community, which was shocked and overwhelmed by the speed of South Sudan's unravelling. It was also the message they sent on the ground. In Malakal and Bentiu, state and army officials framed the conflict as a political competition between the elite to contain opposition and above all gain time: this was not an ethnic conflict, they said.[13] Of course, this political conflict was ethnic, and denials were meant to contain what was the largest systematic massacre in South Sudan's recorded history. Thus the government's framing of the violence served its perpetration.

The Juba Massacre

Chronology

Killings started on the evening of December 15, 2013 (before Kiir's speech), when the Nuer and Dinka contingents of Tiger Battalion split following an attempt to disarm the Nuer.[14] Fighting spread at night from the SPLA barracks in Giyada (the general headquarters) to the SPLA ammunition store in New Site (near the Bilpam barracks) when both sides tried to secure control over weapons.[15]

A Nuer government official living in the Jebel Kujur area at the time remembered, "Many Nuer live behind the Jebel market . . . I was close to the SPLA's general HQ in Jebel, at the old Joint Integrated Units compound, where the Tiger Battalion was. On December 15 at 8pm, the fighting started. From 9 to 10pm, it intensified with big tanks. Fighting went on to 1am and then stopped. It then resumed at 4 or 5 am at Bilpam on December 16, then from 5 or 6 am until 11am at Jebel. Then again at 3pm, they started again. This was on December 16."[16]

Fighting especially accelerated in the early morning of December 16 because the Dinka militia of Dut Ku Beny, recruited by Kiir and Malong and including members of Mathiang Anyoor, had come in as a reinforcement on the government's side.[17] Some say that the Dut Ku Beny, also nicknamed the "Luri boys," numbered about one thousand.[18] But other estimates circulated: "Three thousand Dinka militia recruits from Aweil were in Luri camp. Salva Kiir brought these people in December 2013 to Juba. They were killing people, looking for Nuer house to house," a Nuer member of Parliament in Juba at the time explained.[19] This is indeed when fighting spread to residential areas.

On December 16, killings started at dawn and civilians started fleeing to the UN base. A Nuer government official recalled, "The massacres started on December 16 in the morning, first in New Site on Bilpam road and then in Gudele, and then thirdly, in Mia Saba."[20] That same day, government security organs gave dormant Dinka recruits planted in the earlier months in Juba both guns and uniforms. These recruits joined in the fighting and massacre.[21] After recapturing the headquarters by midmorning, government troops turned to the rest of the town.[22] By 1pm, they had routed out the Nuer soldiers south of Juba.[23] Left with Nuer civilians to target, the massacre most likely accelerated in the afternoon of the 16th: "Then it extended to Lologo area, behind the SPLA barracks in Jebel in the afternoon, and to Kor William," recounted the same survivor. "Then the people ran to the UN house. In Gudele and New Site and Mia Saba, people ran to the UN Tongping site."[24]

For the next week, different groups of perpetrators took part in the massacre: Tiger was reinforced by Dut Ku Beny, the National Security Services (NSS), Mathiang Anyoor, the SPLA, the military police, wildlife services, and commandoes, as well as some armed civilians.[25] They all killed, raped, and tortured Nuer civilians in the neighborhoods of Munuki 107, Khor William, New Site, Gudele One, Mangaten, Mia Saba, Customs, and Nyakuran.[26] Four SPLA Dinka generals from the Bahr El Ghazal region coordinated the killings in their own respective operation sectors.[27] Considering ethnic ranking favoring the Dinka Bahr El Ghazal constituency, the recruitment of parallel Dinka militias in that region in 2010–11, and their involvement in the massacre, the majority of the perpetrators and their commanders were most likely Dinka hailing predominantly from Bahr El Ghazal.

Equatorian inhabitants in Juba witnessed "seven days of killings, from house to house," an Acholi man and his wife in one of these neighborhoods said. "After four days, we saw six soldiers through the fence. A Nuer man just opened his door and was shot in the head."[28] The killings also extended to the Konyo Konyo area, New Site, Bilpam, Gudele around Buwaba and Lou areas, Gudele police station, Jebel, the military headquarters of 116, and Lologo.[29] "I was indoor for two days," recalled a Nuer survivor. "I came out on December 18. The massacres lasted from

December 16 to December 22, with the deadliest days from the 16 to the 20. On December 21 and 22, people started coming out, and the SPLA was not doing it so openly."[30]

Killings were sometimes performative: some were done outside to show what happened to anyone contesting Kiir's rule.[31] They also meant to signify extreme ethnic ranking and hierarchy by dehumanizing the victim. For example, in the Gudele One area, perpetrators forced some of their victims to eat the flesh of people they had just pushed into a bonfire, and to drink the blood of a victim they had poured into a plate.[32]

But efficiency also mattered. For example, the Nuer government official who survived recalled how some of the killings were performative while others were done in haste or with the clear intent to destroy both people and their residence: "My neighbor was shot in front of his gate. People were not always drawn out of their houses . . . In Lologo, Kor William, New Site, Gudele, Mia Saba and Mangaten (between New Site and Mia Saba—people also fled to UN Tongping), people were drawn out of their houses. The killings were done with guns. But sometimes in Kor William and Lologo, the SPLA came with trucks and crushed people within their houses."[33]

In some other instances, government troops also threw people in shipping containers or in prison. One of the deadliest episodes of the massacre occurred at around 8pm on December 16. Between two hundred and four hundred Nuer men were crowded into a 17.5 square meter (188.3 square feet) room of the Gudele police station, shot several times at close range through the windows, while others allegedly died from suffocation.[34]

Killings also achieved an ethnic purge of high- and mid-level Nuer politicians and members of the security apparatus. As for the higher-ups who managed to escape or were not in Juba, their immediate and extended families were not spared.[35] "All the compounds of Peter Gadet and James Hoth Mai had people killed inside," recalled a former Dinka battalion commander. "James Hoth's brothers were killed. Families were killed. The ministers of Jonglei were killed as well."[36] Even though Dinka perpetrators especially focused on killing the men, they also killed women and children. They gang-raped women, killing some of them afterwards.[37]

Although most of the victims were Nuer, other ethnic groups associated with the Nuer were killed in the massacre too.[38] For example, Equatorian women married to Nuer men were killed, along their children.[39] There was violent in-group policing of the Dinka as well. Some who opposed the killing and torture of Nuer civilians and who were from different Dinka sections than the perpetrators from Northern Bahr El Ghazal and Warrap were persecuted on grounds of being too close ethnically to the Nuer.[40]

The perpetrators had a particularly broad understanding of Nuer ethnicity, extending to non-Nuer relatives and lookalikes. This illustrated their extremist, uncompromising, and ultimately genocidal views.[41]

Intent to Kill

The perpetrators made clear to their victims that they felt threatened by Machar's presidential ambitions and would never allow the Nuer to preside over the country.[42] This was quite telling of their extreme sense of Dinka group entitlement.

Nuer victims were executed by shots to the head, abdomen, or back, which indicated that the intent was to kill. The goal was to kill as many Nuer as possible, across all Nuer sections, and to let no one escape. The security forces searched house to house for Nuer civilians. Policemen and soldiers blocked the roads and checked for Nuer.[43]

Since Dinka and Nuer look similar, fleeing civilians at roadblocks were asked to speak Dinka. If they did not, they were shot.[44] Dinka soldiers also tricked Nuer civilians by greeting them in Nuer. Dinka civilians were occasionally mistaken for Nuer since some Dinka groups have the same facial scarification rituals as the Nuer (six lines on the forehead).[45] A Nuer explained, "I have six marks on my forehead—I'm a Nuer, and the Nuer always have six marks . . . But the Dinka from Baliet and from Pigi county can have six marks. In Pariang and Abiemnohm, the Dinka can have six or seven marks, as in Abyei. The Dinka of Lakes have five or more marks. The Nuer always have six."[46]

Death Toll

No one knows how many people died in the Juba massacre, but the African Union accorded credibility to the estimate of fifteen to twenty thousand Nuer deaths.[47] The security forces, after carrying out the massacre, hid or destroyed the evidence. They thoroughly cleaned up the Gudele police station and buried the bodies in haste in mass graves. In the Giada barracks, the SPLA also removed the bodies to prevent the UN from seeing any evidence.[48]

It was clear that the killing targeted not just Nuer soldiers but the Nuer as a people.[49] Most people were killed in Juba between December 15 and 18, 2013.[50] Nearly every Nuer in the country lost some relatives, friends, or acquaintances in the massacre. A Nuer civilian who escaped the massacre illustrated its impact: "In Juba alone I lost ten relatives. Two were my brothers from different mothers, one was my nephew, two were my brothers-in-law to my sisters and uncles, plus the in-laws. They were killed in the Gudele area, in the same house. They were twelve in that same house. There were others who were suffocated in the Gudele area in a container where they locked them in. In this family, three survived."[51]

The Functions of the Juba Massacre

Of course, the Juba massacre was not just intended to achieve mass killings and traumatize the Nuer as a group. It made civil war inevitable in less than eight hours, from the start of fighting within the Presidential Guards at 10:30pm on December 15 to the dawn of December 16. Kiir's faction used it to crush the opposition and cement power right when it was hotly contested. Because the Juba massacre was the largest systematic massacre in South Sudan's recorded history, it mobilized the Nuer communities for revenge against the Dinka on an unprecedented scale. In reaction, the Nuer assembled into the "White Army," a collection of Nuer community defense groups.[52] They joined hands with the Nuer SPLA soldiers who had split from their Dinka SPLA peers throughout the country. A long-time Dinka SPLM/A member and former high-ranking government official stressed the political magnitude of the Juba massacre: "Even 1991 could not divide the SPLA as much as now. Now it's much worse."[53]

The Question of Planning

Leaders rarely plan a genocide as their main objective: they conceive of genocide as their plan B or C, when other plans have failed. Genocides are the result of processes of escalation.[54] In the case of the Juba massacre, genocide was a very natural extension of crushing the opposition (plan A). It may not have been "conceived" as genocide by its organizers, but most likely only because punishing the Nuer for their unsufferable insubordination was such a given.

Indeed, the scale and the planning behind this massacre were unprecedented, precisely compared to the 1991 Bor massacre that Kiir referred to in his speech on December 16. "The Juba massacre was tougher than the 1991 Bor massacre," noted a former Dinka SPLA battalion commander who fought there. "The Juba massacre, it was not Riek Machar who started it. It was the SPLA. Riek was going to be killed even before the massacre."[55] A Dinka former high-ranking SPLA and government official from Rumbek who had also fought Machar's troops in Bor in 1991 explained, "Juba was intended as a massacre and designed by intellectuals, unlike what happened in cattle camps like in Bor in 1991. Juba was an organized massacre."[56] And the goal of the massacre was quite clear to him: it was to have "one nation for one tribe."[57]

Did the perpetrators succeed in Juba? A Nuer government official who survived the massacre had an interesting theory. According to him, the massacre was planned but unsuccessful because incomplete. The Nuer soldiers fought back and some of them managed to escape alongside Nuer civilians. "I think the massacre was planned," he said. "Otherwise it would not have been so quick. They thought that they would capture Riek Machar. They wanted to make people shut up. If you are killed, you have to be quiet. But it didn't happen as was planned. The Nuer were not captured and they were not quiet . . . The fact that people were able to run to UN camps makes it different from Rwanda."[58]

He was not wrong. Indeed, there was planning for at least a military escalation, and one of the organizers who had acted in the shadows for two to three years, Malong, was seen actively participating in the fighting and massacre in Juba.[59] And true enough, international presence did play a role in mitigating the duration of the massacre. "The deadliest days were from the 16 to the 20," said the Nuer official. "On December 21 and 22, people started coming out and the SPLA was not doing it so openly."[60] This decline corresponded to a speech given by Kiir that now called for calm. Kiir had to contend with Western backers aghast at how quickly the country had been plunged back into war. His instructions confused the perpetrating troops, who relaxed the intensity of their killings without stopping it entirely. But by the same token, Kiir tested the international community with the Juba massacre, and the lack of a strong international response to the Juba massacre signaled to him that he could get away with the first phase of what would turn out to be a multiethnic genocide.

The First Phase of a Genocide

As such, the Juba massacre would set the tone for genocidal violence. First, genocidal violence against the Nuer quickly expanded to other areas—particularly Unity state, the birthplace of Machar. The atrocities perpetrated in Juba against Nuer civilians were mirrored upstate in several locations (particularly in Unity state), which illustrated a transference of violence. Second, the Juba massacre also removed the taboo of killing non-Dinka groups other than the Nuer in a systematic manner.[61] The massacre affected Equatorian groups: "Even the people from the Bari and Mundari were killed in the December massacre," noted a Bari civil society member.[62] It also hit ethnic groups from Western Bahr El Ghazal, already victimized by the Dinka state in the past eight years. A Balanda doctor from Wau, at the time in Juba, recalled, "My neighbor was killed driving from there on the way home when hearing of the fighting. He's a Kresh from Raja."[63]

During the Juba massacre, the cotargeting of non-Dinka groups—including Equatorians, the Balanda and Kresh, and the Shilluk—sent a message to these groups and set a precedent. After the massacre, these groups continued to be targeted in Juba, before their home areas fell prey to campaigns of genocidal violence. A student in Juba recounted, "My neighbor, a Balanda, was in Gudele and she was killed in February. Killings continued after December, even in May 2014 . . . On a smaller scale, but still."[64]

The Juba massacre had so efficiently removed the taboo of eliminating non-Dinka groups that the perpetrators made sure to convey to these groups that it was just the beginning. SPLA Dinka soldiers warned Equatorian groups, during the massacre and in the months following, that they would be next. This was especially flagrant in Yei (Central Equatoria), a future target of genocidal violence. "In December 2013, when the Nuer commander defected, the SPLA brought a Dinka to take over the leadership in Yei," a Kakwa civil society member explained. "He came with the mindset that every Nuer was a rebel. By then the SPLA in Yei was mixed. But then the commander and deputy commander, the head of the store ammunition, were Dinka. They could remove the guns from the hands of the Equatorians," just like they had to the Nuer in Juba in December 2013. He continued, "They said to the Equatorians in December 2013, 'You people are cowards.' 'You Equatorians are still here but the day we're done with the Nuer, we're coming for you and you won't like it.' They said it openly, in the market. They said: 'The next people killed should be you.' They said 'you people [from Equatoria], your time is coming. When we're through with these people,' the Nuer."[65]

A Kakwa (Equatorian) SPLA captain from Yei county, then fighting alongside the government in Jonglei and Upper Nile, also confirmed hearing similar threats from his colleagues early in the war—two weeks after the Juba massacre: "By that time, we were fighting the Nuer and my colleagues—Dinka—were telling me, when they were drunk: 'Once we're finished with the Nuer, we'll turn to the Equatorians.' They said it openly."[66] The Juba massacre was thus the first phase of a genocide targeting non-Dinka ethnic groups.

Yet none of this means that this multiethnic genocide was a plan designed by Kiir's faction from as early as the 2011 independence. It may have been a plan designed later, or it may not have been designed at all before the 2013 Juba massacre. Instead, the plan to target other non-Dinka groups may have emerged during the massacre itself and in the following days. This may account for the discourse by Dinka SPLA troops to Equatorian civilians in Juba during the massacre and in other towns. After all, local perpetrators can also push for genocidal violence from the ground, anticipating orders from the top. This would be a generous interpretation.[67] But in the absence of more information on the topic, we are left to speculate. At any rate, not every genocide needs planning, and genocides are often not fully conceived strategies.[68]

Looking back at the period from December 2013 to July 2017, what is most likely is that the multiethnic genocide that unfolded was the culmination of at least two things. First, it was the result of planning for at a minimum a military confrontation following a political crisis in Juba. Second, it was the consequence of an escalation of government violence led by the elite and driven by the will to crush the unbearable threat posed by a growing number of non-Dinka groups, a perception explained by an ideology of extreme group entitlement, or ethnic supremacy, long bred.

If there was no planning for a genocide in 2013, key conditions were at least present for one to unfold: the government had prepared for an absolutely crushing military confrontation; the perpetrators practiced ethnic groupism in identifying targets for destruction from the start, including targets other than the Nuer; and the military elite displayed an impressive capacity to adapt to and anticipate the changing military landscape on the ground.[69] It expected conflict spill-over from its military campaigns and sent in more troops to control new areas, sometimes in advance (as in Equatoria). The increased SPLA presence pushed non-Dinka communities against the wall. The ideology driving military decisions thus became a self-fulfilling prophecy: government violence forced non-Dinka communities to flee or take up arms to defend themselves or die. In fleeing or resisting, these communities unwittingly confirmed the ethnic supremacist narrative, along the lines of: "See? I told you those (non-Dinka) were always rebels. They are not South Sudanese. We are."

Denationalizing and Conquering

The Juba massacre was "typical" not just because the violence perpetrated there was a blueprint for future violence. This first phase also expanded the Dinka conquest cemented since 2005 in Juba. In eliminating the Nuer in Juba and chasing them away from their houses, the perpetrators cleared the way for Dinka settlers. In addition to looting Nuer houses, Dinka soldiers moved into those houses deserted by the Nuer who had either died or taken refuge at the United Nations Mission in South Sudan protection of civilians camp (UNMISS POC).[70] An Acholi man and his wife recalled, "On the road to Bilpam, they killed all the Nuer. In Jebel Kujur, all the Dinka moved into the houses of the Nuer, even if the Nuer are still alive and in Juba . . . They're all staying in the villas of the Nuer who fled in December."[71]

The despoiling of the Nuer conveyed the Dinka perpetrators' sense of group entitlement. The perpetrators attacked the residents whenever they risked returning home to collect their belongings.[72] Returning home was out of the question, including for the Nuer from the formerly ethnically diverse dominant class.

"The worst is that they take your house," lamented a Nuer politician six months after the massacre. "Even now I live in a hotel. Because you never know, I might be pulled out of my house and killed. Even now there's stealing."[73]

The sense of entitlement on the part of the Dinka settlers who silenced the Nuer was not lost on the Equatorians either. A Latuka civil society activist in Juba noted, "In the mixed areas, the Dinka who remained will not say that the Nuer were killed, because they're happy about it. And the Nuer fled so it's very difficult to get information."[74] Ultimately, the Nuer would not return to their homes until the time of writing (six years after the massacre). But losing their homes to the perpetrators was just the beginning.

Indeed, Dinka perpetrators also confiscated the passports, phones, and other belongings of the Nuer who survived and were crowded in the UNMISS POC. Passport confiscation symbolically excluded them from citizenship and as such was a clear attempt at denationalizing them. It also prevented them from leaving the country, which along with the seizure of their wealth and means of communication was meant to bury—both socially and politically—the thirty thousand Nuer crammed into the open-sky prison of the UNMISS POC.[75] The Nuer could not leave the Juba POC without risking death or rape by marauding SPLA soldiers planted on its outskirts. Killings and kidnappings continued at lower rates after the Juba massacre ended. Six months after the massacre, a Nuer politician described how "killings at night still continue. Most of the Nuer are in UNMISS."[76] The SPLA thus sent a clear message to the Nuer: "If you come out, we will kill you."[77] The Nuer's stay in the POC presaged a long social, political, and mental death under UN auspices instead of a swift gruesome one at the hands of their government.

For the first time, the UNMISS POC had effectively averted the death of many more Nuer by providing them with a refuge. But in doing so, the UN had been instrumentalized by the government. In effect, the POC refuge saved the government the logistical burden and the international opprobrium of massacring more Nuer. At the same time, the Juba massacre still accomplished the several functions I described earlier—starting a civil war, a multi-phased genocide, and expanding the Dinka conquest. As the government painted the massacre as an offshoot of Machar's attempted coup, the fact that some Nuer civilians survived it by fleeing to the POC meant to prove that the massacre was not genocidal but rather the result of uncontrollable troops with emotions running high. Combined with the beginning of the third civil war and the retaliatory violence by Nuer troops, the government easily painted the massacre as an unfortunate side-effect of fighting. This could not be further from the truth given its timing and resonance throughout the country—for example, a few kilometers south, in Yei.

Resonance of the Juba Massacre

Expansion and the Case of the Equatorians

The Juba massacre was exceptional in its execution and magnitude. But this event masked the fact that Nuer civilians were being massacred at the same time in other towns. In Yei, similar events to what happened in Juba took place. On December 13–14, 2013, the Nuer SPLA soldiers were not given assignments in preparation for the NLC. On the 15th, fighting broke out between the Dinka and Nuer when the Dinka tried to disarm the Nuer.[78] A Nuer student residing in Yei at the time remembered, "On December 15, 2013, our home was very close to the barracks in Yei. The soldiers divided themselves. One of my friends was a soldier and he came to me to tell me that what happened in Juba was not only targeting soldiers and said I should move away from the barracks. On December 16, I evacuated my relatives 10km (6.2 miles) away . . . In Yei, around five Nuer families were neighbors to me. When the war started in Juba, the government closed all cell networks, and we heard all five families were killed when [fleeing on foot] to Uganda. Salva Kiir has a house in Yei with many soldiers, with heavy weapons. Those people staying around and who were Nuer and renting houses to send their children to school—all those were killed. They were very close to the barracks . . . they were killed by the bodyguards of Salva Kiir."[79]

The political crisis and fighting in Juba radiated especially quickly in Yei. Indeed, these "bodyguards"—potentially comprising some Mathiang Anyoor but most likely Tiger—had been deployed there as early as 2012. They were hosted in an area called New Site, which is not to be confused with Juba's New Site where Salva Kiir had a house. They were most likely joined by new recruits from the Dut Ku Beny militia, and all served in the Presidential Guards. The Nuer student recalled how Mathiang Anyoor soldiers started to flock Yei town in 2012: "Those were Salva Kiir's relatives from Warrap, this Mathiang Anyoor . . . Some of these men were in school, but when they came back home in the evening, they came back to their guns. When the crisis started, those people at school surprised us with their guns. They were fully active—they had guns, uniforms, salaries."[80]

The speed at which events unfolded in Yei again indicated planning for at least a military confrontation following a political crisis. There as well, Nuer civilians were quickly massacred.[81] The Juba massacre against the Nuer also radiated to Kajo Keji, another town of Central Equatoria bordering Uganda—also the scene of future genocidal violence against Equatorian civilians. In both Kajo Keji and Yei, Equatorian inhabitants hid Nuer civilians. A trader in Kajo Keji at the time recalled, "In December 2013, I took some Nuer in my house to protect them in Kajo Keji. The government was shooting the Nuer."[82]

All in all, the Juba massacre radiated to future sites of genocidal violence against Equatorian groups, where some civilians refused to be bystanders. As I explain later, the Juba massacre had a role in attracting Equatorian sympathy for the Nuer. This sympathy caught the attention and fed the paranoia of the Dinka hardliners and perpetrators. But would Equatorian groups have been spared if they had been more passive bystanders? In other words, did the Equatorian saviors provoke the Dinka hardliners? It was more complicated than that, as I explain later.

Early Fighting, Nuer Displacement, and Dinka Settlements

Tensions would continue to simmer in Equatoria for at least another year, while fighting quickly expanded to the Upper Nile region, where both Dinka and Nuer groups cohabited. But no party seemed to have the upper hand. Machar lacked control over the White Army, even though he claimed control when it was convenient, especially in cases of victory. The White Army descended on Bor and Malakal and intended to reach Juba. Bor town changed hands six times before Uganda's Popular Defense Forces (UPDF) secured control for the government on January 16, 2014, including through cluster bombs.[83] Malakal and Bentiu also changed hands numerous times in the first few months. In less than a year, violence would displace over 1.5 million people.[84]

Paul Malong, then governor of Northern Bahr El Ghazal, went to assist the SPLA troops in Jonglei. His trip to Jonglei coincided with the deployment of Mathiang Anyoor troops from Juba to Jonglei and Upper Nile, within two weeks of the Juba massacre.[85] Four months later (in April 2014), Malong was appointed as the new SPLA chief of staff, replacing the Nuer James Hoth Mai. There was no more ethnic window-dressing. Malong and the Dinka from Bahr El Ghazal dominated the SPLA, and Mathiang Anyoor integrated the SPLA.

Despite the "messiness" of war, the aftermath of violence in Bor mirrored that of the Juba massacre. First, the displacement of the Nuer served Dinka settlers. After civilians ran for safety to the Bor UNMISS POC on December 18, 2013, the government came to the POC and ordered the Dinka civilians to leave the POC. For those who stayed, the POC quickly became a prison.[86]

Second, the displaced Nuer in the Bor POC also felt threatened. Yet what distinguished Bor (and other locations) from Juba was that it was much more removed from international scrutiny. This allowed government officials like the Dinka minister of information Michael Makuei, a staunch Kiir supporter from Bor, to threaten the internally displaced persons (IDPs) directly in February 2014.[87] And two months later, on April 17, 2014, between three and five hundred Dinka government security personnel (from the SPLA and from the prison and wildlife departments) and Dinka civilians surrounded and attacked the Bor UNMISS POC compound, killing forty-six civilians and injuring thirty.[88]

The government's daring incursion within a UN POC set a precedent that would be repeated—most notoriously in Malakal two years later, in February 2016. At that point, this was one way for Kiir's faction to signal its sovereignty to the UN, and to the Nuer (and Shilluk) their own precariousness. Just like in Juba, the government crippled the Nuer displaced in Bor. It consistently refused to evacuate them for medical treatment in Juba. It screened Nuer people at the airport and prevented them from leaving from Bor and Juba. And, quite significant, the violent ethnocracy displayed its belief in ethnic ranking, Dinka group legitimacy, ownership, and entitlement by offering compensation to the Dinka for their property loss but not to the Nuer. Much like in Juba, violence went hand in hand with conquest in Bor. After the SPLA "victory" through UPDF cluster bombs, new Dinka occupants also quickly moved into the houses of the residents who had fled to the POC.[89]

The problem was that these trends got quickly buried under the pile of atrocities perpetrated by revengeful Nuer troops. Indeed, the Nuer White Army troops (descending from Uror, Ayod, Nyrol, and Akobo) who joined forces with the Nuer soldiers defecting from the SPLA to create the new SPLA-In-Opposition (IO) were obsessed with retaliating for the Juba massacre on any Dinka in their way. Much like their Dinka counterparts targeting Nuer civilians, the Nuer troops searched houses for Dinka residents in Bor. They targeted them on grounds of their Dinka ethnicity and perpetrated systematic rapes and killings that were incredibly violent and ethnically motivated.[90]

In Malakal, around December 23, 2013, SPLA troops started to search for Nuer house to house.[91] There, Nuer civilians compared their scarifications to a "death certificate." But IO troops also killed and raped.[92] Throughout the rest of the country, the Nuer retaliated on the Dinka when they could, for example killing Dinka who had intermarried with the Nuer.[93] Conversely, in Dinka areas such as Bahr El Ghazal, some Dinka targeted Nuer who had intermarried with the Dinka.[94]

Anti-Dinka and anti-Nuer hatred did not take in every Dinka or Nuer area. In Lakes, six months after the Juba massacre, the Dinka who had intermarried with the Nuer protected them. Yet this was the exception, and as violence pitted groups further against one another, it reinforced their group identity. This was particularly the case in the majority-Nuer Unity state, the most conflict-affected state of all.

THE SECOND PHASE OF THE GENOCIDE IN UNITY STATE

2014–15

Oil-rich Unity state was the only Nuer-majority state in the country. It was also the home state of Riek Machar, born in Leer. As such, it saw most of the fiercest fighting and violence until the end of 2015. By the end of 2015, over 140,000 civilians had fled to the UNMISS POC of Bentiu.[1] Mass displacement was the result of two gruesome military campaigns against Nuer civilians in 2014 and 2015. These campaigns, during which the most shocking acts of violence equaled those of the December 2013 Juba massacre, were the result of a transference of violence against the Nuer from the capital onto the countryside. The state coordinated multiple actors to carry out these attacks. Even if perpetrators were increasingly Nuer, their violence fulfilled the goals of a Dinka supremacist agenda, and their rhetoric referred to that ideology. Salva Kiir's faction merely made use of the perpetrators' own immediate goals of resource accumulation and group ascension. The perpetrators' class interests took precedence over Nuer ethnicity. The two military campaigns in Unity state formed the second phase of the genocide.

The First Military Campaign of 2014: The SPLA and JEM

The first government military campaign against the civilians of Unity state started in early 2014. After the SPLA splintered in Bentiu on December 17, 2013, in reaction to the Juba massacre, fighting quickly engulfed Bentiu, Unity's capital.[2] The SPLA—including Mathiang Anyoor troops brought in through Bahr

FIGURE 8.1.   SPLA chief of staff General Paul Malong in the foreground, with General Marial Chanuong in the background wearing military berets at a peace agreement signing ceremony in Juba, South Sudan, on August 26, 2015. Photo by Jason Patinkin.

El Ghazal and the Darfuri rebel group JEM, going by the local name of "Toro-Boro"—chased and targeted Nuer civilians on grounds of their ethnicity.[3] As a result, civilians fled to the UN POC or to where the IO troops had established some presence (in Guit, Koch, Leer, or Mayendit). This propelled the start of the first military campaign against civilians in Unity state.

From Bentiu, government troops and JEM went south too in January and February 2014.[4] "When the Toro Boro came last time, they put women in the tukul and set them on fire," explained a man from Ding-Ding, in Rubkona county. They also hung people from the trees.[5] The SPLA gained control of much of the territory except in Panyijaar and parts of Mayendit.[6] That is when the government appointed county commissioners instrumental in the second military campaign, as I explain later.[7]

Throughout the months of January–April 2014, government and JEM troops burned houses (*tukuls*) and killed civilians, including women, girls, and the elderly all throughout Unity but particularly in southern Unity, Machar's home region. The county commissioner Stephen Thiak Riek, the area commander Brigadier General Deng Mayik, and the operation commander for the state Major General Matthew Puljang were all implicated.[8] The locations under attack by the government were rarely rebel strongholds. But the government shelled civilians and pursued them into the swamps, where they starved and drowned.[9] The government prevented aid from reaching affected Nuer communities and looted the Nuer food reserves, and government officials lured the Nuer into coming out of hiding to kill them.[10] Still, government troops were just using cars with mounted heavy machine guns and trucks, which left some areas untouched.[11]

Things changed on the ground in April 2014, when the government troops withdrew from Leer as IO attacked Bentiu on April 14. JEM troops supported the SPLA in Bentiu, but this was not enough: "Government troops got their reinforcement from the Bul Nuer, in addition to JEM," explained a Nuer civilian from Leer.[12] The government then retook Bentiu from the IO in early May 2014.[13]

The Second Campaign of 2015:
Nuer Perpetrators

In April–June 2015, the government embarked on its second scorched-earth military campaign against civilians, to dislodge both the remainder of IO troops and civilians it perceived as IO sympathizers. "At that time, there were small IO forces outside of Leer, attacked by the government," recounted a Nuer civilian from Leer.[14] An aid worker summarized the change in this military landscape: "Until May 2015, the frontline was at Nyaldiu, and from there, IO controlled the south of Unity. From April to July 2015, everything was taken by the SPLA in Unity state except Panyjaar."[15]

Again, government troops rarely encountered IO troops, who had largely been defeated, and instead inflicted violence mostly on civilians.[16] Human Rights Watch noted that despite the government's rhetoric of "flushing out the rebels," the government and its allied militias deliberately targeted civilians in what could amount to war crimes and crimes against humanity.[17]

In targeting Rubkona, Guit, Koch, Leer, Mayendit, and Panyijaar counties, the government displaced over a hundred thousand people. Attacks were meant to displace civilians from their villages and settlements. The perpetrators told their victims never to come back; they killed and raped in public to spread fear and looted cattle to compromise survival.[18] It worked: by the end of 2015, 90 percent of the population had been displaced. The Nuer of Unity state were by far the most displaced population in the country, some of them crowded in the most populous UNMISS POC in the country, others hiding in the swamps, others dead.[19]

What differentiated the second military campaign was that local Nuer militias—especially at first the Bul Nuer—played a much more prominent role in carrying out the attacks. "In May 2015," a Nuer civilian who fled Leer explained, "the attacks were mostly carried out by the Bul Nuer . . . The Bul Nuer youth was first mobilized by the governor."[20] Juba used the same rhetoric Khartoum had in the past civil war: "The SPLA rhetoric is to say that the Nuer are fighting among themselves," noted a long-time aid worker there.[21]

The state coordination of annihilating violence serving Dinka supremacists' agenda and the Nuer perpetrators' own referencing of Dinka supremacist ideology and intent to destroy, made this violence genocidal. This second military campaign was the apex of subcontracting genocide, and this modus operandi could be replicated in other locations whenever necessary.

Contracting the Bul Nuer

Unity state was a favorable terrain to contract out some of the violence to Nuer militias—particularly to the Bul Nuer. It had already been the site of intra-Nuer ethnic violence during the second South Sudanese civil war, when Khartoum sponsored different Nuer armed groups who fought each other.[22]

By the end of the second civil war, the Bul Nuer of the SSDF had constituted their own dominant class. The Bul Nuer troops were reintegrated into the SPLA only in 2006 via the Juba Declaration signed between Matiep and Kiir. The Bul Nuer dominant class then came to Juba to coexist and temporarily fuse with that of the predominantly Dinka SPLA. Elites coexisted in Juba but continued to compete in the countryside. In Unity, tensions and rivalry between the Bul Nuer and the rest of the Nuer sections (under Machar and Taban Deng's leadership) continued after the 2005 CPA.[23] Kiir made sure to take advantage of this rivalry. He sided increasingly with the Bul Nuer after the 2010 elections to bench Machar's side.[24] This contributed to the Bul Nuer discourse of group entitlement discussed later.

By the beginning of the third civil war, other Nuer sections already had negative stereotypes about the Bul Nuer, who had perpetrated violence against them in the second war and had formed their own discourse of group entitlement.[25] They saw them as brutish thieves, "taking things from people."[26] With this competition and enmity between the Bul and the rest of the Nuer sections, it was easy for the government to contract its campaign mostly to Bul Nuer forces in April–May 2015.[27] Moreover, it was necessary from a military perspective. Of course, regular SPLA forces still played a role in those attacks. But the distinction between Bul Nuer fighters and regular SPLA soldiers was particularly tenuous given the fact that both the political and military leadership in the state were Bul Nuer.[28] This made leveraging support from Mayom, the Bul Nuer's base, easy.[29] Those Bul Nuer troops were vital to the splintered SPLA, which had lost many recruits to the IO in December 2013 and experienced defections.[30]

All in all, the troops attacking southern Unity in the second military campaign generally included a mix of uniformed SPLA troops (including Bul Nuer) and Bul Nuer fighters dressed in civilian clothes. The link between the SPLA and the Bul Nuer fighters was so organic that the SPLA sometimes appropriated victories by Bul Nuer fighters against the IO. Sometimes SPLA troops committed atrocities without the support of the Bul Nuer fighters, including burning houses and raping, abducting, and killing women in central and southern Unity.[31] But SPLA troops still counted regular Bul Nuer soldiers anyway.

The mix of SPLA and Bul Nuer troops descended first on Koch county before moving south to Leer in mid-May 2015. They hung, shot, or burned civilians in their homes, raped and kidnapped women, and chased civilians into the swamps. Children and the elderly (both men and women) were shot, beaten to death, hung, or burned alive in their houses.[32] They used "barches"—amphibian vehicles with mounted machine guns—to chase civilians into the swamps.[33] They attacked Leer repeatedly. "On May 18, 2015, the SPLA went to Leer with the Bul Nuer," explained a Nuer civilian there at the time. "They stayed for three days there. It felt like three years."[34]

Contracting the Koch and other Youth

After June 2015, and especially in September, the government increasingly involved the local youth militias from Koch, Guit, Leer, and Rubkona (and to a lesser extent from Mayendit) counties in this second military campaign. The county commissioners appointed back during the first military campaign around February 2014 were instrumental in providing these reinforcements to the SPLA and Bul Nuer troops. Recruiting the youth was meant to cut down the IO base and coopt potential IO recruits.

The county commissioner who played the most pivotal role was Koang Biel of Koch county, who had been part of the SSDF in the last war (1983–85) under the command of the SSDF Bul Nuer leader Paulino Matiep. "The relationship between the Jagei and Dok Nuer used to be good," recalled Dok Nuer women who fled Leer. "But this changed when Koang Biel was appointed by Kiir and mobilized the youth to go and kill. JEM moved together with the Jagei . . . If they decide to go to Leer, the JEM, Jagei, Bul and Dinka, go to these areas."[35]

Koang Biel formed an alliance with the Bul Nuer militias who had raided Koch county's cattle en masse in 2014 and 2015.[36] So instead of raiding back from the Bul Nuer, Koang Biel recruited, armed, and instructed the Koch county youth to raid Leer county to reclaim cattle. He acted as a typical ethnopolitical entrepreneur by steering up intersectional enmity, telling the Koch youth and cattle keepers that their cattle had been previously looted not by the Bul Nuer from

Mayom county but by the Dok Nuer from Leer (Machar's home). He was not the only county commissioner to manipulate his fighters, explained a young Nuer woman from Koch who survived being shot: "The commissioners from Koch and Rubkona don't want the cattle keepers to get their cows back from the Bul Nuer. They want them to go fight other counties to get cows. The county commissioners from Rubkona and Koch cooperate together and say that the raiding is done by the people from Leer. But cattle from Mayendit, Leer, Koch, Rubkona, Adok have all been taken by the Bul Nuer."[37] Koang Biel also paid for this campaign by letting the youth keep part of the cattle they raided.[38]

Koang Biel, himself a victim of in-group policing, also made sure to practice violent in-group policing.[39] People in Koch were divided. On the one hand, there were those who agreed to join him and the SPLA to protect their cattle and properties from looting and destruction by the SPLA and were given a chance to loot others and aggrandize their own herds.[40] On the other hand, some decided to join IO, others were bystanders who joined neither group, and finally, some left for fear of being killed. "Some key people of the Jagei Nuer are still in the bush up to now," claimed a civilian from Leer.[41] The neutral bystanders who remained in Koch town only did so because they had old or disabled relatives in town who were unable to walk the journey to UNMISS POC. They were regularly accused of being IO supporters. One of them explained: "They say to us: 'If you don't want to join us, we will take your properties' . . . Koch town is divided in two: those who side with the county commissioner, and those who don't loot and are regularly accused of being IO."[42]

In collaboration with the Rubkona county commissioner Salam Maluet, Biel went further than intimidating those reluctant to join him. He commissioned the Bul Nuer in September 2015 to fight Koch and Rubkona counties' cattle keepers who wanted to raid Mayom for their looted cattle and who were opposed to raiding Leer. In-group policing also affected Leer county, as a Nuer who fled Leer noted: "After this assembly [at Biel's county headquarters] in July 2015, they [the Jagei armed youth] were based in Leer, to mobilize people and get rid of people. 'You're either with us, or against us.' They tried to mobilize the youth from Leer, but it was difficult to mobilize them, and a lot of them refused and joined IO instead." So the government resorted to forced recruitment: "The recruitment in Leer was forced. The youth refused to join, which led to killings to scare them into joining."[43]

The distinction between regular SPLA soldiers and the youth was here again often very flimsy, since some of the recruited (but untrained) youth were given SPLA uniforms. With increased involvement from the local armed youth, fewer SPLA soldiers coordinated these attacks. They were less "necessary" than they used to be. Civilians who fled the attacks in Guit county in August 2015 pointed out that the troops were largely Nuer, coordinated by just a few SPLA commanders.

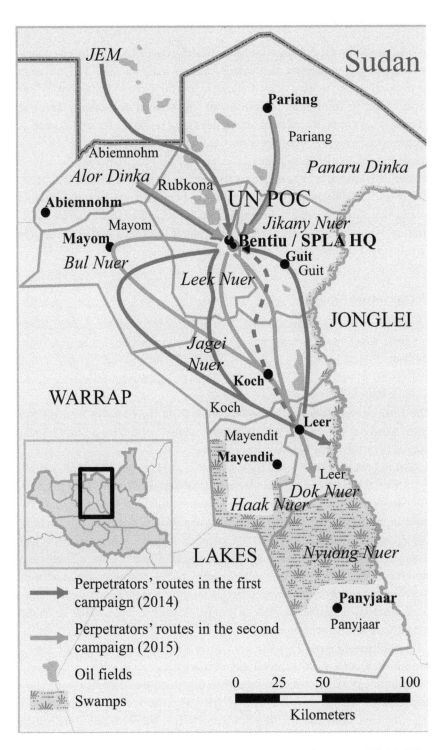

FIGURE 8.2. Map of the two government campaigns in Unity state (2014–15).

The attacks by the Bul Nuer and, most notably, the Koch youth involved their wives, sons, and sometimes their elderly relatives, assigning each age/sex group its own killing and looting tasks. A young man who survived being shot in Leer explained: "The youth from Mayom comes with women and soldiers. Those of Mayom—the youth, the soldiers, young boys aged ten to twelve, and women—are going to Leer now."[44] Another woman from Mayendit reported that "the Koch youth and the soldiers had come to Dalual, near Leer . . . They came with their women, their wives."[45] In Koch county too, perpetrators came with their children and wives.[46] This was, as far as research for this book goes, the form of genocidal attacks the closest to a popular event, as in other genocides involving the mobilization of various segments of the population. It illustrated that entire groups were involved in these attacks, pursuing their own goals.

Perpetrators' Goals

The puzzle with Unity state was that these multiple perpetrators pursued different goals, which made it easy for the government to describe it as another Nuer civil war.

BUL NUER GOALS

The Nuer perpetrators who gained the most from these attacks were the Bul Nuer. As an aid worker put it, "The bloody conquest of southern Unity state in May 2015 by the SPLA Bul Nuer was paid in loot."[47]

The Bul Nuer had developed their own sense of group legitimacy, originating in the role of their SSDF commanders under Matiep's leadership in the past war. They were historically the strongest Nuer section militarily, having received the most support from Khartoum, and their leader Matiep had been Kiir's second in hierarchy in 2006–12, after the 2006 Juba declaration.[48] A dominant class had emerged in SSDF areas through a predatory mode of production, accumulating wealth in things and people, and mirroring that of SPLA areas. From the sense of Bul Nuer group ownership and legitimacy built on this predatory wealth accumulation derived another example of group entitlement. It placed the Bul at the top of Nuer hierarchy.

In implementing government violence, the Bul Nuer SPLA and youth aimed to capture as much wealth as possible from other Nuer sections. After all, extreme group entitlement dictated that it was their due. A displaced civilian from Mayendit county commented that "they've got way more money than before. All the cows have been taken by the Bul Nuer."[49] The Bul Nuer SPLA and youth also made clear during the attacks that they despised other Nuer sections. They wanted to strengthen their position and control of Unity, even more so on the eve of the implementation of the August 2015 peace agreement, signed between the government and Machar's IO after months of international pressure. They were not ready to let the other Nuer sections—especially the Jikany—rob them of their leadership over Unity state. They displayed their own discourse of group entitlement: "In the government, they created another name here: *ther chuong*: 'fighting for their rights'—to be given governorship after Taban Deng," recalled a Nuer civilian from Bentiu. "Taban is from the Jikany Nuer. So *ther chuong* is Bul Nuer language, and the conflict between Nuer and Dinka has become a conflict between Jikany and Bul. This term was created by Joseph Monytuil, who was chosen by Salva Kiir as governor."[50]

The Bul Nuer group legitimacy and entitlement paralleled that of the Dinka from Bahr El Ghazal, especially from Kiir and Paul Malong's areas, at the top of Dinka hierarchy. This created shared class interests in their respective ascension. The Bul Nuer elite had more in common with Kiir's faction because class interests trumped Nuer ethnicity. Its goals were more aligned with those of Kiir's faction (who now ruled the ethnocracy and dominated Dinka ranking) than with those of the other Nuer sections, who were always its closest rivals.

This showed how different versions of extreme ethnic group entitlement could coincide out of dominant class interests, especially when (most likely temporarily) confined to different parts of the country. The convergence of ethnic dominant class interests was not surprising, given the similarities in dominant class formation processes in both SSDF and SPLA areas in the last war. Civilians from other Nuer sections perceived the Bul Nuer as conquerors, in the same way that Equatorians saw the Dinka of the advancing SPLA. Therefore, the dominant Bul Nuer class, at the top of the local ethnic ranking system in Unity state, was the best executant for the policy of Kiir's faction. It used Kiir's faction just as much as it had used Khartoum's support in the past.[51] And the same processes of dominant class formation and consolidation through the accumulation of cattle and its sale and reinvestment into the expansion of kinship networks, continued.[52]

Both Bul Nuer perpetrators themselves and their victims identified the Bul Nuer much more with the Dinka than with the Nuer. They and the Dinka elite benefited the most from the war in Unity state. Class trumped ethnicity to such a degree that Bul Nuer perpetrators adopted and relayed the discourse of Dinka perpetrators. They understood ethnicity as a social radar, a tool for social navigation in times of war.[53] This explains why they offered their victims a chance at ethnic conversion. Of course, it also meant that while ethnic defection to the Dinka was useful to them, it was contingent and as such temporary.[54] Whenever this association with the Dinka would cease to be useful, the Bul Nuer could easily turn their back on the Dinka ethnocrats. For instance, the twenty-eight states decree, passed unilaterally in October 2015 by Kiir in violation of the country's

Transitional Constitution to divide up the country's ten states, effectively redrew boundaries to the advantage of the Dinka constituency, most contentiously in oil-rich areas, and marginalized non-Dinka groups. This created considerable tension between the Bul and the Dinka of Unity as it encroached on their land.[55] The Bul Nuer's allegiance was thus conditional, and they kept their Dinka counterparts on their toes by continuing to recruit in Mayom county. Their ethnic defection did not imply that the Dinka ethnocrats considered them genuine Dinka either—they just needed a strong ally against the rest of the Nuer.

OTHER PERPETRATORS' GOALS

The violence perpetrated by local Nuer groups in Unity looked like a set of dominos. The south of Unity—Leer—was the end of this domino sequence precipitated by Bul Nuer raiding and was hit the hardest.[56] This was partly a function of geography: Leer was raided successively and simultaneously by various perpetrators descending south. Of course, Leer was also hit the hardest because Machar hailed from there, which placed the Dok Nuer at the bottom of Nuer hierarchy, dominated by the Bul, and made Leer the perfect political target. At the bottom of the barrel, Leer was a reservoir for plundering.

In this Nuer ranking, the Jagei Nuer perpetrators from Koch anxiously tried to secure a second position after the Bul Nuer.[57] Both Bul Nuer and Jagei Nuer had the goal of securing and improving their own group's social status through plundering, destruction, and accumulation (including of women and children they did not kill). In June–July 2015, the Jagei Nuer youth "came every day to collect the remaining cattle after the Bul Nuer raids (in May)."[58] They did the same in Leer: "They came every day to collect everything from us," a woman from Leer recalled. "Cattle, clothes, and then they burned the houses."[59]

The fact that the Nuer Jagei perpetrators included women and children illustrates that they all participated in these attacks as a group, just like the Bul Nuer SPLA soldiers and youth in April–July 2015. The wives, armed with machetes, were tasked with finishing off the wounded after the raids and helping to collect and organize the loot in Leer, Koch, and Guit counties. These attacks considerably enriched the perpetrators in cattle, to the extent that it lowered their marriageable age.[60]

Perpetrators from other Nuer sections also fought to preserve or even improve their own personal and group status over ordinary civilians from Leer and those who sided with IO in their own county. This meant that the war also trickled down into local conflicts over cattle raids. "I joined the government in July 2015," explained an armed Nuer government youth from Rubkona. "It's a conflict within Rubkona county. It's also a conflict between IO and the SPLA ... I joined the government because a big part of Rubkona county is near Mayom, and the youth from Mayom comes to Rubkona and takes the cows."[61] This anxiety pushed recruitment and invariably escalated in tit-for-tat cattle raids. But overall, group ranking remained determined by the perpetrators' position in the local-national network controlled by the center in Juba.

State Coordination of the Attacks

Indeed, the state (Juba) regulated events on the ground via its key intermediaries: SPLA commanders, SPLA soldiers from different divisions (especially from Bahr El Ghazal), and the instrumental county commissioners. There was effectively no difference between the government of South Sudan (GoSS) and the SPLA; as an aid worker put it, "The SPLA and the GoSS are the same thing: all the county commissioners are appointed by the SPLA."[62] "The SPLA division commander gives orders to the county commissioners," explained a civilian from Leer. "Decisions are made at the Juba level."[63]

The county commissioners coordinated those attacks on the ground. Before and after the attacks on Leer, troops gathered at Biel's headquarters to receive instructions, report back on the attacks, and organize the division of the loot after the attacks. A Nuer civilian from Leer described these assemblies in June and July 2015: "First Koang Biel had a general assembly with the soldiers and gave them directives, [and the soldiers] then report back to him. There were few Bul Nuer—the majority of them were Jagei. And then there were a few Dinka soldiers from Aweil and a few from Rubkona . . . The Dok Nuer hid their cattle, hence the eleven attacks and the pursuits in the swamps. On July 17, Koang Biel had another general assembly: he said that if these people (Dok Nuer) did not accept [being] raided, then they shall be killed and their houses burned. Assemblies are carried to count looted cattle and plan new raids."[64]

Biel coordinated his attacks with his other county commissioner peers.[65] All county commissioners involved in the attacks received their share of the loot.[66] "Every county commissioner is instructed by Salva to destroy their own place," said a Nuer woman from Koch who survived being shot. "They get a lot of money because they support Salva's side . . . Koang Biel is the worse."[67] A Nuer civilian described Jagei Nuer troops from Koch descending on Leer: "Koang Biel was their commander, the county commissioner of Koch. Wal Yach was the commissioner of Leer and they coordinated together the troops' movement."[68]

The county commissioners were expert ethnopolitical entrepreneurs: they channeled group anxieties at being socially demoted into actions serving the group goals of both the Dinka leadership and the local Nuer perpetrators. They spread rumors to motivate attackers. A Nuer woman from Koch further explained: "The county commissioners from Rubkona and Koch cooperate together and say that the raiding is done by the people from Leer."[69] Leer's own county commissioner (Wal Yach) also pinned Bul Nuer raiding on Leer inhabitants, as Biel instructed.[70]

Ideology, Intent, and Genocide

A few elements made these state-coordinated attacks genocidal. First, Nuer perpetrators—ethnic defectors—appropriated the center's Dinka supremacist ideology. Second, they identified their target group in a form of groupism typical of genocides. Third, they expressed their intent to kill that group in both direct and indirect ways.

Dinka Supremacist Ideology and Ethnic Defection

I have noted that the perpetrators were increasingly Nuer. Yet the Dinka were still present all throughout the military campaigns in Unity state.[71] Dinka from Abiemnohm and Pariang (northern Unity) were spotted in attacks on Leer in August 2015. SPLA Divisions 3, 6, and 5 came through Warrap, Aweil, Bentiu, and Leer. Most Dinka perpetrators in Leer came from Division 5.[72] All in all, the Dinka perpetrators in Unity state were mostly from the northern and western Bahr El Ghazal region.

Survivors of attacks pointed out that the perpetrators, even when they were Nuer—and the vast majority were—depicted themselves as Dinka.[73] The youth from Mayom and Koch counties identified themselves to their victims as Dinka instead of Nuer, presumably because they associated Dinka ethnicity with the central power and wealth. They did not feel any sort of Nuer solidarity with the civilians they victimized. A young man from Leer who survived being shot said of the Koch youth (the Jagei Nuer), "When they took control of Leer, they killed everyone and they said, 'We're Dinka, we're not Nuer' . . . All the Nuer supporters to the SPLA say they're Dinka, not Nuer. And Salva Kiir says 'I'm Dinka and I'm fighting the Nuer.'"[74] Another young woman from Koch, also a gunshot victim, said the same thing of the Rubkona youth who descended on Koch in July 2015: "They were also calling themselves 'Dinka.' When they catch you, they beat you and they tell you, 'Call yourself Dinka, otherwise I'll kill you.' These men were the youth, not the SPLA. But they were instructed by the county commissioner to do that."[75] Another young woman from Leer demonstrated how much the Koch and Leer youth shared the same rhetoric than Dinka attackers: "The people who attacked are from Leer, and from Koch: they're together . . . Some of the attackers were Dinka . . . They're from Bahr El Ghazal, Pariang (northern Unity), etc. They shot my mother in the hand. If they ask you, 'Are you a Dinka?,' then they ask you, 'Are you a rebel?' My mother didn't say anything and she was shot in the hand. The Koch Jagei Nuer also ask the same question . . . If they find you, they kill you."[76]

Overall, victims' testimonies pointed to the same rhetoric in all main Dinka and Nuer perpetrating groups—from the Bul Nuer attackers to the Koch, Leer, and Rubkona youth. In all perpetrators' groups, Dinka ethnicity became a synonym for political legitimacy and the right to live. The reverse was also true: Nuer ethnicity was equated with rebellion; it implied death. This rhetoric illustrated how much Dinka group legitimacy and entitlement had degenerated into an exclusionary ideology adopted by subcontracted Nuer perpetrators. "When they ask you 'are you a Dinka?,' you're lucky," another man from Leer said of his attackers. "Then they say, 'You cannot be outside if you're not a rebel. If you're not a Dinka, you're not with the government.'"[77]

Following their own ethnic defection from the Nuer to the Dinka group, Nuer perpetrators thus practiced a form of ethnic miscuing (passing as Dinka).[78] This may have been an attempt to diffuse responsibility and accountability for their crimes against their original Nuer peers as well. "When they come to Leer and do all these things, they come as 'Dinka,'"[79] explained the gunshot survivor from Leer.[80]

Ethnic defection did not equate to the perpetrator's' literal integration into the Dinka, especially given the supremacist ideology of the Dinka hardliners. Yet the perpetrators did not come up with it on their own. This was communicated to them—whether explicitly, as victims posited ("they were instructed by the county commissioner to do that"), or implicitly.[81] Either way, it was the result of a command.

Both ethnic defection and miscuing were expressions of the perpetrators' attempt to navigate the war socially. Ethnic affiliation worked as a kind of social radar: something to hold on to to make the most of this war or just survive it. From the government's side, Juba was implementing the same strategy as Khartoum in the last war: playing Nuer groups against each other to weaken the opposition (IO) and displacing Nuer populations to secure control over the oil fields. A Nuer civilian from Jonglei, at the time in Unity state, noted, "It's as if the Dinka wanted the Nuer to have internal problems. Last time, the Arabs did the same. They tell you, 'You're my friend,' they give you a gun, ammunition, and then, 'Go and fight your friend.'"[82]

Nuer communities under attack took full measure of the ethnocracy's role in coordinating the attacks against them. They chose to express this by calling the perpetrators "Dinka Jagei" and "Dinka Bul."[83] While countering the government narrative of a Nuer civil war, this name-calling of perpetrators also marked the success of the government's divisive strategy of the Nuer, resulting in the unravelling of Nuer groupness and the eroding of overarching Nuer ethnicity.

The Nuer perpetrators disassociated themselves so much that they tried to force—at least rhetorically—ethnic conversion upon their victims. They threatened to kill civilians who refused to say that they were Dinka ("call yourself Dinka, otherwise I'll kill you").[84] In doing so, they were professing Dinka ethnic domination. Yet these Nuer perpetrators still differed from the Dinka perpetrators of the December 2013 Juba massacre, who had offered no chance at Dinka conversion at all to their victims. This was consistent with the government's polarizing strategy, which through violent cooptation chipped away at Nuer groupness.

Finally, the fact the Bul Nuer and Jagei Nuer were both trying to secure their place in Nuer hierarchy in the context of local-national alliances most likely made them more compliant than Dinka perpetrators (more present in the first campaign) in fulfilling the objectives of the Dinka ethnocracy. In other words, anxious about their own status, subcontracted Nuer perpetrators were overzealous. A woman from Koch explained: "Among them, there are Dinka . . . The Bul Nuer want to be appreciated by Salva Kiir . . . They want to be appreciated by their boss for killing people."[85] This overzealeousness by local perpetrators, often watched or coordinated by a few regular SPLA Dinka soldiers, thus contributed to a crescendo in violence, in both scale and frequency. Between 2014 and 2015, the population of the Bentiu UN POC nearly tripled to reach over 140,000 people, while households in Unity state got 20 percent smaller.[86]

Intent to Destroy

GROUPISM

The flip side of the Nuer perpetrators' ethnic defection to the Dinka was that they targeted their victims by associating Nuer ethnic identity with rebellion—with Machar's IO.[87] In doing so, they revived the old negative ethnic stereotype about the Nuer (*nyagat*, rebels) that had plagued the SPLA in the second civil war.

This association between Nuer ethnicity and rebellion was a form of groupism that differentiated the perpetrators from their victims. Nuer civilians, so long as they were choosing not to live in garrison towns and villages with perpetrators identifying themselves as Dinka, were considered a "rebel group" to be eliminated. "The government says, 'These Nuer people are rebels,'" explained a civilian from Leer.[88] Another man from Rubkona related, "The SPLA tells people, 'If you leave town, we consider you IO, we kill you and we take your cows.'"[89] According to a young woman from Leer, "The people who are not staying with them (the government's side) are considered rebels. If they find you, they kill you."[90]

The only way for a man not to be killed while exiting "legally" was to disprove his given rebel identity through an official piece of paper signed by a government official and showed at a checkpoint.[91] This was reminiscent of the killings at checkpoints during the Juba massacre of December 2013. The only difference now was that the men manning those checkpoints were Nuer and not Dinka. But they identified as Dinka and their Nuer victims identified them as Dinka too.

INTENT TO KILL

For the victims, it was clear that the attacks were meant to kill, not just loot or scare into submission. Perpetrators often outnumbered their victims in these attacks.[92] Civilians were so keenly aware of their perpetrators' intent to kill them that they did not build barges or canoes for fear of helping the SPLA troops to reach them into the swamps.[93] Speaking of attacks in Leer county (in Thonyor and Thurial) in August 2015, a Nuer civilian who fled to an island recalled, "Attacks were not about taking cattle, they were about raping, killing. From 6am they attacked, and people fled to the swamps. If they found a girl or woman, they take her. If they found a man, they shoot him."[94] Old people were not spared either: "The youth flees and leaves the elderly behind," two women from Leer narrated. "So when they come, they kill the old people. Whenever they find someone in Leer, they kill him/her, whether from IO or not."[95]

Other civilians from Leer recounted how "the SPLA gathered people in one house and burnt it."[96] "Sometimes they hung people, beat them with guns, and collected people to burn them."[97] Such extreme violence did not just affect Leer county: for example, less than an hour's car ride from Bentiu, in a town named Ding-Ding in Rubkona county, Bul Nuer troops, after shooting down civilians, also hung six people up the village tree in May 2015: three women and three men. The dehumanizing character of the violence was not lost on the victims: "I wonder," asked another man from Leer, "when these people come and get you—is that a person or an animal that they kill like that? Has the world forgotten we're human beings?"[98]

COMPROMISING SURVIVAL

Annihilating violence and a scorched-earth policy inducing starvation indicated an intent to destroy the group of Nuer civilians defined as "rebels" by the perpetrators. The fact that perpetrators did everything to compromise the victims' survival manifested their intent to kill, this time by attrition.[99] They left nothing behind for the civilians to survive. They took the cattle, burned the food they did not take with them, and destroyed humanitarian material (including seeds, medical equipment, and drugs) to diminish these communities' chances at survival. They burned a lot (if not most) of the houses in these counties, along with food supplies they did not loot.[100] They looted the civilians' clothes, down to their shoes. Some civilians fled in their underwear.

Those who managed to escape and tried to head north to the UN POC had to walk for days, weeks, or months, depending on the route. They faced SPLA attacks on the road, resulting in looting, killing, and rapes. While the UN POC offered shelter, the trick for civilians from central and southern Unity was to make it there alive. A woman from Guit recounted how out of her group of a hundred civilians who fled her county in May 2015, "they [Dinka soldiers] killed twenty of us after hunting us down on the road."[101] Another woman recounted, "We saw them, they wanted to kill us, we ran away again."[102]

As a result, families scattered to multiply their chances at survival.[103] A Nuer civilian from Leer described how he dispersed his seventeen children: "Seven are still there [in Leer county's swamps], ten are here [in Bentiu POC]. I was hiding on some island."[104] Another woman from Rubkona related the same survival tactics: "Some of my children remained in Jazeera. My husband is in the bush with them."[105]

By May, the counties of Guit, Koch, Mayendit, and Leer risked famine. A young woman from Leer explained, "There's nothing to eat . . . There's no food to eat and killing is still going on."[106] The only reason why the international monitoring body of food emergencies, the Integrated Phase Classification (IPC), did not declare famine then was that bodies could not be accessed and counted in this war zone.[107]

Yet the implications were clear to the civilians from southern Unity: "People who are still in the swamps, hunger will kill them," those of Leer predicted.[108] Indeed, some starved, others drowned—especially young girls.[109] "The heaviest cost of war is on adults, who channel all the resources to children," explained an aid worker in Unity. "And the cost of war is especially heavy on pregnant women."[110] The attrition of Nuer civilians in the swamps crippled the group and obliterated its demographic future. "There's no household who hasn't lost a relative," said a civilian who fled Leer.[111]

Civilians in the swamps also still faced government attacks, as a Nuer refugee on an island in late July 2015 reported: "They attacked from Leer the people in swamps, in the islands."[112] Some people, desperate for food and hoping to cultivate, returned to their villages. They were immediately exposed to new waves of attacks by different armed groups, sometimes minutes after they had arrived.

Consequently, in 2015, mortality rates exceeded twice the emergency threshold, and that was still a conservative estimate. The United Nations Office for the Coordination of Humanitarian Affairs (UNOCHA) calculated that, among the twenty-four communities it had accessed (the equivalent of a quarter of the population of Unity state), a total of 10,553 people had died over the course of the year. This figure included 7,165 violent deaths and 829 deaths from drowning. The 7,165 violent deaths were just the tip of the iceberg and did not factor in sexual violence.[113]

GENOCIDAL RAPE

Yet sexual violence killed, crippled, and displaced the Nuer as a group during both military campaigns in Unity state. The perpetrators' intent to destroy the group through rape was clear. This is what made those rapes genocidal.[114]

During the first campaign, government and JEM troops raped women in particularly cruel ways, for example sticking a woman's dead baby's arm into her vagina.[115] In Leer, rapes were followed by acts of forced cannibalism and killing.[116] Rapists aimed to rape as many women as possible. They used stones, guns, and sticks to rape their victims. They meant to destroy women's reproductive capacity, and victims often died from gang rapes. The mental toll on the victims and their communities was evident and affected them physically too.[117]

Rape continued to be used as a tool for genocide in the second military campaign of Unity. Most women raped were still gang-raped, following threats of murder and beatings.[118] Rape was a collective punishment on the Nuer group: "They call civilians 'people from Riek Machar.' That's why they rape," explained a woman from Koch. "It's to punish the women."[119]

The intent to kill was still clear in those rapes. A young woman raped by two Bul Nuer soldiers in Guit, related, "They saw people, they grabbed me, they said, 'If you run, we'll kill you.'"[120] "They tell the women, 'If you don't want us, we'll kill you,'" two other women from Leer reported. "And rape is another way of killing civilians. It's not only one person who rapes—it's ten. Sometimes the women die."[121] In fact, the number of perpetrators could exceed ten. "My mother died of rape in May 2015," recounted a young woman from Koch. "She was raped in May by twenty men from the Bul Nuer militias."[122]

Gang-rapes were often succeeded by torture, murder, or death from rape injuries. "One person was raped by ten men, and later on, when they finished with her, they killed her," attested women from Leer. "It happened a lot, every day."[123] Another woman from Koch proclaimed, "Rape is a form of killing. Rape is killing the community."[124] Gang-rapes were often witnessed by others and done in public, intended as a performance, with some of the victims too injured to leave their village. SPLA soldiers gang-raped both women (including pregnant women) and female children, and castrated both men and boys. Bul Nuer troops also consistently threatened women they had just raped that other troops would come later to kill them if they did not leave.[125]

Therefore, rape was both "torture and a form of killing."[126] The association of rape with killing was so strong that women from age fifteen all the way into their sixties were considered a liability on the road paved with SPLA ambushes.[127] Indeed, any male civilian who refused to surrender cattle and female relatives was considered an IO supporter who should be annihilated.

Nuer men and boys were also the targets of genocidal sexual and gender-based violence. Men were being killed for being men, considered potential IO recruits. They were especially targeted by killings, and many fewer survived the journey to the UN POC in 2015 than in 2014.[128] They were more likely to be killed immediately than women, who were gang-raped and killed, or died later of rape injuries.[129]

The use of rape as a tool of genocide did not stop once women reached the POC. Forced to reexit the camp in search of firewood to cook food provided by aid agencies, they met the perpetrators again: "When you go out, they rape you, they beat you, they kill you. The women who are raped outside the POC, some of them come back, but some of them are killed."[130]

The state did not just use rape to destroy its victims. Indeed, as in other contexts such as Sierra Leone, gang-rapes were meant to redress low cohesion among diverse and forcibly recruited troops.[131] They solidified ties among perpetrators by diffusing responsibility from the individual to the group. These rapes were so systematic that they amounted to a collective "job," or "task": "These people, when they come, they catch the ladies. If the ladies run, they shoot," explained a woman gang-raped in Guit by Bul Nuer soldiers. "These were SPLA soldiers with uniforms . . . about ten other women were raped with me, next to one another, outside the houses."[132] The performance of tasks is typically the most efficient at binding groups—more than collective trauma, for example.[133] Here, these gang-rape tasks meant to involve as many soldiers as possible. Another woman from Rubkona recounted, "I was raped while 9 months pregnant . . . The attackers wore military uniforms . . . Four other women were raped as well. Only one of these men did not take part in the raping."[134]

Mass collective rape thus made groups—that of the perpetrators, and that of the victims. It reinforced group cohesion among the Bul Nuer and other Nuer armed youth, not immune to in-group policing and forced recruitment.[135] It also reinforced the victim groups' cohesion, who now refused to marry from within the perpetrators' groups.[136]

Mass gang-rapes also participated in the process of ethnic ranking within the state and among Nuer sections. Indeed, the women from Leer were most frequently gang-raped, followed by women from other counties; by contrast, the Bul Nuer women from Mayom, associated with the government, were least frequently raped. This was a demonstration of group worth, with real demographic implications.

Gang-rapes were an expression of Bul Nuer group entitlement, through both the acquisition and the destruction of women's individual bodies, and as such they were also a form of conquest. Perpetrators raped, abducted, and killed pregnant women and breastfeeding mothers, induced labor in dramatic conditions, and separated mothers from young babies left to die.[137] Perpetrators spread HIV as well, which even if unintentional would still contribute in the long run to the demographic destruction of the victim group.[138]

The rape and killing of women and the abduction of young women and girls destroyed the collective material wealth of the other Nuer sections—especially the Dok Nuer—since women represented wealth in cattle through bridewealth exchange. "They take the girls and kill the mother. You look for the cows, you look for the girls," explained a Nuer civilian from Bentiu. "The girls, you'll take them. You kill the mother, you'll take the children. Small boys, you kill . . . Anyone big, you kill them."[139] Perpetrators accumulated labor and capital supporting their group ascension.[140] "More children mean strength: militarily, politically, and raiding will be easier," recounted a Nuer civilian from Leer. "They [the Bul Nuer] think that they can have more children and more power."[141] The same applied to the Koch youth: "The armed youth gets the benefit of birthing a new generation with the women they captured, without paying any dowry," attested a man from Leer.[142]

Expanding the Dinka Conquest: From Ten to Twenty-Eight States

The second genocidal phase in Unity also expanded the Dinka conquest. Indeed, mass displacement of Nuer civilians from central and southern Unity state freed up space for the SPLA to move in—similar to the first phase of genocidal violence in Juba.

The goal of government attacks was not to defeat the underarmed, underfunded, and undermanned IO, but to uproot civilians of the "wrong" ethnicity, packed in the UN POC or in the bush and swamps, and to capture their land. It was clear that "the government's rhetoric that IO surrounds Bentiu is meant to allow the SPLA to go attack the villages."[143] Aid workers on the ground at the time of the second military campaign (2015) noticed that "on the way to Koch, the schools are empty, the villages are empty. The oil refineries are empty. The SPLA moved in and around it."[144] A man from Rubkona who survived being shot explained, "The government wants to clear off the area. Civilians in the POC know that . . . they know that nowhere is safe."[145]

In addition to the involvement of Dinka SPLA soldiers from the Bahr El Ghazal region in most attacks, Dinka civilians—including from the northern part of Unity—tagged along: "People who're not soldiers, who are Dinka but not SPLA, came to take civilians' clothes, to loot. They also come from Pariang, and Abiemnohm, these Dinka."[146] Civilians were reluctant to leave their homes, even under deadly attacks, precisely "because they want to protect their land," observed an aid worker in southern Unity.[147]

In Bentiu, SPLA soldiers and their families quickly moved into the homes of civilians who fled to the POC. Nuer civilians noticed that "Dinka from Wau, Pariang, Bor, Aweil, Abienmnohm, and Rumbek" came to settle, encouraged by the Dinka Division 4 commander Deng Wol, from Warrap.[148] Those who refused to move to the POC to protect their homes had to contend with threats, violence, curfews, and night searches by SPLA soldiers.[149]

Among Dinka sections, the Dinka from northern Unity benefited from a decree passed unilaterally by Kiir on October 2, 2015, in violation of South Sudan's Transitional Constitution.[150] This decree redivided South Sudan from ten into twenty-eight states. Government rhetoric held that the redivision of South Sudan would mitigate conflict through power devolution to the people. Kiir's legal advisor repeatedly referred to the SPLA leader John Garang's moto of "taking the towns to the people" to dress this reform in legitimate attire and appeal to Garang's followers.[151]

In fact, the twenty-eight states decree consolidated the ethnocrats' military power on the ground and accelerated resource accumulation to advance the Dinka conquest. This fait accompli was an attempt to behead IO through a system of cooptation, before any implementation of the peace agreement (ARCSS) signed in August 2015 between Kiir and Machar.

Ambrose Riiny Thiik, the JCE chairman, was one of the speakers at the only public debate on the twenty-eight states in Juba, even though he no longer was chief justice. He vocally expressed his opposition to the August 2015 peace agreement "imposed" by the international community while seated next to the presidential legal advisor.[152] This spoke volumes about the role of the JCE in the twenty-eight states decree, yet it was impossible to date this expansionist plan of the Dinka land.

In effect, the twenty-eight states decree amounted to an expansion of Dinka territory while pushing non-Dinka communities out of their homeland through violence: to the UN POCs, to the bush, or to neighboring countries. Unity state was a case in point. There, the twenty-eight states decree pushed the boundary of Dinka land south. It expanded the Dinka Abiemnohm and Pariang counties in northern Unity, united them into a new Dinka state called "Ruweng" encroaching southward on Mayom (Bul Nuer land), Guit, and Rubkona county. "Abiemnohm and Pariang will try to take the river down to Kilo Talatin (Kilo 30)," explained two civilians from Bentiu. "It will become part of Pariang. So land in Rubkona will be taken. This twenty-eight states decree will change colonial borders."[153] A former Nuer oil worker from Rubkona noted, "Unity oil fields belong to Rubkona. Manga belongs to Guit. Both are taken by Pariang county.

Kaikang in Mayom has oil wells [wells dug, but not connected]. This is also taken by Abiemnohm."[154]

The twenty-eight states decree was "all about the oil and the land," in the words of a civil society member.[155] This created anxiety even among the subcontracted Nuer perpetrators, especially the Bul Nuer. The victims recognized this conquest: "Kiir wants the oil-producing areas to be owned by the Dinka people," said women who escaped from Leer. "That's why they're killing us."[156] "Kiir wants to take the oil of Rubkona, to Dinka land," noted another civilian from Rubkona. "The same thing is happening in Malakal."[157]

Indeed, there was a pattern. Not only was it reminiscent of Khartoum's displacement of Nuer civilians in the last civil war through the SSDF.[158] What happened in Unity state also prefigured another genocidal phase in the other oil-rich state of Upper Nile, this time against the Shilluk, shortly after the full start of the Equatorian campaign.[159] Violence in Upper Nile had not yet reached its apex. But there, the twenty-eight states decree also encroached on oil-rich traditional Shilluk land in the capital of Malakal.

Therefore, the subcontracted Nuer perpetrators who uttered a rhetoric rooted in exclusionary Dinka ideology and acted under the watch of a few Dinka soldiers served the expansion of the Dinka conquest while pursuing their own group ascension. They contributed to expand the Dinka conquest by waging violence—including rape, the equivalent of "planting a flag" on another man's territory.[160] Violence eliminated civilians and crammed them in the UN POC and in the swamps, thus freeing their land both for the government to exploit oil and for the local Dinka, who were the minority group in the mostly Nuer Unity state, to expand their territory.

Unity's War Economy

Predatory wealth accumulation was part of the expanding conquest and increased with violence and displacement. Government troops consistently pillaged the homes and looted the cattle of civilians in their *luaks* (cattle barns) and their cattle camps. In May 2015, armed Bul Nuer youth, supported by the SPLA, raided and plundered cattle from every county in southern Unity except Panyjaar (too far down south) and most of Mayendit, which was looted by SPLA soldiers and armed youth coming in south from Lakes.[161] Cattle looting continued for the rest of the year and afterwards, as the armed youth from Koch played an increasing role in violence. The raiders amassed the looted cattle in their own cattle camps.[162]

Beneficiaries included the county commissioners coordinating the attacks and providing troops.[163] The division of the looted cattle followed precise rules of allocation. "A list even circulates every day to distribute the cattle depending on ranks," a Nuer civilian explained. "Wal Yach gets fifteen, the Koch commissioner gets twenty, Khor Gatmai gets fifteen. The rest is taken by the youth. Paul Malong takes his share from the governor of Unity. The share to the state governor is not given in name to a particular person, but to an office, a department."[164]

The county commissioners all quickly expanded their kinship networks thanks to these profitable genocidal campaigns.[165] Looted cattle went up to the governor of Unity state—the Bul Nuer Joseph Monytuil—who reallocated some of his share to the central government in Juba. The looted cattle also made its way to the Bul Nuer SPLA leadership in Bentiu, with numbers tattooed on the looted cattle distinguishing who owned what.[166] The armed local youth was last in getting its share, after part of the cattle was traded.[167]

Of course, it was impossible to know for certain how many cattle each of those stakeholders received after each raid. But the estimate of twenty cattle delivered to the Koch commissioner Koang Biel was in the realm of possibilities.[168] The Koch youth was very frequently involved in raids. In June 2015 alone, they raided Leer eleven times.[169] They seemed to raid more than once a week—say two to three times a week. If averaged to 2.5 raids per week, over a six month-period, Biel could have accumulated 1,200 heads of cattle. With a low estimate of cattle price (US$80 per head of cattle), this meant a biannual revenue of $96,000—or $192,000 over a year.[170] This is likely an underestimate, and to the political elite it was pocket money.

Predatory wealth accumulation continued to be ethnically differentiated. Even someone like Biel had to contend with a hierarchy reflecting Nuer ethnic ranking in the distribution of looted cattle between the county commissioners. All the county commissioners paid tribute in looted cattle to the Bul Nuer.[171] This tribute was both for military support and as a form of racketeering reminiscent of wartime SSDF and SPLA practices. This was typical of a state-building process, and logical since the Bul Nuer dominated the state administration in Unity. Therefore, cattle looting and its conversion into tribute enriched the Bul Nuer the most out of all the Nuer subcontracted by the government. This consolidated the Bul Nuer dominant class constituted in the second civil war. In doing so, it also reinforced Nuer ethnic ranking. But the trade of looted cattle, especially between the Bul Nuer and the Dinka, also continued to illustrate shared dominant class interests between the two ethnic groups.

The capture of Nuer civilians' resources was highly profitable. Cattle were so abundant that those not feeding the troops thus had to be sold as quickly as possible or moved for grazing and health.[172] The trade of looted cattle from Leer and other counties involved several intermediaries. While still at the site of the attacks, the various perpetrators resold the cattle they looted to traders, mostly

Bul Nuer.[173] Those traders transported it to Bentiu and then Mayom to sell to Bul Nuer buyers from Mayom and to Dinka buyers from Warrap and from Abiemn-ohm and Pariang counties in northern Unity state.

Of course, it was impossible to separate the traders from the SPLA. "Some traders are still with the SPLA, they're the ones buying these looted cattle," explained women from Leer.[174] "Without support from the government [the SPLA]," said two civilians from Bentiu, "they could not have traded."[175] "The government has all the cows!" proclaimed other civilians. "The majority of the traders are from Mayom, and then the wealthy soldiers buy the cows. They're usually from Bul Nuer and Dinka, and Toro Boro (JEM): they are all buying the bulls." Wealthy soldiers were especially Bul and Dinka from both Mayom and Warrap, Kiir's home state.[176] They shared the same dominant class interests, resting on the same types of predatory and ethnically differentiated wealth accumulation, which shaped discourses of extreme group entitlement.

"Some [looted] cattle also reach Juba," a Nuer civilian from Leer explained. "And Aneth, between Abyei and Abiemnohm—that's where the Arabs and Dar-furi come to take the cattle."[177] The "Arab" (Messiriya and Darfuri) and Dinka traders from Northern Bahr El Ghazal and Warrap thus congregated in this SPLA-run market of Aneth in Abyei (near Warrap), and in the markets of Agok, Mayom, Pariang, and Abiemnohm.[178] Some of the looted cattle eventually wound up in Sudan via Abyei and then Darfur and Southern Kodofan. Northern Baggara traders cooperated with Bul Nuer traders to transport and sell the looted cattle to the Omdurman cattle market, famous for trading looted cattle in the last war.[179] Thus the perpetrators reactivated the last war's economic networks.

Launching the Third Phase in Equatoria

A genocidal mode of production, resting on ethnic supremacy and consisting of annihilating predation and a profitable war economy, contributed to precipitate the third genocidal phase. The SPLA brought some of the cattle looted en masse from Unity state into Western and then Central Equatoria via Lakes state to graze and to protect and aggrandize the Dinka elite's herds.[180]

The routing of the looted Nuer cattle by Dinka cattle herders and the SPLA into Western Equatoria was the first step toward further expanding the Dinka conquest, this time into Equatoria. The problem was that the local Moro (Equatorian) from Mundri (Western Equatoria), were already frustrated with the Dinka. Grievances dated back to the last war and worsened after December 2013.[181] Still, the Moro noticed the change in 2015: "There's more cattle now, because they take it and loot it." Unity state's cattle also wound up in Wonduruba, in Central

Equatoria, south of Mundri and Juba. As the SPLA brought the looted cattle from Unity on their land, both the Moro (from Mundri) and the Pojulu (from Wonduruba) started joining the IO.[182]

They had good reasons: with the SPLA came the Dinka cattle herders from Lakes and Warrap who benefited from its protection and who started raiding the Equatorians' cattle too.[183] Again, it seemed impossible to really distinguish the cattle herders from the SPLA. A Pojulu man from Wonduruba whose cattle was raided said, "The Dinka have taken on the cattle . . . The Dinka out in the bush with cattle also have the SPLA uniform . . . There are many men keeping the cattle. They have weapons, even the big guns—PKMs, RPGs, Kalashnikovs." The Dinka cattle herders came with their families, the Pojulu man noticed: "They keep the cattle in groups and with their wives and children, they reach about fifty people . . . There are many cattle, even with women and children. They're all Dinka."[184]

As the SPLA was trying to bring its cattle from Western Equatoria (Mundri) into Central Equatoria (Yei county), it continued to route the cattle deeper into Western Equatoria, to Maridi. "Mundri was the first place to blow up," explained two civilians. "It was on May 27, 2015." This was right at the height of the second military campaign in Unity state, with mass cattle raiding. "There was a lot of cattle brought [into Equatoria] by the Dinka. People started resisting because the cattle was destroying the crops and people were shot after protesting. This led to the formation of militias to resist."[185] An inhabitant from Mundri West, whose crops were trampled on by cattle, explained: "When we said something, the Dinka fought us . . . It started in April 2015. . . people started joining the IO because the government supported the cattle keepers . . . From Mundri, it affected Maridi and Yambio."[186] Fighting between the SPLA, its cattle herders, and the local inhabitants joining IO, the Arrow Boys, or some other militia engulfed Mundri, Maridi, and Yambio from June 2015 onward.

As a result, the SPLA moved cattle again, both expanding its conquest and frustrating the locals. Dinka SPLA soldiers and associated Dinka cattle herders and their families all made their way into Yei county from Maridi. "They—the SPLA—were coming with lines of cattle, on their way to Central Equatoria," a bemused civilian recalled. "The cattle were [walking] with the children and women—especially Dinka"—symbolic of the expanding Dinka conquest. "People in Yei heard that they were coming with big lorries and started to become angry."[187] By September 2015, war had spread to Western Equatoria and tensions were mounting in Central Equatoria.

Meanwhile, the international community had pressured IO and the government into signing a peace agreement in August 2015 (ARCSS). Kiir expressed serious reservations about it after it was plainly rejected by the JCE. IO, wary of

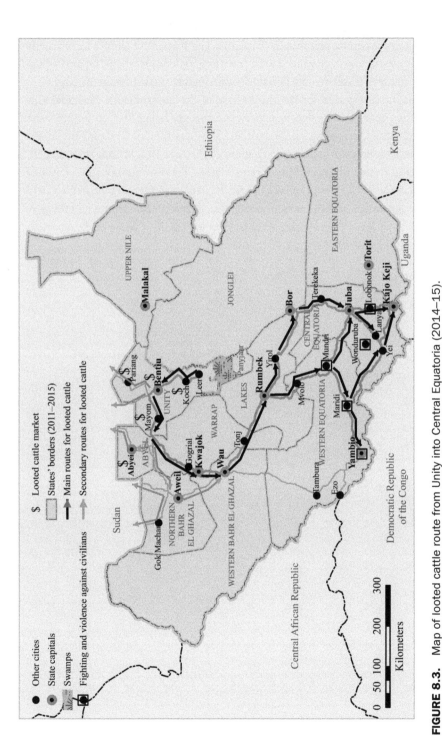

FIGURE 8.3. Map of looted cattle route from Unity into Central Equatoria (2014–15).

another military confrontation and massacre in Juba, especially with Machar's return, increased its presence in Equatoria. The imprint of Unity's looted cattle on Equatorian land, combined with increased violence by the SPLA and Dinka cattle herders, frustrated the Equatorians enough to push them to the edge.

Equatoria was ripe for the third phase of the government's genocidal violence. Extreme violence started in Western Equatoria in late May–June 2015—the looted cattle's trampling on Equatorian crops was the last straw for the locals. Violence escalated in September–October 2015, when Paul Malong ordered helicopter gunships to attack Mundri and Maridi. Yet it would take the arrival of Machar and his IO troops in Juba in March 2016, implementing the August 2015 peace agreement, and the subsequent fighting between these troops and the government in July 2016 to precipitate the apex of this third phase of the genocide in Central Equatoria.

THE THIRD PHASE OF THE GENOCIDE IN EQUATORIA

2015–17

The rippling effects of the second genocidal phase in Unity state contributed to launch the third phase in Central Equatoria. All three phases illustrated a transference phenomenon from one phase to the next—not just in triggering violence in the next location but also in repeating acts of genocidal violence (such as forced anthropophagy, genocidal gang-rapes, or killing checkpoints meant to sort out non-Dinka civilians, to name but a few). But while the second phase was largely subcontracted, the perpetrators of the third were overwhelming Dinka, as this chapter shows.

This chapter explores the articulation of the Dinka supremacist ideology in this third genocidal phase and how it justified the perpetrators' genocidal conquest. Its components became especially evident when the government was not able to subcontract genocidal violence to local co-opted armed groups. This exclusionary ideology was not new. But Dinka perpetrators grew emboldened in the Equatoria region in 2015, before the start of the third genocidal phase in 2016. Until then, the Equatorians had mostly stayed out of this war. But they were not simple bystanders either.

The Equatorians in the Beginning of the Third Civil War

At the beginning of the conflict, some Equatorian civilians had welcomed the fleeing Nuer into their homes, and some Equatorian SPLA soldiers had tried to

FIGURE 9.1.   Bodies of civilians killed during the July 2016 battle of Juba lie wrapped in plastic bags for burial. Photo taken on July 16, 2016, on Yei Road, near Checkpoint Market, by Jason Patinkin.

stand between their Dinka peers and Nuer civilians. "In Juba already in December 2013, and Yei and Kajo Keji, already IO had sympathizers," explained a Kakwa civil society member from Yei, "because the Equatorians saw killings and massacres."[1] The Equatorians, although reluctant to get involved, felt much more sympathy for the Nuer than for the Dinka. They had grievances rooted in the past war's Dinka protoconquest cemented after 2005. Besides, the Juba massacre and its resounding effect in other towns made it clear to other minority groups that killing non-Dinka civilians was deemed acceptable and even encouraged by the violent Dinka state. It was incredibly swift, which suggested planning for at least a military confrontation, and it set a precedent for the systematic state killing of non-Dinka people.

Yet Equatorians understood the mounting tensions culminating into the third war to have been caused not so much by greed but rather by the ancient ethnic hatred and political competition between the Dinka and the Nuer. There were, in the beginning, very few Equatorians among the IO.[2] Most of the Equatorians wanted to be left out of the violent competition with Kiir's faction. "As time went on, we were looking at Dinka and Nuer as one and the same, and we were buying time and looking for an ally," a Kakwa civil society member said.[3]

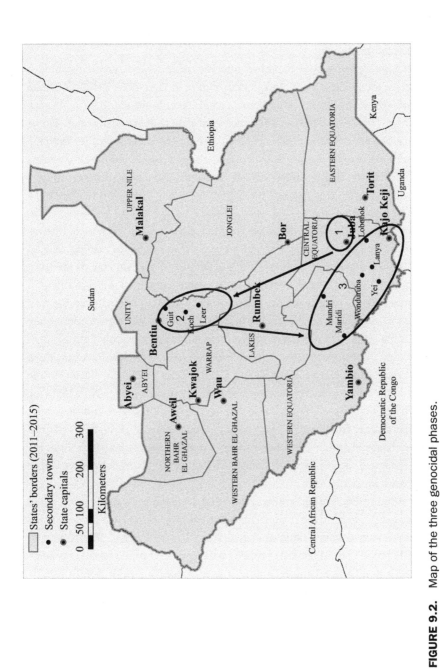

FIGURE 9.2. Map of the three genocidal phases.

The Equatorians, who had seen it all play out before with the 1991 split, were hoping to collect the crumbs of whatever would be left once the Dinka and Nuer had fought it out. In other words, this was not their war. Yet they also were victims of the state. The Equatorians were at the very bottom of the Dinka ethnic ranking because they were not considered a threat by the Dinka and as such they were not worth accommodating.

The Equatorians would be drawn into the conflict, whether they wanted it or not. As soon as the conflict exploded in Juba in December 2013, the Dinka elite brought its cattle and cattle herders from Lakes to the south, into Western Equatoria. This created tensions and increased state violence against non-Dinka civilians perceived as potential dissenters.[4] It only got worse with the repercussions of massive cattle looting in Unity state, when the SPLA and the Dinka elite's cattle herders and their families brought the looted cattle into Western and then Central Equatoria. This marked the beginning of the expansion of the Dinka conquest into Equatoria.

Aware of Equatorian sympathies for the Nuer and of increased frustration with Dinka cattle herders, the SPLA leadership wanted to take no risk. So it rotated the Equatorian soldiers of SPLA Division 2 very quickly to the front lines of the Greater Upper Nile region in 2014 and accelerated this movement in September 2015—right when the situation was becoming untenable in Western Equatoria.[5] A Pojulu trader lamented that the "Yei youth was taken to Unity state to be in the SPLA—75 percent of the youth in 2014. There was big fighting there and we don't know if our boys are alive."[6] Ethnic ranking in the SPLA continued on the front lines, just as it had in the decades since 1983. This meant, in the words of an Equatorian SPLA soldier who defected from Upper Nile, that "the majority of Dinka have higher ranks and so they're all relatives and they don't send them to the front lines."[7] The wife of an Equatorian SPLA soldier explained that her husband and his ethnic comrades "complain about being in front of the other Dinka, so they die first. So there is a lot of loss of life in the greater Upper Nile region for Equatorians."[8]

By rotating Equatorian soldiers, the SPLA leadership meant to prevent IO from gaining ground in the region. It also wanted to decapitate any serious armed rebellion trying to defend Equatorian land from the conquering SPLA troops and Dinka herders. The Equatorian soldier's wife explained of her husband's comrades, "Most of them are located in the greater Upper Nile region because otherwise they will turn away from the SPLA if they're located in Equatoria . . . There are very few desertions because the sites Bentiu and Malakal are very risky to escape, and it's difficult to reach out to Equatoria."[9] "This was a policy," believed the Pojulu man, "because we didn't have youth to protect us."[10]

The rotation of these Equatorian SPLA soldiers into this region was likely intended to free up space for a third genocidal phase. Indeed, while the Equatorian soldiers were assigned to the Greater Upper Nile region, fighting a war they did not consider was theirs against the Nuer, they were told that they would be next.[11] Equatorian civilians who stayed in Yei were told the same thing.[12] Several factors contributed to launch this third genocidal phase—most notably the July 2016 fighting in Juba between IO and the SPLA. But the bottom line is that the very conceptualization of this third genocidal phase was already there among Dinka SPLA troops in early 2014, to the extent that some low-level Dinka soldiers communicated it to other low-level Equatorian SPLA soldiers on the front lines.[13]

Western and Central Equatoria in 2015

Of course, in 2014, this third phase was still just an idea, and waging genocidal violence at the same time in both Unity and Equatoria was not a good idea, nor was it feasible—or necessary—yet. Yet in 2015, violence took on genocidal attributes in Western and Central Equatoria. It started in May 2015 in Mundri and in June in Maridi, when local inhabitants started joining local rebel groups (including the well-known local militia of the Arrow Boys, subcontracted by the SPLA to defend territory against LRA incursions in 2010) out of frustration with having their land trampled on by the SPLA and its cattle.[14] The SPLA, a mix of Tiger, Commando, and Division 6, retaliated violently.[15] "They already started burning houses in the morning (on June 8, 2015) and shooting any person non-Dinka," explained civilians who fled.[16]

The perpetrators deployed the Dinka supremacist ideology they later used in Central Equatoria (explored more at length later). A civilian from Mundri, who protested having the Dinka herders' cattle trample his land, related, "They said: 'It's us who fought with the Arabs to lead South Sudan' . . . 'Don't talk, we're the ones to be your leaders, not you. You're not to lead us.'"[17]

The key elements of the perpetrators' Dinka supremacist ideology were thus already articulated in 2015 in Western Equatoria. Dinka group legitimacy, strengthened in 2005–13, culminated in extreme group Dinka entitlement. This justified conquest through the denationalization of non-Dinka groups and the myth of a Dinka "master race": "They say the Equatorians have no land, that we're from Uganda. They say that the land of Equatoria is not mine—it's theirs. They say South Sudan is for them, that I'm not South Sudanese."[18]

At the time, the replacement and imprisonment of the popular Western Equatoria state governor (Joseph Bakassoro) by Salva Kiir in July–August 2015 created further resentment, and accelerated recruitment into the local militia of the

Arrow Boys in Western Equatoria, who declared allegiance to IO.[19] Men from Western Equatoria were now caught in the same bind as their peers in Unity state: they either joined the opposition or faced government violence. "The SPLA collects people from Western Equatoria—young men—and they're never seen afterwards," explained a civil society member.[20]

Things went from bad to worse in Western Equatoria after the passing of the twenty-eight states decree on October 2, 2015. The day after, the government imposed a strict curfew on Yambio, the state capital, after sporadic gunfire erupted in town. Fighting between local opposition groups and the SPLA engulfed Mundri east and west and Maridi on October 4–7, 2015.[21] Civilians perceived that SPLA Dinka soldiers, with large herds of cattle, were coming to take their land to graze it.[22] The crisis threatened to spread to Yei in Central Equatoria.[23]

The situation deteriorated in neighboring parts of Central Equatoria too—especially in Lanya county, where Mathiang Anyoor arrived in 2014 and increased in presence in 2015, particularly in Wonduruba, Lanya town and Gerya.[24] There, the SPLA and its herders had brought cattle looted from Unity, and groups loosely affiliated with the IO gained footing under Wesley Welebe's leadership. By April 2016, an international observer warned, "In the areas between Lanya, Gerya, Mundri, and Wunduruba, the UN has absolutely no visibility—no UN patrols are allowed. In Gerya [near Juba], the SPLA attacks with helicopters."[25]

The Agreement on the Resolution of the Conflict in South Sudan (ARCSS) and the Run-up to the July 2016 Juba Fighting

But the situation did not just deteriorate in this zone because of the influx of looted cattle, the imprisonment of Bakassoro, and the twenty-eight states decree of October 2015. Indeed, the factor that would act as the strongest accelerant was the upcoming implementation of the peace agreement of August 2015 between Riek Machar and Kiir. The agreement would bring IO back to the country's capital of Juba for the first time since the December 2013 massacre. In preparation, a foreign observer recounted, "Paul Malong sent all his Dinka commandoes to Western, Central, and Eastern Equatoria for prepositioning to wait for IO to come back into the government so that it becomes impossible to form strong local militias and strong alliances between those and the IO."[26] Tiger Battalion—the Presidential Guards—also increased its presence in all three Equatorian states in 2015.[27] The security apparatus—especially the NSS—added pressure on civilians through arrests and killings in all three Equatorian states.[28]

Meanwhile, Malong was still recruiting more Dinka militias between 2014 and 2015.[29] One of these bore the name of Akher Mathar (the "last rain" in Arabic).[30] "They were recruited for the same purpose as Mathiang Anyoor," explained a

Nuer civilian, "for the 'last war.'"[31] In Dinka, the militia was called Amiath Noon, a Dinka former NSS recruit from Aweil explained: "*Noon* means grass in Dinka. Amiath Noon means stomping on the grass."[32] In other words, the militia would crush whatever opposition to the Dinka ethnocrats was hiding in the grass. "They call themselves the 'defence force for the nation,'" added a Nuer IO soldier.[33]

These recruits were reassigned to Wau and Juba, and some of them would be spotted during the fighting of July 2016 in Juba.[34] This new batch of Dinka recruits from Bahr El Ghazal was shrouded in secrecy: "For Akher Mathar, there's no exact date [of recruitment]," a Nuer civilian noted, "apart from the fact the recruitment took place between 2013 and 2015... They were trained during the peace process [ARCSS] negotiations. No one knows exactly when the graduation happened ... They have the same objective than Mathiang Anyoor: 'If we don't recruit them to protect the president, they [the Nuer] will come and finish us, we have to protect ourselves.'"[35]

The rationale remained the same: Dinka hardliners, promoting a discourse of extreme group entitlement, perceived Machar and his troops' arrival in Juba as an intolerable threat. Alluding to the new Dinka militias, a Nuer civilian in July 2016 posited that "they were sent to Juba to fight IO now ... Apparently Malong said he'd be dead before Machar can be first vice-president."[36] Whether Malong really said that or not, everyone was aware of his and the JCE's uncompromising views on ARCSS. They thought of the agreement as a disgrace, an assault on their sovereignty by the international community.

Malong made sure to block the exits to extinguish the threat. He positioned Mathiang Anyoor troops at the Ugandan and Congolese borders after the ARCSS was signed in August 2015: "A lot of Mathiang Anyoor were stationed at the border with DRC—from Kajo Keji to Western Equatoria—everywhere. There were too many!" recalled a Kakwa civil society member in Yei at the time. "That was before Riek Machar came to Juba. That's when they brought more soldiers in Lanya, Kajo Keji, and Nimule and Juba [the main target]. They knew they'd block all the ways."[37]

Civilians noticed an influx of Dinka troops in Yei after the ARCSS was signed, masquerading as students. "They came individually as town migrants. They were below twenty-five years—they were in secondary schools. Many of us taught them," said a Kakwa teacher. Such positioning of troops was reminiscent of 2012, when Dinka soldiers from Warrap came to Yei disguised as civilians. In December 2013, they were "activated" to kill Nuer civilians in Yei and Kajo-Keji. But this time in 2015, the Kakwa teacher recollected, "We were told should there be an issue, we'd be murdered at the border."[38] The Equatorians were warned.

As the presence of Dinka SPLA soldiers, Dinka militias answering to Malong, and Dinka cattle herders and their families increased in Western Equatoria and parts of Central Equatoria, so did extreme violence. The SPLA presence and violence created a coalescing opposition in Central Equatoria, which IO cultivated by sending in a few of its Nuer officers in both Western and Central Equatoria, and into which it could tap in if things turned sour after arriving in Juba as part of the peace agreement.[39] Meanwhile, emboldened Dinka soldiers openly suspected their Equatorian colleagues of treason. They went as far as shooting them, which effectively pushed some SPLA soldiers to defect (when they could) and join the opposition.[40]

The SPLA was keenly aware of IO's growing influence in Equatoria and tightened its grip over the capital. By November 2015, in Juba, a civil society member observed that "every night the SPLA and government kills people."[41] Instead of demilitarizing Juba, the SPLA was increasing its presence there in preparation for IO's arrival. Referring to the ARCSS security arrangements, the civil society member said, "The plan is to turn Mathiang Anyoor into the police so they can stay in Juba and not move away to the 25 km (15.5 miles) radius, and to bring some Dinka from Rumbek, Aweil, and Warrap, to be integrated into the National Security."[42] By February 2016, two months before IO's arrival in town, another civil society member observed that "New Site [Bilpam] and Giada [where the Presidential Guards are] are full of SPLA forces. Thousands are still there . . . The SPLA has been moving a few hundred soldiers, but there's no implementation of the security arrangements."[43] And the SPLA was not the only one in town: "The UPDF [Uganda's Popular Defense Forces] stayed in Juba, wearing civilian clothes. There are also lots of IO men coming into the Juba POC."[44] Other civilians reported that the UPDF was also given SPLA and police uniforms and patrolled the road between Juba and Nimule.[45]

Therefore, six months before the fighting in Juba, the capital was already a powder keg. "IO's return to Juba has meant about two thousand pretty well-armed Nuer troops," a foreign observer warned in June 2016. Machar went ahead with implementing the peace agreement: "Riek Machar shifted all his senior military people to Juba, he's establishing his command."[46] Of course, Machar also made sure IO's influence in Central and Western Equatoria grew to support his position and facilitate his troops' evacuation in the event of another Juba massacre.[47]

IO's arrival in Juba and rebel activity in Central Equatoria most likely helped divert the SPLA's attention from Western Equatoria. In the end, the government also had to contend with the strong local rebellion of the Arrow Boys and other satellite rebel groups linked to the IO. The government was largely unable to co-opt and subcontract local groups to the degree that it had in Unity state. Local rebel Wesley Welebe gained footing in Western Equatoria with support in Ezo and Yambio and parts of Central Equatoria (in Gerya).[48] He was helped by the strong tradition of rebellion in lush and forested Western Equatoria, where civilians had kept guns to defend themselves against the SPLA: "In Western Equatoria, most people have guns and so they could defend themselves," explained Ugandan civilians who were living at the time in Maridi and married to Equatorians. "One household can have two, three, or five guns, even anti-aircraft in their *tukuls* . . . A lot have kept the guns of the first civil war. They also have PKMs [machine guns]. The Arabs were many in Maridi County in the second civil war." Speaking of the locals, they added: "They never trusted the SPLA government."[49]

Therefore, a few factors still restrained extreme government violence. First, the government was unable to co-opt local actors as they had in Unity, and civilians were well-armed. But more important, the SPLA was being kept busy elsewhere: it had to send its Dinka troops and herders into Central Equatoria (up to Yei) to care for the looted cattle from Unity state and contain the influence of the groups loosely affiliated with IO there. It reassigned some of its Equatorian soldiers to Western Equatoria and contented itself with controlling the garrison towns and some of the main roads, giving up on the countryside (at least for now).

Yet civilians affected by extreme government violence in those parts of Western and Central Equatoria before July 2016 still felt that their area had experienced "a rehearsal" of the third genocidal phase later implemented in Central Equatoria.[50] They associated government violence with a Dinka conquest and pointed out that Mundri was rich in gold and uranium.[51] The same pattern was observed in Wau, the capital of Western Bahr El Ghazal state (home to other smaller ethnic communities such as the Balanda, the Fertit, and the Kresh), where IO had also established a presence through its influence on local rebel groups rising against the same violent Dinka conquest.[52] Government violence in Wau was extreme too. But it was still not as annihilating as the campaign about to start in Central Equatoria, because Machar and his troops were not brought to Wau but to Juba, and therefore dispersed into Central Equatoria rather than Western Bahr El Ghazal. Yet the perpetrators' discourse in both Wau and Western Equatoria in 2015 indicated that violence had the same annihilating potential as in Central Equatoria.

The Start of the Third Genocidal Phase in Equatoria

Fighting in Juba between IO and the SPLA in July 2016 would mark an escalation in ethnic violence against non-Dinka civilians. It illustrated how much more exclusionary and pervasive Dinka supremacist ideology had become since December 2013 and precipitated genocidal violence into Central Equatoria.

The Match: Fighting in Juba, July 8–11, 2016

Machar and his IO troops arrived in Juba in April 2016. By then, IO had established a strong influence and relationship with local rebel groups who fought the SPLA in Western and Central Equatoria and Western Bahr El Ghazal. From its arrival, tensions with the government in Juba escalated. In early July 2016, the IO accused the government of arresting 139 of its soldiers, killing two of them, and assassinating one of its senior officers.[53]

Tensions culminated on July 8, 2016, when fighting erupted at the Presidential Palace (J1) between Kiir's and Machar's bodyguards. It quickly engulfed the areas around J1.[54] IO could only flee south and west, into Central and Western Equatoria.[55] On July 11, Machar and his troops managed to withdraw from Juba. A Nuer civilian explained, "Now the situation for IO is very difficult . . . it experiences losses, has no reinforcement, no bullets, no big tanks . . . The only people who can help them are the Equatorians."[56] This was precisely the problem.

The international community had ignored the warning signs. The most salient was the militarization of Juba, which indicated not just bad faith on the government's side but also potential planning for another military confrontation: "CTSAM had seen that an SPLA mortar was pointed towards sites 1 and 2 where Machar was going to go when he came to Juba," remembered a foreign observer.[57] "A mortar was directly pointed towards the POC 1. Early April 2016, there were more tanks around UN House."[58]

Kiir continued to subcontract the UPDF to guarantee the SPLA's victory and his own safety.[59] "The UPDF was already surveying for tomorrow's fight," civilians in and out of Juba said.[60] The UPDF also positioned troops at the border in Nimule.[61] On July 14, a Kakwa civilian in Juba reported, "Fifteen trucks of Ugandans entered South Sudan today . . . Ugandans are saying that they're coming to evacuate the army, but in fact . . . they're bringing in more troops to help them, the Dinka."[62]

It was clear that IO was too weak, especially in the rainy season, to try taking over Juba. "The international community forced IO to come to Juba," explained a Nuer civilian, referring to the hesitation of the rebels, who had "no vehicles, no big guns, no nothing."[63] IO's influence had grown enough in Western and Central Equatoria to support a contingency plan, a worst case scenario, but not an offensive. The wives of some of Machar's soldiers, who came along to Juba, recalled, "These were all soldiers who had very good military tactics. They were expecting things to normalize when Riek came back. No one expected things to go like this."[64] If a few of them were distrustful of the government and left their families behind, the level of violence in Juba still took the majority by surprise.

The fighting in Juba continued to demonstrate just how overwhelmed the UN peacekeeping mission was. "UNMISS retaliates against attackers to protect its staff and properties," a baffled foreigner commented. "While IO is in the POC and uses it as a rear base . . . SPLA mortars have landed within the UNMISS base, in the special representative of the secretary-general's house backyard."[65] Caught in the crossfire, UN peacekeepers were unable to protect civilians within the vicinity of the base and had to engage with the SPLA to defend themselves. South Sudanese women were raped under the nose of the peacekeepers, and the international female aid workers who lived less than a few kilometers away from the UN House and were gang-raped by SPLA troops in their compound (Terrain hotel complex) on July 11 were not rescued either.[66]

Ethnic Violence during the July 2016 Fighting in Juba

Ethnically targeted killings quickly started as well, right on July 8, 2016.[67] Killings spread to various neighborhoods of Juba, targeting at first the Nuer. A civilian living in Mia Saba reported that in her neighborhood, "two Nuer boys were killed during the first day of the fighting—shot in the head."[68] The Bul Nuer wives of Machar's soldiers, some of whom narrowly escaped, attested: "Our life was in danger in Juba because we're Nuer. Many Nuer were killed. Even the women, because they're Nuer. We know one boy who was killed in the house of Nhial Gang, a businessman in Mia Saba. By the SPLA, because they knew he was Nuer."[69] Nuer men (civilians) who were married to Dinka women and who worked for the government were not spared either. To the Dinka perpetrators, their ethnicity took precedence above all else, and they were called "rebels."[70]

Yet killings soon expanded to the Equatorian group: "Civilians were killed in Jebel when they were fleeing towards Khator church; Equatorians are identified as IO and sometimes were shot in their house around Jebel."[71] Another civil society member reported that "on July 11, 2016, SPLA soldiers were searching house to house during the fighting in Gudele in Juba. One Equatorian journalist and one Nuer journalist were killed."[72] Kakwa and Kuku women living in Juba reported that "soldiers were entering houses: in Gudele, Munuki, around the Parliament, Tongping and Jebel. Those areas were destroyed, some places were set on fire. We heard of cases of executions of civilians." One of them related, "My neighbors were killed by a grenade. The soldiers put a grenade in the house, saying they were Nuer. In fact they were Equatorians." But this was no mistake: "They singled out the house . . . The Dinka know how to differentiate Nuer from Equatorians because of the marks, the scarification."[73]

To the Dinka perpetrators, Equatorians were guilty by association with the Nuer, and the troops announced their intention to kill the Equatorians. "I heard we are the next to be killed," said a Kakwa inhabitant of Juba on July 14, three days after the fighting subsided. "A threatening Dinka said to me, 'After the Nuer, you Equatorians are next.' He was a civilian and a relative to a Dinka SPLA soldier. I sensed he might have heard it from his people. They have armed relatives . . . That was the neighbor at my work place. They said they're born to rule . . . The boss is a Dinka."[74]

The same Dinka supremacist ideology expressed in 2015 in Western Equatoria, championing a "master race," persisted. This time it was manifested not by the perpetrators but by their relatives who felt emboldened. Some Equatorian civilians tried not to succumb to panic when faced with the fact that this ideology had spread beyond SPLA circles. But others gave in: "People are now emptying my neighborhood, leaving," said an inhabitant of Mia Saba. "They're all leaving, printing flight tickets frantically."[75] The Nuer civilians still had it worse: in addition to being chased and killed, they were—much like in December 2013—still stopped at the airport and prevented from fleeing, including those with U.S. and Australian passports.[76]

During the fighting and the killings of July 2016, Dinka perpetrators made clear references to their ideology of Dinka supremacy, which equated Dinka ethnic membership with the right to live in South Sudan—or live at all. "We were told to leave Equatoria," recounted a Kuku woman in Juba. This was a "soft" warning, which still referred explicitly to Dinka supremacist ideology, bred during the interwar period on Dinka group legitimacy and entitlement: "The Dinka say that all the Equatorians should leave the land because they are taking care of the grave of John Garang . . . One of my neighbors in Rock city, who is a Dinka man and who is in the SPLA, said that."[77] But Mathiang Anyoor elements in Yei in the past year had warned civilians that "should there be an issue"—i.e., should IO fight back—the civilians "would be murdered at the border."[78] So this discourse did not really offer an "out" to the Equatorians.

Other non-Dinka groups were also increasingly threatened, compared even with the 2013 Juba massacre. A Shilluk woman in Juba at the time related, "In Juba, my neighbor wanted to kill me. He was a Dinka man, a soldier from the SPLA. He was planning to kill me. He shot at me. I realized my life was in danger simply because I was a Shilluk. Some other people were killed because of their ethnicity in the neighborhood—just shot—Bari people."[79] The expansion of threats and ethnic killings to non-Dinka civilians other than the Nuer, and not just by the SPLA but also by their Dinka relatives, illustrates how the Dinka supremacist ideology had grown more exclusionary since 2013 and its perpetrators more emboldened. Symptomatically, during the fighting in Juba in July 2016, the Dinka perpetrators also forgot about their Nuer allies' ethnic defection.[80]

The ethnic character of the killing was becoming more impossible to deny. Yet a few skilled Nuer politicians still reaped the benefits from an alliance with the Dinka.[81] Their circle became even smaller as violence against the Nuer increased. Meanwhile, in-group policing among the Dinka increased against Dinka politicians and soldiers who had joined Machar in December 2013 and early 2014 and were now caught in Juba.[82]

All in all, the fighting in Juba in July displayed how much more exclusionary and pervasive Dinka supremacist ideology had become since December 2013. The Dinka perpetrators continued to target Nuer civilians while expanding their ethnic targeting to other non-Dinka groups. They did not tolerate political and intimate relations between Dinka and Nuer. The thought of Nuer IO troops escaping from Juba south through Equatoria was intolerable, and violence against civilians quickly escalated in the larger Equatorian region.

The Development of the Third Phase of Genocidal Violence

From July 2016 onward, the government deployed the same type of violence against civilians in towns under SPLA control as it had in Unity state. But it employed different perpetrators, mostly Dinka NSS and military intelligence in towns, and Dinka SPLA soldiers and militias (Mathiang Anyoor) in the countryside.

The Expansion of Government Violence in Central Equatoria

In Yei town, a civilian illustrated how targeted killings on July 12, 2016, quickly expanded: "In the beginning they started with people with good jobs—a doctor, and then a family of eight children."[83] "Government soldiers chopped people with *pangas* (machetes) because they're Kakwa," explained a Kakwa man. "The Pojulu were killed in the market as well . . . The reason being: 'You people are all rebels.'"[84] In September-October 2016, SPLA soldiers went on to target Nimule.[85] Around the same time, they burned villages in Yei county.[86]

In Magwi county in Eastern Equatoria, where tensions had mounted in 2015 with the IO presence, things took a turn in June 2016.[87] More SPLA troops deployed to Magwi and Torit town.[88] In early April 2017 (April 3), the SPLA launched an extremely violent and well-coordinated operation against Pajok, as IO was gaining ground in the area.[89] But extreme violence did not reach further east, for fear of triggering a Lokoya and Toposa uprising against the Dinka SPLA.[90]

What happened in Pajok—a transference of the violence in Central Equatoria—did not (yet) reach Torit, where killings were targeted but not intended to decimate an entire community identified as rebel.[91]

The Perpetrators

The second genocidal phase in Unity state had been largely subcontracted to local Nuer perpetrators. In contrast, the third genocidal phase in Central Equatoria was mostly carried out by Dinka SPLA troops.

The attacks were planned and organized in the SPLA barracks, not in the county commissioners' headquarters like in Unity state. But the government still co-opted some local politicians and military commanders (more so in Pajok) and some local informants who showed them the locations of IO bases in the bush.[92]

The SPLA based itself out of towns and villages. Within the main towns, the NSS and the SPLA's military intelligence (MI) played an instrumental role in controlling civilians who did not leave. In addition to spying on these civilians, they restricted and controlled their movements.[93] The military intelligence was involved in ruthless acts of torture in the SPLA barracks, along with Mathiang Anyoor troops: "That was the SPLA military intelligence who took me [in September 2016]," recalled a man from Magwi county. "Every day they take you out and they interrogate you and beat you with a stick—150 strokes at morning, 150 in the afternoon, and 150 in the evening. They beat you everywhere. They kill you . . . Two people are doing this at the same time . . . They were Dinka Bahr El Ghazal: from Warrap, from the president's side."[94] Again, civilians were tortured the same way as in Unity state: they were crowded and starved in containers, where they died of sickness, suffocation, and heat. A victim recalled how intentional this form of killing was: "They cut out the trees that covered the container. Other people died in the container—five of them."[95]

By July 2017, the SPLA had bases in Jale, Cansook, Wudu, and Bamure in Kajo Keji county; in Bereka, Limbe, Kenyi payam, and Lokaround in Lanya county; and in Ombashi, Jambo (or Jombo), Mugo, Tore, Guimunu, Wudabi, Kaya, Basi, and Morobo town in Yei county.[96] In Magwi county (Eastern Equatoria), it had bases in Owinkibul, Palua, Magwi town, Panyakwara, and Lobone.[97] It targeted civilians in those bases at night and attacked civilians outside during the day.[98]

The SPLA soldiers "roamed around and killed people when they found them."[99] From Ombashi, they targeted villages such as Mosa, Yeiba, and Mongo.[100] In Kupera village, victims recalled that SPLA soldiers "came about every three days."[101] And there was a lot of territory for the government to roam.[102] Civilians stayed behind IO lines to be protected, but that also attracted government violence and retaliation when IO was defeated.[103] Whenever it wished to engage the IO, the SPLA came well-armed.

The government occasionally used helicopter gunships, just like in Western Equatoria the previous year.[104] But it was the exception, and the SPLA mostly operated in small soldiers' units of poorly trained recruits when it attacked civilians.[105] SPLA soldiers travelled in groups of ten to thirty, sometimes fifty, by foot.[106] They hid to chase, kill, and rape as many civilians as they could.[107]

Mathiang Anyoor troops were often cited as perpetrators of the "silent killing."[108] They were part of SPLA Divisions 2 and 6. Division 2 was even commanded by the head of Mathiang Anyoor from May 2016 onward in Yei.[109] But Mathiang Anyoor was still its own group within the SPLA.[110] They were better treated than other SPLA soldiers, though still less favored than Salva Kiir's Presidential Guards, the Tiger Battalion.[111] The Tiger Battalion stayed mostly around Juba and on Nimule road, and soldiers roaming from towns and villages in Central Equatoria were mainly from the SPLA Divisions 6 and 7 stationed in Lanya, Morobo, Kajo Keji, and Yei. They included a minority of Equatorian soldiers, who mostly stayed out of atrocities against people of their ethnic groups—at least in Central Equatoria.[112]

All in all, attacks outside the main towns on civilians were carried out by perpetrators including both Mathiang Anyoor and regular SPLA soldiers. Perpetrators were sometimes "old"(in their thirties and forties), but sometimes younger (from eighteen to twenty-five years old).[113] Yet few were below 18.[114] Most perpetrators were Dinka from different parts of the country.[115] Victims identified them by the language they spoke. The perpetrators spoke to their victims in Arabic, and some of them did not know Arabic and spoke only Dinka.[116] A few SPLA soldiers were Nuer as well, most likely Bul or Jikany once Taban Deng defected to the government.[117]

Most of the perpetrators wore SPLA uniforms, but some did not.[118] They included cattle herders who came with their families, armed by the SPLA and keeping the elite's cattle and their own.[119] This illustrated the fact that the genocidal conquest was somewhat of a popular event.

Some perpetrators changed on the ground in the summer 2017, after Kiir dismissed Malong in May 2017. But attacks on non-Dinka civilians continued. This was not surprising, because Malong alone was not behind the genocidal violence. If anything, his dismissal was convenient for Kiir: "Kiir can blame Malong for everything. It doesn't mean he's not a tribalist," a former NSS Dinka officer pointed out. The reintegration of Mathiang Anyoor troops into the SPLA's various divisions, spread across the country, had partly cut down Malong's personal power.[120] Yet some Mathiang Anyoor troops started to defect and make their way back to Juba, while some stayed in Yei's Kogul area. They continued to commit atrocities both in Yei town (where by July 2017 they numbered about a thousand) and on their path.[121]

Other Mathiang Anyoor recruits left various parts of the country—including Malakal—and made their way through territory controlled by IO, who mostly let them pass to weaken the SPLA.[122] Some even crossed into Uganda, escaping to refugee camps near Gulu and hiding among Dinka civilians from Jonglei that Mathiang Anyoor troops there had contributed to displace.[123] But Kiir (and reportedly the NSS chief Akol Kuur) continued to recruit Dinka militias in their home state of Warrap while trying to co-opt local Equatorian soldiers to keep a non-Dinka veneer.[124]

Killing and Destroying Equatorian Civilians as a Group

Killings in Central Equatoria quickly turned genocidal. The perpetrators lumped together civilians into a group they identified as a threat, and expressed their intent to destroy it.

Defining the Target Group: The Equatorian

Dinka supremacists used to consider people from Equatoria "cowards" not worth accommodating.[125] But from the moment the IO gained ground in Equatoria, the Dinka started to refer to the Equatorians as "rebels" (*nyagat*)—a term initially reserved for the Nuer. The confluence between the "Equatorian" and "rebel" categories greatly accelerated in July 2016, with the fighting in Juba between Machar's IO troops and the SPLA. A Kakwa civil society member recalled how in Yei, "after July 2016, they started telling all Equatorians were IO."[126]

By 2017, a Pojulu man from Lanya explained that the "SPLA says that civilians are all brothers of IO."[127] In other words, the Equatorians and the Nuer belonged to the same "family"—a family of rebels, of traitors. Of course, just like Nuer civilians, most of the civilians from Equatoria were not part of, or were not actively supporting, the IO. They were defenseless and therefore easily kidnapped, killed, beaten, raped, looted, and tortured. And just like the Nuer who fled SPLA-controlled towns in Unity state, whoever was 5 miles outside of one of the towns in Central Equatoria was accused of "being IO," arrested, tortured, or killed.[128] There was just no good solution: either one gave in and waited for the eventual accusation of being IO because of being Equatorian—and for murder, torture, and/or rape—or one hit the road.

The perpetrators' use of the pronouns "they" and "we" clearly showed that they intended violence against a group. Women recalled how "in Kajo Keji, in Bamure camp, the Dinka were raping women and slaughtering people saying that *they* [Equatorians] were supporting the Nuer."[129] "They said that we are the ones hiding IO," recalled a woman who was gang-raped.[130] Another woman, beaten after seeing her house burned in Gimunu in Yei county and then gang-raped, recalled: "We were beaten up because the SPLA said it was beating the IO."[131] Perhaps the most explicit quote was that of perpetrators who, before raping a woman, yelled to her from their trucks: "*You people, we* are killing you, raping you, we are beating you."[132] "You people" was the definition of a target group for genocidal violence. It was yelled from a position of superiority, from onlooking Dinka perpetrators who thought themselves better than their victims.

It was clear that survivors were raped and beaten because the perpetrators thought that they belonged to a group, made of various ethnic groups lumped together as "Equatorians." The perpetrators identified this group as the enemy of the ethnocracy and therefore the enemy of the Dinka. A gang-rape victim explained of her perpetrators, "They said the ladies and children are going to become enemies for the Dinka."[133]

The SPLA continued to ask civilians their ethnicity at checkpoints—just like in Juba in December 2013. "There are roadblocks on Nimule roads: the SPLA asks which tribe you are. When you say that you are a Kakwa from Yei, you have a problem," said a Kakwa man.[134] Alternatively, non-Equatorian civilians were less at risk, which was still telling of the intent to kill Equatorian civilians as a group. For example, a Shilluk woman, whose house was looted by Dinka SPLA soldiers in Yei, insisted, "If I were a Kakwa, they would have killed me . . . They said this to me: that if I were a Kakwa, they would kill me."[135]

Killing and Destroying the Equatorian Group

The perpetrators did not let the Equatorian group escape their grip. They chased and killed their victims. Once victims managed to flee the villages, they encountered SPLA troops who, as one woman gang-raped by three SPLA soldiers recalled, "hid in the bush," waiting for people to pass and attack them.[136] "The SPLA adapts to people's changing routes to kill them," explained a Kakwa civilian. "Between Morobo and Basi, the SPLA kills people to prevent them from crossing the border." Perched on the Poki mountain near Kaya, the SPLA meant to let no one pass.[137] It was clear the SPLA did not mean to just forcibly displace people. "If the government knows civilians are fleeing, they chase them. If it was just ethnic cleansing, the government would just let them flee," noted a Kuku civil society member.[138]

A woman raped in her village while SPLA soldiers beat and kidnapped her husband illustrated how government violence was meant to annihilate: "When the SPLA came to the village, they said, 'If you want to move to the camps or outside, you can.' But they kill people on the way to the camps too. Men are killed the most, but sometimes women too."[139] Men were killed so that they would not take refuge in Uganda and use it as a rear base to fight the government. Those kidnapped were used as slave laborers or soldiers for the SPLA troops.[140] Boys were at risk of being killed or kidnapped too. A mother who was gang-raped recalled how the perpetrators debated whether to kill her boys after killing her husband and their father: "They wanted to kill the boys because they would grow up as IO, and become their enemies."[141]

Perpetrators clearly expressed their intent to kill to their victims. A woman who was gang-raped recalled that "the SPLA said it wanted to kill all the people so that only birds remain in South Sudan. They did not want to see any human being. This was in January 2017, that they said this to me, in Logo in Yei county . . . In Yei, the SPLA said they wanted to kill people and did not want to see any human being, anyone alive there."[142] Looking back, from early 2014 on, the perpetrators kept on warning the Equatorians that they would kill them. And they did what they said they would do.

In fact, the perpetrators meant to kill as many members of the target group as possible. Most people fleeing were not successful. Out of a family of fifteen people, eight were killed on the way, according to aid workers surveying new arrivals in the Ugandan refugee camps.[143] If they had verbally expressed warnings to their victims before, silence was key in the execution of the killing itself.

"What happens most is 'silent killing': coming to your house, they slaughter you and kill you," noted South Sudanese aid workers welcoming new fellow refugees in the Ugandan camps.[144] Perpetrators burned houses after killing entire families inside, their history disappearing with them; they shot, kidnapped, raped, tortured, and beat civilians. But "silent killing is the most prevalent," the aid workers insisted. "The silent killing is done using *pangas* and knives. They slice the throats . . . You wake up in the morning to find the neighbor is dead, or people are dead on the road."[145]

Therefore, while the SPLA soldiers showed off their military superiority to the IO loudly, they did the complete opposite with defenseless civilians.[146] They terrified them into submission so they could kill and rape them in silence, without shooting a bullet. Of her rapists, a woman recalled, "They said, 'Equatorians should leave the land, and if you do not want to leave, we won't shoot you, we will slaughter you, because guns make noise.'"[147]

In addition to killing, the goal was to destroy, both physically and psychologically. Burning houses with people inside was intended to be much more painful and performative than executions by shooting. "SPLA soldiers come to a house and instruct the children to call on their father. Then they slaughter the one who has called, and then the father. That happened in Kajo Keji in February–March 2017," recalled a psychological aid worker in the camps.[148] People—including older men—broke down with loud cries in the refugee camps when they learned that their entire families had been burned in their homes back in South Sudan.[149] Some survivors suffered from depression and survivor's guilt, others from acute levels of psychosis. "The goal is to traumatize people so much that they never come back."[150]

Waging Genocidal Rape

KILLING AND DESTROYING THROUGH RAPE

Genocidal intent was particularly manifest in sexual atrocities. Rape mirrored the génocidaires' intent to kill and destroy the group. The victims, usually walking in groups of women and (sometimes) men, were caught by lurking perpetrators hiding in the bush.[151] The perpetrators' intent to kill was clear through the same habitual question, reminiscent of the genocidal campaigns in Unity state. A Kakwa gang-rape victim said of her Dinka SPLA perpetrators: "They brought us together and said, 'We want to rape you, and if you don't want to, we will kill you.'"[152] Another gang-raped Abukaya (Equatorian) woman attested: "They asked us if we wanted to live or die. If we wanted to live, we had to be raped."[153]

This forced exchange of rape for survival was widespread. It was a tool for dehumanization, and of course, this was only a rhetorical choice for the victims.[154] Indeed, rapes—especially gang-rapes—often led to the death of the victim or to her physical and emotional crippling, which could also result later in death. Rapes were instrumental in destroying the group—including by causing infertility.[155] Rapes were not meant to "produce Dinka babies," explained a gang-rape victim. "They are doing that because they want to take the land . . . because when they get the people, they kill them."[156] As in Unity state, the perpetrators intended rape as a form of killing in Central Equatoria: "They asked me if I preferred to be killed or raped," recalled a woman gang-raped by four Dinka SPLA soldiers.[157] If there was a "choice" between raping and killing, it was precisely because rape was no better than killing.

Rapes were genocidal because women were raped as members of the group the perpetrators intended to destroy. Rapes communicated the perpetrators' ideology of Dinka supremacy justifying atrocities.[158] Elements of this ideology were uttered by the perpetrators during the rapes, which I later turn to. Rapes were meant to terrorize, traumatize, and shatter relationships—constitutive of the group—and not just by destroying intimacy. Indeed, they occurred together with the kidnapping—or most often the execution—of the victims' husbands. One of these women, gang-raped by five Dinka SPLA soldiers along with six other women, cried, "I saw my husband being killed with a knife in front of me . . . My husband was killed before I was raped, and three other husbands were killed."[159] The execution or beating to death of husbands, or their kidnapping, often leading to death, emasculated the victim group and empowered the perpetrators.

Killing unborn and newborn babies was not a "side effect" of the violence either. The perpetrators intended to kill future rebels. Some survivors said they had witnessed perpetrators cut open pregnant women with *pangas* to "make sure it's not a boy."[160] Perpetrators told pregnant women that "they did not know if the baby would be born and become a soldier and be their enemy. So, 'if the baby comes out during the rape, let it come.'"[161] They often killed the rape victims' infants after beating them.[162]

Commanders often raped girl children above the age of ten (on average). Troops invariably killed or kidnapped boys, especially above the age of thirteen, and killed infants and unborn babies of both sexes, but especially male. They mostly spared the lives of girls and young boys they did not see as threats (yet)—those who could understand their death threats so that the "silent killing" could go on. "They said if the children cried, they would also kill them. All of this happened in silence," recalled a woman gang-raped in front of her children after the execution of her husband.[163]

Children, very often beaten, were invariably forced to watch the murder or kidnapping of their male relatives and the rape or death of their mothers (either by rape or by slaughtering).[164] The perpetrators sadistically gloated to these children that the murder of their parents would decrease their chances of survival when they trekked for days on their way to Uganda or the DRC.[165] Raping and killing in front of children sent a clear message to the new generations: they would associate South Sudan with death and rape and never want to come back. There was arguably more glory in leaving some witnesses because it made the perpetrators' annihilating domination—and therefore absolute sovereignty—that much more performative and long-lasting.[166] As for the adult women, the killing and abduction of their male relatives meant to traumatize them: rape did kill, but often perpetrators told their victims how "lucky" they were to be raped instead of killed, which (purposefully or not) reinforced survivor's guilt.[167]

The SPLA routinely desecrated the dead, throwing bodies on the roads, in rivers, scattering them.[168] Gang-raping on a potential mass grave further desecrated the long dead, the recently dead, and the rape victims. Reaffirming their absolute supremacy while revealing the implacable logic of their killing enterprise, the perpetrators told a woman they gang-raped along with ten others on the site of naked dead bodies (possibly a mass grave) after slaughtering the fifteen men accompanying them, "'It is good luck we rape you. If we do not rape you, you will be killed like the men.'"[169]

As a matter of fact, the perpetrators often debated whether to rape or to kill their victims. Those who survived and were raped attested, "Before raping me, this soldier said, 'These people should be killed.' Others said they should not, but said, 'We rape them and we release them to go.'"[170] They still debated whether to kill women *after* their rape, which was telling of how generalized the intent to kill was among troops.[171] Sometimes, a more senior perpetrator (a commander) in charge of the troops stepped in and ordered the rape instead of the kill. Victims explained that other women were not as "lucky" as them, including in the villages, where they were sometimes also killed alongside men.[172]

After the rape, the perpetrators intended to continue humiliating their victims. They often left them with nothing to wear, and when they did leave them with a piece of clothing, it was not their skirts but their tops, in order to expose their rape, or it was an article of their clothing that the perpetrators had used to wash themselves of blood and then thrown back at them.[173]

ACHIEVING GROUPNESS THROUGH GENOCIDAL RAPE

The vast majority of rapes were gang-rapes performed on women, though some cases were reported of male victims as well.[174] Rapes—and especially gang-rapes—were formative of the perpetrators' group while also destroying the victims' groupness.[175]

The perpetrators aimed to rape as many women as possible. A woman gang-raped by six SPLA soldiers noted how "some of the soldiers went to hide themselves as well to wait for some women on the same road to rape them."[176] Since the goal was to catch as many women as possible, the gang-rapes were essentially a "job" or a "task" performed by a group. In other words, there was nothing "out of control" about those rapes, another characteristic of genocidal rape.[177] In some cases, soldiers exchanged women so they could be raped as much as possible by as many men as possible. A victim recalled, "The two soldiers who raped me went on to rape other women, so they exchanged women among themselves. Once they were done, they exchanged, so every woman could be raped."[178]

It was clear that these gang-rapes were tasks assigned, supervised, and endorsed by the commanders, who waited for their soldiers to be done raping and killing the victims' male relatives. "Among the hundred soldiers, some remained in the vehicles," remembered a woman gang-raped by six Dinka SPLA soldiers. "Others came out to rape us, while the rest waited for them to be done raping us."[179]

Military hierarchy was displayed in these rapes. The more senior commanders raped younger women, often children, individually.[180] They did not debase themselves to take part in gang-rapes that spread STIs.

Of course, the SPLA also continued to use women to support its troops. Before raping their victims, SPLA troops forced women to carry their loot from the villages they had descended on. "We were beaten and were given a lot to carry on our heads before the rape, for like one hour and a half," one of them recalled. "I was forced to carry stuff in a convoy and if you move slowly they beat you. They tied our arms . . . There were soldiers in front and behind and next to me so I could not run. There were about fifty soldiers."[181] Women continued to be used as forced porters—or slave laborers—just like in the last war. There were fewer cases of abduction of women as sex slaves than in Unity state, but Equatorian women were also arrested and tortured in the SPLA barracks in towns.[182]

The Perpetrators' Ideology

Dinka Supremacy and Dinka Groupness

Throughout all these atrocities, the perpetrators displayed the exclusionary ideology of Dinka supremacy that went hand-in-hand with extreme ethnic group entitlement.

Extreme Dinka group entitlement was based on Dinka group legitimacy, itself founded on the idea that the overwhelmingly Dinka SPLA had "liberated" South Sudan and delivered its independence. This legitimacy was the foundation of extreme Dinka group entitlement, which had already manifested itself in everyday life and common spaces before the third war but was increasingly present after.

The performance of mass violence as a group after December 2013 reinforced Dinka groupness and as such further radicalized the perpetrators. By the third phase, the perpetrators' group had gotten away with two previous phases of genocidal violence in Juba and Unity state and waged violence against non-Dinka civilians in Wau and Western Equatoria, violence that, in its ideological underlining, was very similar (as I explain later). This emboldened the perpetrators in the third genocidal phase.

The July 2016 fighting in Juba, in merging the categories of "Equatorian" and "rebels," also further radicalized the Dinka perpetrators' views of their own group legitimacy and entitlement. In Magwi, civilians recalled that "the SPLA takes things by force on the markets. When we ask for a better price, they say, 'Where were you during the war?' . . . It was in August 2016. Mostly the Dinka are the ones talking like this and you should not react."[183]

Dinka perpetrators lumped together all non-Dinka groups there as "non-Sudanese." Their denationalization of non-Dinka civilians, typical in genocide, derived from Dinka group legitimacy equating South Sudanese nationality with Dinka ethnic membership. It justified Dinka conquest, which was rooted in the last war's ethnically exclusionary mode of production. Denationalization was consistent with discourses of Dinka settlers in Equatoria from 2005 to 2013, consolidating the last war's protoconquest.[184] There was a continuum but also an escalation by July 2016, based on two previous genocidal phases and on the perceived Equatorian threat.

Now, whoever was not Dinka and therefore not associated with the SPLA was not South Sudanese. Of the "Kuku, Pojulu, and Kakwa, the Dinka say that they are not South Sudanese because they claim that they are the people who are South Sudanese, not us," explained a civilian from Lanya.[185] This idea permeated SPLA troops from the top down and instructions were given: "Mathiang Anyoor were deployed and were told by their commander that Congolese and Ugandans were in Ombashi—these are the Equatorians. So they were told to settle there to oust the people," a Kakwa former SPLA soldier explained.[186]

This ideology prescribed that the Dinka were the "true" South Sudanese, to the detriment of the people they ousted. The non-Dinka did not "own" the country. In effect, this ideology was rooted in decades of real dispossession through the SPLA's exclusionary and predatory mode of production in non-Dinka areas. A Kakwa woman from Kayaya who witnessed Dinka SPLA soldiers kill two other women harvesting cassava in her village said of the perpetrators: "They wanted to eat the harvest collected by their own wives [not by Kakwa women] . . . They think South Sudan belongs to them."[187] The ethnocracy had turned genocidal, illustrating that genocide is the most violent culmination of discrimination.[188] Because these non-Dinka ethnic groups did not belong to the political community—and did not "own" the country—they were not equal to the Dinka. After July 2016, they had no right be in South Sudan at all—and by extension, no right to life there.

Scarification expressed some of the most acute—because immutable—form of ethnic ranking: they showed to the perpetrators who was a South Sudanese and who they thought wasn't, who had the privilege to live and who did not.[189] Although not all Dinka perpetrators practiced face scarification, many did. A former trader in Yei explained that "when you don't have marks on your forehead, you're not a real South Sudanese. They say that."[190] Central Equatoria was not the only place where the perpetrators held this discourse on scarification, as I explain later.

Whoever was not Dinka, was not South Sudanese, and no longer even existed administratively. Non-Dinka men who were still allowed to cross the border from Magwi to Uganda early in the third phase (August 2016) before it reached

Magwi in April 2017 had their passports confiscated, along with extremely valuable documents.[191] Confiscating passports prevented return to the country and travel outside the refugee camps, de facto imprisoning the survivors.

The perpetrators expressed their supremacy as their right by virtue of birth to dictate who lived or died. A victim of torture recalled, "They beat you with the aim of killing you and they tell you when they beat you 'we are born to rule, you're supposed to die. We're supposed to rule you people.'"[192] Group entitlement based on group legitimacy and group ownership rooted both in an exclusionary mode of production practiced in and since the last war and the shared memory of past humiliations thus combined with an essentialized supremacist vision of Dinka ethnicity, understood as "naturally" superior from birth. The perpetrators echoed the discourses already deployed in Western Equatoria (Mundri) in 2015: they asserted that the Dinka were a sort of "master race" tasked with "clearing" the inferior non-Dinka.

The name of Mathiang Anyoor itself—"brown caterpillar" in Dinka, one of the most destructive crop-eating pests—was already quite evocative: "A 'caterpillar' eats the grass—everything, it clears everything," explained a Kakwa civilian. "They're told to clear everything. And that's why they kill everyone."[193] The name of the new batch of Dinka recruits after Mathiang Anyoor, called Akher Mathar ("the last rain") in Arabic or Amiath Noon in Dinka, also spoke of extreme group entitlement and racism. "'Amiath Noon' means stomping on the grass [not cutting]—putting the grass down or flattening the grass," explained a former Dinka NSS officer from Aweil. "It refers to people who don't care: because when you do that, it means you don't care what's inside the grass."[194] In other words, anything in the grass that was associated with opposition was not Dinka and needed to be crushed. Perpetrators were not to care about nuance: all non-Dinka ethnic groups were to be "flattened."

The perpetrators' mythology and essentialization of Dinka ethnicity motivated them to crush the non-Dinka. Dinka ethnicity was so primordialized that perpetrators thought their supremacy was god-given. After capturing a crowd of civilians in Ombashi in May 2017, soldiers from Mathiang Anyoor "said that the country belongs to the Dinka. They believe God said the country and the government is for the Dinka."[195]

As Dinka supremacist ideology climaxed, the presence of high-ranking non-Dinka officers within the SPLA became intolerable. Just like the high-ranking Nuer SPLA officers from Unity state in Juba in July 2016, some of the high-ranking non-Dinka SPLA officers from Equatorian groups were purged—assassinated in their homes or on the job after July 2016.[196] Dinka supremacist and exclusionary ideology permeated the troops and the Dinka cattle herders so completely that the question became whether they would even listen to orders to stop if they were given. This was impossible to know given the duplicity of Kiir's public statements against the violence, which often amounted to mere posturing.[197]

As violence continued, the ideology of Dinka supremacy consolidated. Mass gang-raping undoubtedly reinforced the perpetrators' groupness and with it the group's self-aggrandizement. It gave them, in subjugating the victim group, more opportunities to verbally express their supremacy as a group above all forms of accountability, further dehumanizing their victims. "They said, 'What we feel like doing, we will do,'" recalled a woman of her two Dinka SPLA rapists.[198]

Mass gang-raping also increased the perpetrators' cohesion, since they were otherwise little trained and therefore had little bonding them together. This was evident from their discourse, as a woman who was gang-raped recalled: "They said, 'If IO thinks that they are powerful on their land, then they will see what we the Dinka do.'"[199] The words "we the Dinka" and "do" illustrate the degree to which violence performed as group tasks reaffirmed and enhanced the power of the Dinka, first in units, then as an ethnic group. This was evident in executions, gang-rapes, and looting.[200] Every member of the group was "doing" something— accomplishing a "task," the most efficient form of military cohesion-building. No perpetrator was idle, as a gang-raped woman illustrated: "As for the rest of the soldiers: five were killing my stepfather, while two were collecting the properties inside. They burned the house too."[201]

In addition to the rape itself, forcing Equatorian men into submission through compelling them to participate (by holding the victims' legs and arms for the rapists) also fostered the groupness of the perpetrators as superior to both these women and men.[202] In other words, it fostered the perpetrators' groupness as opposed to that of the victims and therefore continued to build up Dinka supremacy.

Fostering Dinka groupness through violence reaffirming supremacy was key because the Dinka were of course not a naturally unified group but rather a myriad of Dinka groups (sections) who all competed. The small SPLA units attacking civilians in Equatoria were mixed with different Dinka sections.[203] They were supported by other security organs (such as MI and NSS) and cattle herders from various Dinka sections.[204] Dinka civilians from various sections also came to settle in the houses of the disappeared.[205] All of these Dinka perpetrators and beneficiaries came together and mixed, even if some were competing for resources and prestige.

Fostering Dinka Groupness despite Divisions

Genocidal violence, in fostering Dinka groupness, helped mask in-group competition and a narrowing ethnic supremacist center of power rooted in Kiir's home state. Indeed, in-group competition continued among the Dinka, between the two traditional blocks of western and eastern Dinka. This competition was mostly won by the western Dinka from the Bahr El Ghazal region. Not only was Mathiang Anyoor, instrumental in the Equatorian campaign, above all from Northern Bahr El Ghazal. The Dinka cattle herders who kept the SPLA's cattle in the region largely also came from the Bahr El Ghazal region. They were more numerous than the Bor Dinka, spotted in Lanya county.[206] A civilian explained the larger contingent of western Dinka by the fact that "the Dinka Bahr El Ghazal want to take over the SPLA from the Dinka Bor."[207] He was not wrong: in-group competition still ran through the SPLA and the ethnocracy, and the Bor Dinka elite's arming of its youth was a manifestation of its attempt to compete with the Bahr El Ghazal group in defending its interests and protecting itself.[208]

Yet the Bahr El Ghazal group itself was increasingly split by competition. First, the Dinka from Lakes (Dinka Agar and Gok) thought they were losing out to the other Dinka sections from Bahr El Ghazal and Bor.[209] They thought of themselves as the lumpen Dinka group. "Most people benefiting from the current war are from Aweil, Warrap, and some from Bor," explained a former SPLA battalion commander from Lakes. "People in Lakes are not happy with people from Aweil and Warrap ruling the country," he complained.[210] This sentiment was echoed by members of other Dinka sections, such as the Dinka Padang in Upper Nile, who were also competing within their own group of eastern Dinka, with the Bor Dinka for land in Equatoria.[211]

Second, the Dinka constituency from Northern Bahr El Ghazal, under the leadership of Paul Malong, whose political ambitions were obvious, exasperated Kiir's constituency. The fact that most of Mathiang Anyoor had been recruited from Northern Bahr El Ghazal by Malong did not fool his constituents: "Malong argued it was for Salva's protection. But there were maybe less than a thousand men from Warrap in Mathiang Anyoor," argued a Dinka politician in Aweil. "All the people in Aweil know that he's preparing himself to become the next president."[212] After Kiir dismissed his rival in May 2017, in-group policing affected cadres from Malong's home area of Aweil and his entourage.[213]

This in-group competition among the western Dinka, between especially the Northern Bahr El Ghazal and Warrap constituencies, meant that the ethnic center of gravity—or power—of the Dinka hardliners was getting smaller and smaller, and more and more centered in Warrap state. This is where Kiir, Akol Kuur (the NSS chief), and the JCE Chairman Ambrose Riiny Thiik all hailed from. The fact that the génocidaires' ethnic center of gravity became narrower was not unusual. Indeed, just like for other perpetrators, it was much easier for them to define who was inferior than who was the right and the best kind of Dinka. Appearances mattered, though, and Kiir's faction widened the JCE's membership—including by appointing a Dinka Padang as Ambrose's deputy—to foster Dinka groupness.

This was a function of military necessity too, a former high-ranking Bor Dinka government official explained: "When war broke out, other regions were not providing troops—Bahr El Ghazal was not enough. And so the JCE expanded to other regions to include Dinka from Upper Nile too." Referring to the cooptation of other Dinka sections, he explained how the JCE "expanded to include the Jieng from Bor, Baliet, Pariang, Renk [including Melut]."[214] Yet most of the troops who came to Central Equatoria and elsewhere were still from Bahr El Ghazal, and the western Dinka still dominated most of the security apparatus. Widening the JCE's membership masked the fact that the gravitational center of Kiir's faction was still firmly rooted in Warrap.

Expanding the Dinka Conquest

Expanding the Dinka conquest through genocidal violence considerably helped Dinka groupness and enabled Kiir's faction to remain unchallenged. Indeed, conquest was a function of the Dinka supremacist ideology. Conquest was rooted in the SPLA's exclusionary mode of production from the last war, itself emanating from the legacy of slavery and its expanding frontier. This supremacist ideology, as an expression of extreme Dinka group entitlement, naturally culminated in the idea of group grabbing and expansion, which on a large scale amounted to conquest.

The SPLA troops, numerous and well-armed, established themselves in the villages of Central Equatoria. By the summer of 2017, very few civilians were left in Kajo Keji and Lanya town, or in Morobo.[215] Less than five hundred Pojulu and Kakwa civilians lived in Yei town, aggregated around the market.[216] The SPLA chased civilians from their houses and their fields, a young man from Kenyi payam in Lanya county recalled.[217]

Dinka soldiers and cattle herders—some with SPLA uniforms and some without, but always armed—came to settle with women and children in the homes and on the land of their victims.[218] A man from Bereka village in Lanya recounted of the SPLA, "They stay in our homes after chasing us. They chase you and then they stay in your homes."[219] A woman from Yei county, gang-raped in her house in Mangalatore village, noted, "Only a few houses they burned so that people would not stay there. So that just *they* [the Dinka SPLA soldiers] would stay there ... They're doing that so that they will settle there." "They're doing this [killing] so that the land belongs to them," another gang-rape victim said.[220]

Dinka perpetrators made explicit these long-term goals and sometimes mocked their victims, asking them "who was going to stay on our land," one victim of gang-rape recalled.[221] Some gloated to their victims. A woman gang-raped by four Dinka soldiers who first slaughtered her husband and her baby recalled, "They said they were happy because they killed many people and they're about to take the land now."[222]

There is nothing surprising about the fact that conquest and genocide went together. After all, Raphael Lemkin, who coined the term "genocide," understood the process as an inherently imperialist venture.[223] This conquest was also symbolic, and the perpetrators rebranded the places they conquered, a typical feature of genocide. Names started changing in Juba, and places such as Jebel Ladu became commonly known as "that of the Dinka": "Jebel Dinka."[224] The Dinka conquerors were thus rewriting history.[225]

Conquest also continued to enrich the perpetrators, who sold their loot not only in Torit, Magwi, and Juba but also in Uganda.[226] They engaged in racketeering with their victims in multiple ways (from ransoming to confiscating goods).[227] In wealth accumulation, ethnic ranking continued too (just like in Unity state).[228] The Dinka perpetrators from Northern Bahr El Ghazal and Warrap amassed the most wealth among all Dinka groups because they could transport it and sell it. Equatoria was rich in minerals, and the NSS was also involved in mining.[229]

The link between genocidal violence and coveted natural resources did not escape the Equatorians—much like the Nuer in Unity state. "In Kajo Keji, there's gold, uranium, iron, cement, tanganyite (which you put on the phones), even diamonds," explained an IO commissioner.[230] Yet the many mineral resources and arable land throughout Equatoria could not solely explain the drive behind state genocidal violence against non-Dinka civilians.

Ideology drove the profitable genocidal violence and took precedence over accumulation. On the ground, Dinka supremacist ideology motivated the perpetrators. Of course, this did not mean the ethnocrats were not also guided by various other motives. But one motive did not exclude the other—quite the opposite. Extreme Dinka group entitlement incorporated the idea of group ownership. Group grabbing (of properties, resources, people, and land) and the resulting group expansion elaborated on group entitlement. The perpetrators portrayed their genocidal conquest as merely recuperating what was always theirs. In effect, supremacy went hand in hand with a profitable conquest throughout the entire country, not just in Unity state and in Western and Central Equatoria.

ETHNIC SUPREMACY AND GENOCIDAL CONQUEST

Other instances of mass violence against non-Dinka civilians reveal a similar pattern to that of the three genocidal phases examined in this book (Juba, Unity, Central Equatoria). They illustrate how an exclusionary ideology of Dinka supremacy culminated both in military campaigns intended to kill non-Dinka civilians and in expanding Dinka conquest. I examine briefly the most salient elements below, focusing on ideology, intent, and conquest.

Reflecting on other Cases of Mass Violence in South Sudan

The Perpetrators' Ideology

Just like in Central Equatoria, this ideology revolved around Dinka group legitimacy and ownership leading to extreme group entitlement. It embraced the idea of a "master race" whose ethnic identity was primordial. From 2015 to 2017, the perpetrators manifested this exclusionary ideology of Dinka supremacy in Western Bahr El Ghazal and Upper Nile.

This ideology merged ethnic and national identities and de facto denationalized—before dehumanizing—members of non-Dinka groups. Just like the Nuer and the Equatorian groups, these other non-Dinka groups (such as the Balanda, the Fertit and the Shilluk) overlapped neighboring countries as well. They had not joined the SPLA en masse in the second civil war due to ethnic ranking and discrimination against them. As a result, they were not considered "legitimate" enough to be South Sudanese.

In Wau (in Western Bahr El Ghazal), Mathiang Anyoor troops from Aweil deployed the exact same exclusionary ideology in 2015 that was used in Western Equatoria the same year and in Central Equatoria later. "The Dinka come and take the land and say, 'Now, you've not been in the SPLA to the bush to fight, so we're taking the land,'" explained a Balanda civilian. "When you want to ask about this land, they'll kill you." There as well extreme group entitlement merged with exclusionary ethnic ranking: "When they have scarifications on their forehead, they say, 'When you're not cut, you're not South Sudanese.' They said this to me."[1] In Wau too the perpetrators equated Dinka ethnicity with South Sudanese nationality.

Their delegitimization of non-Dinka civilians went together with denationalization: since no non-Dinka had truly "earned" the right to the land (shed "buckets full of human blood"), no non-Dinka was a "true" South Sudanese.[2] In Upper Nile, where Dinka SPLA soldiers deployed the same supremacist rhetoric, the Shilluk knew they shared the same destiny with most non-Dinka groups: "The Dinka say that the Equatorians should go back to Uganda, Kenya, and the DRC. Also in Malakal, they say that the Shilluk should go back to Khartoum," reported a Shilluk woman. "It's the same for the Fertit (the Balanda are part of it): they should go back to Khartoum. They say the Balanda and Fertit came from Chad, and the area should remain vacant for the Dinka. The Nuer, because there are Nuer in Ethiopia, should go back to Ethiopia."[3]

In other words, every non-Dinka group was eventually denationalized by the Dinka perpetrators. But this was not the only similarity between all five places—Unity, Western and Central Equatoria, Western Bahr El Ghazal, and Upper Nile.

The Perpetrators' Intent to Kill

The perpetrators also seemed to intend to kill non-Dinka civilians both in Western Bahr El Ghazal and Upper Nile. As a matter of fact, in Central Equatoria perpetrators had warned civilians that genocidal violence had and would expand beyond their group. When SPLA soldiers told victims that they "wanted to kill all the people," a woman raped in March 2017 in her village in Yei county recounted, "They were talking about the entire country, not just Central Equatoria."[4] In Wau in 2015, Mathiang Anyoor troops, mostly from Aweil, had also sought to annihilate non-Dinka civilians: "When they come, they see you, they speak Dinka, they don't ask anything, they just shoot," recalled a Balanda civilian.[5]

The third genocidal phase shared many commonalities with what looked like a fourth one in Upper Nile against the Shilluk. "I think that what is happening to the Shilluk and the Kakwa is the same," said a Shilluk woman who fled Yei.[6] "Most people were slaughtered, others shot, others burned inside their houses in Malakal, Wau Shilluk, and Kodok," explained another Shilluk woman. "Slaughtered, burned, shot. Others died of lack of water." And the perpetrators were the same as in Equatoria. "The SPLA soldiers do the killing. And it is dominated by the Dinka. Those soldiers are Dinka from Lakes, Bahr El Ghazal, Jonglei."[7]

The victims and the vocabulary were also the same: "Whether you are a civilian, a woman, a child, they will do the same to you: they will *clear* you." The atrocities were incredibly reminiscent: "In Shilluk land they did the same as in Unity and Equatoria: especially the men were killed. Even the children, as long as it's a baby boy. So many women have been raped and sometimes killed." Finally, the perpetrators worked toward the same mission: to expand their group through an annihilating and profitable conquest: "Those people have a long-term plan: they want to own all the resources . . . They are raping to scare and torture—in front of your husband or on top of him—just to traumatize you so that you don't go back."[8]

In a nutshell, civilians were witnessing a multiethnic genocide by the same group of perpetrators: "The Dinka is the biggest tribe and they take advantage of it to kill the other tribes to remove them from their lands."[9] The guiding principle was simple (one versus all), yet the execution was challenging: if the Dinka was the biggest single group, when all other non-Dinka groups were aggregated the Dinka became the minority. Therefore, as demonstrated most in Unity, the ethnocrats had become experts at constantly co-opting members of the victim groups to blur the political landscape to outsiders and disorganize their opponents.

Expanding Dinka Conquest and Dinka Groupness

While their opponents were disorganized, the perpetrators' annihilating violence advanced Dinka conquest and fostered Dinka groupness. In Malakal (Upper Nile), after chasing most Shilluk civilians to the UN POC, Dinka settlers changed the name of the streets, just like they had in Juba.[10] A Shilluk woman noted that the Dinka wives who settled with their children in the deserted houses came from different sections and subsections (clans): "After sending us away, the SPLA soldiers come with their wives and children . . . They are the Dinka from Melut, Akogo, Atar. It's not only a single clan, but the Dinka tribe uniting against other tribes to extend their territory." This was a national trend, as Dinka from as far away as Bahr El Ghazal now settled on Shilluk land, across the country from their area of origin. "Even Dinka from Bahr El Ghazal come to settle on Shilluk land: from Yirol, and from Bahr El Ghazal, Warrap. Since they all speak the same language, they empower the local Dinka tribes."[11] In November 2016, the ethnocracy even assisted about two thousand Dinka in this land rush, flying them from Juba to Malakal.[12] A Dinka Padang civilian, after pointing out that Mathiang Anyoor troops were in Malakal, noted, "The Dinka are the Dinka. But many of us don't know the other Dinka. The war brought people together. But we in Upper Nile don't [didn't] know the Dinka from Bahr El Ghazal. The Dinka in Ruweng [Unity] we know, and the Dinka from Jonglei. But from Bahr El Ghazal, we didn't know."[13]

While conquest fostered Dinka groupness, it also continued to reveal Dinka in-group competition. The center of gravity of military power remained firmly rooted in Bahr El Ghazal: "still, the western Dinka [from Bahr El Ghazal] were more, demographically speaking," a Bor Dinka insider noted of the SPLA's composition.[14] In fact, Dinka in-group competition fueled the Dinka conquest. Mathiang Anyoor soldiers were spotted settling on the Shilluk's land, and each Dinka section defended its interests.[15]

This national Dinka migration and conquest, reinforcing overarching Dinka groupness when confronting non-Dinka civilians, hid an inner conquest among Dinka sections. Indeed, the western Dinka displaced other eastern Dinka civilians, especially from Bor, the rival constituency. Bor Dinka women lamented that Mathiang Anyoor troops had made it impossible for them to cultivate: "They grab the food, if you resist, they shoot you. They're scattered, not staying in one place. They've been there for almost two years. Most of them are from Bahr El Ghazal, from Warrap and Northern Bahr El Ghazal." It was clear that the Dinka civilians from Bor, who started flooding the Ugandan refugee camps as well, were also being conquered by their rival Dinka constituency.[16]

The inner Dinka conquest was the prolongation of the supremacist Dinka ideology rooted in Kiir's faction: the western Dinka constituencies of Northern Bahr El Ghazal and Warrap. Symptomatically, that rival western Dinka constituency, where the Dinka hardliners mostly sprung from and then extended their reach east, was itself fractured by competition, most openly after Kiir dismissed Malong, who orchestrated violence for him from 2013 to 2017.

The Wider Trends

State Coordination and Supremacist Ideology

In every genocidal phase studied in this book, the state coordinated attacks against civilians. This violence was extremely similar in every phase. The state waged war against non-Dinka civilians. State-coordinated perpetrators lumped them into groups the state considered a threat. The perpetrators dehumanized their victims and sought to destroy them as members of their group. The perpetrators, including ethnic defectors in Unity state, deployed the same exclusionary ideology of Dinka supremacy.

This exclusionary ideology of Dinka supremacy linked together what might otherwise look like multiple separate instances of ethnic cleansing. This ideological thread, combined with obliterating violence, made it a genocide led by one group against all others. The ideology was rooted in the country's *longue durée* and the legacy of slavery in multiple ways. It was a version of extreme group entitlement, the sum of both group ownership and group legitimacy developed together during the second civil war. It had grown during the interwar period under the aegis of a growing ethnocracy supported in turn by the international community. The exclusionary ideology equated Dinka ethnic membership with South Sudanese nationality. Dinka perpetrators most fully expressed it to their victims.

This one-versus-all genocide was the result of an escalation of violence throughout all three phases since December 2013 and the Juba massacre. Each phase emboldened the state and its perpetrators, who widened the membership of the target group from the Nuer to include other non-Dinka civilians. Perpetrators lumped all of non-Dinka civilians into the category of "rebels." In equating Dinka ethnicity with South Sudanese nationality, the perpetrators denationalized their victims. From there came destruction: the victims had no right to life in South Sudan.

Class, Ethnicity, and Genocide Perpetration

Ethnic and class memberships played different roles in the implementation of each genocidal campaign. A legacy of strong ethnic ranking meant that ethnicity would take precedence over class in the perpetration of genocidal violence. Where the SPLA had a strong presence in the last war and enforced a strong system of ethnic ranking between the Dinka and other groups (as in Equatoria), it was impossible for the ethnocracy to subcontract genocidal violence via shared class interests. Members of the target group had little interest in implementing government violence. In Western and Central Equatoria, where the perpetrators were mostly Dinka, ethnicity trumped class.

But where processes of dominant class formation and in-group competition mirrored that of the Dinka ethnocrats, class won out over ethnicity in the perpetration of genocidal violence. In Unity state, processes of dominant class formation in Nuer SSDF areas similar to those in SPLA-controlled areas and in-group competition between different Nuer sections helped the SPLA subcontract genocidal violence. The Bul Nuer especially shared more dominant class interests with the Dinka ethnocrats than with ordinary non-Bul Nuer civilians. Ethnicity played a role at the level of in-group competition, and genocidal violence consolidated Nuer ethnic ranking. But at the national (Dinka versus Nuer) level, class took precedence over ethnicity in co-opting Bul Nuer and other ethnic defectors and turning them into perpetrators.

Therefore, this one-versus-all genocide drew perpetrators on the basis of, alternatively, either class or ethnic membership, depending on the legacy of ethnic ranking and in-group competition, different in each location. The one constant remained that in all phases, this genocide targeted other groups defined by their non-Dinka ethnic membership. Where perpetrators were Dinka, they expressed the ethnocracy's supremacist ideology most explicitly.

Violence, Conquest, and Groupness

The supremacist ideology, combining extreme group entitlement and an essentialized vision of Dinka ethnicity as a "master race," culminated in a conquest. Group expansion through violent acquisition (of things, land, people) was the ideological extension of group entitlement. The perpetrators were merely recuperating what they thought was always theirs. In effect, supremacy went hand in hand with a profitable conquest throughout the entire country that expanded Dinka land.

Genocidal violence and conquest fostered Dinka groupness to mask in-group competition since the second civil war and the ever-narrowing ethnic center of power. Dinka perpetrators settled on the land of their victims. But this type of modern settler colonialism also hid an inner conquest among Dinka sections, whereby the land and properties of eastern Dinka sections were being taken over by their rival Dinka constituency.

Becoming a Genocidal State

How did South Sudan become a predatory and genocidal state? The short answer is that unchecked predation and strengthened group legitimacy fostered extreme group entitlement, which turned into ethnic supremacy after the second civil war. Political competition and a political crisis in 2013 provided the impetus for the ethnocratic regime to veer into genocide against non-Dinka groups. But the underlying processes of ethnicized violence and the denationalization of non-Dinka had been underway since the early 1980s. Moreover, the deeper answer to this question lies in the *longue durée*: in the country's legacy of slavery and colonialism. The history of racist exploitation and ethnic ranking can be seen in the SPLA's discrimination against non-Dinka recruits and in its mode of production from the beginning. Unrestrained ethnic ranking and ethnically exclusive wealth accumulation made the formation of an ideology of Dinka ethnic supremacy possible.

An intra-Dinka coalition and proto pan-Dinka ideology of group entitlement had already emerged during the first interwar period of the 1970s. They masked Dinka in-group competition then too. As the Dinka expanded their presence, especially into Equatoria, anti-Dinka racism increased, climaxing during the *kokora* events—the (re)division of the South into three regions. These events were instrumental in shaping the discourse of Dinka group legitimacy within the newly created SPLA in 1983.

The predominantly Dinka SPLA reenacted interethnic hostility and the political themes of the 1970s–80s in its ranks. In practicing ethnic discrimination against non-Dinka recruits, it promoted ethnic homogeneity. Together with the performance of violence directed at ethnic outsiders, ethnic ranking steered Dinka exclusive groupness. The split of the SPLA in 1991 further ethnicized it, and the Bor massacre contributed to define the Dinka around the Bor constituency of its leader John Garang. This did not contain intra-Dinka competition, which had traversed the armed group from the start. Corruption and ethnic patronage fostered the rise of a competing Dinka political faction rooted in the northeast of Bahr El Ghazal, whose leaders would become instrumental in the third civil war.

The international endorsement of the political myth of SPLA national liberation during those years masked the armed group's ethnicization and the tensions between its two Dinka constituencies. The myth of SPLA national liberation promoted Dinka group legitimacy and resonated with the proto pan-Dinka ideology of the 1970s.

Garang's dependence on the West most likely restrained SPLA violence against civilians during the second civil war. Yet deeper processes were at work, with long-term consequences: the SPLA had started a protoconquest of non-Dinka areas while building a state (with the support of the international community) on predation. Both processes of protostate-building and protoconquest were driven by the violent, ethnically exclusionary, and exploitative SPLA's mode of (re)production. It consisted of socioeconomic and sexual predation and forced labor, while restricting control of the war economy to the preferred ethnic group. It was reminiscent of slavery's racist system of socioeconomic exploitation, which operated in part through the accumulation of women and their forced labor. As such, this mode of (re)production was prone to foster extreme ethnic group entitlement.

The SPLA's Dinka dominant class emerged through the control of this mode of (re)production, amassing and concentrating material wealth and wealth in people, expanding kinship networks, and trickling down some benefits to its lower strata. Through the violent accumulation of resources, people, and land, this mode of (re)production made and expanded Dinka groupness, Dinka group ownership over the territory (the protoconquest), and as such, Dinka group legitimacy.

As a result of support from the international community and aid agencies, SPLA state-making routinized and maximized predation. It benefited mostly this new Dinka dominant class. It reinforced structural inequalities based on ethnic ranking, a blueprint for the postwar ethnocracy. The increased international presence also aggravated group entitlement by reviving past humiliations from slavery and colonialism.

By 2005, SPLA nationalism largely catered to the Dinka. The international community endorsed the SPLA's predatory and exclusionary protostate through the CPA. It continued to feed it and strengthen it with aid. It supported the SPLA's usurpation of collective memory. It endorsed the violent 2010 elections and applauded the undisputed 2011 independence. Yet the international community's presence in South Sudan, in reviving racist colonial stereotypes, continued to negatively impact group worth and to irritate feelings of Dinka group entitlement.

The SPLA political myth of national liberation became the founding narrative of Dinka hardliners after Garang's death, in an international context favorable to war-mongering nationalism. Extreme group entitlement translated into an ideology of Dinka supremacy. Intraethnic competition between the two Dinka factions and against other ethnic competitors drove ethnic ranking in the state and the army.

The state turned into a violent ethnocracy under the growing influence of the hardliners from the Dinka Bahr El Ghazal faction around Salva Kiir. It eliminated Dinka dissenters through in-group policing while recruiting Dinka militias to both promote groupness and accomplish a takeover of the SPLA—and, ultimately, fully control the state. Ethnic ranking permeated society through ethnic prejudices, xenophobia, and attempts to denationalize non-Dinka groups. The past war's mode of (re)production continued in those postwar years, consolidating the conquest of non-Dinka areas, manifesting extreme group entitlement, and expanding the imagined confines of Dinka land.

The state's repression against political competitors culminated in a political crisis within the authoritarian party-state of the SPLM. The largest systematic and ethnic mass killing of Nuer by government forces in Juba on December 16, 2013, started the third civil war. The government framed this violence as a civil war and the massacre as an unfortunate side-effect of fighting. The fact that some Nuer were able to seek protection from the UN in its POC camps and that Riek Machar began a rebellion played into the government's manipulation of the "meta-conflict." The lack of international response emboldened the government.

Settling into the houses of their victims in Juba, Dinka perpetrators continued to practice ethnically exclusive wealth accumulation—but this time preceded by annihilating violence. The Juba massacre set a precedent for the targeting of non-Dinka civilians. It was the first phase of the multiethnic genocide against non-Dinka civilians, which was the result of an escalation of government violence ensuing from elite decisions rooted in an ideology of ethnic supremacy.

Violence quickly transferred to oil-rich Unity state, the only Nuer-majority state of the country and home state of Machar. The government unleashed two gruesome military campaigns against Nuer civilians in 2014 and 2015, which formed the second phase of the genocide. The state coordinated and organized multiple actors to carry out attacks, subcontracting especially its second military campaign to local Nuer perpetrators who pursued their own goals of resource accumulation and group ascension. The state used the legacy of local ethnic ranking, founded on similar dynamics in both SSDF and SPLA areas in the second civil war. This had yielded a Bul Nuer version of extreme ethnic group entitlement that worked with the Dinka ethnocracy out of dominant ethnic class interests. Perpetrators implemented violence that displaced, traumatized, and destroyed the Nuer as a group. Genocidal rape helped define the perpetrators' group in multiple ways, and violent wealth accumulation continued to be ethnically differentiated.

The rippling effects of this second genocidal phase and the military build-up following the 2015 peace agreement contributed to launch the third genocidal phase in Central Equatoria. This third phase started with the fighting in Juba between IO and the SPLA July 2016. All three genocidal phases were connected by the transference of violence from one area to the next and by extremely similar acts of genocidal violence. But there was also an escalation by July 2016, based on the two previous genocidal phases and on the perceived Equatorian threat. The perpetrators of the third phase were overwhelming Dinka. The fighting in Juba in July displayed how much more exclusionary and pervasive Dinka supremacist ideology had become since December 2013. Just like in Unity, the perpetrators lumped together civilians into a group they identified as a threat to destroy.

The perpetration of violence, including mass gang-rapes, fostered the perpetrators' groupness and consolidated the ideology of Dinka supremacy. This supremacist ideology, as an expression of extreme Dinka group entitlement, naturally culminated in the idea of group expansion through acquisition, which on a large scale amounted to conquest.

In contrast to the last civil war, this conquest was accelerated and annihilating. The SPLA's ethnically exclusionary mode of production turned genocidal, with a profitable war economy. SPLA violence was no longer mostly exploitative: it was obliterating and driven by exclusionary ideology. Yet genocidal violence was still profitable, and its proceeds were distributed on an ethnic basis.

Other instances of state military campaigns against non-Dinka civilians in Western Bahr El Ghazal and Upper Nile pointed to a similar pattern of annihilating violence, driven by the same supremacist ideology and the expansion of Dinka land. In all cases, genocidal violence fostered Dinka groupness to mask in-group competition, an ever-narrowing Dinka ethnic center of power, and an inner conquest among Dinka sections.

From the post-CPA years through this third civil war, the international community's own stereotypes about the South Sudanese and wishful thinking made it easy for the ethnocrats to remain underestimated and manipulate their former Western backers. In turn, the former backers interpreted their own failure at steering democracy in South Sudan as validation that its people were just too violent to govern themselves. They fell back on the same old colonial stereotypes inherited from military slavery and the tradition of "martial races." Yet the problem was not that the people of South Sudan were naturally aggressive and the country ungovernable. It was rather that the Western backers had sought to rid the country of its northern oppressor while supporting the rise of a predatory and violent ethnocracy. Doing so had crushed any hope for a democratic state, merely replacing one oppressor with another.

LIST OF INTERVIEW LOCATIONS

South Sudan

Aweil, Northern Bahr El Ghazal
Bentiu POC and Bentiu town, Unity
Bor, Jonglei
Ding Ding, Unity
Juba, Central Equatoria
Kajo Keji, Central Equatoria
Kerua, Central Equatoria
Koch town, Unity
Lankien, Jonglei
Lanya, Central Equatoria
Logo, Central Equatoria
Malakal, Upper Nile
Morobo, Central Equatoria
Nimule, Eastern Equatoria
Nyal, Unity
Rumbek, Lakes
Torit, Eastern Equatoria
Wau, Western Bahr El Ghazal
Yei, Central Equatoria
Yuai, Jonglei

Uganda

Bidi Bidi refugee camp
Imvepi refugee camp
Kampala
Lamwo refugee camp
Rhino refugee camp
Yumbe

Ethiopia

Addis Ababa

Kenya

Nairobi

USA

New York
Washington, DC

France

Paris

Notes

FROM PREDATION TO GENOCIDE

Epigraphs: Member of Civil Society 10, February 2, 2016; Thirty-five-year-old displaced woman from Lomuku village, Yei county, June 16, 2017

1. Douglas H. Johnson, "Briefing: The Crisis In South Sudan," *African Affairs* 113, no. 451 (April 2014): 300.

2. The exception may be South Sudanese intellectual Peter Adwok Nyaba's latest book, largely ignored by international circles, most likely due to his affiliation with the opposition. Peter Adwok Nyaba, *South Sudan. Elites, Ethnicity, Endless Wars and the Stunted State* (Dar es Salaam: Mkuki Na Nyota Publishers Ltd, 2019).

3. Benjamin Lieberman, "'Ethnic Cleansing' Versus Genocide?," in *The Oxford Handbook of Genocide Studies*, ed. Donald Bloxham and A. Dirk Moses (New York: Oxford University Press, 2010), 42, 44.

4. Member of Civil Society 4, June 14, 2017. I use the term "civil society" very broadly to protect the anonymity of local nonstate and unarmed organized actors I interviewed.

5. Thirty-two-year-old displaced woman from Malakal town, interview with the author, June 21, 2017.

6. United Nations General Assembly, Convention on the Prevention and Punishment of the Crime of Genocide, 1021 § (1948), https://treaties.un.org/doc/publication/unts/volume%2078/volume-78-i-1021-english.pdf. I later turn to the wealth of academic definitions of genocide.

7. Replace "Holocaust" with "Rwanda" in Moses and Bloxham's remark: "If the Holocaust is taken as an 'ideal type' genocide, scholars and advocates of particular cases often seek to fit theirs within a 'Holocaust paradigm' at the expense of careful contextualization." A. Dirk Moses and Donald Bloxham, "Editor's Introduction: Changing Themes in the Study of Genocide," in *The Oxford Handbook of Genocide Studies*, 4.

8. "Rulers and their associates resemble a mafia rather than a government if one thinks of the latter as necessarily serving some collective interest, however faint and by whatever means, to be distinguished from the mafia." William Reno, *Warlord Politics and African States* (Boulder, CO: Lynne Rienner Publishers, 1999), 3.

9. The "Equatorians" are not an ethnic group but a regional label for various ethnic groups. I return to the issue later.

10. I borrow the expression from Donald Bloxham in the case of the Armenian genocide: "The expulsion during the First World War of the majority of the Ottoman Armenians, including the murder of approximately one million of them, was part of a drive for Ottoman-Turkish population homogeneity in Anatolia . . . and in adjacent Cilicia on the Mediterranean coast. An intrinsic part of this drive, indeed, a trigger at certain points, was the settlement of Muslims in the stead of the Armenians in a sort of 'inner colonization,' as one contemporary observer described it: an attempt to consolidate Ottoman control of the land by the installation of 'ethnically-reliable' subjects in the stead of 'untrustworthy' ones." Donald Bloxham, "Internal Colonization, Inter-Imperial Conflict and the Armenian Genocide," in *Empire, Colony, Genocide: Conquest, Occupation and Subaltern Resistance in World History*, ed. A. Dirk Moses (New York: Berghahn Books, 2008), 326.

11. Mark Levene, *Genocide in the Age of the Nation State*, vol. 1 (London: I.B. Tauris & Co. Ltd, 2005), 163; A. Dirk Moses, ed., *Genocide and Settler Society: Frontier Violence and Stolen Indigenous Children in Australian History* (New York: Berghahn Books, 2004), xvi; A. Dirk Moses, "Empire, Colony, Genocide: Keywords and the Philosophy of History," in *Empire, Colony, Genocide*, ed. Moses, 9, 34.

12. Donald Horowitz, *Ethnic Groups in Conflict* (Berkeley: University of California Press, 1985), 186.

13. I find Horowitz's notion of group entitlement most useful to analyze South Sudan, but other notable works on conflict and intergroup comparisons include Ted Robert Gurr, *Why Men Rebel* (Princeton, NJ: Princeton University Press, 1970); W.G. Runciman, *Relative Deprivation and Social Justice: A Study of Attitudes to Social Inequality in Twentieth-Century England* (Berkeley: University of California Press, 1966); Jim Sidanius and Felicia Pratto, *Social Dominance: An Intergroup Theory of Social Hierarchy and Oppression* (New York: Cambridge University Press, 1999); Roger D. Petersen, *Understanding Ethnic Violence Fear, Hatred, and Resentment in Twentieth-Century Eastern Europe* (Cambridge: Cambridge University Press, 2002). See for a review of the literature Christopher Claassen, "Group Entitlement, Anger and Participation in Intergroup Violence," *British Journal of Political Science* 46, no. 1 (2016): 127–48.

14. Horowitz, *Ethnic Groups in Conflict*, 201–2.

15. Rogers Brubaker, *Ethnicity without Groups* (Cambridge, MA: Harvard University Press, 2004), 12.

16. Jane I. Guyer, "Wealth in People, Wealth in Things—Introduction," *Journal of African History*, no. 36 (1995): 83–90.

17. "The concept of mode of production, therefore, involves a complex interaction between economy, society, and the state in a form that reproduces these relationships. The essential ingredients include the prevalence of slave labour in vital sectors of the economy, the development of class relationships based on the relegation of slaves to the bottom of the social order, and the consolidation of a political and commercial infrastructure that can maintain these forms of exploitation ... other relationships, such as those based on kinship, tribute, taxation, and plunder, are usually affected and may become dependent on relationships associated with slavery." Paul E. Lovejoy, *Transformations in Slavery: A History of Slavery in Africa*, 1st ed. (Cambridge: Cambridge University Press, 1983), 9–11, 269–70.

18. For a history of the Marxian concept of mode of production, neglected in favor of Immanuel Wallerstein's "world systems" since the 1980s, and for parallels between capitalism and slavery (capitalism being a transformation of slavery), see David Graeber, "Turning Modes of Production Inside Out: Or, Why Capitalism Is a Transformation of Slavery," *Critique of Anthropology* 26, no. 1 (2006): 61–85. My point of view differs since I see a historical connection in South Sudan, when Graeber focuses on logical terms and industrial capitalism elsewhere.

19. I have argued elsewhere that wartime predation was the engine of the process of dominant-class formation. See Pinaud, "South Sudan: Civil War, Predation And The Making Of A Military Aristocracy," *African Affairs* 113, no. 451 (April 2014): 200, 210; "'We Are Trained to Be Married!' Elite Formation and Ideology in the 'Girls' Battalion' of the Sudan People's Liberation Army,'" *Journal of Eastern African Studies* 9, no. 3 (2015): 10; "Military Kinship, Inc.: Patronage, Inter-Ethnic Marriages and Social Classes in South Sudan," *Review of African Political Economy*, June 2016, 253.

20. A critique articulated by Michael Mann, *The Dark Side of Democracy: Explaining Ethnic Cleansing* (Cambridge: Cambridge University Press, 2005), 5.

21. Civilian support was key in running the SPLA, which exhibited traits of both an "activist" and an "opportunist" rebellion in the second civil war. Jeremy M. Weinstein,

Inside Rebellion: The Politics of Insurgent Violence. (Cambridge: Cambridge University Press, 2007), 7, 9.

22. Marielle Debos, *Living by the Gun in Chad: Combatants, Impunity and State Formation* (London: Zed Books, 2016), 10.

23. Ana Arjona, Nelson Kasfir, and Zachariah Mampilly, "Introduction," in *Rebel Governance in Civil War*, ed. Ana Arjona, Nelson Kasfir, and Zachariah Mampilly (Cambridge: Cambridge University Press, 2015), 10.

24. Stathis N. Kalyvas, *The Logic of Violence in Civil War* (New York: Cambridge University Press, 2006), 21–22, 363; Laia Balcells, *Rivalry and Revenge: The Politics of Violence during Civil War* (Cambridge: Cambridge University Press, 2017); Debos, *Living by the Gun in Chad*, 4–5.

25. "A way to distinguish between the two is to ask whether at least one political actor intends to govern the population it targets for violence; an empirical indicator of this intention is whether the targets of violence have the option to surrender." Kalyvas, *The Logic of Violence in Civil War*, 26.

26. I integrate analyses of sexual violence as a weapon of war and as a tool for genocide, with multiple functions. But I also use some findings from the next wave of literature arguing for other explanations than sexual violence as a policy. See Doris E. Buss, "Rethinking 'Rape as a Weapon of War,'" *Feminist Legal Studies*, no. 17 (2009): 146–49; Kerry F. Crawford, *Wartime Sexual Violence: From Silence to Condemnation of a Weapon of War* (Washington, DC: Georgetown University Press, 2017), 47; Elisabeth Jean Wood, "Variation in Sexual Violence during War," *Politics and Society* 34, no. 3 (September 2006): 307–41; Maria Eriksson Baaz and Maria Stern, "Why Do Soldiers Rape? Masculinity, Violence, and Sexuality in the Armed Forces in the Congo (DRC)," *International Studies Quarterly* 53, no. 2 (June 2009): 495–518; Dara Kay Cohen, *Rape during Civil War* (Ithaca, NY: Cornell University Press, 2016), 17–56.

27. "Governments and rebel groups with narrow domestic and international constituencies tend to be more isolated from domestic and international criticism, thus reducing the costs of violence and the incentives for restraint." Jessica A. Stanton, *Violence and Restraint in Civil War Civilian Targeting in the Shadow of International Law* (Cambridge: Cambridge University Press, 2016), 10.

28. The way in which the West has shaped the ideology of ethnic supremacy in South Sudan includes steering feelings of humiliation, which is not atypical. See Louisa Lombard, *State of Rebellion: Violence and Intervention in the Central African Republic* (London: Zed Books, 2016), 14.

29. This was particularly evident in the souring relationship of South Sudan with its biggest backer, the United States. See for a history of the relationship between South Sudan and the U.S. John Young, *South Sudan's Civil War: Violence, Insurgency and Failed Peacemaking* (London: Zed Books Ltd, 2019).

30. I consulted some of the national archives regarding the colonial period and the first interwar period in Washington, DC, and Juba; some of the latter I cite in the first chapter. They constitute a minority of my sources.

31. Mahmood Mamdani, *When Victims Become Killers: Colonialism, Nativism and Genocide in Rwanda* (Princeton, NJ: Princeton University Press, 2001); Dan Stone, "Genocide and Memory," in *The Oxford Handbook of Genocide Studies*, ed. Moses and Bloxham, 108, 118.

32. I carried out 150 interviews over a period of two years in 2009–10, 75 interviews in July–August 2014, 215 interviews in September 2015–March 2016, and 110 interviews in June–July 2017.

33. "We remember insults and injuries best . . . When something terrifying happens, like seeing a child or a friend hurt in an accident, we will retain an intense and largely

accurate memory of the event for a long time . . . the more adrenaline you secrete, the more precise your memory will be. But that is true only to a certain point. Confronted with horror—especially the horror of 'inescapable shock'—this system becomes overwhelmed and breaks down." Bessel Van Der Kolk, *The Body Keeps The Score. Brain, Mind And Body In The Healing of Trauma*. (New York: Penguin Books, 2015), 177–78, 192, 196.

34. "The fact that people can say that 'this has happened' remains the starting point for historiography." Stone, "Genocide and Memory," 104.

35. For example, Alexander Laban Hinton, *Why Did They Kill? Cambodia in the Shadow of Genocide* (Berkeley: University of California Press, 2005).

36. Scott Straus, *Making and Unmaking Nations: War, Leadership and Genocide in Modern Africa* (Ithaca, NY: Cornell University Press, 2015), xi.

37. I also use the administrative delineations prior to the presidential decree of October 2015 that divided South Sudan into twenty-eight states for the sake of clarity, since administrative units keep on being added and divided since then.

38. Straus, *Making and Unmaking Nations*, 34.

39. Hence my imperfect decision to include in this case, whenever possible and relevant, the respondent's ethnicity, since "Equatorian" is originally a regional identity (unlike Nuer or Dinka) with ethnic connotations. For example, I will write Madi (Equatorian). Madi refers to the respondent's ethnic group, while Equatorian is the overarching regional category by which the respondent is identified and/or identifies.

40. Brubaker, *Ethnicity without Groups*.

41. Mann, *The Dark Side of Democracy*, 21.

42. In other words, similar historical processes could have befallen another group than the Dinka—for example, the Nuer. But they did not, and this book explains why.

43. See for a summary of different approaches to defining genocide Straus, *Making and Unmaking Nations*, 1–7; Scott Straus, "Contested Meanings and Conflicting Imperatives: A Conceptual Analysis of Genocide," *Journal of Genocide Research* 3, no. 3 (2001): 349–75.

44. In this, I sympathize with Leo Kuper: "I shall follow the definition of genocide given in the UN Convention. This is not to say that I agree with the definition. On the contrary, I believe a major omission to be in the exclusion of political groups from the list of groups protected . . . However, I do not think it helpful to create a new definition of genocide, when there is an internationally recognized definition and a Convention on Genocide which might become the basis for some effective action, however limited the underlying conception." Leo Kuper, *Genocide: Its Political Use in the Twentieth Century* (New Haven: Yale University Press, 1981), 39.

45. Straus, *Making and Unmaking Nations*, 1.

46. Straus, 10, 20–24.

47. Eric D. Weitz, *A Century of Genocide: Utopias of Race and Nation* (Princeton, NJ: Princeton University Press, 2003), 9.

48. A lot of documents claiming to originate from the government of South Sudan but presumed to be fake have circulated online.

49. Mann, *The Dark Side of Democracy*, 208.

50. Levene, *Genocide in the Age of the Nation State*, 1:157.

51. Levene, 1:157.

52. It is again consistent with other studies documenting various motivations among perpetrators, including in Darfur, as noted by Dominik J. Shaller, "From Lemkin to Clooney: The Development and State of Genocide Studies," *Genocide Studies and Prevention: An International Journal* 6, no. 3 (2011): 252.

53. Henry Hale, "Explaining Ethnicity," *Comparative Political Studies* 37, no. 4 (May 2004): 458–85.

54. Writing of Rwanda's masterminding elite, the "director" of violence, Lee Ann Fuji noted that "no director's vision is ever hegemonic. Realization of the director's ideas depends on the actors themselves—their skills, interests, and commitment level." Fuji, *Killing Neighbors: Webs of Violence in Rwanda* (Ithaca, NY: Cornell University Press, 2009), 13.

55. The US State Department labeled Darfur a genocide, unlike the UN Security Council, who referred the case to the ICC but whose international Commission of Inquiry on Darfur found no evidence of genocidal intent. I will highlight here the main differences between Darfur and the third civil war in South Sudan. The first phase of genocidal violence in South Sudan was not started as a counterinsurgency like in Darfur; instead, it triggered the civil war. Perpetrators in South Sudan are largely (with the exception of some of the violence in Unity state) of the same ethnicity as the state ordering the violence—Dinka—contrary to Darfur, where the state subcontracted local Arab militias. The state perpetrated most of the violence in South Sudan on foot, in contrast to the much more prominent role of aircrafts in Darfur. Extreme violence affected multiple groups and on a longer time span in South Sudan (2003–4 were by far the most violent years in Darfur). Sudanese state officials (for example Ahmed Haroun) and the militias they supported were much less shy in outlining their decimating plans and claiming responsibility (until they opted for denial and deception), as opposed to the South Sudanese state, which was much more careful to cover its tracks from the beginning. There are still multiple links between these two events. The history of the Sudanese state's extractive relation and racism with its (traditionally) non-Arab peripheries still permeates South Sudanese politics and the making of a supremacist ideology, since the South Sudanese situation is partly a reaction to and a consequence of it. It played out differently in Darfur, where the Arab supremacist ideology originated in regional politics (particularly Libya since the 1980s) and was supported by the state. For more, see Alex De Waal and Julie Flint, *Darfur: A New History of a Long War*, 2nd ed. (London/New York: Zed Books, 2008), 121, 70, 133, 147, 179–83, 47–52; Gérard Prunier, *Darfour, Un Génocide Ambigu* (Paris: La Table ronde, 2005), 195, 226–29; Clémence Pinaud, "Genocides in the Sudans," in *The Cambridge World History of Genocide*, vol. 3, ed. Wendy Lower, Ben Kiernan, Norman Naimark, and Scott Straus (Cambridge: Cambridge University Press, forthcoming).

56. Thirty-four-year old displaced man from Wau, interview with the author, July 7, 2017.

57. Independent International Commission of Inquiry on the Syrian Arab Republic, "'They Came to Destroy': ISIS Crimes Against the Yazidis" (Geneva: Independent International Commission of Inquiry on the Syrian Arab Republic, June 15, 2016), 29.

58. Straus, *Making and Unmaking Nations*, x.

59. A metaconflict is a "conflict over the nature of the conflict." Brubaker, *Ethnicity without Groups*, 111.

60. Observer 5, interview with the author, October 31, 2017.

61. Independent International Commission of Inquiry on the Syrian Arab Republic, "'They Came to Destroy,'" 22, 27.

62. Member of civil society 4, interview with the author, June 14, 2017.

63. Catharine A. MacKinnon, "Genocide's Sexuality," *Nomos*, Political Exclusion and Domination, 46 (2005): 315.

64. Lieberman, "'Ethnic Cleansing' Versus Genocide?," 42–61.

65. Thirty-year-old displaced woman from Kayaya village, Yei county, interview with the author, June 16, 2017.

66. Member of civil society 3, interview with the author, July 4, 2017.

67. Destruction can be "in part" according to the 1948 UN Convention. A. Dirk Moses, "Raphael Lemkin, Culture, and the Concept of Genocide," in *The Oxford Handbook of Genocide Studies*, 21, 38.

68. United Nations Office of the Deputy Humanitarian Coordinator for South Sudan (UNOCHA), *Crisis Impacts on Households in Unity State, South Sudan, 2014–2015: Initial Results of a Survey* (Juba: UNOCHA, January 2016), 5.

69. Médecins Sans Frontières, "Retrospective Survey: South Sudanese Refugees Journey to the Uganda," Internal (Paris: Médecins Sans Frontières, May 2017), 7.

70. Aid Worker 14.

71. "The conflict in South Sudan has likely led to nearly 400,000 excess deaths in the country's population since it began in 2013, with around half of the lives lost estimated to be through violence." The figure of fifty thousand deaths, reportedly first issued by the International Crisis Group in 2014, had been floating around until then. "War in South Sudan Estimated to Have Led to Almost 400,000 Excess Deaths," *London School of Hygiene and Tropical Medicine* (blog), September 24, 2018, https://www.lshtm.ac.uk/new sevents/news/2018/war-south-sudan-estimated-have-led-almost-400000-excess-deaths; "U.N. Official Says at Least 50,000 Dead in South Sudan War," *Reuters*, March 2, 2016, https://www.reuters.com/article/us-southsudan-unrest-un/u-n-official-says-at-least-50000-dead-in-south-sudan-war-idUSKCN0W503Q.

72. Young, *South Sudan's Civil War*, 73; Observer 6, interview with the author, June 2, 2019. This was not the first time the UN seemed to drag its feet. See Helen Fein's description of problematic evidence gathering and analysis during the Cambodian genocide by international human rights organizations, in a context of international apathy. Helen Fein, "Genocide by Attrition 1939–1993: The Warsaw Ghetto, Cambodia, and Sudan: Links Between Human Rights, Health, And Mass Death," *Health and Human Rights* 2, no. 2 (1997): 20–21.

73. High-ranking government official 2 and wife, interview with the author, July 24, 2014; thirty-four-year-old displaced man from Wau; African Union (AU) Commission of Inquiry on South Sudan, *Final Report of the African Union Commission of Inquiry on South Sudan* (Addis Ababa: AU Commission of Inquiry on South Sudan, October 15, 2014).

74. By lack of strategic thinking I mean failing to ask the right questions or not knowing how to interpret data in a particular local context.

75. The Khmer Rouge was still given a share of Cambodia's seat at the UN after it was ousted from power in 1979. Cambodia was isolated until it was finally accepted back into the international community in 1993, regaining its seat at the UN. The Khmer Rouge only came to an end in late 1998, twenty years after the genocide. See Fein, "Genocide by Attrition," 20–21; Hinton, *Why Did They Kill?*, 6–7, 13–15; Seth Mydans, "11 Years, $300 Million and 3 Convictions. Was the Khmer Rouge Tribunal Worth It?," *New York Times*, April 10, 2017, https://www.nytimes.com/2017/04/10/world/asia/cambodia-khmer-rouge-united-nations-tribunal.html.

1. FROM THE TURKIYYA TO THE SECOND CIVIL WAR

1. Douglas H. Johnson, *The Root Causes of Sudan's Civil Wars*, 2nd ed. (Bloomington: Indiana University Press, 2007), 2.

2. Alicia C. Decker, *In Idi Amin's Shadow. Women, Gender and Militarism in Uganda* (Athens: Ohio University Press, 2014), 20.

3. Douglas H. Johnson, "Sudanese Military Slavery from the Eighteenth to the Twentieth Century," in *Slavery and Other Forms of Unfree Labour*, ed. Léonie J. Archer, History Workshop (London: Routledge, 1988), 148.

4. Stephanie Beswick, *Sudan's Blood Memory: The Legacy of War, Ethnicity, and Slavery in Early South Sudan* (Rochester, NY: University of Rochester Press, 2004), 201.

5. Johnson, *The Root Causes*, 6.

6. G. P. Makris, "Slavery, Possession and History: The Construction of the Self among Slave Descendants in the Sudan," *Africa: Journal of the International African Institute* 66, no. 2 (1996): 161–62.

7. Johnson, *The Root Causes*, 6.

8. Douglas H. Johnson, "Recruitment and Entrapment in Private Slave Armies: The Structure of the Zarä'ib in the Southern Sudan," *Slavery and Abolition* 13, no. 1 (1992): 165–67.

9. Douglas H. Johnson, "The Structure of a Legacy: Military Slavery in Northeast Africa," *Ethnohistory*, 1989, 76–77; Johnson, "Sudanese Military Slavery," 145–46.

10. Øystein H. Rolandsen and M. W. Daly, *A History of South Sudan: From Slavery to Independence* (Cambridge: Cambridge University Press, 2016), 17, 19.

11. *Zariba* refers to fortified camps hosting traders, armed retainers, slaves, and camp followers, and from which slave raids were carried out. Johnson, "Sudanese Military Slavery," 143; Rolandsen and Daly, *A History of South Sudan*, 15.

12. Johnson, "Sudanese Military Slavery," 148–49.

13. Rolandsen and Daly, *A History of South Sudan*, 14, 15.

14. Georg August Schweinfurth, *The Heart of Africa. Three Years Travels and Adventures in the Unexplored Regions of Central Africa From 1868 to 1871*, 3rd ed. (London: S. Low, Marston, Searle & Rivington, 1878), 1:148–50.

15. Douglas H. Johnson, "The Fighting Nuer: Primary Sources and the Origins of a Stereotype," *Africa* 51, no. 01 (1981): 511, 512.

16. Rolandsen and Daly, *A History of South Sudan*, 14.

17. Johnson, "The Structure of a Legacy," 79.

18. Johnson, *The Root Causes*, 6–7; Rolandsen and Daly, *A History of South Sudan*, 10, 26.

19. Johnson, *The Root Causes*, 7.

20. Matthew LeRiche and Matthew Arnold, *South Sudan: From Revolution to Independence.* (London: Hurst & Company, 2012), 9.

21. The Sudanese troops, under British, Sudanese, and Egyptian troops, started the conquest of the southern Sudan in 1900. David Keen, *The Benefits of Famine: A Political Economy of Famine and Relief in Southwestern Sudan, 1983–1989*, 2nd ed. (Oxford: James Currey, 2008), 28–29; Robert O. Collins, *Land beyond the Rivers: The Southern Sudan 1898–1918*, 1st ed. (New Haven, CT: Yale University Press, 1971), 15.

22. Keen, *The Benefits of Famine*, 28–29; Collins, *Land beyond the Rivers*, 90.

23. Johnson, *The Root Causes*, 83; Peter Woodward, *Sudan, 1898–1989: The Unstable State* (Boulder, CO: Lynne Rienner Publishers Inc, 1990), 26; Francis Mading Deng, *War of Visions: Conflict of Identities in the Sudan* (Washington, DC: Brookings Institution Press, 1995), 77; Douglas H. Johnson, "The Nuer Civil War," in *Sudanese Society in the Context of Civil War. Papers from a Seminar at the University of Copenhagen, 9–10 February 2001*, ed. Maj-Britt Johannsen and Niels Kastfelt (Copenhagen: University of Copenhagen North/South Priority Research Area, 2001), 3; David Keen, *The Economic Functions of Violence in Civil Wars*, 1st ed., Adelphi Paper 320 (Oxford: International Institute for Strategic Studies, 1998), 29; Rolandsen and Daly, *A History of South Sudan*, 41.

24. Johnson, *The Root Causes*, 9–10. The Anglo-Egyptian Condominium was established after the Anglo-Egyptian conquest of Sudan and allowed the British to rule Sudan with Egyptian intermediaries.

25. Øystein H. Rolandsen, "The Making of the Anya-Nya Insurgency in the Southern Sudan, 1961–64," *Journal of Eastern African Studies* 5, no. 2 (2011): 213.

26. Johnson, *The Root Causes*, 12; Robert O. Collins, *The Southern Sudan in Historical Perspective* (University of Tel Aviv: Shiloah Center for Middle Eastern and African Studies, 1975), 52; Johnson, "The Fighting Nuer," 514. The administration in the south was

developed further along "African" rather than "Arab" lines, since the south was closer to East Africa than to the Middle East. Johnson, *The Root Causes*, 11; Deng, *War of Visions*, 96–97.

27. Lilian Passmore Sanderson and Neville Sanderson, *Education, Religion & Politics in Southern Sudan, 1899–1964* (London: Ithaca Press, 1981), 421, 430–31.

28. Johnson, *The Root Causes*, 11, 16–17.

29. Makris, "Slavery, Possession and History," 163.

30. Johnson, "Sudanese Military Slavery," 150; Johnson, "The Structure of a Legacy," 81–82.

31. Johnson, "Sudanese Military Slavery," 150, 152.

32. Johnson, *The Root Causes*, 11, 16–17.

33. Douglas H. Johnson, "Enforcing Separate Identities in the Southern Sudan: The Case of the Nilotes of the Upper Nile," in *Les ethnies ont une histoire*, ed. Gérard Prunier and Jean-Pierre Chrétien, 2nd ed. (Karthala, 2003), 239–40; Edward Lord Gleichen, *Handbook of the Sudan*, Intelligence Division, War Office of Great Britain (London: Harrison and Sons, 1898), 107.

34. Johnson, "Enforcing Separate Identities," 240; Lord Gleichen, *Handbook of the Sudan*, 117, 125.

35. Rolandsen and Daly, *A History of South Sudan*, 50.

36. Decker, *In Idi Amin's Shadow*, 29.

37. Lord Gleichen, *Handbook of the Sudan*, 120–21.

38. Johnson, "The Fighting Nuer," 508, 511–13, 522; Douglas H. Johnson, "Evans-Pritchard, the Nuer, and the Sudan Political Service," *African Affairs* 383, no. 81 (April 1982): 232.

39. Douglas H. Johnson, "Political Ecology of Upper Nile: The Twentieth Century Expansion of the Pastoral 'Common Economy,'" in *Herders, Warriors and Traders, Pastoralism in Africa*, ed. John G. Galaty and Pierre Bonte (Boulder, CO: Westview Press, 1991), 106.

40. Johnson, "Enforcing Separate Identities," 241–44; Johnson, "The Fighting Nuer," 515–16, 520; S.G.D. H. A. Romilly, District Commissioner, Western Nuer, "Letter to the Governor of Upper Nile Province," May 3, 1932, box no. 919, South Sudan National Archives; Governor of Kordofan, "Dinka Administration," May 27, 1929, box no. 298, South Sudan National Archives; Governor of Kordofan, "Upper Nile Province-Kordofan Province Boundaries," March 19, 1930, box no. 298, South Sudan National Archives.

41. Johnson, "Enforcing Separate Identities," 241–44; Johnson, "The Fighting Nuer," 515–16, 520.

42. Rolandsen and Daly, *A History of South Sudan*, 45.

43. Governor of Kordofan, "Dinka Administration."

44. Beswick, *Sudan's Blood Memory*, 1–2.

45. Johnson, "Enforcing Separate Identities," 241–44; Johnson, "The Fighting Nuer," 515.

46. Johnson, "The Fighting Nuer," 516–17, 520.

47. Rolandsen and Daly, *A History of South Sudan*, 58.

48. Johnson, *The Root Causes*, 12, 18.

49. Former high-ranking SPLA and government official, interview with the author, August 7, 2014.

50. Johnson, *The Root Causes*, 13, 15, 17, 18–19.

51. Forty-year-old displaced man from Pigi Canal county, Jonglei, interview with the author, July 5, 2017.

52. Johnson, *The Root Causes*, 13, 15, 17, 18–19.

53. Johnson, 22; LeRiche and Arnold, *From Revolution to Independence*, 9; Woodward, *The Unstable State*, 64–65.

54. Johnson, *The Root Causes*, 22.

55. Deng, *War of Visions*, 129; Gérard Prunier, "Rebel Movements and Proxy Warfare: Uganda, Sudan and the Congo (1986–99)," *African Affairs* 103, no. 412 (July 1, 2004): 363.

56. Johnson, *The Root Causes*, 27; Dunstan M. Wai, *The African-Arab Conflict in the Sudan* (New York: Africana Publishing Company, 1981), 85; Deng, *War of Visions*, 135.

57. LeRiche and Arnold, *From Revolution to Independence*, 13–14.

58. Makris, "Slavery, Possession and History," 163.

59. Øystein H. Rolandsen, "A False Start: Between War and Peace in The Southern Sudan, 1956–62," *Journal of African History* 52, no. 1 (2011): 109. Torit is located in the region of Equatoria, renamed Eastern Equatoria with the signature of the CPA in 2005. At the time it was the headquarters of the Equatorial Corps. The mutiny has been associated with the beginning of the first civil war, which historians like Johnson and Rolandsen have contradicted, arguing that it started rather in 1963–64.

60. Johnson, *The Root Causes*, 28; Rolandsen, "A False Start," 111; LeRiche and Arnold, *From Revolution to Independence*, 12.

61. Rolandsen, "A False Start," 112; Rolandsen, "The Making of the Anya-Nya," 105; Rolandsen and Daly, *A History of South Sudan*, 73.

62. LeRiche and Arnold, *From Revolution to Independence*, 14, 15.

63. Johnson, *The Root Causes*, 22.

64. Johnson, 30; Rolandsen, "The Making of the Anya-Nya," 214.

65. Douglas H. Johnson, "Twentieth-Century Civil Wars," in *The Sudan Handbook*, ed. John Ryle et al. (New York: James Currey, 2011), 124.

66. Rolandsen, "The Making of the Anya-Nya," 214; Deng, *War of Visions*, 12.

67. LeRiche and Arnold, *From Revolution to Independence*, 12; Rolandsen, "A False Start," 121.

68. LeRiche and Arnold, *From Revolution to Independence*, 15.

69. Rolandsen, "A False Start," 106, 122.

70. Johnson, "Twentieth-Century Civil Wars," 122–23, 125.

71. The SANU was initially called the Sudan African Closed Districts National Union (SACDNU), created in February 1962 by Willian Deng, Father Saturnino Lahure, and Joseph Oduho. Rolandsen, "The Making of the Anya-Nya," 215.

72. Rolandsen, "The Making of the Anya-Nya," 211.

73. The Upper Nile region comprises the modern-day states of Upper Nile, Jonglei, and Unity, and the region of Bahr El Ghazal encompasses the modern-day states of Lakes, Warrap, Northern Bahr El Ghazal, and Western Bahr El Ghazal.

74. Johnson, *The Root Causes*, 28, 32–33; Edgar O'Balance, *The Secret War in the Sudan, 1955–1972* (Hamden, CT: Archon Books, 1977), 83.

75. Johnson, *The Root Causes*, 35; O'Balance, *The Secret War*, 84.

76. Johnson, *The Root Causes*, 34; O'Balance, *The Secret War*, 80–81; Political representative 1, interview with the author, October 24, 2010.

77. Benaiah Yongo-Bure, "The Underdevelopment of the Southern Sudan since Independence," in *Civil War in the Sudan*, ed. M. W. Daly and Ahmad Alawad Sikainga (London: British Academy Press, 1993), 53; O'Balance, *The Secret War*, 80.

78. O'Balance, *The Secret War*, 82, 86.

79. Rolandsen, "The Making of the Anya-Nya," 227.

80. Douglas H. Johnson and Gérard Prunier, "The Foundation and Expansion of the Sudan People's Liberation Army," in *Civil War in the Sudan*, ed. M. W. Daly and Ahmad Alawad Sikainga (London: British Academic Press, 1993), 118.

81. Rolandsen, "The Making of the Anya-Nya," 227; O'Balance, *The Secret War*, 79, 85.

82. Johnson, *The Root Causes*, 32–33.

83. Johnson, 31–33, 34.

84. Rolandsen, "A False Start," 117.

85. Johnson, *The Root Causes*, 34, 36.

86. Øystein H. Rolandsen, "Civil War Society?: Political Processes, Social Groups and Conflict Intensity in the Southern Sudan, 1955–2005" (PhD diss., University of Oslo, 2010), 181; Johnson and Prunier, "Foundation and Expansion," 133. (Reversely, the SPLA already counted about 20,000 men in 1985.)

87. Johnson and Prunier, "Foundation and Expansion," 119; O'Balance, *The Secret War*, 116.

88. Johnson, *The Root Causes*, 34; Rolandsen, "A False Start," 117; O'Balance, *The Secret War*, 81, 96, 103; Deng, *War of Visions*, 12.

89. Johnson, *The Root Causes*, 32–33; O'Balance, *The Secret War*, 96.

90. O'Balance, *The Secret War*, 115–16.

91. Johnson, *The Root Causes*, 36–37; Johnson and Prunier, "Foundation and Expansion," 119.

92. O'Balance, *The Secret War*, 127; Johnson, *The Root Causes*, 36–37.

93. Woodward, *The Unstable State*, 142.

94. Johnson, *The Root Causes*, 39–41; Woodward, *The Unstable State*, 143; Deng, *War of Visions*, 136.

95. The Nuer and Dinka Anyanya units were among the most reluctant parties to the Addis Ababa Agreement. Johnson, "The Nuer Civil War," 4.

96. Johnson and Prunier, "Foundation and Expansion," 120.

97. Sharon Elaine Hutchinson, *Nuer Dilemmas: Coping with Money, War, and the State* (Berkeley: University of California Press, 1996), 27; Yongo-Bure, "The Underdevelopment of the Southern Sudan," 53–54.

98. Johnson, *The Root Causes*, 42–43.

99. Yongo-Bure, "The Underdevelopment of the Southern Sudan," 64–65.

100. Johnson, *The Root Causes*, 50.

101. Johnson, *The Root Causes*, 43–44; Deng, *War of Visions*, 12.

102. Apart from oil, the south's main economic asset was water. In 1974, the government launched the project of the Jonglei canal to meet the agricultural expansion of both Egypt and the Sudan. The southern regional government was not involved in the Jonglei scheme and the central government decided everything. The area of the Jonglei Canal saw very little development. Johnson, *The Root Causes*, 48–49; Woodward, *The Unstable State*, 160.

103. Johnson, *The Root Causes*, 46–47.

104. Johnson, *The Root Causes*, 42–43, 52–53; Peter Woodward, *The Unstable State*, 145.

105. Even after the official end of the civil war, ex-Anyanya fighters remained in Ethiopia and were active throughout the late 1970s and early 1980s. Johnson, *The Root Causes*, 42–43.

106. Political representative 2, interview with the author, August 1, 2014.

107. Member of civil society 1, interview with the author, June 30, 2017; member of civil society 2, interview with the author, July 8, 2016.

108. Member of civil society 3, interview with the author, July 4, 2017.

109. Rolandsen and Daly, *A History of South Sudan*, 92.

110. Edward Thomas, *South Sudan: A Slow Liberation* (London: Zed Books Ltd, 2015), 99–100.

111. Clémence Pinaud, "South Sudan: Civil War, Predation And The Making Of A Military Aristocracy," *African Affairs* 113, no. 451 (April 2014): 192–211; Alex De Waal, "When Kleptocracy Becomes Insolvent: Brute Causes of the Civil War in South Sudan," *African Affairs*, 113, no. 452 (2014): 347–69.

112. Johnson, *The Root Causes*, 29; O'Balance, *The Secret War*, 84; Rolandsen and Daly, *A History of South Sudan*, 100.

113. Johnson, *The Root Causes*, 29; O'Balance, *The Secret War*, 84; Rolandsen and Daly, *A History of South Sudan*, 100.

114. Member of civil society 4, interview with the author, June 14, 2017; John Young, *The Fate of Sudan: The Origins and Consequences of a Flawed Peace Process* (London: Zed Books, 2012), 104, 139.

115. Member of civil society 3.

116. Longtime observer 1, interview with the author, January 3, 2018; former high-ranking government official 1, interview with the author, July 11, 2017; South Sudanese intellectual 1, interview with the author, November 21, 2017.

117. Rolandsen and Daly, *A History of South Sudan*, 100–101; Douglas H. Johnson, "Federalism in the History of South Sudan Political Thought," Rift Valley Institute Research Paper (London: Rift Valley Institute, 2014), 19.

118. Thomas, *A Slow Liberation*, 101–2.

119. Johnson, *The Root Causes*, 51–52.

120. Rens Willems and David Deng, "The Legacy of Kokora in South Sudan. Intersections of Truth, Justice and Reconciliation in South Sudan," briefing paper, South Sudan Law Society, University for Peace, Pax Christi, November 2015, 7; Joseph Lagu, *Sudan: Odyssey through a State: From Ruin to Hope* (Omdurman Sudan: M.O.B Center for Sudanese Studies Omdurman Ahlia University, 2006), 376.

121. Johnson, *The Root Causes*, 52–53.

122. Johnson, 51.

123. Forty-year-old displaced man from Pigi Canal county, Jonglei.

124. Former high-ranking government official 1.

125. Johnson, *The Root Causes*, 18.

126. Thomas, *A Slow Liberation*, 101–2. My emphasis.

127. Donald Horowitz, *Ethnic Groups in Conflict* (Berkeley: University of California Press, 1985), 226.

128. Sixty-year-old displaced man from Ikotos / IO major general, interview with the author, July 8, 2017.

129. South Sudanese intellectual 1.

130. Beswick, *Sudan's Blood Memory*, 245.

131. Member of civil society 3.

132. Beswick, *Sudan's Blood Memory*, 139, 176–83, 190.

133. Johnson, *The Root Causes*, 18.

134. South Sudanese intellectual 2, interview with the author, July 11, 2017.

135. Horowitz, *Ethnic Groups in Conflict*, 110.

136. Willems and Deng, "The Legacy of Kokora," 8.

137. Rolandsen and Daly, *A History of South Sudan*, 95–96.

138. Thomas, *A Slow Liberation*, 99.

139. Willems and Deng, "The Legacy of Kokora," 7.

140. Beswick, *Sudan's Blood Memory*, 207.

141. High-ranking government official 1, interview with the author, August 5, 2014.

142. Rolandsen and Daly, *A History of South Sudan*, 101.

143. Member of civil society 5, interview with the author, July 4, 2017.

144. Clémence Pinaud, "Military Kinship, Inc.: Patronage, Inter-Ethnic Marriages and Social Classes in South Sudan," *Review of African Political Economy*, June 2016, 249.

145. Former SPLA commander, interview with the author, August 4, 2014.

146. Beswick, *Sudan's Blood Memory*, 177.

147. Pinaud, "Military Kinship, Inc.," 249.

148. Fifty-five-year-old displaced man from Agoro payam, Magwi county, June 27, 2017.

149. Political representative 2, interview with the author, August 1, 2014.

150. Beswick, *Sudan's Blood Memory*, 134, 138.

151. Johnson, *The Root Causes*, 53–55.

152. Rolandsen and Daly, *A History of South Sudan*, 100–101; Willems and Deng, "The Legacy of Kokora.," 1.

153. Willems and Deng, "The Legacy of Kokora.," 14.

154. Political representative 2.

155. High-ranking government official 2, interview with the author, July 24, 2014.

156. Political representative 2.

157. High-ranking government official 2.

158. Johnson, *The Root Causes*, 56–57; Woodward, *The Unstable State*, 153.

159. Johnson, *The Root Causes*, 54; Woodward, *The Unstable State*, 180.

160. Woodward, *The Unstable State*, 159.

161. Peter Adwok Nyaba, *Politics of Liberation in South Sudan: An Insider's View* (Kampala: Fountain Publishers, 1997), 26; Deng, *War of Visions*, 12–13.

162. Johnson, *The Root Causes*, 60–61.

163. Alex De Waal, "Some Comments on the Militias in the Contemporary Sudan," in *Civil War in the Sudan*, ed. M. W. Daly and Ahmad Alawad Sikainga (London: British Academic Press, 1993), 150–51.

164. Johnson and Prunier, "Foundation and Expansion," 122–23; Woodward, *The Unstable State*, 161.

165. Johnson, "Twentieth-Century Civil Wars," 125.

166. Johnson, *The Root Causes*, 60–62.

167. Johnson and Prunier, "Foundation and Expansion," 122–23.

168. Johnson, *The Root Causes*, 57–58; Woodward, *The Unstable State*, 162.

169. Johnson, *The Root Causes*, 61–62.

170. Johnson, "Twentieth-Century Civil Wars," 127.

171. Johnson, *The Root Causes*, 62; Johnson and Prunier, "Foundation and Expansion," 126; Woodward, *The Unstable State*, 162.

172. Woodward, *The Unstable State*, 162.

173. Johnson, *The Root Causes*, 67.

174. Rolandsen and Daly, *A History of South Sudan*, 39.

175. Johnson, "Sudanese Military Slavery," 144, 154–55.

176. Johnson, "The Structure of a Legacy," 73.

177. Decker, *In Idi Amin's Shadow*, 20.

178. Johnson, "Sudanese Military Slavery," 150.

179. Beswick, *Sudan's Blood Memory*, 202.

180. Johnson, "Recruitment and Entrapment"; Clémence Pinaud, "Are 'Griefs of More Value Than Triumphs'? Power Relations, Nation-Building and the Different Histories of Women's Wartime Contributions in Postwar South Sudan," *Journal of Northeast African Studies* 13, no. 2 (2013): 151–76; Clémence Pinaud, ""We Are Trained to Be Married!" Elite Formation and Ideology in the 'Girls" Battalion" of the Sudan People's Liberation Army,'" *Journal of Eastern African Studies*, no. 9:3 (2015): 375–93; Pinaud, "Military Kinship, Inc."

181. Johnson, "The Structure of a Legacy," 83–84; Decker, *In Idi Amin's Shadow*, 23, 35.

182. Johnson, "The Structure of a Legacy," 83–84.

183. Decker, *In Idi Amin's Shadow*, 166.

184. Rolandsen and Daly, *A History of South Sudan*, 32, 36, 53, 61.

185. Member of civil society 5, interview with the author, July 4, 2017.

186. Horowitz, *Ethnic Groups in Conflict*, 135.

187. Beswick, *Sudan's Blood Memory*, 159, 206.

188. Horowitz, *Ethnic Groups in Conflict*, 144.

189. Christopher Vaughan, Mareike Schomerus, and Lotje De Vries, eds., *The Border-lands of South Sudan: Authority and Identity in Contemporary and Historical Perspectives*, Palgrave Series in African Borderlands Studies (New York: Palgrave Macmillan, 2013), 3; Pinaud, "Are 'Griefs of More Value Than Triumphs'?"

190. Horowitz, *Ethnic Groups in Conflict*, 166.

191. Horowitz, 167, 172, 175, 185.

192. Horowitz, 177–78.

193. Beswick, *Sudan's Blood Memory*, 199; Vaughan, Schomerus, and De Vries, *The Borderlands of South Sudan.*, 5.

194. Beswick, *Sudan's Blood Memory*, 140.

195. Beswick, 140.

196. Beswick, 208.

2. THE SPLA AND THE MAKING OF AN ETHNIC DINKA ARMY

1. Jeremy M. Weinstein, *Inside Rebellion. The Politics of Insurgent Violence* (Cambridge, UK: Cambridge University Press, 2007), 9–10.

2. Douglas H. Johnson, *The Root Causes of Sudan's Civil Wars*, 2nd ed. (Bloomington, IN: Indiana University Press, 2007), 59–60.

3. Johnson, *The Root Causes*, 62; Francis Mading Deng, *War of Visions: Conflict of Identities in the Sudan* (Washington, DC: Brookings Institution Press, 1995), 13.

4. Johnson, *The Root Causes*, 63.

5. Two former high-ranking government officials and high-ranking members of IO, interview with the author, February 22, 2017.

6. Johnson, *The Root Causes*, 63.

7. Two former high-ranking government officials and high-ranking members of IO. On the SPLA's ambiguities in messaging its constituency, see Zachariah Mampilly, "Performing the Nation-State: Rebel Governance and Symbolic Processes," in *Rebel Governance in Civil War*, ed. Ana Arjona, Nelson Kasfir, and Zachariah Mampilly (Cambridge: Cambridge University Press, 2015), 90.

8. Peter Adwok Nyaba, *Politics of Liberation in South Sudan: An Insider's View* (Kampala: Fountain Publishers, 1997), 26; Johnson, *The Root Causes*, 63.

9. Douglas H. Johnson, "Twentieth-Century Civil Wars," in *The Sudan Handbook*, ed. John Ryle et al. (New York: James Currey, 2011), 63–64, 127; Peter Woodward, *Sudan, 1898–1989: The Unstable State* (Boulder, CO: Lynne Rienner Publishers Inc, 1990), 162.

10. These problems included unemployment, inflation, and oppression by the state security organization.

11. Johnson, *The Root Causes*, 64–65.

12. Johnson, 64–65.

13. Nyaba, *Politics of Liberation*, 39; African Rights, *Food and Power in Sudan: A Critique of Humanitarianism* (London: African Rights, 1997), 65; "Stated Position of the Rebels: Background and Manifesto of the Sudan People's Liberation Movement (SPLM)," *Horn of Africa*, 1985; Clémence Pinaud, ""We Are Trained to Be Married!" Elite Formation and Ideology in the 'Girls" Battalion" of the Sudan People's Liberation Army,'" *Journal of Eastern African Studies*, no. 9:3 (2015): 375–93.

14. On August 28, 1991, two senior SPLA commanders from Upper Nile, Riek Machar and Lam Akol, declared the "overthrow" of John Garang, which signified the beginning of the "split" of the SPLA into two factions at first. Johnson, *The Root Causes*, 94–98.

15. Robert F. Melson, *Revolution and Genocide: On the Origins of the Armenian Genocide and the Holocaust* (Chicago: University of Chicago Press, 1992), 264, 267.

16. Arop Madut-Arop, *Sudan's Painful Road to Peace: A Full Story of the Founding and Development of SPLM/SPLA* (self-pub., Booksurge LLC, 2005), 77.

17. The first wave of South Sudanese refugees to Ethiopia arrived between the Bor mutiny in May and the launching of the SPLM in late July 1983. Johnson, *The Root Causes*, 70, 147–48; Madut-Arop, *Sudan's Painful Road to Peace*, 66, 77; Nyaba, *Politics of Liberation*, 35.

18. Nyaba, *Politics of Liberation*, 35.

19. Madut-Arop, *Sudan's Painful Road to Peace*, 86.

20. The SPLA tried to broaden its base by recruiting a few soldiers from local communities, who would in turn also recruit others. By 1988, the SPLA had Mundari and Toposa in its ranks. Johnson, *The Root Causes*, 86.

21. Madut-Arop, *Sudan's Painful Road to Peace*, 86.

22. Madut-Arop, 88; Nyaba, *Politics of Liberation*, 35.

23. Nyaba, *Politics of Liberation*, 25, 35, 39.

24. Member of civil society 6, interview with the author, August 9, 2014.

25. Nyaba, *Politics of Liberation*, 33, 38, 49, 53.

26. Nyaba, 37.

27. High-ranking government official 3, interview with the author, November 11, 2010. Later, SPLA zonal commanders such as Riek Machar, in charge of Western Upper Nile in the late 1980s, would also remove cultural taboos among the Nuer by promoting the idea that gun slayings were far more impersonal, distant, and therefore less sacrilegious than death by the spear. Jok Madut Jok and Sharon Elaine Hutchinson, "Sudan's Prolonged Second Civil War and the Militarization of Nuer and Dinka Ethnic Identities," *African Studies Review* 42, no. 2 (1999): 125–45; Sharon Elaine Hutchinson, "Nuer Ethnicity Militarized," *Anthropology Today* 16, no. 3 (June 1, 2000): 10.

28. SPLA high-ranking officer 1, interview with the author, April 4, 2009; SPLA high-ranking officer 1, interview with the author, October 5, 2010; Pinaud, "We Are Trained to Be Married!," 375–93.

29. Nyaba, *Politics of Liberation*, 35, 36–40.

30. Clémence Pinaud, "Women, Guns and Cattle: A Social History of the Second Civil War in South Sudan" (Université Paris 1 Panthéon-Sorbonne, 2013); Pinaud, "We Are Trained to Be Married!"

31. Nyaba, *Politics of Liberation*, 37.

32. "Sudan: Stalling Speed," *Africa Confidential*, May 22, 1985.

33. New Dinka recruits trying to reach Ethiopia in 1984–86 had left a trail of violence in Nuerland. They became the target of the (mostly Nuer) Anya Nya II in retaliation against the violence they had committed against Lou, Gajak, and Gawaar Nuer civilians. Nyaba, *Politics of Liberation*, 37, 45–49.

34. Two members of civil society 1, interview with the author, November 13, 2015; member of civil society 6, interview with the author, August 9, 2014.

35. Two members of civil society 1; three members of civil society 1, interview with the author, October 15, 2015.

36. Member of civil society 6, interview with the author, August 9, 2014.

37. Maria Eriksson Baaz and Maria Stern, *Sexual Violence as a Weapon of War? Perceptions, Prescriptions, Problems in the Congo and Beyond* (London: Zed Books, 2013), 72; Nyaba, *Politics of Liberation*, 50.

38. "Group crystallization and polarization were the result of violence, not the cause." Rogers Brubaker, *Ethnicity without Groups* (Cambridge, MA: Harvard University Press, 2004), 14.

39. Thomas Kühne, *The Rise and Fall of Comradeship: Hitler's Soldiers, Male Bonding and Mass Violence in the Twentieth Century* (Cambridge: Cambridge University Press, 2017), 4.

40. Kühne, 28–30; Clémence Pinaud, "Military Kinship, Inc.: Patronage, Inter-Ethnic Marriages and Social Classes in South Sudan," *Review of African Political Economy*, June 2016.

41. Kühne, *The Rise and Fall of Comradeship*, 10.

42. Garang had attended school in East Africa and had obtained his bachelor of arts from the United States. He had gained military training both in the Sudan and in America, where he also pursued a PhD in agricultural economics at Iowa State University. Johnson, *The Root Causes*, 66.

43. The Ethiopians denied Akuot Atem (a Bor Dinka from the Anya Nya II) the opportunity to be chairman of the political wing of the SPLA and proposed that Samuel Gai Tut (the Anya Nya II Nuer leader) and Garang lead the movement instead.

44. Douglas H. Johnson and Gérard Prunier, "The Foundation and Expansion of the Sudan People's Liberation Army," in *Civil War in the Sudan*, ed. M. W. Daly and Ahmad Alawad Sikainga (London: British Academic Press, 1993), 126.

45. Stephanie Beswick, *Sudan's Blood Memory: The Legacy of War, Ethnicity, and Slavery in Early South Sudan* (Rochester, NY: University of Rochester Press, 2004), 219.

46. Øystein H. Rolandsen, "Another Civil War in South Sudan: The Failure of Guerrilla Government?," *Journal of Eastern African Studies* 9, no. 1 (January 2015): 167.

47. Beswick, *Sudan's Blood Memory*, 219.

48. "If the presence of ethnic strangers provides an unflattering contrast with one's own group, that is a good reason to emphasize demands for the exclusion of strangers. Homogeneity would remove the irritating comparison." Donald Horowitz, *Ethnic Groups in Conflict* (Berkeley: University of California Press, 1985), 186.

49. Hutchinson, "Nuer Ethnicity Militarized," 6. I follow the approach of Brubaker, in *Ethnicity without Groups*, 10, 12, 19, 54, 67. Brubaker understands an ethnopolitical entrepreneur as a leader who seeks to organize an ethnic group, speaks and acts in its name and uses ethnopolitical rhetoric to reify and shape the identity of this group.

50. Member of civil society 7, interview with the author, October 15, 2015.

51. Nyaba, *Politics of Liberation*, 47; former SPLA commander, interview with the author, August 6, 2014.

52. Two members of civil society 2, interview with the author, January 30, 2016.

53. Member of civil society 7, interview with the author, October 15, 2015.

54. Former SPLA commander, August 6, 2014.

55. Former government official and high-ranking member of IO 1, interview with the author, July 13, 2014; three members of civil society 1.

56. Three members of civil society 1; member of civil society 7.

57. Former government official and high-ranking member of IO 1.

58. Sixty-year-old displaced man from Ikotos / IO major general, interview with the author, July 8, 2017. The Lango are a people of Lokua language found in Ikotos, in eastern Equatoria.

59. Pinaud, "We Are Trained to Be Married!"

60. Longtime observer 1, interview with the author, January 3, 2018.

61. Member of civil society 4, interview with the author, June 22, 2017.

62. These civilian figures included the veteran politician Joseph Oduho and the renowned judge Martin Majier. Douglas H. Johnson, "The Sudan People's Liberation Army and the Problem of Factionalism," in *African Guerrillas*, ed. Christopher Clapham (Oxford: Indiana University Press, 1998), 56–57; Johnson, *The Root Causes*, 91–92.

63. Johnson, *The Root Causes*, 91.

64. Nyaba, *Politics of Liberation*, 44, 49.

65. Kerubino Kuanyin was arrested after he tried to organize the overthrow of Garang. So was Arok Thon Arok, who had challenged Garang's authority and made contact with the Sudanese government. Johnson, *The Root Causes*, 92.

66. Julia Aker Duany, *Making Peace and Nurturing Life: A Memoir of an African Woman About a Journey of Struggle and Hope*. (Bloomington IN: 1st Books Library, 2003), 140–41; two former high-ranking government officials and high-ranking members of IO.

67. Only after the reconciliation and reunification with the Anya Nya II started in 1986 did peace and stability return to Nuer land. Nyaba, *Politics of Liberation*, 48.

68. Nyaba, 48.

69. Nyaba, 35; African Rights, *Food and Power*, 74–75.

70. These men had also enrolled mainly because of local grievances or to protect their homes, and their bitterness at the leadership would incur defections from 1991 onwards. Nyaba, *Politics of Liberation*, 177.

71. Johnson, *The Root Causes*, 94–98.

72. Nuer officers like William Nyuon left the SPLA in 1992, reportedly "because of the poor treatment he received as a Nuer." Member of civil society 7.

73. Sixty-year-old displaced man from Ikotos / IO Major General.

74. Member of Civil Society 4.

75. Member of Civil Society 1.

76. Small Arms Survey, *Armed Groups in Sudan. The South Sudan Defence Forces in the Aftermath of the Juba Declaration*, Sudan Issue Brief, Human Security Baseline Assessment (Geneva: Small Arms Survey, October 2006), 3.

77. Groupness is an event and its intensity can vary depending on events. Brubaker, *Ethnicity without Groups*, 12.

78. Brubaker, 99.

79. Former high-ranking government official 1, interview with the author, July 11, 2017.

80. South Sudanese Intellectual 2, interview with the author, July 11, 2017.

81. Member of civil society 4, interview with the author, June 14, 2017.

82. Sixty-year-old displaced man from Ikotos / IO major general.

83. Kiir was promoted by Garang to second in command to represent the greater Bahr El Ghazal region in the SPLA leadership after Kerubino Kuanyin Bol tried to organize a coup in 1987–88. Rolandsen, "Another Civil War in South Sudan," 168.

84. I still follow the approach of Brubaker, in *Ethnicity without Groups*, 13.

85. Pinaud, "Military Kinship, Inc.," 247–48.

86. Member of civil society 8, interview with the author, February 5, 2016.

87. Former high-ranking government official 1.

88. Clémence Pinaud, "Briefing Note—The War in South Sudan" (Bordeaux: Observatoire des Enjeux Politiques et Sécuritaires dans la Corne de l'Afrique, March 2015), 19, http://lam.sciencespobordeaux.fr/sites/lam/files/note7_observatoire.pdf.

89. International Crisis Group, *The Khartoum-SPLM Agreement: Sudan's Uncertain Peace*, Africa Report (International Crisis Group, July 25, 2005), 15; John Young, *The Fate of Sudan: The Origins and Consequences of a Flawed Peace Process* (London: Zed Books, 2012), 76.

90. Young, *The Fate of Sudan*, 14, 66, 93–96.

91. "By delaying in signing, Khartoum will gain $2.5 billion from the oil revenues, which we must prevent by all means possible. Khartoum was unhappy with the Power Sharing and 3 areas protocols. Neither I nor Cdr. Salva had any interest in delaying the peace agreement. I have nothing to gain by dismissing Cdr. Salva." "Minutes of Historical SPLM Meeting in Rumbek 2004." (*Sudan Tribune*, March 10, 2008), http://www.sudantribune.com/spip.php?article26320.

92. Former high-ranking government official 1.

93. Sixty-year-old displaced man from Ikotos / IO major general.

94. Young, *The Fate of Sudan*, 84.

95. "Minutes of Historical SPLM Meeting in Rumbek 2004."

96. International Crisis Group, "The Khartoum-SPLM Agreement," 15; Young, *The Fate of Sudan*, 76; "Minutes of Historical SPLM Meeting in Rumbek 2004." (Sudan Tribune, March 10, 2008), http://www.sudantribune.com/spip.php?article26320.

97. Horowitz, *Ethnic Groups in Conflict*, 146–47, 148–49, 166–67, 185, 188.

98. Pinaud, "Military Kinship, Inc."

99. "Cdr. James Oath. I greet the gathering. When the movement started you were seven (7) and now you are only two (2)—five died having problems with you (Dr. John)... Cdr. Oyai Deng. I want to add my voice of being happy to participate in this meeting. When the movement started, you were seven (7) and now you are only two (2) remaining. Some said that you conspired against those who died and now you are conspiring against yourselves." "Minutes of Historical SPLM Meeting in Rumbek 2004."

100. Young, *The Fate of Sudan*, 196, 303.

101. Rolandsen, "Another Civil War in South Sudan," 168.

102. "To understand the concept of group legitimacy, it is necessary to link it to ownership. Legitimacy goes to one's rightful place in the country. To be legitimate is therefore to be identified with the territory." Horowitz, *Ethnic Groups in Conflict*, 201, 207.

103. "Group entitlement, conceived as a joint function of comparative worth and legitimacy, does this—it explains why the followers follow, accounts for the intensity of group reactions, even to modest stimuli, and clarifies the otherwise mysterious quest for public signs of group status." Horowitz, 226.

104. Brubaker, *Ethnicity without Groups*, 14.

105. "Cdr. Oyai Deng.... I am shocked to hear Cdr. Salva talk here only about Bahr El Ghazal and not the South in general given he is a leader for all." "Minutes of Historical SPLM Meeting in Rumbek 2004."

106. Pinaud, "Military Kinship, Inc."

107. Member of civil society 4.

108. Melson, *Revolution and Genocide*, 21, 267.

109. "Minutes of Historical SPLM Meeting in Rumbek 2004."

110. Longtime observer 1; former high-ranking government official 1.

111. Thirty-four-year-old displaced man from Wau, interview with the author, July 7, 2017.

3. THE WAR ECONOMY AND STATE-MAKING IN SPLA AREAS

1. Philippe Le Billon, *Geopolitics of Resource Wars: Resource Dependence, Governance and Violence* (London: Frank Cass, 2005), 288.

2. Charles Tilly, "How War Made States, and Vice Versa," in *Coercion, Capital, and European States, AD 990–1990* (Cambridge, MA: Basil Blackwell, 1990); Charles Tilly, "War Making and State Making as Organized Crime," in *Bringing the State Back In*, ed. Peter Evans, Dietrich Rueschemeyer, and Theda Skocpol (Cambridge: Cambridge University Press, 1985), 169.

3. This process is similar to what is described by Tilly, "State Making as Organized Crime," 183.

4. Anne Walraet, "Displacement in Postwar Southern Sudan: Survival and Accumulation within Urban Perimeters," MICROCON: A Micro Level Analysis of Violent Conflict (Brighton: Institute of Development Studies at the University of Sussex, 2011), 20; Rens Twijnstra, "On the State of Business: Trade, Entrepreneurship and Real Economic Governance in South Sudan" (PhD diss., Wageningen University, 2014), 75, 119.

5. Douglas H. Johnson and Gérard Prunier, "The Foundation and Expansion of the Sudan People's Liberation Army," in *Civil War in the Sudan*, ed. M. W. Daly and Ahmad Alawad Sikainga (London: British Academic Press, 1993), 132, 135–36.

6. Alex De Waal, "Starving out the South," in *Civil War in the Sudan*, ed. M. W. Daly and Ahmad Alawad Sikainga (London: British Academic Press, 1993), 167; David Keen, *The Benefits of Famine: A Political Economy of Famine and Relief in Southwestern Sudan, 1983–1989*, 2nd ed. (Oxford: James Currey, 2008), 115.

7. Thomas Kedini, "The Challenge to Survive," in *War Wounds: Development Costs of Conflict in Southern Sudan*, ed. Nigel Twose and Benjamin Pogrund (Washington: Panos Institute, 1988), 29; De Waal, "Starving out the South," 167; four members of civil society 1, interview with the author, May 21, 2009; three members of civil society 2, interview with the author, April 9, 2009.

8. Peter Adwok Nyaba, *Politics of Liberation in South Sudan: An Insider's View* (Kampala: Fountain Publishers, 1997), 53.

9. Kedini, "The Challenge to Survive," 29; De Waal, "Starving out the South," 167; Keen, *The Benefits of Famine*, 220.

10. See on Blue Nile state Wendy James, *War and Survival in Sudan's Frontierlands: Voices from the Blue Nile* (Oxford: Oxford University Press, 2007), 16.

11. Keen, *The Benefits of Famine*, 147.

12. Mancur Olson, "Dictatorship, Democracy, and Development," *American Political Science Review* 87, no. 3 (September 1993): 567.

13. This strategy consisted of organizing the movement of people into Ethiopian refugee camps and restricting government military activity in the rural areas while attacking militia organizations and the population they were drawn from.

14. Douglas H. Johnson, "The Sudan People's Liberation Army and the Problem of Factionalism," in *African Guerrillas*, ed. Christopher Clapham (Oxford: Indiana University Press, 1998), 65–66, 105, 147–48, 165; Zachariah Cherian Mampilly, *Rebel Ruler: Insurgent Governance and Civilian Life during War* (Ithaca, NY: Cornell University Press, 2015), 145.

15. Øystein H. Rolandsen, *Guerrilla Government: Political Changes in the Southern Sudan during the 1990s* (Uppsala: Nordic Africa Institute, 2005), 71.

16. Member of civil society 6, interview with the author, August 10, 2014.

17. Douglas H. Johnson, *The Root Causes of Sudan's Civil Wars*, 2nd ed. (Bloomington: Indiana University Press, 2007), 152.

18. Cherry Leonardi, "Violence, Sacrifice and Chiefship in Central Equatoria, Southern Sudan," *Africa* 77, no. 4 (2007): 540; Mampilly, *Rebel Rulers*, 145.

19. Keen, *The Benefits of Famine*, 89.

20. Thirteen members of civil society 1, interview with the author, April 23, 2009.

21. Former SPLA child soldier, interview with the author, August 7, 2014.

22. Former SPLA child soldier.

23. Member of civil society 6.

24. David Keen, *Useful Enemies: When Waging Wars Is More Important Than Winning Them* (New Haven, CT: Yale University Press, 2012), 14–15.

25. Rolandsen, *Guerrilla Government*, 64–67, 68–70.

26. Human Rights Watch, *Civilian Devastation: Abuses by All Parties in the War in Southern Sudan* (Human Rights Watch, 1994), 115; African Rights, *Facing Genocide: The Nuba of Sudan* (London: African Rights, July 1995), 312.

27. Member of SPLM electoral team in 2010, interview with the author, March 28, 2010.

28. SPLA high-ranking officer, interview with the author, October 5, 2010; seven women from the Joint Integrated Units (JIU), interview with the author, November 9, 2010; political representative 3, interview with the author, November 6, 2010; fourteen members of civil society 1, interview with the author, May 14, 2009; four members of civil society 1, interview with the author, May 21, 2009; member of SPLM electoral team in 2010; Kedini, "The Challenge to Survive," 29; De Waal, "Starving out the South," 167; Keen, *The Benefits of Famine*, 220.

29. Thirteen members of civil society 1.

30. Four members of civil society 1.

31. Leonardi, "Violence, Sacrifice and Chiefship," 540; Johnson and Prunier, "Foundation and Expansion."

32. Four members of civil society 1.

33. Four members of civil society 1.

34. Three members of civil society 3, interview with the author, October 21, 2010.

35. Francis Namutina and Lewis William Kandi, "W. Equatoria People Denounce Appointment of Corrupt New Governor," *Sudan Tribune*, January 18, 2007, http://www.sudantribune.com/spip.php?page=imprimable&id_article=19815.

36. Paul E. Lovejoy, *Transformations in Slavery: A History of Slavery in Africa*, 1st ed. (Cambridge: Cambridge University Press, 1983), 126.

37. Claire C. Robertson and Martin Klein, *Women and Slavery in Africa* (Madison: University of Wisconsin Press, 1983), 3.

38. Lovejoy, *Transformations in Slavery*, 269–70.

39. See on the patronage of marriage within the SPLA Clémence Pinaud, "Military Kinship, Inc.: Patronage, Inter-Ethnic Marriages and Social Classes in South Sudan," *Review of African Political Economy*, June 2016, 243–59.

40. A survey directed for UNHCR during field research in five cities (Juba, Rumbek, Bor, Torit and Malakal) found that 27 percent of female respondents and 29 percent of male respondents had been involved at some point in war-related activities. South Sudan Center for Census SSCCSE Statistics and Evaluation et al., *Gender-Based Violence and Protection Survey* (Juba, South Sudan: 2010).

41. Johnson and Prunier, "Foundation and Expansion," 133.

42. Member of civil society 6.

43. Thirteen members of civil society 1.

44. Thirteen members of civil society 1.

45. Member of civil society 9, interview with the author, June 15, 2017.

46. Member of civil society 9.

47. Cordaid, *Mining in South Sudan: Opportunities and Risks for Local Communities. Baseline Assessment of Small-Scale and Artisanal Gold Mining in Central and Eastern Equatoria States, South Sudan* (Cordaid, January 2016), 24, https://www.cordaid.org/nl/wp-content/uploads/sites/2/2016/03/South_Sudan_Gold_Mining_Report-LR_1.pdf.

48. Member of civil society 10, interview with the author, July 8, 2016.

49. Lovejoy, *Transformations in Slavery*, 125.

50. Douglas H. Johnson, "Sudanese Military Slavery from the Eighteenth to the Twentieth Century," in *Slavery and Other Forms of Unfree Labour*, ed. Léonie J. Archer, History Workshop (London: Routledge, 1988), 151–52.

51. Johnson, *The Root Causes*, 147–48.

52. Pinaud, "Military Kinship, Inc."

53. Former SPLA commander, interview with the author, August 4, 2014.

54. Sam Gonda and William Mogga, "Loss of the Revered Cattle," in *War Wounds: Development Costs Of Conflict In Southern Sudan* (Washington, DC: Panos Institute, 1988), 74–75; "Sudan: Stalling Speed," *Africa Confidential*, May 22, 1985, 5–6; thirteen members of civil society 1; Nyaba, *Politics of Liberation*, 36–37.

55. The SPLA was involved in Ethiopia's internal war, which was meant to repay Mengistu for its support but also to continue fighting the war against Khartoum's militias. Johnson, *The Root Causes*, 88.

56. Johnson, 147–48; political representative 4, interview with the author, August 1, 2014.

57. Former SPLA child soldier.

58. Johnson, *The Root Causes*, 124, 152.

59. Member of civil society 11, interview with the author, November 20, 2015.

60. Tilly, "State Making as Organized Crime," 171.

61. Former SPLA child soldier; former SPLA commander, August 4, 2014.

62. Former SPLA child soldier.

63. Tilly, "State Making as Organized Crime," 182.

64. Member of civil society 12, interview with the author, August 9, 2014.

65. Johnson, *The Root Causes*, 145; Ataul Karim et al., *OLS—Operation Lifeline Sudan, A Review* (UNICEF, July 1996), 14.

66. Johnson, *The Root Causes*, 145; Karim et al., *OLS*, 14.

67. For example, in 1993, various units of the SPLA-Nasir started attacking one another around Waat, as the Lou Nuer received little support from neighboring forces and were frustrated by the lack of access to food assistance from humanitarian agencies and from their Dinka neighbors, in the context of the removal of a single SPLA administration. Johnson, *The Root Causes*, 118.

68. Riek Machar simultaneously requested both that the government airlift supplies and ammunitions and the UN send relief to Ayod and Waat. Johnson, *The Root Causes*, 115–16, 150.

69. Rolandsen, *Guerrilla Government*, 39, 80; African Rights, *Food and Power in Sudan*, 317.

70. Two former high-ranking government officials and high-ranking members of IO, interview with the author, February 22, 2017.

71. Rolandsen, *Guerrilla Government*, 125.

72. Mampilly, *Rebel Rulers*, 145.

73. Rolandsen, *Guerrilla Government*, 115.

74. Rolandsen, 81–82, 109, 116.

75. South Sudanese intellectual 1, interview with the author, November 21, 2017. The National Liberation Council (NLC) and a formal judicial system were also established. Johnson, "The Sudan People's Liberation Army and the Problem of Factionalism," 69–70; Rolandsen, *Guerrilla Government*, 115–16.

76. South Sudanese intellectual 1.

77. Former SPLA child soldier; former SPLA commander, August 4, 2014.

78. African Rights, *Imposing Empowerment? Aid and Civil Institutions in Southern Sudan* (African Rights, December 1995), 10–11.

79. African Rights, *Food and Power in Sudan*, 319.

80. African Rights, 334; former SPLA commander, August 4, 2014.

81. Nyaba, *Politics of Liberation*, 162; Mampilly, *Rebel Rulers*, 146.

82. Rolandsen, *Guerrilla Government*, 81–82, 109.

83. African Rights, *Food and Power in Sudan*, 320.

84. Volker Riehl, *Who Is Ruling in South Sudan? The Role of NGOs in Rebuilding Socio-Political Order*, Studies on Emergencies and Disaster Relief (Sweden: Nordiska Afrikainstitutet, 2001), 4.

85. OLS operated in the south beginning in 1989 following an agreement between the government of Sudan and the rebel movements to allow for the passage of aid to their respective areas.

86. Volker Riehl, "Who Is Ruling in South Sudan?," 6.

87. Mark Bradbury, Nicholas Leader, and Kate Mackintosh, *The "Agreement on Ground Rules" in South Sudan*, Humanitarian Policy Group, The Politics of Principle: The Principles of Humanitarian Action in Practice (London: Overseas Development Institute (ODI), March 2000), 33–34.

88. Mampilly, *Rebel Rulers*, 152.

89. Riehl, "Who Is Ruling in South Sudan?," 13.

90. Rolandsen, *Guerrilla Government*, 158.

91. In this case, complaints were raised at the 1996 conference supposed to bolster civil administration. Rolandsen, *Guerrilla Government*, 157.

92. Cherry Leonardi, *Dealing with Government in South Sudan: Histories of Chiefship, Community and State* (Woodbridge: James Currey, 2013), 177.

93. Former SPLA child soldier.

94. Former SPLA commander, interview with the author, August 6, 2014.

95. Former SPLA commander, August 4, 2014.

96. Former SPLA commander, August 6, 2014.

97. This practice of taking a commission would continue after 2005.

98. Johnson, *The Root Causes*, 92–93, 105–6.

99. Former SPLA child soldier.

100. Anne Walraet, "Violence et Géographie du Pouvoir et de l'Enrichissement dans la Zone Frontière de Chukudum (Sud Soudan)," *Politique africaine* N° 111, no. 3 (October 1, 2008): 95.

101. Mampilly, *Rebel Rulers*, 152.

102. African Rights, "Imposing Empowerment?," 6.

103. The names of these companies would change after the war. Former SPLA commander, August 6, 2014, interview with the author.

104. A respondent recalled how in 1997, a local commander made a fortune by selling about sixty trucks captured in Tonj (Warrap) to Uganda. Individual commanders' companies rented trucks and cars to relief agencies such as the World Food Program to deliver aid. Former SPLA child soldier; former SPLA commander, August 6, 2014.

105. One of those U.S. companies was Jarch Capital. Former SPLA commander, August 6, 2014; Luke A. Patey, "Crude Days Ahead? Oil and the Resource Curse in Sudan," *African Affairs* 109, no. 437 (October 1, 2010): 630.

106. Mampilly, *Rebel Rulers*, 153.

107. Keen, *Useful Enemies*, 201–2.

108. Ataul Karim et al., *OLS*, 170.

109. John W. Burton, "Development and Cultural Genocide in the Sudan," *Journal of Modern African Studies* 29, no. 3 (September 1991): 511, 518–19.

110. On the relationship between trauma and entitlement ideologies, see Vamık D. Volkan and J. Christopher Fowler, "Large-Group Narcissism and Political Leaders with Narcissistic Personality Organization," *Psychiatric Annals* 39, no. 4 (April 2009): 214.

111. Tilly, *Coercion, Capital, and European States*.

112. Clémence Pinaud, "South Sudan: Civil War, Predation And The Making Of A Military Aristocracy," *African Affairs* 113, no. 451 (April 2014): 192–211.

113. Patrick Chabal and Jean-Pascal Daloz, *Africa Works: Disorder As Political Instrument* (Oxford: James Currey Publishers, 1999), 85.

114. African Rights, *Food and Power in Sudan*, 79.

115. Anne Walraet, "Governance, Violence and the Struggle for Economic Regulation in South Sudan: The Case of Budi County (Eastern Equatoria)," *Afrika Focus* 21, no. 2 (2008): 53–70.

116. A concept forged by Keen, *The Benefits of Famine*, 109–11.

117. This included state-building projects such as thirteenth century's Mediterranean Europe, where King Frederick II made sure that no independent class of merchants could destabilize the landowning aristocracy. Tilly, *Coercion, Capital, and European States*, 142.

118. African Rights, *Food and Power*, 80.

119. Thirteen members of civil society 1; former SPLA child soldier.

120. De Waal, "Starving out the South," 174–75; Millard Burr and Robert O. Collins, *Requiem for the Sudan: War, Drought, and Disaster Relief on the Nile* (Boulder, CO: Westview Press, 1995), 47, 84; Johnson, *The Root Causes*, 108, 154; Human Rights Watch,

Sudan: How Human Rights Abuses Caused the Disaster. Background Paper on the 1998 Famine in Bahr El Ghazal (Human Rights Watch, July 23, 1998); Keen, *The Benefits of Famine*, 115; George Tombe Lako, *Southern Sudan: The Foundation of a War Economy* (Peter Lang Pub Inc, 1994), 79; Johnson, *The Root Causes*, 154, 165.

121. Anne Walraet, "State-Making in Southern Sudan-Kenyan Border Area," in *The Borderlands of South Sudan. Authority and Identity in Historical Perspectives.*, ed. Christopher Vaughan, Mareike Schomerus, and Lotje De Vries (New York: Palgrave Macmillan, 2013), 175; Walraet, "Governance, Violence and the Struggle for Economic Regulation," 67.

122. Walraet, "Governance, Violence and the Struggle for Economic Regulation," 67.

123. Walraet, "State-Making in Southern Sudan-Kenyan Border Area," 182.

124. Political representative 2, interview with the author, August 1, 2014.

125. Walraet, "Governance, Violence and the Struggle for Economic Regulation," 62; Walraet, "Violence et Géographie du Pouvoir," 98.

126. Different armed actors including the SPLA but also the Ugandan People's Defense Forces (UPDF), the Lord's Resistance Army (LRA), and the Equatoria Defense Forces (EDF) regularly purchased weapons from this market. Walraet, "Displacement in Post-War Southern Sudan;" Walraet, "Violence et Géographie du Pouvoir;" Walraet, "Governance, Violence and the Struggle for Economic Regulation," 60, 62, 65; Darlington Akabwai and Priscillar E. Ateyo, *The Scramble for Cattle, Power and Guns in Karamoja* (Boston: Feinstein International Center, December 2007).

127. Walraet, "Violence et Géographie du Pouvoir," 94.

128. Walraet, "Governance, Violence and the Struggle for Economic Regulation," 60.

129. South Sudanese intellectual 3, interview with the author, August 7, 2014; Walraet, "Violence et Géographie du Pouvoir," 94.

130. Sixty-year-old displaced man from Ikotos / IO major general, interview with the author, July 8, 2017.

131. Member of civil society 9.

132. South Sudanese intellectual 3.

133. Former SPLA child soldier; forty-year-old displaced man from Yei, interview with the author, June 21, 2017.

134. See, on Khartoum's interest in Marijuana, Johnson, *The Root Causes*, 80.

135. Former SPLA child soldier; South Sudanese intellectual 3.

136. Former SPLA child soldier.

137. Former SPLA soldier from Yei, interview with the author, July 4, 2017.

138. "Sudan: Independent Report on Blue Nile Province," *IRIN News*, May 21, 1998, http://www.africa.upenn.edu/Hornet/irin_52198.html.

139. Former SPLA child soldier.

140. South Sudanese intellectual 3.

141. Member of civil society 12; former SPLA child soldier; political representative 2.

142. Member of civil society 12; former SPLA child soldier; political representative 2.

143. Sixty-year-old displaced man from Ikotos / IO major general.

144. Member of civil society 9.

145. Member of civil society 9.

146. Namutina and Kandi, "W. Equatoria People Denounce Appointment of Corrupt New Governor"; South Sudanese intellectual 1.

147. The national economic commission existed before 1994, officially to "initiate public investment especially in natural resources such as gold, livestock, and fisheries." Benaiah Yongo-Bure, *Economic Development of Southern Sudan* (Lanham, MD: University Press of America, Inc, 2007), 197; forty-year-old displaced man from Yei.

148. Namutina and Kandi, "W. Equatoria People Denounce Appointment of Corrupt New Governor." One of Abu-John's feats included selling in advance the teak plantations of Western Equatoria (Maridi and Ibba) to an Indian tycoon.

149. Walraet, "Violence et Géographie du Pouvoir," 103; Walraet, "Governance, Violence and the Struggle for Economic Regulation," 57, 62, 65.

150. Pinaud, "Military Kinship, Inc." Patrimonial capitalism is inheritance-based capitalism in which capital ownership remains key, wealth is concentrated at the top, and income can be generated without the pain of work. Branko Milanovic, "The Return of 'Patrimonial Capitalism': A Review of Thomas Piketty's Capital in the Twenty-First Century," *Journal of Economic Literature* 52, no. 2 (2014): 519–34; Thomas Piketty, *Capital in the Twenty-First Century* (Cambridge, MA: Belknap Press of Harvard University Press, 2014), 84, 113–14.

151. Walraet, "State-Making in Southern Sudan-Kenyan Border Area," 178, 180.

152. Former SPLA child soldier.

153. Member of civil society 13, interview with the author, August 9, 2014.

154. Tilly, "State Making as Organized Crime," 175.

155. Member of civil society 13.

156. Karl Vick, "Ripping Off Slave 'Redeemers.' Rebels Exploit Westerners' Efforts to Buy Emancipation for Sudanese," *Washington Post Foreign Service*, February 26, 2002, http://www.hartford-hwp.com/archives/33/173.html.

157. Vick, "Ripping Off Slave 'Redeemers.'" Elijah Majok, a Bor Dinka close to Garang, could have been the head of the SRRA the article referred to. He served from 1989 to 1993, when he was replaced by Justin Yac. He was appointed in 2005 as deputy governor of the Central Bank of Sudan (CBOS) and president of the Bank of Southern Sudan (BOSS).

158. Former high-ranking government official 1, interview with the author, July 11, 2017.

159. Tilly, "State Making as Organized Crime," 183.

160. Vick, "Ripping Off Slave 'Redeemers.'"

161. Horowitz writes, "Group entitlement, conceived as a joint function of comparative worth and legitimacy, does this—it explains why the followers follow, accounts for the intensity of group reactions, even to modest stimuli, and clarifies the otherwise mysterious quest for public signs of group status." Donald Horowitz, *Ethnic Groups in Conflict* (Berkeley: University of California Press, 1985), 226.

162. Declan Walsh, "Sudan's Great Slave Scam," *News24*, February 27, 2002, https://www.news24.com/xArchive/Archive/Sudans-great-slave-scam-20020227-2.

163. Former high-ranking government official 1.

164. Walsh, "Sudan's Great Slave Scam."

165. Malok was reinstated in February 1999. He had directed the SRRA first from 1989 to 1993. The slave redemption scandal was alleged to have started circa 1994. If Malok was involved, this continued to demonstrate that despite the competition between the two constituencies mobilized by the ethnopolitical entrepreneurs, these individuals were capitalists at heart first and identified with similar dominant class interests.

166. Vick, "Ripping Off Slave 'Redeemers.'"

167. Walsh, "Sudan's Great Slave Scam."

168. Pinaud, "Military Kinship, Inc."; Vick, "Ripping Off Slave 'Redeemers.'"

169. Vick, "Ripping Off Slave 'Redeemers.'"

170. Former SPLA commander, August 6, 2014.

171. Pinaud, "Military Kinship, Inc."

172. High-ranking government official 4, interview with the author, November 5, 2010; Nyaba, *Politics of Liberation*, 129. John Garang himself admitted the economic appeal of the armed struggle in the South: "The marginal cost of rebellion in the South became very small, zero to negative; that is, in the South it pays to rebel." Ali Abdel Gadir Ali, Ibrahim A. Elbadawi, and Atta El-Batahani, "Sudan's Civil War: Why Has It Prevailed for So Long?," in *Understanding Civil War: Evidence and Analysis, Vol. 1—Africa*, ed. Nicholas Sambanis and Paul Collier (Washington, DC: The World Bank, 2005), 193.

173. Nyaba, *Politics of Liberation*, 58; former SPLA child soldier.

174. Former SPLA child soldier.

175. For example, Kuol Manyang in Eastern Equatoria or Garang Mabil in Bahr El Ghazal Former SPLA child soldier; Johnson, *The Root Causes*, 165–66.

176. Member of civil society 10.

177. Kwathi Ajawin, "NCP-SPLM, Corruption Fireworks," *Sudan Tribune*, March 30, 2006, http://www.sudantribune.com/spip.php?article14828.

178. Julia Aker Duany, *Making Peace and Nurturing Life: A Memoir of an African Woman About a Journey of Struggle and Hope* (Bloomington IN: 1st Books Library, 2003), 206; high-ranking government official in Juba, interview with the author, November, 5, 2010.

179. Johnson, *The Root Causes*, 165–66.

180. Nyaba, *Politics of Liberation*, 7, 131.

181. Member of civil society 12.

182. Tilly, "State Making as Organized Crime," 172.

183. I borrow the expression from Larry Diamond, "Class Formation in the Swollen African State," *Journal of Modern African Studies* 25, no. 4 (1987): 567–96.

184. I follow Diamond's definition of a dominant class as "a category encompassing those who have similar economic motivation because they have similar economic opportunities . . . dominant if it owns or controls the most productive assets, appropriates the bulk of the most valued consumption opportunities, and commands a sufficient monopoly over the means of coercion and legitimation to sustain politically this cumulative socio-economic pre-eminence. Necessarily, the members of such a class will have 'controlling positions in the dominant institutions of society.' They will also have high degrees of class consciousness and social coherence—constituting in the Marxian sense a 'class-for-itself'—as this is a precondition for the class action necessary to preserve and extend class domination . . . the transmission of this status across generations will be seen as a particular mark of the consolidation of class domination." Diamond, "Class Formation in the Swollen African State," 578.

185. Elements of the colonial system persisted as well. Feudalism was based on land tenure (fiefs or administrative units) ruled by lords invested with political power to the service of a military oligarchy, and slavery was founded on the exchange and commodification of people, both of which—land and people—were forms of capital (in the case of people, "slave capital"). Different definitions of feudalism and how they could apply to Africa exist. I borrow from Marc Bloch, Max Weber, and Joseph Strayer. See Jack Goody, "Feudalism in Africa?," *Journal of African History* 4, no. 1 (1963): 3; Marc Bloch, *Feudal Society: Social Classes and Political Organisation*, 3rd ed. (London: Routledge, 1989), 2:167. On the relationship between capitalism and slavery, see Piketty, *Capital in the Twenty-First Century*, 46.

186. Tilly, "State Making as Organized Crime," 183–84.

187. Nyaba, *Politics of Liberation*, 52; Keen, *Useful Enemies*, 9.

188. Keen defines "war systems" as "Wars that actually serve complex functions for a variety of groups." Keen, *Useful Enemies*, 236.

189. Lovejoy, *Transformations in Slavery*, 125.

190. Horowitz links group legitimacy to ownership: "To be legitimate is therefore to be identified with the territory . . . group legitimacy provides a foundation for the recurrent psychological denial that another group owns an equal share in the land." Horowitz, *Ethnic Groups in Conflict*, 201–2.

191. Walraet, "Governance, Violence and the Struggle for Economic Regulation," 67.

4. SPLA VIOLENCE, GROUP-MAKING, AND EXPANSION

1. Peter Adwok Nyaba, *Politics of Liberation in South Sudan: An Insider's View* (Kampala: Fountain Publishers, 1997), 36–37.

2. Political representative 4, interview with the author, July 25, 2014.

3. Douglas H. Johnson and Gérard Prunier, "The Foundation and Expansion of the Sudan People's Liberation Army," in *Civil War in the Sudan*, ed. M. W. Daly and Ahmad Alawad Sikainga (London: British Academic Press, 1993), 131.

4. Nyaba, *Politics of Liberation*, 36–37.

5. Douglas H. Johnson, "The Sudan People's Liberation Army and the Problem of Factionalism," in *African Guerrillas*, ed. Christopher Clapham (Oxford: Indiana University Press, 1998), 68–69.

6. Nyaba, *Politics of Liberation*, 36–37; David Keen, *The Benefits of Famine: A Political Economy of Famine and Relief in Southwestern Sudan, 1983–1989*, 2nd ed. (Oxford: James Currey, 2008), 220.

7. I use the term "protoconquest" to distinguish the second civil war from the third. I consider this protoconquest the first phase of three, the third phase (2013–) culminating in annihilation.

8. Three members of civil society 2, interview with the author, April 9, 2009; Nyaba, *Politics of Liberation*, 52.,

9. Fourteen members of civil society 1, interview with the author, May 14, 2009.

10. Thirteen members of civil society 1, interview with the author, April 23, 2009.

11. Member of civil society 14, interview with the author, April 21, 2009.

12. Fourteen members of civil society 1.

13. Member of civil society 15, interview with the author, November 17, 2015.

14. Member of civil society 14.

15. Four members of civil society 1, interview with the author, May 21, 2009; member of civil society 6, interview with the author, August 9, 2014.

16. Four members of civil society 1.

17. See Jok Madut Jok, "Militarism, Gender and Reproductive Suffering: The Case of Abortion in Western Dinka," *Africa* 69, no. 2 (1999): 203; Jok Madut Jok, *Militarization, Gender and Reproductive Health in South Sudan* (Lewiston, NY: Edwin Mellen Press, Ltd., 1998), 138, 198; Jok Madut Jok, "Militarization and Gender Violence in South Sudan," in *JAAS XXXIV, 4* (Koninklijke Brill NV, Leiden, 1999), 33.

18. Joanna Bourke, *Rape: Sex, Violence, History* (London: Virago, 2007), 378. Cited in Dara Kay Cohen, *Rape during Civil War* (Ithaca, NY: Cornell University Press, 2016), 10.

19. See Cohen, *Rape during Civil War*, 11, 19.

20. Three members of civil society 3, interview with the author, October 21, 2010.

21. Four members of civil society 1.

22. Three members of civil society 2.

23. Catharine A. MacKinnon, *Are Women Human? And Other International Dialogues* (Cambridge, MA: Harvard University Press, 2007), 171.

24. Three members of civil society 3. "In patrilineal societies . . . men could acquire a slave concubine more cheaply than a wife, and build up their lineages with the free off-spring of these unions." Frederick Cooper, "The Problem of Slavery in African Studies," *Journal of African History* 20, no. 1 (1979): 117. "Slavery and male dominance converged in the institution of concubinage." Margaret Strobel, *Muslim Women in Mombasa 1890–1975* (New Haven, CT: Yale University Press, 1979), 48; Claire C. Robertson and Martin Klein, *Women and Slavery in Africa* (Madison: University of Wisconsin Press, 1983), 6, 9.

25. Political representative 2, interview with the author, August 1, 2014.

26. Member of civil society 16, interview with the author, November 11, 2015. The respondent referred to Mundri, in Western Equatoria.

27. Thirteen members of civil society 1.

28. Fourteen members of civil society 1; four members of civil society 1; three members of civil society 3; thirteen members of civil society 1.

29. Clémence Pinaud, "Are 'Griefs of More Value Than Triumphs'? Power Relations, Nation-Building and the Different Histories of Women's Wartime Contributions in

Post-War South Sudan," *Journal of Northeast African Studies* 13, no. 2 (2013): 151–76; Clémence Pinaud, "'We Are Trained to Be Married!' Elite Formation and Ideology in the 'Girls" Battalion" of the Sudan People's Liberation Army,'" *Journal of Eastern African Studies*, 9, no. 3 (2015): 375–93.

30. "Women's class status is significantly mediated by women's relation to men." Catharine A. MacKinnon, *Toward a Feminist Theory of the State* (Cambridge, MA: Harvard University Press, 1989), 48. Therefore women are not just victims of male control either, and can sometimes act to perpetuate their own subordination as a group to defend their own interests, including class interests. See Pierre Bourdieu, *Outline of a Theory of Practice* (Cambridge, MA: Cambridge University Press, 1977).

31. Here Marx's reflections on slavery are illuminating: "What is a Negro slave? A man of the black race . . . He only becomes a slave in certain relations. A cotton spinning jenny is a machine for spinning cotton. It becomes capital only in certain relations." Replace slave here with woman and a cotton spinning jenny with sex. Karl Marx, *Wage-Labor and Capital* (New York: International Publishers, 1971), 28. Cited in MacKinnon, *Toward a Feminist Theory of the State*, 26.

32. Thomas Piketty, *Capital in the Twenty-First Century* (Cambridge, MA: Belknap Press of Harvard University Press, 2014), 46.

33. Paul E. Lovejoy, *Transformations in Slavery: A History of Slavery in Africa*, 1st ed. (Cambridge: Cambridge University Press, 1983), 4–5.

34. Considering the level of coercion and the absence of benefits from the work, this forced labor most paralleled slavery, not other forms of forced labor such as serfdom, clientage, wage-labor, pawning, or communal work. For a description of those, see Lovejoy, *Transformations in Slavery*, 5.

35. "Attributing a monetary value to the stock of human capital makes sense only in societies where it is actually possible to own other individuals fully and entirely." Piketty, *Capital in the Twenty-First Century*, 163.

36. Clémence Pinaud, "Military Kinship, Inc.: Patronage, Inter-Ethnic Marriages and Social Classes in South Sudan," *Review of African Political Economy*, June 2016, 243–59.

37. Member of civil society 17, interview with the author, June 28, 2017.

38. Understanding women as capital does not mean that bridewealth does not fulfill other key social functions—quite the opposite. For a summary of the different views of bridewealth with special reference to the Nuer and women's autonomy, see Stanley J. Tambiah et al., "Bridewealth and Dowry Revisited: The Position of Women in Sub-Saharan Africa and North India [and Comments and Reply]," *Current Anthropology* 30, no. 4 (October 1989): 414–16.

39. Explaining her use of the phrase "choiceless decision" to explain female fighters' trajectories in Sierra Leone, Chris Coulter wrote, "Sometimes the only choice was between becoming a fighter/lover or dying, which is not really much of a choice, more a matter of bare survival." Chris Coulter, *Bush Wives and Girl Soldiers: Women's Lives Through War and Peace in Sierra Leone* (Ithaca, NY: Cornell University Press, 2009), 146, 150.

40. Government official and member of civil society 1, interview with the author, November 3, 2010.

41. It was practiced in other regions too, such as Upper Nile. Sharon Elaine Hutchinson, *Nuer Dilemmas: Coping with Money, War, and the State* (Berkeley: University of California Press, 1996), 208; high-ranking government official 3, interview with the author, November 11, 2010; Pinaud, "Are 'Griefs of More Value Than Triumphs'?, 151–76.

42. Member of civil society 18, interview with the author, November 10, 2010; SPLA lieutenant, interview with the author, November 8, 2010; Sharon Elaine Hutchinson, "Nuer Ethnicity Militarized," *Anthropology Today* 16, no. 3 (June 1, 2000): 11.

43. "Introduction to the Laws of New Sudan," *Gurtong*, n.d., http://www.gurtong.net/Governance/ConstitutionLaws/tabid/106/Default.aspx. For more on the topic, see

Zachariah Cherian Mampilly, *Rebel Rulers. Insurgent Governance and Civilian Life during War* (Ithaca, NY: Cornell University Press, 2015), 156–58; "Introduction to the Laws of New Sudan."

44. Member of civil society 18.

45. Johnson, "The Problem of Factionalism," 68; member of civil society 2, interview with the author, October 16, 2015.

46. These officers included Kerubino Kuanyin Bol, Arok Thon Arok, William Nyuon Bany, and Lam Akol, or the lesser known Samuel Abu-John. Douglas H. Johnson, *The Root Causes of Sudan's Civil Wars*, 2nd ed. (Bloomington: Indiana University Press, 2007), 92–93; Nyaba, *Politics of Liberation*, 55, 67; Johnson, "The Problem of Factionalism," 68–69; member of civil society 18.

47. Johnson, *The Root Causes*, 91; Nyaba, *Politics of Liberation*, 58.

48. Johnson, "The Problem of Factionalism," 68–69; three police officers, interview with the author, June 14, 2010; Cherry Leonardi, "Violence, Sacrifice and Chiefship in Central Equatoria, Southern Sudan," *Africa* 77, no. 4 (2007): 535–58.

49. Johnson and Prunier, "The Foundation and Expansion of the Sudan People's Liberation Army," 135–36; Julie Flint, "Yousif Kuwa. The Lost Leader of Africa's Persecuted Nuba People, He Tempered Armed Resistance with Justice," *Guardian*, April 1, 2001, https://www.theguardian.com/news/2001/apr/04/guardianobituaries; former SPLA child soldier, interview with the author, August 7, 2014; Francis Namutina and Lewis William Kandi, "W. Equatoria People Denounce Appointment of Corrupt New Governor," *Sudan Tribune*, January 18, 2007, http://www.sudantribune.com/spip.php?page=imprimable&id_article=19815.

50. SPLA high-ranking officer, interview with the author, October 5, 2010; member of civil society 18.

51. New Sudan Council of Churches, *Come Let Us Reason Together: Report of the Historic Dialogue Held between the Sudan's People Liberation Movement (SPLM) and the New Sudan Council Of Churches (NSCC), Yei-Keijiko, New Sudan, 21–24 July 1997* (Nairobi: New Sudan Council of Churches, 1998), 6–7, 22–23; political representative 1, interview with the author, October 24, 2010; Justin S. Holcomb, "Southern Sudanese Chaplains: Human Rights and the Embodiment of Peace," *Other Journal* 6 (August 8, 2005), http://theotherjournal.com/2005/08/08/southern-sudanese-chaplains-human-rights-and-the-embodiment-of-peace/; SPLM cadre, interview with the author, November 2, 2010; member of civil society 18; high-ranking government official 4, interview with the author, November 5, 2010.

52. Johnson, *The Root Causes*, 109.

53. Nyaba, *Politics of Liberation*, 70.

54. Maria Eriksson Baaz and Maria Stern, *Sexual Violence as a Weapon of War? Perceptions, Prescriptions, Problems in the Congo and Beyond* (London: Zed Books, 2013), 74.

55. Nyaba, *Politics of Liberation*, 99; Jok Madut Jok and Sharon Elaine Hutchinson, "Sudan's Prolonged Second Civil War and the Militarization of Nuer and Dinka Ethnic Identities," *African Studies Review* 42, no. 2 (1999): 133; Johnson, *The Root Causes*, 109–10; Jok and Hutchinson, "Militarization of Nuer and Dinka Ethnic Identities," 142–43.

56. Eriksson Baaz and Stern, *Sexual Violence as a Weapon of War?*, 76–77; Clémence Pinaud, "South Sudan: Civil War, Predation and the Making of a Military Aristocracy," *African Affairs* 113, no. 451 (April 2014): 192–211; Pinaud, "Military Kinship, Inc."

57. I certainly do not mean that the lack of a definition for rape within the SPLA was an explanation, but it was an added advantage to the rapists on the ground and to the leadership, who tolerated and facilitated sexual violence through the patronage of marriage aka women's accumulation. On issues of cultural definition of rape in South Sudan, see Jok, *Militarization, Gender and Reproductive Health in South Sudan*, 198; Jok, "Militarism, Gender and Reproductive Suffering," 209.

58. Training in the Ethiopian camps initially lasted from one year to six months but was hardly sustainable given the demands for new recruits especially after the 1991 split, the SPLA's ousting from these camps, its relocation to Eastern Equatoria, and the increased forced recruitment to replace deserters. Member of civil society 6.

59. Member of civil society 2, interview with the author, November 29, 2015.

60. Cohen, *Rape during Civil War*, 30, 41.

61. SPLA lieutenant.

62. Three members of civil society 1, interview with the author, October 15, 2015.

63. Violence also fostered the groupness of the non-Dinka groups.

64. I take inspiration from Vamık D. Volkan and J. Christopher Fowler, "Large-Group Narcissism and Political Leaders with Narcissistic Personality Organization," *Psychiatric Annals* 39, no. 4 (April 2009). On the topic of narcissism, see Kenneth Levy et al., "Narcissistic Pathology: Empirical Approaches," *Psychiatric Annals* 39, no. 4 (April 2009): 203–13.

65. Stuart J. Kaufman, *Nationalist Passions* (Ithaca, NY: Cornell University Press, 2015), 59.

66. Hutchinson, "Nuer Ethnicity Militarized," 6.

67. Johnson, *The Root Causes*, 114–15; Johnson, "The Nuer Civil War," 14.

68. "The way relations between ethnic groups play out in any country depends on four main factors: symbolic predispositions, perceived threat, leadership, and organization." Kaufman, *Nationalist Passions*, 12.

69. "What is usual in a large-group regression is the reactivation of 'chosen traumas,' shared mental representation of a past historical event that has caused the ancestors of a large group to face drastic losses." Volkan and Fowler, "Large-Group Narcissism," 217, 218.

70. On rational choice theory and its shortcomings, see Kaufman, *Nationalist Passions*, 11–16.

71. Volkan and Fowler, "Large-Group Narcissism," 218.

72. The "White Army" was composed mainly of the Lou Nuer youth from the cattle camps in central and eastern Upper Nile. It was made up of multiple armed bands, which rarely came under one united leadership. John Young, *The White Army: An Introduction and Overview* (Geneva: Small Arms Survey, 2007), 9, 16.

73. Johnson, *The Root Causes*, 97–98, 117; Millard Burr and Robert O. Collins, *Requiem for the Sudan: War, Drought, and Disaster Relief on the Nile* (Boulder, CO: Westview Press, 1995), 301; Nyaba, *Politics of Liberation*, 94; Johnson, "The Nuer Civil War," 10; three members of civil society 1.

74. Former government official and high-ranking member of IO 1, interview with the author, July 13, 2014; former SPLA commander, interview with the author, August 4, 2014; member of civil society 6.

75. Former SPLA commander, August 4, 2014.

76. This included interethnic fighting between the Nuer and the Dinka; the Dinka and the Didinga; the Toposa, Buya, and Latuko in eastern Equatoria; the Murle and the Dinka in Upper Nile; and between Nuer sections in Upper Nile.

77. Immediately after the Bor massacre, the SPLA burned Yuai, Waat, Ayod, Pulchol, and Pathai (in Jonglei) in retaliation against Machar's troops (especially the Lou Nuer from the White Army), who ran to Akobo east and Nyirol. Dinka troops from Bahr El Ghazal also participated (with some Bor Dinka) in massacres of the Nuer and Nuer-speaking Dinka in Yuai, Waat, and Ayod in counterattacks in 1992–93. Member of civil society 19, interview with the author, October 14, 2015; Johnson, *The Root Causes*, 114–15; Johnson, "The Nuer Civil War," 14.

78. Nyaba, *Politics of Liberation*, 98; Johnson, *The Root Causes*, 97.

79. Nuer civilians from Akobo and Ayod joined the attack on Bor; Nuer and Dinka civilians from western Upper Nile and Lakes started raiding each other; and Garang's SPLA in Pibor encouraged the Murle to start raiding the Nuer in Akobo and Waat districts. Johnson, *The Root Causes*, 114.

80. The NGO Norwegian People's Aid reported that by the end of November 1991, up to five thousand Dinka, mainly civilians, had been killed by Machar's faction. Burr and Collins, *Requiem for the Sudan*, 301.

81. Former SPLA commander, August 4, 2014.

82. Johnson, *The Root Causes*, 98.

83. Former high-ranking SPLA and government official, interview with the author, August 7, 2014.

84. Member of civil society 7, interview with the author, October 15, 2015.

85. Nyaba, *Politics of Liberation*, 94.

86. Member of civil society 6, interview with the author, August 10, 2014.

87. For a discussion of the history of ethnicity among the Nuer, the Dinka, and other Nilotic people in the nineteenth century, see Douglas H. Johnson, "Enforcing Separate Identities in the Southern Sudan: The Case of the Nilotes of the Upper Nile," in *Les Ethnies Ont Une Histoire*, ed. Gérard Prunier and Jean-Pierre Chrétien, 2nd ed. (Paris: Karthala, 2003), 235–45.

88. Hutchinson, "Nuer Ethnicity Militarized," 11.

89. Nyaba, *Politics of Liberation*, 95.

90. Nyaba, 95; Young, *The White Army*, 16.

91. Former high-ranking SPLA and government official.

92. SPLA high-ranking officer.

93. Former government official and high-ranking member of IO; member of civil society 6.

94. Clémence Pinaud, "Women, Guns and Cattle: A Social History of the Second Civil War in South Sudan" (Université Paris 1 Panthéon-Sorbonne, 2013).

95. This, of course, does not invalidate what Hutchinson collected about women being killed on the basis of their ethnicity. The issue here is nevertheless the scale of this phenomenon and its relative importance compared to other types of violence against women.

96. Cohen, *Rape during Civil War*, 5, 14, 17, 18, 21; Rebecca Littman and Elizabeth Levy Paluck, "The Cycle of Violence: Understanding Individual Participation in Collective Violence," *Advances in Political Psychology* 36, suppl. 1 (2015): 95.

97. Marcel Mauss, *The Gift: Forms and Functions of Exchange in Archaic Societies* (Eastford, CT: Martino Fine Books, 2011), 18.

98. Member of civil society 18; SPLA lieutenant.

99. SPLA lieutenant. Bridewealth is popularly called "dowry" in South Sudan.

100. I take inspiration from Pierre Bourdieu, *Choses Dites*, Le Sens Commun (Paris: Les Éditions de Minuit, 1987), 153, 155–58.

101. I follow Mauss, *The Gift*, 6.

102. Douglas H. Johnson, *Nuer Prophets: A History of Prophecy from the Upper Nile in the Nineteenth and Twentieth Centuries* (Oxford: Clarendon Press, 1994), 126, 146; Francis Mading Deng, *The Man Called Deng Majok: A Biography of Power, Polygyny and Change* (Lawrenceville, NJ: Red Sea Press, 2009), 193.

103. According to Max Weber, "the patrimonial ruler is linked with the ruled through a consensual community which also exists apart from his independent military force and which is rooted in the belief that the ruler's power are legitimate insofar as they are *traditional*." Max Weber, *Economy and Society: An Outline of Interpretive Sociology*, ed. Guenther Roth and Claus Wittich, 4th ed. (Berkeley: University of California Press, 1978), 1020.

104. Deng, *The Dinka of the Sudan*, 9.

105. Member of civil society 18.

106. Former SPLA lieutenant colonel, interview with the author, August 7, 2014.

107. Former SPLA commander, interview with the author, August 6, 2014; Pinaud, "Military Kinship, Inc."

108. The exchange of some bridewealth cattle was still traditionally preferable despite the rise of "credit" marriages. Government official and members of civil society 1; SPLA high-ranking officer; member of civil society 18; Hutchinson, *Nuer Dilemmas*, 81–93, 100–102; former SPLA commander, August 4, 2014.

109. A letter of guarantee of payment stipulated that the soldier would pay for the bridewealth if he survived the war. In the event of his death, children born by his bride would be claimed by his relatives who would pay for her bridewealth. Member of civil society 18; former SPLA commander, August 6, 2014.

110. Among the Dinka, the head of the family (the father) normally paid his son's bridewealth, assisted by his brothers, extended kin, and friends. Francis Mading Deng, *The Dinka of the Sudan* (New York: Holt, Rinehart and Winston, Inc., 1972), 106, 211.

111. Thirteen members of civil society 1; former SPLA commander, August 6, 2014; four members of civil society 2, interview with the author, July 21, 2014.

112. SPLA high-ranking officer; high-ranking government official 3.

113. High-ranking government official 3; government official and members of civil society 1.

114. SPLA high-ranking officer.

115. Lovejoy, *Transformations in Slavery*, 20, 177.

116. Nyaba, *Politics of Liberation*, 72n22.

117. Former SPLA commander, August 4, 2014.

118. Nyaba, *Politics of Liberation*, 55; David Hoile, "Has Canadian Church Money Bought Wives and Weapons in Sudan?: The Rev Cal Bombay, Crossroads, Fraud and Naivety," *Media Monitors*, April 5, 2002, https://www.mediamonitors.net/has-canadian-church-money-bought-wives-weapons-in-sudan/.

119. Johnson, *The Root Causes*, 158; Karl Vick, "Ripping Off Slave 'Redeemers.' Rebels Exploit Westerners' Efforts to Buy Emancipation for Sudanese," *Washington Post Foreign Service*, February 26, 2002, http://www.hartford-hwp.com/archives/33/173.html.

120. Member of civil society 2, interview with the author, November 11, 2016.

121. Member of civil society 18.

122. Former SPLA commander, August 6, 2014.

123. Gérard Prunier, *The Rwanda Crisis: History of a Genocide* (London: Hurst & Company, 1995), 13–14.

124. Henry Hale, "Explaining Ethnicity," *Comparative Political Studies* 37, no. 4 (May 2004): 461.

125. Fifty-five-year-old displaced woman from Narus, Kapoeta East county, interview with the author, June 27, 2017.

126. The endurance of a foreign ethnic identity was not surprising in an agnatic society.

127. Deng, *The Man Called Deng Majok*, 191.

128. SPLA lieutenant; member of civil society 20, interview with the author, January 29, 2016.

129. Member of civil society 18.

130. Two members of civil society 3, interview with the author, November 8, 2010; Hutchinson, *Nuer Dilemmas*, 336.

131. Three members of civil society 1.

132. Two members of civil society 3; member of civil society 18.

133. SPLA lieutenant.

134. Member of civil society 18; Pinaud, "Military Kinship, Inc."

135. Two members of civil society 1, interview with the author, November 13, 2015.

136. The exact number of wives is debated, and Malong is reportedly still currently marrying more, as is Peter Gadet. Two members of civil society 1.

137. Member of civil society 13, interview with the author, August 9, 2014.

138. Member of civil society 8, interview with the author, November 19, 2015.

139. The likes of John Koang (the Upper Nile SPLA governor), Bol Kong, Elijah Hontop, Peter Gadet (who had about eighty wives, including from Dinka groups), Paulino Matiep (around forty-two wives), Gatluak Gai (around fifty wives), Gordon Kong Chol (over twenty wives), and William Duol Chol (eight to ten wives), accumulated many wives this way, although only a few of them, like Matiep, were reputably wealthy enough to have their bridewealth paid in full at once. Former SPLA commander, August 6, 2014; government official 1, interview with the author, Juba, July 25, 2014; former SPLA child soldier; member of civil society 21, interview with the author, October 26, 2015; two members of civil society 1; member of civil society 22, interview with the author, November 25, 2015; member of civil society 20.

140. Member of civil society 2.

141. Member of civil society 18.

142. Member of civil society 20. This sends us back to the very capacity and function of "paying"—which endows with prestige the purchaser who uses it to command others. Marcel Mauss, "Les Origines de La Notion de Monnaie," in *Comptes-Rendus Des Séances*, vol. 2, tome 1, Supplément à l'Anthropologie (Institut français d'anthropologie, 1914), 8.

143. Member of civil society 20.

144. Weber, *Economy and Society*, 1010–11.

145. Member of civil society 2. For example, Koang Biel, notorious as well for his role in coordinating the military campaign against civilians in 2015 in Unity state, is the nephew of the now deceased Gatluak Gai, who opposed Kiir's government in 2010 and was Paulino Matiep's bodyguard during the second civil war. Member of civil society 22; forty-three-year-old woman from Mayom county, thirty-eight-year-old woman from Mayendit, and forty-four-year-old woman from Mayom, interview with the author, October 27, 2015.

146. Two members of civil society 2, interview with the author, February 6, 2016.

147. Member of civil society 23, interview with the author, August 9, 2014; member of civil society 13.

148. Member of civil society 20.

149. Pinaud, "The Making of a Military Aristocracy."

150. Noteworthy is the fact that "rape increases the social status of its perpetrators" among peers. Cohen, *Rape during Civil War*, 28.

151. Patrick Chabal and Jean-Pascal Daloz, *Africa Works: Disorder As Political Instrument* (Oxford: James Currey Publishers, 1999), 44.

152. SPLA high-ranking officer; J. P. Olivier de Sardan, "A Moral Economy of Corruption in Africa?," *Journal of Modern African Studies* 37, no. 1 (March 1, 1999): 39, 40.

153. Weber, *Economy and Society*, 1012.

154. Former SPLA lieutenant colonel; former SPLA child soldier.

155. Government official and members of civil society 1.

156. Inner colonization is defined here following A. Dirk Moses as the "settlement of peoples, usually in frontier areas, loyal to the metropole to ensure security and encourage economic development of semi—or unoccupied land within a national or imperial territory." Moses, "Empire, Colony, Genocide: Keywords and the Philosophy of History," in *Empire, Colony, Genocide: Conquest, Occupation, and Subaltern Resistance in World History*, ed. by A. Dirk Moses (New York: Berghahn Books, 2008), 23.

157. Stephanie Beswick, *Sudan's Blood Memory: The Legacy of War, Ethnicity, and Slavery in Early South Sudan* (Rochester, NY: University of Rochester Press, 2004), 134, 138.

158. Jok, "Militarization and Gender Violence in South Sudan," 429.

159. Fifty-five-year-old displaced man from Agoro payam, Magwi county, interview with the author, June 27, 2017.

160. MacKinnon, *Are Women Human?*, 170–71.

161. Four members of civil society 1; three members of civil society 3.

162. High-ranking government official 3.

163. I do not subscribe to the thesis that sexual violence was costly to the perpetrator in terms of reputation. Many reports on SPLA human rights violations were published and mostly ignored. On the opportunism/greed argument of rape, see Cohen, *Rape during Civil War*, 47.

164. Former SPLA commander, August 4, 2014.

165. Member of civil society 15.

166. Three members of civil society 2.

167. Member of civil society 14; thirteen members of civil society 1.

168. Member of civil society 15; member of civil society 16.

169. Not every dominant class or aristocracy is a "nobility." Marc Bloch, *Feudal Society: Social Classes and Political Organisation*, 3rd ed., (London: Routledge, 1989), 2:2; Joseph Morsel, *L'Aristocratie Medievale. La domination sociale en Occident (Ve-XVe siècle)*, Histoire (Paris: Armand Colin, 2004), 6–7; Pinaud, "The Making of a Military Aristocracy."

170. I borrow the expression from MacKinnon, *Are Women Human?*, 170–71.

171. Member of civil society 12, interview with the author, August 9, 2014.

172. I am adding a materialist twist to Donald Horowitz's conception of group legitimacy: "To understand the concept of group legitimacy, it is necessary to link it to ownership. Legitimacy goes to one's rightful place in the country. To be legitimate is therefore to be identified with the territory. Georg Simmel shrewdly notes that the ethnic stranger is "no 'owner of the soil'—soil not only in the physical but also in the figurative sense of a life-substance which is fixed, if not in a point in space, at least in an ideal point in the social environment." As patrimony confronts equality, group legitimacy provides a foundation for the recurrent psychological denial that another group owns an equal share in the land." Horowitz, *Ethnic Groups in Conflict* (Berkeley: University of California Press, 1985), 201–2.

173. Moses, "Empire, Colony, Genocide," 38.

5. NATIONALISM, PREDATION, AND ETHNIC RANKING

1. John Young, *The Fate of Sudan: The Origins and Consequences of a Flawed Peace Process* (London: Zed Books, 2012), 15, 61; Small Arms Survey, *Armed Groups in Sudan: The South Sudan Defence Forces in the Aftermath of the Juba Declaration*, Sudan Issue Brief, Human Security Baseline Assessment (Geneva: Small Arms Survey, October 2006), 3.

2. Peter Adwok Nyaba, *South Sudan: The State We Aspire To* (Cape Town: Centre for Advanced Study of African Society, 2011), 14, 18.

3. Gerard Prunier, *Darfur: The Ambiguous Genocide* (Ithaca, NY: Cornell University Press, 2005), 155.

4. Member of civil society 12, interview with the author, August 9, 2014.

5. Øystein H. Rolandsen and M. W. Daly, *A History of South Sudan: From Slavery to Independence* (Cambridge: Cambridge University Press, 2016), 137.

6. The SSDF was an umbrella for armed groups sponsored by Khartoum and united through the Khartoum Peace Agreement in 1997. It included the South Sudan Independence Movement (SSIM), the Equatorian Defence Forces (EDF), the SPLM Bahr El Ghazal Group, the South Sudan Independence Group (SSIG), and the Bor Group, as well as other groups such as Murle, Fertit, and other ethnic militias. Young, *The Fate of Sudan*, 14; John Young, *The South Sudan Defence Forces in the Wake of the Juba Declaration* (Geneva: Small Arms Survey, Graduate Institute of International Studies, November 2006), 17.

7. Young, *The Fate of Sudan*, 14.

8. "The Addis Ababa Agreement was a deal between the Southern bourgeoisie and the Northern bourgeoisie . . . the Southern bourgeoisie compromised the interests of the

masses, in return for the jobs that had long been denied to them." "Stated Position of the Rebels: Background and Manifesto of the Sudan People's Liberation Movement (SPLM)," *Horn of Africa*, 1985, 41; Young, *The Fate of Sudan*, 46.

9. Young, *The Fate of Sudan*, xv.

10. Young, *The Fate of Sudan*, 125–28.

11. Brian Da Silva (Department of Agriculture), Roger Winter (USAID), Andrew Natsios (special envoy to President George W. Bush).

12. Johnson was Norway's international development minister. Young, *The Fate of Sudan*, 8, 125–28.

13. The Juba Declaration was signed between Paulino Matiep's SSDF and Salva Kiir's SPLA. Young, *The Fate of Sudan*, 14.

14. According to Straus, the ideas forming ideologies identifying a specific group of people whose interests are promoted by the state, are the stuff of genocide. These ideas are what he calls "founding narratives." Scott Straus, *Making and Unmaking Nations: War, Leadership and Genocide in Modern Africa* (Ithaca, NY: Cornell University Press, 2015), x, 63.

15. Mona Siegel, "'History Is the Opposite of Forgetting': The Limits of Memory and the Lessons of History in Interwar France," *Journal of Modern History* 74, no. 4 (December 2002): 770–800; Christof Dejung, "Dissonant Memories: National Identity, Political Power, and the Commemoration of World War Two in Switzerland," *Oral History* 35, no. 2 (Autumn 2007): 57–66; Andrew Bank, "The Politics of Mythology: The Genealogy of the Philip Myth," *Journal of Southern African Studies* 25, no. 3 (1999): 461–77; Clémence Pinaud, "Are 'Griefs of More Value Than Triumphs'? Power Relations, Nation-Building and the Different Histories of Women's Wartime Contributions in Post-War South Sudan," *Journal of Northeast African Studies* 13, no. 2 (2013): 151–76; Zachariah Mampilly, "Performing the Nation-State: Rebel Governance and Symbolic Processes," in *Rebel Governance in Civil War*, ed. Ana Arjona, Nelson Kasfir, and Zachariah Mampilly (Cambridge: Cambridge University Press, 2015), 78–79.

16. A political myth is defined here as a powerful oversimplification merging "complex and contradictory experiences into one formula." Thomas Kühne, *The Rise and Fall of Comradeship: Hitler's Soldiers, Male Bonding and Mass Violence in the Twentieth Century* (Cambridge: Cambridge University Press, 2017), 18, 27.

17. Robert F. Melson, *Revolution and Genocide: On the Origins of the Armenian Genocide and the Holocaust* (Chicago: University of Chicago Press, 1992).

18. On ethnic prejudices, see Stuart J. Kaufman, *Nationalist Passions* (Ithaca, NY: Cornell University Press, 2015), 42.

19. The Nuer were seen by the Dinka as traitors to the nation much like the Jews in Nazi Germany or the Armenians in the Ottoman Empire. Straus, *Making and Unmaking Nations*, 71; Mark Levene, *Genocide in the Age of the Nation State* (London: I.B. Tauris & Co. Ltd, 2005), 1:72.

20. Straus, *Making and Unmaking Nations*, 11, 20.

21. Two former high-ranking government officials and high-ranking members of IO, interview with the author, February 22, 2017.

22. Counternarratives can be essential in deescalating genocidal violence. Straus, *Making and Unmaking Nations*, 12.

23. For example, the state promoted the mostly Dinka SPLA women's battalion Ketiba Banat in the postwar period, in contrast to its total neglect of the history of camp followers— one of forced recruitment, forced union, abduction, forced labor (including sexual labor), and unpaid bridewealth. See Pinaud, "Are 'Griefs of More Value Than Triumphs'?"

24. The Juba Declaration was signed on January 9, 2006, a year exactly after the CPA.

25. See, for example, Douglas H. Johnson, *South Sudan: A New History for a New Nation*, Ohio Short Stories of Africa (Athens: Ohio University Press, 2016).

26. High-ranking government official 2, interview with the author, July 25, 2014.

27. Symptomatically, in the third civil war, Machar would attempt to issue a new currency and flag in areas his troop controlled. Anne Quito, "Branding the World's Newest Country," *Works That Work*, 2015, https://worksthatwork.com/4/branding-south-sudan.

28. Quito, "Branding the World's Newest Country;" Jason Patinkin, "Spoiled by War: South Sudan Loses Its First and Only Brewery," *Beeradvocate*, March 2016, https://www.beeradvocate.com/articles/13445/spoiled-by-war-south-sudan-loses-its-first-and-only-brewery/; Ranjit Bhaskar, "In Pictures: Cattle for Wealth," January 3, 2011, https://www.aljazeera.com/news/africa/2011/01/20111361220925156.html; Nyaba, *The State We Aspire To*, 128.

29. Gwendolyn Leick, *Tombs of the Great Leaders: A Contemporary Guide* (London: Reaktion Books, 2013), 272–80; Majok Arol Dhieu, "Dr. John Garang's Mausoleum Is NOT a Cleansing Ground for Sinful Elites," *Paanluel Wel* (blog), April 13, 2016, https://paanluelwel.com/2016/04/13/dr-john-garangs-mausoleum-is-not-a-cleansing-ground-for-sinful-elites/.

30. The leadership had briefly hesitated to anoint Ramciel in Lakes, Dinka land, as the country's capital.

31. To summarize, the lack of political will (and commitment) on both sides to disarm, the lack of institutional capacity in both northern and southern DDR commissions (who seldom cooperated and coordinated), and the lack of transparency and accountability in the DDR process (amounting to widespread corruption)—hence the lack of monitoring of disarmament—all impeded and slowed down the DDR process. The first phase of the demilitarization process concerned the "special needs" category (women, the elderly, and the wounded/disabled) and was a way to buy time until the referendum and independence of the south.

32. Ian Rowe and Laurent Banal, *Sudan: Assessment of the Disarmament and Demobilisation Process*, (Khartoum: United Nations Integrated DDR Unit, November 28, 2009), 14–15.

33. Ernest Renan, when writing about the processes at work in the formation of a nation, insisted that "forgetting, I would even go so far as to say historical error, is a crucial factor in the creation of a nation." Ernest Renan, "What Is a Nation?," in *Nation and Narration*, ed. Homi K. Bhabha (London: Routledge, 1990), 11.

34. Member of civil society 3, interview with the author, July 4, 2017.

35. Member of civil society 12.

36. Lombard noted a similar process of social exclusion and the creation of a master narrative through DDR programs in the Central African Republic. Louisa Lombard, *State of Rebellion: Violence and Intervention in the Central African Republic* (London: Zed Books, 2016), 141–46.

37. Pinaud, "Are 'Griefs of More Value Than Triumphs'?," 158.

38. This is typical of ethnic groups considered "primitive," "backwards," and at the bottom of ethnic ranking. Kaufman also writes of the SPLM during the second civil war that "while the SPLM rhetoric did not refer explicitly to slavery, many of its themes are best understood against the background narrative of past resistance to northern discrimination." See Donald Horowitz, *Ethnic Groups in Conflict* (Berkeley: University of California Press, 1985), 144; Kaufman, *Nationalist Passions*, 114.

39. Rolandsen and Daly, *A History of South Sudan*, 147; International Crisis Group, *Sudan's Comprehensive Peace Agreement: Beyond the Crisis*, Africa Briefing, Policy Briefing (Nairobi/Brussels: International Crisis Group, March 13, 2008), 3.

40. Johnson, *A New History for a New Nation*, 164.

41. Rolandsen and Daly, *A History of South Sudan*, 149–50.

42. Young, *The Fate of Sudan*, xx.

43. Rolandsen and Daly, *A History of South Sudan*, 144.

44. Khartoum supported rebellions in the south after the April 2010 elections and with the renewal of the war in South Kordofan in the summer 2011.

45. Rolandsen and Daly, *A History of South Sudan*, 141.

46. David Keen, *Useful Enemies: When Waging Wars Is More Important Than Winning Them* (Yale University Press, 2012), 236.

47. On war systems, see Keen, *Useful Enemies*, 238.

48. American Embassy, Khartoum, "Defense White Paper Energizes SPLA Budget Process, While Expectations of USG Assistance Are Heightened By Its Completion" (Wikileaks Cable: 08KHARTOUM971_a, July 2, 2008), http://wikileaks.org/plusd/cables/08KHAR TOUM971_a.html; American Embassy, Khartoum, "SE Gration Meeting with SPLA Leadership" (Wikileaks Cable: 09KHARTOUM508_a, April 14, 2009), http://wikileaks.org/plusd/cables/09KHARTOUM508_a.html.

49. International Crisis Group, *Beyond the Crisis*, 5.

50. Rolandsen and Daly, *A History of South Sudan*, 147; Christopher Vaughan, Mareike Schomerus, and Lotje De Vries, eds., *The Borderlands of South Sudan. Authority and Identity in Contemporary and Historical Perspectives* (New York: Palgrave Macmillan, 2013), 3.

51. Young, *The Fate of Sudan*, 97.

52. The SPLM/A and Khartoum could not agree on proposals by international bodies defining Abyei's borders. Rolandsen and Daly, *A History of South Sudan*, 137–38, 146–47.

53. Heglig is an oil-rich contested border point between Abyei and South Kordofan. See Joshua Craze, "Unclear Lines: State and Non-State Actors in Abyei," in *The Borderlands of South Sudan*, ed. Vaughan, Schomerus, and De Vries, 47, 56.

54. Two former high-ranking government officials and high-ranking members of IO. More research is needed on the relationship between Kiir's faction and the SPLA-North. But Kiir's faction seems to have instrumentalized the SPLM/A-North to serve its own separatist and nationalist aims. See Nyaba, *The State We Aspire To*, 31.

55. Former high-ranking government official 1, interview with the author, July 11, 2017.

56. Two former high-ranking government officials and high-ranking members of IO.

57. I take inspiration from Charles Tilly, "War Making and State Making as Organized Crime," in *Bringing the State Back In*, ed. Peter Evans, Dietrich Rueschemeyer, and Theda Skocpol (Cambridge: Cambridge University Press, 1985), 184.

58. Former high-ranking government official 1.

59. Former high-ranking government official 1.

60. Two former high-ranking government officials and high-ranking members of IO

61. Alex De Waal, "When Kleptocracy Becomes Insolvent: Brute Causes of the Civil War in South Sudan," *African Affairs*, no. 113/452 (2014): 364–65.

62. De Waal, "When Kleptocracy Becomes Insolvent," 365; Waakhe Simon Wudu, "South Sudanese Accuse Khartoum after Village Bombed," *Voice of America*, November 3, 2014, https://www.voanews.com/africa/south-sudanese-accuse-khartoum-after-village-bombed; "Sudan 'Bombs Refugees' in South Sudan's Unity State," *BBC*, November 11, 2011, http://www.bbc.co.uk/news/world-africa-15678261.

63. Douglas H. Johnson, "Briefing: The Crisis in South Sudan," *African Affairs* 113, no. 451 (April 2014): 303–4; Nyaba, *The State We Aspire To*, 38, 41.

64. Young, *The Fate of Sudan*, 15.

65. Among the shady contractors were the American Erik Prince, the founder of Blackwater. Jeremy Scahill and Matthew Cole, "Echo Papa Exposed: Inside Erik Prince's Treacherous Drive to Build a Private Air Force," *Intercept*, April 11, 2016, https://theintercept.com/2016/04/11/blackwater-founder-erik-prince-drive-to-build-private-air-force/; Daniel Large, "The International Presence in Sudan," in *The Sudan Handbook*, ed. John Ryle et al (Woodbridge: James Currey, 2011), 272–92.

66. American Embassy, Khartoum, "SE Gration Meeting with SPLA Leadership." To give just one example, the South Sudanese government paid the firm Independent Diplomat to focus on the country's relationship with the U.S., the EU, the UN, and the African Union from 2009 to January 2014. Ted Dagne, one of the SPLM/A's most well-known advocates in Washington DC and a former staffer on the U.S. Congressional Research Service, also advised Kiir throughout the CPA period. He wrote the letter to the seventy-five "corrupt officials" in 2012. See Rebecca Hamilton, "Special Report: The Wonks Who Sold Washington on South Sudan," *Reuters*, July 11, 2012, http://www.reuters.com/article/2012/07/11/us-south-sudan-midwives-idUSBRE86A0GC20120711.

67. David Deng, *The New Frontier: A Baseline Survey of Large-Scale Land-Based Investment in Southern Sudan* (Norwegian People's Aid, March 2011), http://reliefweb.int/sites/reliefweb.int/files/resources/6F0B144DA275260B8525785C0069DB6A-Full_Report.pdf.

68. The SPLA already resorted to these metaphors during the war. For example, it opened its 1994 National Convention by describing the period pre-NC as "childhood." Øystein H. Rolandsen, *Guerrilla Government: Political Changes in the Southern Sudan during the 1990s* (Uppsala: Nordic Africa Institute, 2005), 122.

69. This racist attitude is exemplified in a scene from the documentary *State Builders* about the CPA period, featuring Lise Grande, the UN Coordinator for South Sudan. Grande is approving the final draft of a UN brochure about South Sudan, the "key message [of which] is that in South Sudan, people are young, rural, poor, uneducated and lack basic services . . . Our brand is that 15-year-old girl who has a greater chance of dying in childbirth than finishing school." Quito, "Branding the World's Newest Country."

70. On the topic of South Sudan's international relations in the CPA period, see Gérard Prunier, "Sudan's Regional Relations," in *Sudan Handbook*, ed. John Ryle et al. (Woodbridge: James Currey, 2011), 153–63.

71. Young, *The Fate of Sudan*, 133; Michael Mann, *The Dark Side of Democracy: Explaining Ethnic Cleansing* (Cambridge: Cambridge University Press, 2005), 22. In the south, the UN Mission in Sudan (UNMIS) became after 2011 the UN Mission in South Sudan (UNMISS).

72. States going through a process of democratization are more vulnerable to ethno-nationalism, where "ethnonationalist movements claim the state for their own ethnos." Mann, *The Dark Side of Democracy*, 502.

73. Levene argues that the exportation of the very concept of the nation-state after World War II and the related wave of decolonization has been associated with the globalization of genocide. Levene, *Genocide in the Age of the Nation State*, vol. 1, 17, 155, 164; Young, *The Fate of Sudan*, 4–8; Kaufman, *Nationalist Passions*, 41; Mann, *The Dark Side of Democracy*, 22.

74. Young, *The Fate of Sudan*, 4–8; Naseem Badiey, *The State of Post-Conflict Reconstruction: Land, Urban Development and State-Building in Juba Southern Sudan* (Woodbridge: James Currey, 2014), 10–11.

75. Sudan was the third largest recipient of U.S. aid after Afghanistan and Iraq and a large portion of that aid went to the south. Wolfram Lacher, *South Sudan: International State-Building and Its Limits*, SWP Research Paper (Berlin: German Institute for International and Security Affairs, February 2012), 12.

76. *South Sudan: Options in Crisis: Hearings Before the United States Senate Committee on Foreign Relations*, 114th Cong. 2nd (2016) (Statement of Kate Almquist Knopf: "U.S. Options as South Sudan Leaders Fail the Peace"), 6.

77. Global Humanitarian Assistance, *Resource Flows to Sudan: Aid to South Sudan* (Global Humanitarian Assistance, July 2011), 4, http://devinit.org/wp-content/uploads/2011/07/gha-Sudan-aid-factsheet-2011-South-Sudan-focus1.pdf.

78. In terms of ratio, oil revenues provided for a spending of US$340 per capital and aid for US$100 per capita in 2011. Alex De Waal, *The Real Politics of the Horn of Africa* (Cambridge: Polity, 2015), 100.

79. Rolandsen and Daly, *A History of South Sudan*, 137.

80. International oil companies and petty traders from neighboring countries (especially Uganda and Kenya) dominated the economy. Young, *The Fate of Sudan*, 11–12.

81. Rolandsen, *Guerrilla Government*, 148; Young, *The Fate of Sudan*, 164.

82. Diplomat 1, interview with the author, July 23, 2014.

83. High-ranking officer from the Ethiopian Army, interview with the author, July 10, 2014.

84. Nyaba, *The State We Aspire To*, ix, 141.

85. This did not mean the SPLA was not still corrupt. But South Sudan's case illustrated that "as the state becomes wealthier, especially in a rapid or sudden fashion, its centrality in the process of dominant-class formation will increase." Larry Diamond, "Class Formation in the Swollen African State," *Journal of Modern African Studies* 25, no. 04 (1987): 578.

86. Lineage-based societies have adapted remarkably well to new bureaucratic environments. Jean-Francois Bayart, Stephen Ellis, and Beatrice Hibou, *Criminalization of the State in Africa* (Bloomington: Indiana University Press, 2009), 39.

87. Clémence Pinaud, "South Sudan: Civil War, Predation and the Making of a Military Aristocracy," *African Affairs* 113, no. 451 (April 2014): 208.

88. Member of civil society 10, interview with the author, February 3, 2016.

89. This is inspired from Ernest Harsch's reflections on the role of corruption: in some countries, it "is the cement that holds together the entire system of political and class domination." Ernest Harsch, "Accumulators and Democrats: Challenging State Corruption in Africa," *Journal of Modern African Studies* 31, no. 1 (March 1, 1993): 37.

90. According to the Sudd Institute, a Juba-based think tank, less than 17 percent of the national budget was transferred from Juba to the state capitals. Once in the capitals, most of the state revenues stayed there and never reached the county level: only about 10 percent reached rural areas. Edward Thomas, *South Sudan: A Slow Liberation* (London: Zed Books Ltd, 2015), 143–46; Anne Walraet, "South Sudan: Violence as Politics," in *Africa's Insurgents. Navigating an Evolving Landscape.*, ed. Morten Bøås and Kevin C. Dunn (Boulder, CO: Lynne Rienner Publishers, 2017), 207.

91. Alex De Waal, "What Actual Spending Tells Us About South Sudan's Governance," *World Peace Foundation. Reinventing Peace* (blog), March 6, 2014, https://sites.tufts.edu/reinventingpeace/2014/03/06/what-actual-spending-tells-us-about-south-sudans-governance/.

92. Global Humanitarian Assistance, *Resource Flows to Sudan. Aid to South Sudan*, 6.

93. African Rights, *Imposing Empowerment? Aid and Civil Institutions in Southern Sudan* (African Rights, December 1995), 7.

94. "Joint Donors Warn S. Sudan Government over Corruption," *Sudan Tribune*, April 12, 2011, http://www.sudantribune.com/spip.php?article38552.

95. Bayart was referring to the case of Senegal. Jean-François Bayart, "Preface to the Second English Edition: Africa in the World; A History of Extraversion," in *The State in Africa: The Politics of the Belly*, 2nd ed. (Malden, MA: Polity, 2009), xxviii.

96. South Sudan's Anti-Corruption Commission did submit the names of five officials in May 2012. "Warrap Parliament Backs South Sudan's Fight Against Corruption," *Sudan Tribune*, June 8, 2012, http://www.sudantribune.com/spip.php?article42864.

97. Since 2005, only one top official, the SPLM secretary general Pagan Amum (one of the "Garang boys"), was tried (in March 2012), in a court in Juba—and not through the SSACC. He was acquitted. Ngor Arol Garang, "South Sudan: SPLM's Amum Acquitted

of $30 Million Scam," *Sudan Tribune*, March 21, 2012, http://www.sudantribune.com/South-Sudan-SPLM-s-Amum-acquitted,41992; South Sudanese academic 3, interview with the author, July 11, 2017.

98. Global Witness, "Attack on Activist Threatens Anti-Corruption Efforts in South Sudan," press release, July 12, 2012, http://www.globalwitness.org/library/attack-activist-threatens-anti-corruption-efforts-south-sudan.

99. The corruption of the elite was demonstrated by the "dura saga" (dura means sorghum) scandal that surfaced in 2008. It was, a Juba resident recalled, "a gold rush, except for grain . . . Most people opening companies were instigated by top people. These guys would take a cut . . . Everyone who came from Riek Machar or Salva Kiir with a letter was given registration to deliver maize and dura to hungry people." High-ranking government official 2, interview with the author, July 26, 2014.

100. High-ranking government official 2.

101. On state and county-level administrations, see Thomas, *A Slow Liberation*, 139–41.

102. Political representative 4, interview with the author, July 25, 2014.

103. The term "roving bandit" is taken from Mancur Olson, "Dictatorship, Democracy, and Development," *American Political Science Review* 87, no. 3 (September 1993): 567–76; De Waal, "When Kleptocracy Becomes Insolvent," 350.

104. De Waal, *The Real Politics of the Horn of Africa*, 98.

105. "Salva Kiir Furious at Call to Step Down," *Radio Tamazuj*, January 27, 2015, https://radiotamazuj.org/en/news/article/salva-kiir-furious-at-call-to-step-down.

106. The three rebel groups are the South Sudan Democratic Movement/Army, the South Sudan Defense Forces, and the South Sudan Liberation Movement/Army. Walraet, "South Sudan: Violence as Politics," 205–6.

107. Mann, *The Dark Side of Democracy*, 5.

108. They included Pagan Amum, Nhial Deng Nhial, Deng Alor Kuol, Majak D'Agoot, Yassir Arman, Malik Aggar, and Adbalaziz al-Hilu, as well as others from the old Leadership Council.

109. South Sudanese intellectual 2, interview with the author, July 11, 2017.

110. Young, *The Fate of Sudan*, 77.

111. International Crisis Group, *Sudan's Comprehensive Peace Agreement: The Long Road Ahead* (International Crisis Group, March 31, 2006), 20–21.

112. International Crisis Group, *Beyond the Crisis*, 4–5, 7; Nyaba, *The State We Aspire To*, 28.

113. Johnson, "Briefing: The Crisis In South Sudan," 303–4; Nyaba, *The State We Aspire To*, 38, 41.

114. Nyaba, *The State We Aspire To*, 15.

115. Nyaba also mentions the importance of the slave-redemption scandal in coalescing the anti-Garang coalition behind Bona Malual. Nyaba, *The State We Aspire To*, 19, 30.

116. Former SPLA commander, interview with the author, August 6, 2014; Nyaba, *The State We Aspire To*, 15.

117. Longtime observer 1, interview with the author, January 3, 2018.

118. South Sudanese intellectual 1, interview with the author, November 21, 2017.

119. Because the JCE is an official "council," I call it an "organization"—not a "club" or "group" or just a "network" (even if it is also a network of Dinka people from various backgrounds), like in the case of the Hutu Power groups that were not as institutionalized before 1993 as the JCE was as an ethnic organization throughout the CPA period. Hutu groups, by contrast, were present in a variety of former opposition political parties and came together in their ideology of Hutu ethnic domination. The process seems to have gone the other way with the JCE: it was an ethnic organization first that later infiltrated the SPLM party-state. See Gérard Prunier, *The Rwanda Crisis. History of a Genocide.* (London:

Hurst & Company, 1995), 200–201, 220; Scott Straus, *The Order of Genocide: Race, Power and Race in Rwanda* (Ithaca, NY: Cornell University Press, 2006), 42.

120. International Crisis Group, *The Long Road Ahead*, 21.

121. Former high-ranking government official 1.

122. Nations are imagined communities. Benedict Anderson, *Imagined Communities*, 2nd ed. (London: Verso, 1991).

123. They practiced an embittered form of nationalism. Mann, *The Dark Side of Democracy*, 196.

124. Member of civil society 17, interview with the author, June 28, 2017.

125. I borrow this term of "ethno-political entrepreneurs" from Rogers Brubaker, *Ethnicity without Groups* (Cambridge, MA: Harvard University Press, 2004), 10.

126. Nyaba, *The State We Aspire To*, 130, 175; On the topic see Young, *The Fate of Sudan*, 292–93.

127. African Union (AU) Commission of Inquiry on South Sudan, *Final Report of the African Union Commission of Inquiry on South Sudan—Executive Summary* (Addis Ababa: AU Commission of Inquiry on South Sudan, October 15, 2014), 10; member of civil society 4, interview with the author, June 14, 2017; Nyaba, *The State We Aspire To*, 55.

128. I borrow the expression of "ethnic extremism" from Horowitz, *Ethnic Groups in Conflict*, 227.

129. Member of civil society 4.

130. Nyaba, *The State We Aspire To*, 29–30.

131. Thirty-four-year-old displaced man from Wau, interview with the author, July 7, 2017.

132. Kiir, Thiik, and Akol Kuur (the head of national security) all belong to the same Dinka Rek clan, while Bona Malual belongs to the Twic—all are from Warrap. Isaiah Abraham, "Who's the Founding Father of the Republic of South Sudan?," *Sudan Tribune*, December 7, 2011, http://www.sudantribune.com/spip.php?article40936; former high-ranking government official and detainee 3, interview with the author, July 11, 2017.

133. Mann, *The Dark Side of Democracy*, 39, 55, 502, 519.

134. The competition between Kiir and the Garang factions kept them so busy that they devoted little attention to the CPA implementation. Kiir took advantage of the SPLM's reorganization to place his followers in key roles, which made political figures like the Nuer Angelina Teny (Riek Machar's wife) and the Equatorian Joseph Bakassoro decide to run independently in the upcoming elections. International Crisis Group, *Beyond the Crisis*, 4–5, 7; Nyaba, *The State We Aspire To*, 166; two former high-ranking government officials and high-ranking members of IO.

135. Kiir would seek to isolate Amum within the SPLM and later through a corruption trial in 2012. International Crisis Group, *Beyond the Crisis*, 6; Ngor Arol Garang, "South Sudan: SPLM's Amum Acquitted of $30 Million Scam," *Sudan Tribune*, March 21, 2012, http://www.sudantribune.com/South-Sudan-SPLM-s-Amum-acquitted,41992; Nyaba, *The State We Aspire To*, 143.

136. Nyaba, 2–3.

137. Isaac Vuni, "Sudan's Kiir Faces Two Contenders for the SPLM Chairmanship," *Sudan Tribune*, May 14, 2008, http://www.sudantribune.com/spip.php?article27153; Nyaba, The State We Aspire To, 140.

138. Former high-ranking government official 1.

139. South Sudanese intellectual 2.

140. Two former high-ranking government officials and high-ranking members of IO.

141. "Machar Has Apologised to Dinka Bor Community—Army Official," *Sudan Tribune*, August 11, 2011, http://www.sudantribune.com/spip.php?article39795; two former high-ranking government officials and high-ranking members of IO.

142. International Crisis Group, *South Sudan: Jonglei—"We Have Always Been at War,"* Crisis Group Africa Report (International Crisis Group, December 22, 2014), 10.

143. International Crisis Group, 10; American Embassy, Khartoum, "Sudan: SPLA Chief of Staff Says He Might Be Replaced" (Wikileaks Cable: 07KHARTOUM470_a, March 25, 2007), https://wikileaks.org/plusd/cables/07KHARTOUM470_a.html.

144. Straus mentions how "founding narratives" create an "implicit moral hierarchy between, on the one hand, a primary population whom the state should benefit and protect and, on the other hand, secondary populations to whom the state should pay less attention and who should not rule." Scott Straus, *Remaking Rwanda State Building and Human Rights after Mass Violence* (Madison: University of Wisconsin Press, 2011), 57.

145. Member of civil society 4.

146. Member of civil society 23, interview with the author, August 9, 2014.

147. Nyaba, *The State We Aspire To*, 53, 56, 157n23.

148. Oil production would only restart in April 2013, at a slower pace since installations had been damaged by this halt. De Waal, "When Kleptocracy Becomes Insolvent," 364–65.

149. De Waal, "When Kleptocracy Becomes Insolvent," 364–65.

150. Thomas, *A Slow Liberation*, 143.

151. Small Arms Survey, *The 14-Mile Area*, Human Security Baseline Assessment (Small Arms Survey, November 3, 2014), http://www.smallarmssurveysudan.org/facts-figures/borderdisputed-areas/14-mile-area.html; Abraham Agoth, "Governor Delivers Assistance To SPLA Frontline At Kiir-Adem," *Gurtong*, December 30, 2012, http://www.gurtong.net/ECM/Editorial/tabid/124/ctl/ArticleView/mid/519/articleId/8957/categoryId/6/Governor-Delivers-Assistance-To-SPLA-Frontline-At-Kiir-Adem.aspx.

152. Former high-ranking government official 1.

153. Straus, *Making and Unmaking Nations*, 26.

154. Former high-ranking government official 2, interview with the author, August 18, 2014.

155. AU Commission of Inquiry on South Sudan, *Final Report*, 138.

156. Former high-ranking government official 2.

157. The position of the non-Dinka rivals was like that of the Jews and the Armenians—they were also despised by the dominant group, who felt that sense of "moral outrage" when they moved up in society. Melson, *Revolution and Genocide*, 20.

158. Former high-ranking government official 3, interview with the author, August 18, 2014.

159. These newcomers included Alieu Ayeny Alieu, Telar Ring Deng, Michael Makuei, the Nuer Dr Riak Gai Kok (former NCP leader in the South), and Abdallah Deng Nhial (from Gogrial and close to the northerner Hassan Al-Turabi). Johnson, "Briefing: The Crisis In South Sudan," 303, 304.

160. De Waal, *The Real Politics of the Horn of Africa*, 104.

161. Johnson, "Briefing: The Crisis In South Sudan," 303.

162. AU Commission of Inquiry on South Sudan, *Final Report*, 138, 226; Mahmood Mamdani, *A Separate Opinion* (AU Commission of Inquiry on South Sudan, October 20, 2014), 6.

163. AU Commission of Inquiry on South Sudan, *Final Report*, 138, 216, 226; diplomat 2, interview with the author, August 18, 2014; IO member 1, interview with the author, August 18, 2014.

164. High-ranking government official 2 and wife, interview with the author, July 24, 2014.

165. AU Commission of Inquiry on South Sudan, *Final Report*, 128; "Kiir Dissolves All South Sudan's SPLM Structures," *Sudan Tribune*, November 15, 2013, http://www.sudantribune.com/spip.php?article48818.

166. "Press Statement By Riek Machar," *Gurtong*, December 8, 2013, http://www.gurtong.net/ECM/Editorial/tabid/124/ctl/ArticleView/mid/519/articleId/14076/categoryId/120/Press-%20Statement-by-Riek-Machar.aspx.

167. "[Indiscipline in the party] will take us back to the days of the 1991 split . . . [and] we all know where the split took us . . . this could jeopardize the unity and independence of our country and we must guard against such things. My dear comrades, I am not prepared to let this happen again." See "South Sudan's New War Abuses by Government and Opposition Forces" (Human Rights Watch, August 2014), 18; "National Conference of SPLA Board—President's Salva Kiir Speech" YouTube video, 31:46, posted by "South Sudan," December 15, 2013, https://www.youtube.com/watch?v=5y3bp6Oehis.

168. Johnson, "Briefing: The Crisis in South Sudan," 307; Human Rights Watch, *South Sudan's New War Abuses by Government and Opposition Forces* (Human Rights Watch, August 2014), 16–17.

169. Former high-ranking government official 2; Human Rights Watch, *South Sudan's New War Abuses*, 22.

170. This was reminiscent of other pregenocidal situations. Levene, *Genocide in the Age of the Nation State*, vol. 1, 74; Melson, *Revolution and Genocide*, 272.

171. Olson, "Dictatorship, Democracy, and Development," 572.

172. Genocides are subject to processes of both escalation and restraint. Straus, *Making and Unmaking Nations*, 10.

173. I take inspiration from Brubaker, *Ethnicity without Groups*, 12.

6. THE MAKING OF A VIOLENT ETHNOCRACY

1. Øystein H. Rolandsen and M. W. Daly, *A History of South Sudan: From Slavery to Independence* (Cambridge: Cambridge University Press, 2016), 137.

2. John Young, *The Fate of Sudan: The Origins and Consequences of a Flawed Peace Process* (London: Zed Books, 2012), 14; Small Arms Survey, *Armed Groups in Sudan: The South Sudan Defence Forces in the Aftermath of the Juba Declaration*, Sudan Issue Brief, Human Security Baseline Assessment (Geneva: Small Arms Survey, October 2006), 3; Comprehensive Peace Agreement between the Government of the Republic of the Sudan and the Sudan People's Liberation Movement/Sudan People's Liberation Army, January 9, 2005, 88–89.

3. A few of the SSDF militias remained aligned with Khartoum and continued to undermine the SPLA's control of the territory and demilitarization efforts, but they were a minority. Small Arms Survey, *Armed Groups in Sudan*, 3.

4. Fifty-one-year-old displaced man from Makuach boma/payam, Bor county, Jonglei, interview with the author, July 5, 2017.

5. John Young, *The South Sudan Defence Forces in the Wake of the Juba Declaration* (Geneva: Small Arms Survey, Graduate Institute of International Studies, November 2006), 26.

6. Former SPLA commander, interview with the author, August 6, 2014.

7. Former SPLA commander, August 6, 2014.

8. Former SPLA commander, interview with the author, August 4, 2014; Small Arms Survey, *Armed Groups*, 6.

9. American Embassy, Khartoum, "SPLA and Forces Loyal to Former Militia Leader Square Off in Juba" (Wikileaks Cable: 07KHARTOUM613_a, April 19, 2007), https://wikileaks.org/plusd/cables/07KHARTOUM613_a.html.

10. Former high-ranking SPLA and government official, interview with the author, August 7, 2014.

11. Young, *The South Sudan Defence Forces*, 28, 40.

12. Scott Straus, *Making and Unmaking Nations: War, Leadership and Genocide in Modern Africa* (Ithaca, NY: Cornell University Press, 2015), 33.

13. American Embassy, Khartoum, "Sudan: SPLA Chief of Staff Says He Might Be Replaced" (Wikileaks Cable: 07KHARTOUM470_a, March 25, 2007), https://wikileaks.org/plusd/cables/07KHARTOUM470_a.html.

14. I do not mean to say here that Garang wanted the SPLA to be ranked again, since he died before the Juba Declaration and too soon to have any impact on it.

15. Former SPLA commander, August 6, 2014.

16. Member of civil society 10, interview with the author, February 3, 2016.

17. Anne Walraet, "South Sudan: Violence as Politics," in *Africa's Insurgents. Navigating an Evolving Landscape*, ed. Morten Bøås and Kevin C. Dunn (Lynne Rienner Publishers, 2017), 206; longtime observer 1, interview with the author, December 4, 2015.

18. High-ranking officer from the Ethiopian army, interview with the author, July 10, 2014.

19. Procurement and logistics officers were in particularly privileged positions. Peter Adwok Nyaba, *South Sudan: The State We Aspire To* (Cape Town: Centre for Advanced Study of African Society, 2011), 132.

20. Former SPLA commander, August 6, 2014.

21. Alex De Waal, *The Real Politics of the Horn of Africa* (Cambridge: Polity, 2015), 97–98.

22. Aid worker 1, interview with the author, January 27, 2010.

23. High-ranking government official 2, interview with the author, July 26, 2014.

24. Walraet, "Violence as Politics," 206.

25. American Embassy, Khartoum, "SPLA Defense White Paper" (Wikileaks Cable: 08KHARTOUM542_a, April 8, 2008), https://wikileaks.org/plusd/cables/08KHARTOUM542_a.html.

26. Former SPLA commander, August 6, 2014.

27. African Union (AU) Commission of Inquiry on South Sudan, *Final Report of the African Union Commission of Inquiry on South Sudan—Executive Summary* (Addis Ababa: AU Commission of Inquiry on South Sudan, October 15, 2014), 10.

28. High-ranking officer from the Ethiopian army.

29. De Waal, *The Real Politics of the Horn of Africa*, 96.

30. For example, raids between the Lou Nuer and the Murle in August 2011 would result in at least six hundred dead and twenty-six thousand cattle stolen. Eszter Farkas, "South Sudan Clashes Kill 600, U.N. Calls for Talks," *CNN*, August 27, 2011, http://www.cnn.com/2011/WORLD/africa/08/22/southern.sudan.attack.reconciliation/index.html.

31. An expression forged by J. P. Olivier de Sardan, "A Moral Economy of Corruption in Africa?" *Journal of Modern African Studies* 37, no. 1 (March 1, 1999): 27.

32. Nyaba has been the most explicit in the case of Malakal and Jonglei: "The cattle-theft afflicting Malakal has been traced to security and law enforcement agents." Some of the raiding militias were affiliated with the "roving bandits" of the post-2010 elections who received weapons from Khartoum. See Nyaba, *The State We Aspire To*, 57; Young, *The Fate of Sudan*, 309–10; Small Arms Survey, *My Neighbour, My Enemy: Inter-Tribal Violence in Jonglei*, Human Security Baseline Assessment (Geneva: Small Arms Survey, October 2012), 4.

33. Edward Thomas, *South Sudan: A Slow Liberation* (London: Zed Books Ltd, 2015), 218.

34. Former government official and high-ranking member of IO 1, interview with the author, July 13, 2014.

35. High-ranking government official 1, interview with the author, August 5, 2014.

36. Former government official and high-ranking member of IO 1; diplomat 1, interview with the author, July 23, 2014.

37. Aid worker 2, interview with the author, August 4, 2014.

38. Member of civil society 6, interview with the author, August 10, 2014; cattle keeper, interview with the author, August 6, 2014; Clémence Pinaud, "Military Kinship, Inc.: Patronage, Inter-Ethnic Marriages and Social Classes in South Sudan," *Review of African Political Economy*, June 2016, 254.

39. Political representative 5, interview with the author, July 28, 2014.

40. Political representative 4, interview with the author, July 25, 2014.

41. Former government official and high-ranking member of IO 1.

42. On this topic in Lakes, also see Safer World, *Informal Armies: Community Defence Groups in South Sudan's Civil War* (London: Safer World, February 2017), 23.

43. . Rogers Brubaker, *Ethnicity without Groups* (Cambridge, MA: Harvard University Press, 2004), 10.

44. South Sudanese intellectual 4, interview with the author, July 21, 2014. Miscuing is trying to pass as a member of a different ethnic group. See Donald Horowitz, *Ethnic Groups in Conflict* (Berkeley: University of California Press, 1985), 48–49

45. Former government official and high-ranking member of IO 1. Many of the eight thousand Lou Nuer raiders in the December 2011–January 2012 attacks on the Murle wore SPLA and other security uniforms. Small Arms Survey, *My Neighbour, My Enemy*, 2.

46. Small Arms Survey, *My Neighbour, My Enemy*, 1–2. See Rebecca Littman, "Perpetrating Violence Increases Identification with Violent Groups: Survey Evidence from Former Combatants," *Personality and Social Psychology Bulletin* 44, no. 7 (2018): 1–13.

47. I take inspiration from Richard L. Sklar, "The Nature of Class Domination in Africa," *Journal of Modern African Studies* 17, no. 4 (1979): 531–52.

48. American Embassy, Khartoum, "SPLA and Forces Loyal to Former Militia Leader Square Off in Juba;" American Embassy, Khartoum, "Paulino Matiep on SPLM Politics and the SPLA" (Wikileaks Cable: 08KHARTOUM739_a, May 15, 2008), https://wikileaks.org/plusd/cables/08KHARTOUM739_a.html.

49. High-ranking officer from the Ethiopian army.

50. Forty-year-old displaced man from Yei, interview with the author, June 21, 2017.

51. Member of civil society 6. In June 2013, Salva Kiir also dismissed 170 SPLA officers known for their ties to the SPLA-North. Douglas H. Johnson, "Briefing: The Crisis in South Sudan," *African Affairs* 113, no. 451 (April 2014): 304.

52. Johnson, "Briefing: The Crisis in South Sudan," 305.

53. Young, *The Fate of Sudan*, 296.

54. Member of civil society 3, interview with the author, July 4, 2017.

55. Sixty-year-old displaced man from Ikotos / IO major general, interview with the author, July 8, 2017.

56. Former SPLA soldier 1, interview with the author, July 4, 2017.

57. Thirty-six-year-old displaced man from Wonduruba payam in Lanya county, interview with the author, June 20, 2017.

58. Young, *The Fate of Sudan,* 298.

59. Numerous sources have pointed out that the project emerged in 2010, contrary to the widespread assumption that these militias were recruited in 2012 or 2013. Some even went back as far as 2009, referencing Malong's initiative to recruit in Northern Bahr El Ghazal. This contradicts findings from the African Union Commission of Inquiry, which dated the recruitment to April 2012 at the time of the fighting in Heglig. Former SPLA commander, August 6, 2014; member of civil society 6; AU Commission of Inquiry on South Sudan, *Final Report—Executive Summary*, 23.

60. Research shows that contact with movement organizers, the framing of issues resonating with symbolic predispositions (group narratives), and networking are all key in government-led and mass-led mobilization. Stuart J. Kaufman, *Nationalist Passions* (Ithaca, NY: Cornell University Press, 2015), 49–51, 53.

61. Former SPLA commander, August 4, 2014.

62. Events included the SAF bombing of Kir Adem, Majok Yinh Thiou, and Warguit in November/December 2010 and then in 2012; the fighting around Heglig in April 2012; and the SAF/SPLA clashes in Aweil East in September 2012.

63. Former high-ranking government official 1, interview with the author, July 11, 2017.

64. Nyaba, *The State We Aspire To*, 157.

65. Malong used to travel on UNMISS flights to Juba. The fact he no longer did meant that the UN had even less insight into the evolution of the political situation both in Northern Bahr El Ghazal and in Juba. Aid worker 3, interview with the author, August 9, 2014.

66. Former high-ranking government official 3, interview with the author, August 18, 2014.

67. IO member 1, interview with the author, August 18, 2014.

68. Two members of civil society 1, interview with the author, November 13, 2015.

69. IO member 1; thirty-year-old displaced man from Aweil, interview with the author, June 23, 2017.

70. Wol Anyaak is from Yirol, eastern Lakes. One of the very few reports published on Mathiang Anyoor since the writing of this book also posited that General Santino Deng Wol, the SPLA division 3 commander, had been the one to recruit these men into Pantit's training camp. Alan Boswell, *Insecure Power And Violence. The Rise and Fall of Paul Malong and the Mathiang Anyoor* (Geneva: Small Arms Survey, Graduate Institute of International Studies, October 2019), 4.

71. Thirty-year-old displaced man from Aweil; member of civil society 6.

72. Thirty-year-old displaced man from Aweil.

73. Mahmood Mamdani, *A Separate Opinion* (AU Commission of Inquiry on South Sudan, October 20, 2014), 16; "Generals Say Juba Massacres Done by Private Militia, Not SPLA," *Radio Tamazuj*, March 9, 2015, https://radiotamazuj.org/en/news/article/generals-say-juba-massacres-done-by-private-militia-not-spla; "Ambrose Riny Thiik Denies Having Fueled War," *Radio Tamazuj*, December 10, 2015, https://radiotamazuj.org/en/news/article/ambrose-riny-thiik-denies-having-fueled-war.

74. This is neither surprising nor exceptional. For example, during the second half of 1941, "to maintain secrecy, Heinrich Himmler and his key subordinates generally avoided written orders and certainly dispensed with detailed blueprints setting out their plans for the Jews." Richard Breitman, "Himmler and the 'Terrible Secret' among the Executioners," *Journal of Contemporary History* 26, no. 3/4 (1991): 431–32.

75. Thirty-year-old displaced man from Aweil.

76. Twenty-seven-year-old displaced man from Wau payam, Ayod county, Jonglei, interview with the author, July 5, 2017.

77. South Sudanese intellectual 2, interview with the author, July 11, 2017; Former SPLA Commander, August 4, 2014.

78. Twenty-seven-year-old displaced man from Wau payam, Ayod county, Jonglei.

79. The name "Tiger" was a reference to the battalion Salva Kiir had commanded in the last war. De Waal, *The Real Politics of the Horn of Africa*, 104; member of civil society 6.

80. Two former high-ranking government officials and high-ranking members of IO, interview with the author, February 22, 2017.

81. South Sudanese intellectual 2. The only difference between Titweng and Gelueng was the geographic area they covered during the second civil war. Titweng was deployed to the north against government incursions and Gelueng to the south against Nuer raiders. Also see Thomas, *A Slow Liberation*, 206; Safer World, *Informal Armies*, 21; Naomi Pendle, "'They Are Now Community Police': Negotiating the Boundaries and Nature of the Government in South Sudan through the Identity of Militarised Cattle-Keepers," *International Journal On Minority And Group Rights*, no. 22 (2015): 410–34.

82. Member of civil society 6.

83. South Sudanese intellectual 2; member of civil society 6.

84. AU Commission of Inquiry on South Sudan, *Final Report of the African Union Commission of Inquiry on South Sudan* (Addis Ababa: AU Commission of Inquiry on South Sudan, October 15, 2014), 216.

85. IO member 1.

86. Former high-ranking government official 3.

87. Former high-ranking government official 3.

88. Member of civil society 6.

89. South Sudanese intellectual 2; Pendle, "'They Are Now Community Police,'" 432.

90. AU Commission of Inquiry on South Sudan, "Final Report," 138, 216, 226.

91. Diplomat 2, interview with the author, August 18, 2014; IO member 1.

92. Member of civil society 6.

93. Former high-ranking government official 3.

94. Pendle, "'They Are Now Community Police,'" 433; former high-ranking government official 3.

95. International Crisis Group, *South Sudan: Jonglei—"We Have Always Been at War,"* Crisis Group Africa Report (International Crisis Group, December 22, 2014), 10; two former high-ranking government officials and high-ranking members of IO; thirty-year-old displaced man from Aweil.

96. United Nations Security Council, *Final Report of the Panel of Experts on South Sudan Established Pursuant to Security Council Resolution 2206 (2015)* (United Nations Security Council, January 22, 2016), 26.

97. Thirty-year-old displaced man from Aweil.

98. AU Commission of Inquiry on South Sudan, *Final Report—Executive Summary*, 13.

99. International Crisis Group, *South Sudan: Jonglei—"We Have Always Been at War,"* 10.

100. Amnesty International, *South Sudan: Civil Unrest and State Repression; Human Rights Violations in Wau, Western Bahr El Ghazal State* (Amnesty International, February 2013).

101. Amnesty International, *South Sudan: Civil Unrest and State Repression.*

102. Thomas, *A Slow Liberation*, 212, 217–21; Human Rights Watch, *"They Are Killing Us": Abuses Against Civilians in South Sudan's Pibor County* (Human Rights Watch, September 12, 2013).

103. Nyaba, *The State We Aspire To*, 150, 171.

104. International Crisis Group, *South Sudan: Jonglei*, 9.

105. "The Honduran city of San Pedro Sula had the world's highest murder rate, with 159 murders per 100,000 inhabitants in 2011. The figures from Akobo and Pibor correspond with a yearly murder rate of about 1,218 murders per 100,000 inhabitants, more than seven times that of San Pedro Sula." David Deng, "South Sudan: Murder Rates at Wartime Levels In Jonglei," *New Sudan Vision*, September 21, 2013, http://www.newsudanvision.com/commentary-archive/2751-david-k.

106. Kiir and Machar acquired land in Equatoria and elsewhere—in the case of Machar, in Nasir and Akobo, appropriating Anyuak land. In Malakal, senior Dinka Padang ministers appropriated Shilluk land as well in 2009. Nyaba, *The State We Aspire To*, 119–21; government worker, interview with the author, July 31, 2014; Walraet, "South Sudan: Violence as Politics," 204.

107. David Deng, *The New Frontier: A Baseline Survey of Large-Scale Land-Based Investment in Southern Sudan* (Norwegian People's Aid, March 2011), 1, http://reliefweb.int/sites/reliefweb.int/files/resources/6F0B144DA275260B8525785C0069DB6A-Full_Report.pdf.

108. Member of civil society 24, interview with the author, July 24, 2014.

109. It should be noted that Equatorian groups also have cattle, but some more than others and overall much less and with smaller herds than the Dinka—not to mention compared to herds aggrandized through cattle raids.

110. Pendle, "'They Are Now Community Police,'" 423–24.

111. Historically, conflicts have followed droughts. United Nations Development Program, *Factsheet: Climate Change, Food Insecurity and Resilient Livelihoods in South Sudan* (United Nations Development Program, June 28, 2017); BRACED, *Building Climate Resilience in Fragile Contexts: Key Findings of BRACED Research in South Sudan; Improving Resilience to Climate Change in South Sudan.* (BRACED, February 19, 2018), 23–24, 29–30.

112. USGS & USAID, *A Climate Trend Analysis of Sudan*, Famine Early Warning Systems Network—Informing Climate Change Adaptation Series (USGS & USAID, 2011).

113. Government worker, Juba, interview with the author, July 31, 2014.

114. Member of civil society 4, interview with the author, June 14, 2017.

115. Other academics noted the prevalence of Dinka SPLA soldiers from both the Bahr El Ghazal and Upper Nile regions who settled on Equatorians' land and who, when the Equatorians sought to recover their own land, typically asked them, "Where were you (during the war)?" Member of civil society 17, interview with the author, June 28, 2017; Adam Branch and Zachariah Cherian Mampilly, "Winning the War, but Losing the Peace? The Dilemma of SPLM/A Civil Administration and the Tasks Ahead," *Journal of Modern African Studies* 43, no. 1 (March 2005): 1, 11–12; Cherry Leonardi, "Paying 'Buckets of Blood' for the Land: Moral Debates over Economy, War and State in Southern Sudan," *Journal of Modern African Studies*, no. 49 (2011): 220–21.

116. "To understand the concept of group legitimacy, it is necessary to link it to ownership. Legitimacy goes to one's rightful place in the country. To be legitimate is therefore to be identified with the territory." Horowitz, *Ethnic Groups in Conflict*, 201; member of civil society 3; Leonardi, "Paying 'Buckets of Blood,'" 221; Naseem Badiey, *The State of Post-Conflict Reconstruction: Land, Urban Development and State-Building in Juba Southern Sudan* (Woodbridge: James Currey, 2014), 159.

117. To be fair, discourses of indigenous autochthony were practiced by other communities, or by the Dinka in other areas that they had typically inhabited side by side with communities. But this Dinka group entitlement discourse, in these traditionally non-Dinka areas of Equatoria, was different. See Badiey, *The State of Post-Conflict Reconstruction*, 19.

118. Some were returning from neighboring Kenya Kakuma's camp and stopping on their way to Jonglei to settle in Eastern Equatoria. To be sure, Jonglei was insecure. But the Dinka settlers' discourses cannot be ignored.

119. Some Dinka settlers even petitioned Kiir to turn the Dinka enclave of New Cush in Eastern Equatoria into a Dinka county. Mareike Schomerus, *Violent Legacies: Insecurity in Sudan's Central and Eastern Equatoria*, Human Security Baseline Assessment (Geneva: Small Arms Survey, June 2008), 32.

120. See a description of this process by Israel in Oren Yiftachel, "'Ethnocracy': The Politics of Judaizing Israel/Palestine," *Constellations: An International Journal of Critical and Democratic Theory* 6, no. 3 (1999): 364–90.

121. Thirty-four-year-old displaced man from Wau, interview with the author, July 7, 2017.

122. I take inspiration from Ian S. Lustick, *Unsettled States, Disputed Lands: Britain and Ireland, France and Algeria, Israel and the West Bank-Gaza* (Ithaca, NY: Cornell University Press, 1995), 32–33.

123. Horowitz, *Ethnic Groups in Conflict*, 177–78.

124. Former SPLA lieutenant colonel, interview with the author, August 7, 2014.

125. Former SPLA lieutenant colonel. The most densely populated county was Juba, which reflected the postwar rush to settle in the capital, near the increasingly Dinka state. Juba was closely followed by the overwhelmingly Dinka counties of Aweil East in Northern Bahr El Ghazal, Gogrial West in Warrap, and Bor South in Jonglei. In fifth position

came the Nuer county of Nasir in Upper Nile, quickly followed by another Dinka county of Warrap (Twic), and Yei (Central Equatoria), where a lot of Dinka soldiers had settled. And yet according to Nyaba, Aweil was undercounted during the census. IMU OCHA SS, *5th Sudan Census 2008—Total Population Figures by County*, SS-0041 (12–29–2009: IMU OCHA SS, n.d.); Nyaba, *The State We Aspire To*, 70.

126. See Pinaud, "Military Kinship, Inc."

127. "Rarely will it be possible, without the application of considerable coercion, to maintain a system of ethnic stratification." Horowitz, *Ethnic Groups in Conflict*, 35.

128. Human Rights Watch, *Sudan: Government Repression Threatens Fair Elections National and Southern Officials Should End Abusive Practices* (Johannesburg: Human Rights Watch, March 21, 2010); Rolandsen and Daly, *A History of South Sudan*, 148; Young, *The Fate of Sudan*, 152, 165.

129. Member of civil society 25, interview with the author, April 2, 2010.

130. Aid worker 3.

131. Member of civil society 13, interview with the author, August 9, 2014.

132. Young, *The Fate of Sudan*, 169, 175.

133. Kiir postured an interest in resolving postreferendum issues but focused entirely on oil revenue sharing with the NCP. He continued to strongly advocate for separation based on his own personal views, while Pagan Amum implied that the SPLM did not support secession Young, *The Fate of Sudan*, 186–93.

134. Young, *The Fate of Sudan*, 212–13, 216–17, 221; De Waal, *The Real Politics of the Horn of Africa*, 92.

135. Member of civil society 13.

136. For example, Nuer and Equatorian members of the South Sudan Law Society were beaten and harassed for wanting to represent Pagan Amum during his trial for corruption in 2012. Member of civil society 24.

137. In December 2012, protests started over the shooting of civil society activists who opposed the relocation of the county capital Wau to the town of Bagari, which threatened to marginalize non-Dinka communities. The SPLA shot the protesters, and several hundred Dinka youths quickly descended on Wau. They came to avenge the killing of six Dinka farmers killed in Farajallah by unknown persons—murders most likely staged by government security agents. Amnesty International, *South Sudan: Civil Unrest and State Repression*, 11–12.

138. It also endorsed the relocation of the county capital. Amnesty International, *South Sudan: Civil Unrest and State Repression*, 6–7, 12–16.

139. Examples of journalists being jailed abound. For examples, see "S. Sudan Reporters and MPs Arrested in Wau," *Radio Tamazuj*, January 3, 2013, http://radiotamazuj.org/en/article/s-sudan-reporters-and-mps-arrested-wau; Ngor Arol Garang, "South Sudan Denies Arrest of Newspaper Editor," *Sudan Tribune*, October 11, 2011, http://www.sudantribune.com/spip.php?article40293.

140. Waakhe Simon Wudu, "Civil Society Wants Corrupt Officials Prosecuted: The Civil Society Has Called for Investigations into the Embezzlement of Public Funds in South Sudan," *Gurtong*, June 13, 2012, http://www.gurtong.net/ECM/Editorial/tabid/124/ctl/ArticleView/mid/519/articleId/7144/Civil-Society-Wants-Corrupt-Officials-Prosecuted.aspx; "South Sudan Deny Kidnap and Torture of Anti-Corruption Activist," *Sudan Tribune*, June 12, 2012, http://www.sudantribune.com/spip.php?article43254; "South Sudan Police Fire on Student Protest: Witnesses," *Reuters*, October 31, 2012, http://www.reuters.com/article/2012/10/31/us-sudan-south-protest-idUSBRE89U1CS20121031; "In South Sudan, a Town Simmers amid Unrest," CNN, December 20, 2012, http://www.cnn.com/2012/12/20/world/africa/south-sudan-instability/index.html; "Warrap Assembly Summons Governor over MP's 'arrest and Torture,'" *Sudan Tribune*, August 24, 2011, http://www.sudantribune.com/spip.php?article39937.

141. In-group policing is a typical tool to foster ethnic "groupness." Brubaker, *Ethnicity without Groups*, 19–20.

142. This was a problem back in the last war as well: according to a U.S. official, the level of violence against the Dinka in 1986–88 was "acceptable." Keen wrote that "there was nothing 'acceptable' about the catastrophe that befell the Dinka in 1986–1988." David Keen, *The Benefits of Famine: A Political Economy of Famine and Relief in Southwestern Sudan, 1983–1989*, 2nd ed. (Oxford: James Currey, 2008), x.

143. Alan Boswell, "American Expelled from South Sudan for Anti-Corruption Work," *McClatchy Newspapers*, August 20, 2012, http://www.mcclatchydc.com/2012/08/20/162893/american-expelled-from-south-sudan.html#storylink=cpy.; "South Sudan Expels UN Human Rights Official," *Aljazeera*, November 5, 2012, http://www.aljazeera.com/news/africa/2012/11/201211416420561324.html. Alan Boswell, correspondent for the US newspaper *McClatchy*, was labeled an "enemy of peace" by top government officials for his critical columns. Mahir Abu Goukh, "Kiir and Obama: Apologies and Denials," *Niles*, August 29, 2012, http://www.theniles.org/articles/?id=1393.

144. Amnesty International, *South Sudan: Civil Unrest and State Repression*, 9.

145. "Economic Migrants Battle Xenophobia," *IRIN News*, January 30, 2012, https://www.irinnews.org/fr/node/251548; Andrew Green, "South Sudan: Xenophobia Emerges Amidst Local Unemployment," *International Reporting Project*, May 23, 2012, https://internationalreportingproject.org/stories/view/south-sudan-xenophobia-emerges-amidst-local-unemployment; "South Sudan Ambassador Denies Xenophobia Against Ugandans," *Red Pepper*, September 17, 2013, https://www.redpepper.co.ug/south-sudan-ambassador-denies-xenophobia-against-ugandans/.

146. Michael Mann, *The Dark Side of Democracy: Explaining Ethnic Cleansing* (Cambridge: Cambridge University Press, 2005), 502.

147. The Prosecutor vs Théoneste Bagosora, Gratien Kabiligi, Aloys Ntabakuze, and Analtole Nsengiyumva, Judgment and Sentence, No. ICTR-98–41-T (International Criminal Tribunal for Rwanda (ICTR) 2008). Cited in Scott Straus, *Remaking Rwanda State Building and Human Rights after Mass Violence* (Madison: University of Wisconsin Press, 2011), 39.

148. This was also reminiscent of other contexts such as the Ottoman Empire under the CUP's Young Turks before the Armenian genocide. Straus, *Making and Unmaking Nations*, 69–71.

149. Mann, *The Dark Side of Democracy*, 39, 502, 519.

150. Horowitz, *Ethnic Groups in Conflict*, 175.

151. "The fear of extinction is actually a projection. Projection is a psychological mechanism by which unacceptable impulses felt by oneself are imputed to others, often the very targets of those impulses . . . backward groups are overwhelmingly initiators and advanced groups are targets of ethnic riot behavior." Horowitz, *Ethnic Groups in Conflict*, 180.

152. "The more prejudiced group members are, the more likely they are to perceive a threat from the disliked group." Kaufman, *Nationalist Passions*, 45.

153. For example, during this period the SPLA outsourced to a local militia (the Arrow Boys) security against incursions by the Lord's Resistance Army (LRA) into Western Equatoria. De Waal, *The Real Politics of the Horn of Africa*, 97.

154. See Charles Tilly, "War Making and State Making as Organized Crime," in *Bringing the State Back In*, ed. Peter Evans, Dietrich Rueschemeyer, and Theda Skocpol (Cambridge: Cambridge University Press, 1985), 184.

155. Diplomat 2; IO member 1.

156. Kiir relied on Uganda, Egypt, rebel groups such as the Darfuri JEM, SPLM/A-North, the Congolese M23, and mercenaries such as Blackwater's Erik Prince.

7. CIVIL WAR AND THE FIRST GENOCIDAL PHASE

1. Douglas H. Johnson, "Briefing: The Crisis In South Sudan," *African Affairs* 113, no. 451 (April 2014): 301.

2. African Union (AU) Commission of Inquiry on South Sudan, *Final Report of the African Union Commission of Inquiry on South Sudan* (Addis Ababa: AU Commission of Inquiry on South Sudan, October 15, 2014), 152, 171. Human Rights Watch placed Riek Machar's escape earlier, on December 15. Human Rights Watch, *South Sudan's New War Abuses by Government and Opposition Forces* (Human Rights Watch, August 2014), 19–20.

3. They were called the political detainees, and once released months later, they formed the nonaligned group of the "former political detainees." They included Oyay Deng Ajak, Gier Choung, Majak D'Agoot John Luk Jok, Cirino Hiteng, Madur Biar, Ezekiel Lol Gatkuoth, Deng Alor Koul, Madut Bier, and Kosti Manibe, arrested on December 17. On December 19, the SPLM secretary general Pagan Amum and Peter Adwok Nyaba, an ex-minister, were arrested. Human Rights Watch, *South Sudan's New War Abuses by Government and Opposition Forces*, 19.

4. General Peter Gadet, who commanded the SPLA's Division Eight, defected and joined the SPLA/IO. AU Commission of Inquiry on South Sudan, *Final Report*, 164.

5. Lucy Poni and Andrew Green, "Seven South Sudan Political Detainees Released," January 29, 2014, https://www.voanews.com/a/south-sudan-seven-political-detainees-released/1840403.html.

6. Former high-ranking government official 2, interview with the author, August 18, 2014.

7. The African Union came to the same conclusion. See AU Commission of Inquiry on South Sudan, *Final Report*, 27, 125.

8. AU Commission of Inquiry on South Sudan, 126, 129, 131.

9. See, for a description of timing, Human Rights Watch, *South Sudan's New War Abuses by Government and Opposition Forces*, 22.

10. AU Commission of Inquiry on South Sudan, *Final Report*, 124, 210, 238.

11. "President Salva Kiir's Speech on 16 December 2013 Attempted Coup," YouTube video, 17:05, posted by "A. J. Arusi," December 16, 2013, https://www.youtube.com/watch?v=jWVXw0s9S10.

12. AU Commission of Inquiry on South Sudan, *Final Report*, 184–85.

13. See AU Commission of Inquiry on South Sudan, 182.

14. Member of civil society 6, interview with the author, August 10, 2014; former high-ranking government official 3, interview with the author, August 18, 2014. Riek Machar's wife Angelina Teny also reported that targeted killings of Nuer in Juba started on December, 11, 2013. AU Commission of Inquiry on South Sudan, *Final Report*, 130. The best chronology so far on the fighting within Tiger and the SPLA in Juba is in Human Rights Watch, *South Sudan's New War Abuses by Government and Opposition Forces*, 23.

15. Naomi Pendle, "'They Are Now Community Police': Negotiating the Boundaries and Nature of the Government in South Sudan through the Identity of Militarised Cattle-Keepers," *International Journal On Minority And Group Rights*, no. 22 (2015): 433; former high-ranking government official 3; AU Commission of Inquiry on South Sudan, *Final Report*, 26.

16. Government official 1, Juba, interview with the author, July 25, 2014.

17. Pendle, "They Are Now Community Police," 433; former high-ranking government official 3; AU Commission of Inquiry on South Sudan, *Final Report*, 26.

18. The Dut Ku Beny were nicknamed the "Luri boys" for their training on Salva Kiir's farm in Luri near Juba. Human Rights Watch, *South Sudan's New War Abuses by Government and Opposition Forces*, 26.

19. Political representative 4, interview with the author, July 25, 2014.

20. Government official 1, Juba.

21. NSS or Presidential Guards were reportedly the ones delivering the guns. Mahmood Mamdani, *A Separate Opinion* (AU Commission of Inquiry on South Sudan, October 20, 2014), 18.

22. AU Commission of Inquiry on South Sudan, *Final Report*, 131.

23. Human Rights Watch, *South Sudan's New War Abuses by Government and Opposition Forces*, 24.

24. Government official 1, Juba.

25. Major General Marial Chanuong had ordered the disarmament of Tiger's Nuer contingent on the 15th, and he continued to command the reinforced Tiger on the 16th. AU Commission of Inquiry on South Sudan, *Final Report*, 121, 139; Human Rights Watch, *South Sudan's New War Abuses by Government and Opposition Forces*, 29. The SPLA major general Bol Akot commanded the commandoes. Mamdani, *A Separate Opinion*, 17–18. Some elements of Mathiang Anyoor were already part of Dut Ku Beny and integrated in Tiger. If some civilians took up arms, some of them may have been from the group of dormant recruits planted throughout Juba in the earlier months. Human Rights Watch, *South Sudan's New War Abuses by Government and Opposition Forces*, 24.

26. AU Commission of Inquiry on South Sudan, *Final Report*, 133, 140.

27. General Salva Matok commanded operations in Maharat; General Bol Akot in Gudele and Mia Saba; General Garang Mabir in Mangaten; General Marial Chinuong in Khor William. AU Commission of Inquiry on South Sudan, 140.

28. High-ranking government official 2 and wife, interview with the author, July 24, 2014.

29. AU Commission of Inquiry on South Sudan, "Final Report," 140–42.

30. Government official 1, Juba.

31. "Another witness, JWX testified that he saw a captain gathering Nuer soldiers, tying their hands behind their backs, killing them and saying that "they wanted to kill Nuers in the open so that everybody sees what will happen to whoever tries to fight the Dinka government"." AU Commission of Inquiry on South Sudan, "Final Report," 141.

32. AU Commission of Inquiry on South Sudan, 142, 211.

33. Government official 1, Juba.

34. AU Commission of Inquiry on South Sudan, *Final Report*, 141, 142, 145; Human Rights Watch, *South Sudan's New War Abuses by Government and Opposition Forces*, 22, 37.

35. Human Rights Watch, *South Sudan's New War Abuses by Government and Opposition Forces*, 40–41.

36. Former SPLA commander, interview with the author, August 4, 2014.

37. Human Rights Watch, *South Sudan's New War Abuses by Government and Opposition Forces*, 33–34.

38. Mamdani, *A Separate Opinion*, 12.

39. AU Commission of Inquiry on South Sudan, *Final Report of the African Union Commission of Inquiry on South Sudan—Executive Summary* (Addis Ababa: AU Commission of Inquiry on South Sudan, October 15, 2014), 213.

40. AU Commission of Inquiry on South Sudan, *Final Report*, 211.

41. Not every Dinka was either a passive bystander or an active perpetrator—for example, one of the Dinka soldiers present at the site of the Gudele police station killing hid a survivor in his own home. This was unfortunately an exception. AU Commission of Inquiry on South Sudan, 141, 142, 145; Human Rights Watch, *South Sudan's New War Abuses by Government and Opposition Forces*, 22.

42. Human Rights Watch, *South Sudan's New War Abuses by Government and Opposition Forces*, 27, 44.

43. AU Commission of Inquiry on South Sudan, *Final Report*, 136, 140, 219. Also see Human Rights Watch, 23n25.

44. AU Commission of Inquiry on South Sudan, *Final Report*, 176; Human Rights Watch, *South Sudan's New War Abuses by Government and Opposition Forces*, 31.

45. AU Commission of Inquiry on South Sudan, *Final Report*, 176, 210–11.

46. Government official 1, Juba.

47. AU Commission of Inquiry on South Sudan, *Final Report*, 114.

48. AU Commission of Inquiry on South Sudan, 145, 148, 149; Human Rights Watch, *South Sudan's New War Abuses by Government and Opposition Forces*, 38; AU Commission of Inquiry on South Sudan, *Final Report—Executive Summary*, 211.

49. On this topic see Human Rights Watch, *South Sudan's New War Abuses by Government and Opposition Forces*, 26–27.

50. AU Commission of Inquiry on South Sudan, *Final Report*, 225.

51. Member of civil society 10, interview with the author, February 8, 2016.

52. The White Army had been part of South Sudan's military landscape for decades but was not a single cohesive force. See, on the White Army, Ingrid Marie Breidlid and Michael J. Arensen, *"Anyone Who Can Carry a Gun Can Go": The Role of the White Army in the Current Conflict in South Sudan*, PRIO Paper (Oslo: Peace Research Institute Oslo (PRIO), 2014); John Young, *The White Army: An Introduction and Overview* (Geneva: Small Arms Survey, 2007).

53. Former high-ranking SPLA and government official, interview with the author, August 7, 2014.

54. Scott Straus, *Making and Unmaking Nations: War, Leadership and Genocide in Modern Africa* (Ithaca, NY: Cornell University Press, 2015), 36–41.

55. Former SPLA Commander, August 4, 2014.

56. Former high-ranking SPLA and government official.

57. Former high-ranking SPLA and government official.

58. Government official 1, Juba.

59. Paul Malong, then only officially governor of Northern Bahr El Ghazal but instrumental in the recruitment of Tiger/Dut Ku Beny and Mathiang Anyoor since independence, gave orders at the NSS compound and was seen traveling around Juba during the massacre. Human Rights Watch, *South Sudan's New War Abuses by Government and Opposition Forces*, 26.

60. Government official 1, Juba.

61. Mamdani, *A Separate Opinion*.

62. Political representative 5, interview with the author, July 28, 2014.

63. Thirty-four-year-old displaced man from Wau, interview with the author, July 7, 2017.

64. Juba resident, interview with the author, July 26, 2014.

65. Member of civil society 3, interview with the author, July 4, 2017.

66. Former SPLA soldier 1, interview with the author, July 4, 2017.

67. This interpretation would have to be reconciled with the number of high-ranking commanders and officials seen coordinating the massacre on the ground. On Rwanda and the role of local networks and politics in driving genocidal violence, see Scott Straus, *The Order of Genocide: Race, Power and Race in Rwanda*. (Ithaca, NY: Cornell University Press, 2006); Lee Ann Fuji, *Killing Neighbors: Webs of Violence in Rwanda* (Ithaca, NY: Cornell University Press, 2009). On the Holocaust and the role of local SS and police officers in anticipating orders, see for example Jürgen Matthäus, "Controlled Escalation: Himmler's Men in the Summer of 1941 and the Holocaust in the Occupied Soviet Territories," *Holocaust and Genocide Studies* 21, no. 2 (Fall 2007): 228, 232–33.

68. Straus, *Making and Unmaking Nations*, xi.

69. The capacity of the military elite to adapt is exemplified by the cases of Western and Central Equatoria in 2014–15. See chapter 9 on the rotations of SPLA soldiers from these states in 2014.

70. Human Rights Watch, *South Sudan's New War Abuses by Government and Opposition Forces*, 27; AU Commission of Inquiry on South Sudan, *Final Report*, 137.

71. High-ranking government official 2 and wife.

72. Human Rights Watch, *South Sudan's New War Abuses by Government and Opposition Forces*, 31.

73. Political representative 4.

74. Member of civil society 24, interview with the author, July 24, 2014.

75. The estimate of thirty thousand Nuer is from Human Rights Watch, *South Sudan's New War Abuses by Government and Opposition Forces*, 28.

76. Political representative 4.

77. See on the topic Human Rights Watch, *South Sudan's New War Abuses by Government and Opposition Forces*, 35.

78. AU Commission of Inquiry on South Sudan, *Final Report*, 134.

79. Twenty-seven-year-old displaced man from Wau payam, Ayod county, Jonglei, interview with the author, July 5, 2017.

80. Twenty-seven-year-old displaced man from Wau payam, Ayod county, Jonglei.

81. Member of civil society 3.

82. Member of civil society 1, interview with the author, June 30, 2017.

83. AU Commission of Inquiry on South Sudan, *Final Report*, 152, 153, 157, 166, 216.

84. Human Rights Watch, *South Sudan's New War Abuses by Government and Opposition Forces*, 20, 21.

85. Former SPLA soldier 1.

86. AU Commission of Inquiry on South Sudan, *Final Report*, 160, 161.

87. AU Commission of Inquiry on South Sudan, 161–62.

88. AU Commission of Inquiry on South Sudan, 155, 161; Human Rights Watch, *South Sudan's New War Abuses by Government and Opposition Forces*, 55.

89. AU Commission of Inquiry on South Sudan, *Final Report*, 163, 221.

90. AU Commission of Inquiry on South Sudan, 155, 165, 166.

91. It also distributed guns to all other ethnic groups but the Nuer in Melut county. AU Commission of Inquiry on South Sudan, 189, 191.

92. AU Commission of Inquiry on South Sudan, 185, 191.

93. AU Commission of Inquiry on South Sudan, *Final Report—Executive Summary*, 212.

94. Mamdani, *A Separate Opinion*, 23.

8. THE SECOND PHASE OF THE GENOCIDE IN UNITY STATE

1. Joshua Craze, Jérôme Tubiana, and Claudio Gramizzi, *A State of Disunity: Conflict Dynamics in Unity State, South Sudan, 2013–15* (Geneva: Small Arms Survey, December 2016), 8.

2. Craze, Tubiana, and Gramizzi, *A State of Disunity*, 39.

3. Forty-year-old displaced man from Nimne payam, Guit county, Unity, interview with the author, July 5, 2017. See Human Rights Watch, *South Sudan's New War Abuses by Government and Opposition Forces* (Human Rights Watch, August 2014), 60–61.

4. Human Rights Watch, 57; thirty-two-year-old displaced woman from Guit county, interview with the author, October 26, 2015.

5. Sixty-year-old man from Ding Ding, Rubkona county, interview with the author, February 1, 2016.

6. African Union (AU) Commission of Inquiry on South Sudan, *Final Report of the African Union Commission of Inquiry on South Sudan* (Addis Ababa: AU Commission of Inquiry on South Sudan, October 15, 2014), 171.

7. These county commissioners were Steven Taker, Khor Gatmai, Wal Yach, and Koang Biel.

8. AU Commission of Inquiry on South Sudan, *Final Report*, 174–75, 178.

9. Human Rights Watch, *South Sudan's New War Abuses by Government and Opposition Forces*, 63, 65.

10. AU Commission of Inquiry on South Sudan, *Final Report*, 177. Steven Taker, a government official, pretended to be a rebel on the radio and asked civilians to come out of hiding. Once they did, they were killed. AU Commission of Inquiry on South Sudan, 177, 181; Human Rights Watch, *South Sudan's New War Abuses by Government and Opposition Forces*, 64.

11. Member of civil society 20, interview with the author, February 3, 2016.

12. Member of civil society 20.

13. Gadet was replaced with Simon Maguet Gai. Member of civil society 20, interview with the author, February 3, 2016.

14. Member of civil society 20.

15. Aid worker 4, interview with the author, October 12, 2015.

16. IO was defeated due to lack of weapons, ammunitions, and recruits. IO had secured support from Sudan, but supplies were insufficient. Craze, Tubiana, and Gramizzi, *A State of Disunity*, 13.

17. Human Rights Watch, *"They Burned It All": Destruction of Villages, Killings, and Sexual Violence in Unity State, South Sudan* (Human Rights Watch, July 2015), 2–3.

18. Human Rights Watch, 1–2, 4.

19. Craze, Tubiana, and Gramizzi, *A State of Disunity*, 8.

20. Member of civil society 23, interview with the author, November 5, 2015.

21. Aid worker 5, interview with the author, October 7, 2015.

22. Craze, Tubiana, and Gramizzi, *A State of Disunity*, 22, 25–26.

23. Taban Deng was with Machar in the last civil war but sided with Kiir after 2005, retaining Unity's governor seat until he was dismissed by Kiir in July of 2013 (his seat was given to Bul Nuer Nguen Monytuil) after becoming closer to Machar again. He joined IO in December 2013 but he would later rejoin the government again in July 2016. See, on Taban Deng, Craze, Tubiana, and Gramizzi, *A State of Disunity*, 28.

24. Craze, Tubiana, and Gramizzi, *A State of Disunity*, 10–12.

25. The other Nuer sections are the Leek Nuer in Rubkona county, the Jikany Nuer in Guit county, the Jagei Nuer in Koch county, the Haak Nuer in Mayendit county, the Dok Nuer in Leer county, and the Nyuong Nuer in Panyjaar county. Member of civil society 10, interview with the author, February 8, 2016.

26. Member of civil society 25, interview with the author, February 9, 2016.

27. Human Rights Watch, *"They Burned It All,"* 1.

28. Joseph Nguen Monytuil, a Bul Nuer, was the state governor. A former member of the South Sudan Liberation Movement/ Army (SSLM/A), he was the brother of Bapiny Monytuil, formerly in the Sudanese Armed Forces as Puljang's superior. The SPLA Division 4 operations commander in Unity was a Bul Nuer, Matthew Puljang, formerly in Matiep's SSDF and known for recruiting men and boys. Tayeb Gatluak Taitai, another Bul Nuer also formerly in the SSDF as Matiep's deputy, was the SPLA Division 4 commander. Human Rights Watch, 37; Craze, Tubiana, and Gramizzi, *A State of Disunity*, 12, 34.

29. Member of civil society 26, interview with the author, November 22, 2015.

30. Reinforcements from Bahr El Ghazal came from the SPLA under the command of Santino Deng Wol, sanctioned by the UN Security Council. Government official in Juba, member of the SPLA-IO, Addis Ababa, interview with the author, July 13, 2014; member of civil society 20; United Nations Security Council, Santino Deng Wol, SSi.004, https://www.un.org/securitycouncil/sanctions/2206/materials/summaries/individual/santino-deng-wol.

31. Human Rights Watch, *"They Burned It All,"* 18, 37–38.

32. Human Rights Watch, 19, 17–21.

33. The PKM is a machine gun. Member of civil society 20; Human Rights Watch, 5, 22, 37.

34. Member of civil society 20.

35. Two members of civil society 3, interview with the author, October 24, 2015.

36. Aid worker 6, interview with the author, October 11, 2015.

37. Eighteen-year-old female gunshot wound victim from Koch, interview with the author, October 25, 2015.

38. Four displaced women from Leer, interview with the author, October 24, 2015; member of civil society 22, interview with the author, November 25, 2015.

39. In May 2015, Koang Biel was accused of supporting IO for agreeing to transport the wounded out of Koch. Afterwards, he would become much more involved in coordinating massacres. Aid worker 7, interview with the author, November 23, 2015.

40. This is not to say that the IO did not loot, but it did not have the same capacity or rationale, and practiced instead subsistence looting.

41. Member of civil society 2, interview with the author, July 13, 2016.

42. Member of civil society 22.

43. Member of civil society 23.

44. Twenty-one-year-old male gunshot wound victim from Leer county, interview with the author, October 25, 2015.

45. Twenty-three-year-old displaced woman from Mayendit county, interview with the author, October 26, 2015.

46. Forty-year-old displaced woman from Koch county, interview with the author, November 19, 2015.

47. Aid worker 6.

48. See Craze, Tubiana, and Gramizzi, *A State of Disunity*, 24, 28.

49. Member of civil society 26.

50. Member of civil society 25.

51. Craze, Tubiana, and Gramizzi, *A State of Disunity*, 32.

52. Four displaced women from Leer.

53. On ethnicity as a social radar, see Henry Hale, "Explaining Ethnicity," *Comparative Political Studies* 37, no. 4 (May 2004): 458–85. On social navigation in war see Mats Utas, "West-African Warscapes: Victimcy, Girlfriending, Soldiering: Tactic Agency in a Young Woman's Social Navigation of the Liberian War Zone," *Anthropological Quarterly* 78, no. 2 (2005): 403–30.

54. "Ethnic defection is a process whereby individuals join organizations explicitly opposed to the national aspirations of the ethnic group with which they identify and end up fighting against their coethnics. The process of ethnic defection implies a disjunction between ethnic identification and political support for ethnonational goals, without requiring a shift in a person's self-identification." Stathis N. Kalyvas, "Ethnic Defection in Civil War," *Comparative Political Studies* 41, no. 8 (August 2008): 1045. For some Bul Nuer perpetrators, self-identification temporarily shifted when they identified themselves as Dinka to their victims.

55. Member of civil society 27, interview with the author, February 3, 2016; member of civil society 25.

56. The very southern tip of Unity (Panyjaar county) was protected by large swaths of swamps.

57. IO inadvertently made it easier for Biel to recruit the Jagei Nuer when the IO Koch county commissioner Nhial Kam (in Buaw) told them to return the cattle they had raided in Leer and as a result became unpopular.

58. Forty-five-year-old displaced woman from Mayendit county, interview with the author, November 23, 2015.

59. Eighteen-year-old displaced woman from Leer county, interview with the author, November 23, 2015.

60. Member of civil society 22.

61. Twenty-year-old male gunshot victim / cattle herder and SPLA-affiliated youth from Rubkona, interview with the author, November 20, 2015.

62. Aid worker 3, interview with the author, August 9, 2014.

63. Member of civil society 23.

64. Member of civil society 23.

65. Member of civil society 8, interview with the author, November 26, 2015.

66. In late September 2015, attacks on Leer were perpetrated by SPLA soldiers and youth from Mayom as well as Koch and Leer youth. The Koch youth were sent as reinforcements to the soldiers and youth from Leer and Mayom. They were rewarded with loot for their reinforcement and played a key role in perpetrating violence.

67. Eighteen-year-old female gunshot victim from Koch.

68. Member of civil society 23.

69. Eighteen-year-old female gunshot victim from Koch.

70. Wal Yach, the Leer county commissionner, "is controlled by Koang Biel," another Nuer woman from Leer recalled. "Wal Yach and Koang Biel said it was Leer people raiding the cattle of Koch when in fact it was Bul Nuer." Eighteen-year-old displaced woman from Leer county.

71. Forty-year-old displaced woman from Koch county; sixty-year-old displaced woman from Koch county, interview with the author, November 23, 2015; twenty-six-year-old displaced woman from Koch county, interview with the author, November 23, 2015.

72. Member of civil society 23.

73. I insist on the fact that this is a self-depiction, unlike references to the victims calling their perpetrators Dinka.

74. Twenty-one-year-old male gunshot victim from Leer county.

75. Eighteen-year-old female gunshot victim from Koch.

76. Eighteen-year-old displaced woman from Leer county, interview with the author, November 9, 2015.

77. Twenty-seven-year-old displaced man from Leer county, interview with the author, November 9, 2015.

78. On ethnic miscuing in general, see Donald Horowitz, *Ethnic Groups in Conflict* (Berkeley: University of California Press, 1985), 49.

79. Twenty-one-year-old male gunshot victim from Leer county.

80. Yet diffusing responsability by miscuing did not really work. If Nuer victims occasionally called Nuer perpetrators "Dinka Jagei" or "Dinka Bul," they also used another expression—*Nuer Weo*, literally meaning "Nuer money"—to designate the "Nuer who have been sold, and/or who are getting money for the killing of Nuer in Juba in December 2013." Member of civil society 25.

81. Eighteen-year-old female gunshot victim from Koch.

82. Member of civil society 7, interview with the author, October 15, 2015.

83. Member of civil society 23.

84. Eighteen-year-old female gunshot victim from Koch.

85. Forty-year-old displaced woman from Koch county.

86. United Nations Office of the Deputy Humanitarian Coordinator for South Sudan (UNOCHA), *Crisis Impacts on Households in Unity State, South Sudan, 2014–2015: Initial Results of a Survey* (Office of the Deputy Humanitarian Coordinator for South Sudan, UNOCHA, January 2016), 10. UNOCHA reported that in about one quarter of the population of Unity state, "on average, there were 10 people per household in 2014 and 8 people per household in 2015." This was still an average. Indeed, 58 percent of households recorded an average decrease of nearly five people over the year 2014–15. UNOCHA, 15–16.

87. Member of civil society 23.

88. Member of civil society 28, interview with the author, November 19, 2015.

89. Member of civil society 8.

90. Eighteen-year-old displaced woman from Leer county.

91. Twenty-two-year-old displaced woman from Leer county, interview with the author, November 22, 2015; fifteen displaced men, women, and children from Rubkuai, Mayendit county, interview with the author, November 22, 2015.

92. Fifty-five-year-old displaced man from Koch county, interview with the author, November 23, 2015.

93. Aid worker 8, interview with the author, October 8, 2015.

94. Member of civil society 23.

95. Two members of civil society 3.

96. Four displaced women from Leer.

97. Twenty-four-year-old displaced woman from Leer county, interview with the author, October 26, 2015.

98. Twenty-seven-year-old displaced man from Leer county.

99. The expression "genocide by attrition" was forged by Helen Fein, in reference to "a public health crisis threatening the lives of members as well as their ability to procreate. This outcome was a consequence of policies that we infer were 'committed with intent to destroy, in whole or in part, a national, ethnical, racial or religious groups such,' as Article 2 of the Genocide Convention puts it, also 'causing serious bodily or mental harm to members of the group' and 'deliberately inflicting on the group conditions of life calculated to bring about its physical destruction in whole or in part.'" Helen Fein, "Genocide by Attrition 1939–1993: The Warsaw Ghetto, Cambodia, and Sudan: Links Between Human Rights, Health, And Mass Death," *Health and Human Rights* 2, no. 2 (1997): 32.

100. Human Rights Watch, *"They Burned It All,"* 31, 32–33.

101. Fifty-year-old displaced woman from Guit county, interview with the author, January 29, 2016.

102. Thirty-year-old displaced woman from Guit county, interview with the author, October 26, 2015.

103. See UNOCHA, *Crisis Impacts on Households in Unity State*, 24.

104. Sixty-year-old male gunshot victim from Leer county, interview with the author, February 3, 2016.

105. Thirty-five-year-old displaced woman from Rubkona county, interview with the author, October 27, 2015.

106. Twenty-three-year-old displaced woman from Leer county, interview with the author, October 26, 2015.

107. UNOCHA, *Crisis Impacts on Households in Unity State*, 12. The Integrated Phase Classification describes the severity of food emergencies. For a description of the five phases, see: http://fews.net/IPC. Alex De Waal also wrote that "some international officials successfully argued that those who died from drowning (escaping massacre and seeking refuge and sustenance) should be excluded from the numbers—which brought the death rate below the threshold for declaring famine. In January 2017, this assessment was revised and the UN declared famine." Alex De Waal, *Mass Starvation: The History and Future of Famine* (Cambridge: Polity, 2018), 31.

108. Two members of civil society 3.

109. UNOCHA, *Crisis Impacts on Households in Unity State*, 10–11, 19, 26.

110. Aid worker 6.

111. Member of civil society 2, July 13, 2016.

112. Member of civil society 23.

113. UNOCHA, *Crisis Impacts on Households in Unity State*, 5, 19–20, 22–24.

114. "Each act of sexual abuse committed with intent to destroy the (usually) women of a group defined by its nationality, ethnicity, religion, and/or race is therefore legally an act of genocide. Rapes undertaken as part of a genocide in fact are thus genocidal in law, as the Rwanda Tribunal recognized in Akayesu . . . Rape in war is a war crime. It is not genocidal until it is part of an aim to destroy a people as such on one of the listed grounds." Catharine A. MacKinnon, "Genocide's Sexuality," Nomos, Political Exclusion And Domination, 46 (2005): 327. MacKinnon first coined the concept of genocidal rape in "Crimes of War, Crimes of Peace," in *On Human Rights: The Oxford Amnesty Lectures 1993*, ed. Stephen Shute and Susan Hurley (Basic Books, 1993). She was the first to argue the concept of rape as genocide in a court in the case of *Kadic v. Karadzic*, 866 F. Supp. 734 (S.D.N.Y. 1994), 70 F. 3d 232 (2d Cir. 1996), *cert. denied* 518 U.S. 1005 (1996). She and her co-counsel won the case, establishing genocidal rape in international law. Also see International Criminal Tribunal for Rwanda (ICTR), "The Prosecutor vs. Jean-Paul Akayesu," Case No. ICTR-98–44-T (1998), Trial Judgment Para. 731: "Rape and sexual violence . . . constitute genocide in the same way as any other act as long as they were committed with the specific intent to destroy, in whole or in part, a particular group, targeted as such . . . These rapes resulted in physical and psychological destruction of Tutsi women, their families and their communities. Sexual violence was an integral part of the process of destruction."

115. Clémence Pinaud, "Genocidal Rape in South Sudan: Organization, Function, and Effects," *Human Rights Quarterly* 42, no. 3 (August 2020): 667–94.

116. Forced cannibalism may have been a dehumanizing yet meaningful act of revenge for past humiliations. A thirty-two-year-old woman reported to the AU investigators that Nuer civilians were forced to "eat the flesh of dead people": "They were told that you always say Dinka eat people, so now you eat." AU Commission of Inquiry on South Sudan, *Final Report*, 180–81.

117. Including weight loss, sleeplessness, and stress-induced illness. AU Commission of Inquiry on South Sudan, *Final Report*, 194–95.

118. The women raped by one single perpetrator were often abducted after the rape and used to carry loot. There was little chance for them to escape their captor, since the SPLA controlled the road from Leer to Mayom. Biel himself held a few of them in his compound in Koch town, most likely abducted from Mayendit and Leer. Yet abducted women—raped by a single perpetrator before their capture—were the minority of the victims of sexual violence. Human Rights Watch, *"They Burned It All,"* 4–5, 25; Aid worker 7.

119. Sixty-year-old displaced woman from Koch county.

120. Eighteen-year-old displaced woman from Guit county, interview with the author, November 19, 2015.

121. Members of civil society 3, interview with the author, October 24, 2015.

122. Eighteen-year-old female gunshot victim from Koch.

123. Four displaced women from Leer.

124. Sixty-year-old displaced woman from Koch county.

125. Human Rights Watch, *"They Burned It All,"* 21, 24, 25.

126. Two members of civil society 3.

127. Aid worker 9, interview with the author, October 23, 2015.

128. The vast majority of households who reached the POC were female-headed in 2015, nearly double than in 2014. UNOCHA, *Crisis Impacts on Households in Unity State*, 19, 26.

129. UNOCHA, *Crisis Impacts on Households in Unity State*, 20.

130. Four displaced women from Leer.

131. See Dara Kay Cohen, *Rape during Civil War* (Ithaca: Cornell UP, 2016).

132. Eighteen-year-old displaced woman from Guit county.

133. See Thomas Kühne, *The Rise and Fall of Comradeship: Hitler's Soldiers, Male Bonding and Mass Violence in the Twentieth Century* (Cambridge: Cambridge UP, 2017), 45, 137.

134. Thirty-five-year-old displaced woman from Juach, Rubkona county, interview with the author, November 23, 2015.

135. Observer 1, interview with the author, October 8, 2015.

136. "Girls are not allowed to marry other than from Guit, Mayendit, Rubkona and Leer. Others such as Koch and Mayom are forbidden." Eighteen-year-old displaced woman from Leer county.

137. Eighteen-year-old displaced woman from Rubkona county, interview with the author, October 26, 2015.

138. Aid worker 10, interview with the author, November 19, 2015.

139. Member of civil society 8.

140. Member of civil society 2, interview with the author, November 11, 2016.

141. Member of civil society 2, July 13, 2016.

142. "Dowry" popularly refers to bridewealth in South Sudan. Twenty-year-old displaced man from Leer county, interview with the author, November 9, 2015.

143. Thirty-eight-year-old male gunshot victim from Rubkona county, interview with the author, February 3, 2016.

144. Aid worker 10, interview with the author, November 22, 2015.

145. Thirty-eight-year-old male gunshot victim from Rubkona county.

146. Twenty-seven-year-old displaced man from Leer county.

147. Aid worker 11, interview with the author, November 19, 2015.

148. Nineteen, twenty-six, and thirty-two-year old displaced women from Bentiu town, interview with the author, June 30, 2017; forty-year-old displaced man from Nimne payam, Guit county, Unity.

149. Group discussion with Bentiu town residents, January 30, 2016.

150. Specifically in violation of article 162, section 1, stating that South Sudan is composed of ten states. The council of states was the one that should have officially requested a change of number, boundaries, and state capitals from the president, not the other way around, by imposition.

151. "When you have a state, you don't wait for the center to give you money." Heard from the presidential legal advisor by the author at Juba University during the "Public Interest Debate on the Presidential Decree, Order Number 36/2015 for the Decentralized Government of South Sudan" (October 8, 2015). Speakers were the presidential legal adviser in the Office of the President, Hon. Lawrence Korbandy Kodis; the former president of the Southern Sudan Supreme Court and chairman of the Jieng Council of Elders, Justice Ambrose Ring Thiik; Dr. Lam Akol, the chairperson of SPLM for Democratic Change (SPLM-DC) and leader of the national alliance of opposition political parties; and Mr. Edmund Yakani, the executive director of Community Empowerment for Progress Organization (CEPO).

152. Michael Makuei, the minister of information and known to be a Dinka hardliner, also expressed his opposition to the peace agreement.

153. Two members of civil society 2, interview with the author, February 6, 2016.

154. Member of civil society 27.

155. Aid worker 12, interview with the author, February 9, 2016.

156. Two members of civil society 3.

157. Member of civil society 25.

158. See Audrey Macklin, "Like Water and Oil, with a Match: Militarized Commerce, Armed Conflict, and Human Security in Sudan," in *Sites of Violence. Gender and Conflict Zones.*, ed. Wenona Giles and Jennifer Hyndman (Berkeley: University of California Press, 2004), 87; Human Rights Watch, *Sudan, Oil, and Human Rights* (New York: Human Rights Watch, 2003).

159. This book does not address in depth this fourth phase of the genocide, for lack of fieldwork in that region. For more on violence against the Shilluk, see Joshua Craze, *Displaced and Immiserated: The Shilluk of Upper Nile in South Sudan's Civil War, 2014–19* (Geneva: Small Arms Survey, September 2019).

160. "Violating other men's women is planting a flag; it is a way some men say to other men, "What was yours is now mine." . . . As often happens when men plant flags, someone was already living there." Catharine A. MacKinnon, *Are Women Human? And Other International Dialogues* (Cambridge, MA: Harvard University Press, 2007), 170–71.

161. Human Rights Watch, *"They Burned It All,"* 18, 36, 37–38. Mayendit was protected by water, though cattle was looted from Rubkai.

162. Four displaced women from Leer.

163. These county commissioners were Wal Yach of Leer, Biel of Koch, Salam Maluet of Rubkona, Kawai Cheng of Guit, and Bul Ma Yah of Mayom, as well as Khor Gatmai of Mayendit.

164. Member of civil society 23.

165. In 2015 alone, Biel married two more wives, and Salam Meluet, the Rubkona county commissioner, five more. Member of civil society 22; member of civil society 25.

166. Member of civil society 8.

167. This distribution of the loot created such resentment among troops that it led to sporadic in-fighting in Koch, Leer, and Mayendit.

168. Interviewees placed the amount of cattle given to Biel after each raid at between 10 and 30 heads. Member of civil society 22; member of civil society 23.

169. Member of civil society 23, interview with the author, November 16, 2015.

170. I am here accounting for a potentially very low cattle price. In reality, prices vary even throughout Unity—where cattle are scarce, prices rise, and vice-versa.

171. Twenty-year-old male gunshot victim / cattle herder and SPLA-affiliated youth from Rubkona; four displaced women from Leer.

172. The SPLA was trying to get medicine for its livestock to Koch.

173. Dinka SPLA soldiers often thought taking looted cattle to Lakes or Warrap was too burdensome: "For the Dinka soldiers operating now in Unity state," women from Leer explained, "taking the cattle back to Warrap or Rumbek [Lakes] is difficult. So they sell them back in Bentiu, Guit, Koch, Tharjaat, and Mayom. The cows travel, they are taken from Koch, to Buaw, to Wankei, and finally Mayom." Two members of civil society 3.

174. Two members of civil society 3.

175. Two members of civil society 2.

176. Two members of civil society 3.

177. Member of civil society 23.

178. Member of civil society 11, interview with the author, November 20, 2015; two members of civil society 2; member of civil society 25.

179. Member of civil society 8.

180. A common route for the cattle was "from Leer-Koch-Bentiu-Mayom-Warrap-Rumbek-Mundri." Member of civil society 16, interview with the author, November 11, 2015.

181. "After Dec 2013, the elite moved its cattle from Lakes to Mundri. In July/August 2015, they had to take all Salva's personal cattle into trucks to bring it back from Mundri to his home state." Member of civil society 16.

182. Member of civil society 15, interview with the author, November 17, 2015.

183. Observer 2, interview with the author, June 18, 2017.

184. Thirty-six-year-old displaced man from Wonduruba payam in Lanya county, interview with the author, June 20, 2017.

185. Two members of civil society 4, interview with the author, June 27, 2017.

186. Forty-seven-year-old displaced man from Amadi village, Mundri West county, WES, interview with the author, July 5, 2017.

187. Member of civil society 29, interview with the author, June 27, 2017.

9. THE THIRD PHASE OF THE GENOCIDE IN EQUATORIA

1. Member of civil society 3, interview with the author, July 4, 2017.

2. Martin Kenyi and Alfred Ladu Gore were some of the Equatorian members of IO. Member of civil society 3.

3. Member of civil society 3.

4. See African Union (AU) Commission of Inquiry on South Sudan, *Final Report of the African Union Commission of Inquiry on South Sudan* (Addis Ababa: AU Commission of Inquiry on South Sudan, October 15, 2014), 205.

5. Member of civil society 3; IO commissioner for Kajo Keji county, interview with the author, July 2, 2017.

6. Member of civil society 5, interview with the author, July 4, 2017.

7. Former SPLA soldier 1, interview with the author, July 4, 2017.

8. Six midwives, interview with the author, June 15, 2017.

9. Six midwives.

10. Member of civil society 5.

11. Former SPLA soldier 1.

12. Member of civil society 3.

13. Former SPLA soldier 1.

14. Two members of civil society 4, interview with the author, June 27, 2017; Alex De Waal, *The Real Politics of the Horn of Africa* (Cambridge: Polity, 2015), 97.

15. Observer 2, interview with the author, June 18, 2017; fifty-five-year-old displaced man from Agoro payam, Magwi county, interview with the author, June 27, 2017; two members of civil society 4.

16. Two members of civil society 4.

17. Forty-seven-year-old displaced man from Amadi village, Mundri West county, WES, interview with the author, July 5, 2017.

18. Forty-seven-year-old displaced man from Amadi village, Mundri West county, WES.

19. Observer 3, interview with the author, October 28, 2015; member of civil society 30, interview with the author, July 10, 2016.

20. The Arrow Boys also reportedly forcibly enrolled men. Member of civil society 30.

21. UNOCHA Bi-Weekly Emergency Meeting Group, October 7, 2015.

22. Twenty-three-year-old displaced woman from Mundri town, Mundri West county, interview with the author, June 21, 2017.

23. UNOCHA Bi-Weekly Emergency Meeting Group, October 7, 2015.

24. Thirty-six-year-old displaced man from Wonduruba payam in Lanya county, interview with the author, June 20, 2017.

25. Observer 4, interview with the author, April 29, 2016.

26. Observer 4, April 29, 2016.

27. Member of civil society 17, interview with the author, June 28, 2017; two members of civil society 4.

28. Thirty-five-year-old displaced man from Yei, former SPLA and IO soldier, interview with the author, June 15, 2017; member of civil society 17.

29. Member of civil society 2, interview with the author, July 15, 2016.

30. Member of civil society 20, interview with the author, July 13, 2016.

31. Member of civil society 2, interview with the author, July 8, 2016.

32. Thirty-year-old displaced man from Aweil, interview with the author, June 23, 2017.

33. Forty-year-old displaced man from Nimne payam, Guit county, Unity, interview with the author, July 5, 2017.

34. Member of civil society 2, July 8, 2016; Juba resident, interview with the author, July 13, 2016.

35. Member of civil society 2, July 15, 2016.

36. Member of civil society 20.

37. Member of civil society 3.

38. Member of civil society 3.

39. Two members of civil society 6, interview with the author, February 2, 2016. The local opposition was especially strong in Wunduruba, the scene of extreme violence in September 2015 under the rule of a Dinka unit led by Major-General Bol Akot, and in Lobonok in January 2016. Member of civil society 3.

40. Thirty-five-year-old displaced man from Yei former SPLA and IO soldier.

41. Member of civil society 15, interview with the author, November 17, 2015.

42. Member of civil society 15.

43. Member of civil society 30, interview with the author, February 15, 2016.

44. Member of civil society 15.

45. Member of civil society 2, July 8, 2016.

46. Longtime observer 1, interview with the author, June 1, 2016.

47. IO also wanted to consolidate its influence to be in a position of strength—this was most likely wishful thinking given the overwhelming military superiority of the government. As for these rebel satellite groups, they pursued their own goals in formalizing ties with IO, such as being included in future demilitarization plans.

48. Observer 4, April 29, 2016.

49. Two members of civil society 4.

50. Two members of civil society 4.

51. Member of civil society 15.

52. On the formation of these rebel groups, see Sarah Vuylsteke, *Identity and Self-Determination: The Fertit Opposition in South Sudan* (Geneva: Small Arms Survey, December 2018), 7.

53. Member of civil society 2, July 12, 2016.

54. Member of civil society 32, interview with the author, July 8, 2016.

55. Observer 4, interview with the author, July 9, 2016; Observer 4, interview with the author, July 13, 2016.

56. Member of civil society 20.

57. CTSAM, the Ceasefire Transitional Security Arrangement Mechanism, is the international monitoring body of the agreement.

58. Observer 4, July 9, 2016.

59. Longtime observer 2, interview with the author, August 3, 2016.

60. Member of civil society 2, interview with the author, July 10, 2016; Juba resident, July 13, 2016.

61. Observer 4, July 13, 2016.

62. Member of civil society 31, interview with the author, July 14, 2016.

63. Member of civil society 2, July 15, 2016.

64. Nineteen-year-old, twenty-six-year-old, and thirty-two-year old displaced women from Bentiu town, interview with the author, June 30, 2017.

65. Observer 4, July 10, 2016.

66. Amnesty International, *"We Did Not Believe We Would Survive": Killings, Rape and Looting in Juba* (Amnesty International, 2016), 12.

67. Observer 4, July 9, 2016.

68. Juba resident, July 13, 2016.

69. Juba resident, interview with the author, July 14, 2016.

70. Amnesty International, "'We Did Not Believe We Would Survive,'" 13.

71. Juba resident, July 14, 2016.

72. Member of civil society 30, interview with the author, July 13, 2016.

73. Six midwives.

74. Member of civil society 31.

75. Juba resident, July 14, 2016.

76. Member of civil society 2, July 13, 2016.

77. Twenty-five-year-old displaced woman from Juba town, interview with the author, June 19, 2017.

78. Member of civil society 3.

79. Thirty-two-year-old displaced woman from Malakal town, interview with the author, June 21, 2017.

80. The SPLA destroyed the houses of officers such as Peter Bol Koang, a Lou Nuer from Lankien (Jonglei); they attacked the office in Bilpam HQ of Charles Lam, another prominent Nuer; and they arrested the half Bul Nuer, half Dinka SPLA division commander Stephen Buay for trying to curb looting. Member of civil society 2, July 10, 2016; nineteen-year-old, twenty-six-year-old, and thirty-two-year old displaced women from Bentiu town.

81. Taban Deng, on July 13, pulled the rug out from under Machar's feet by defecting to the government and becoming the Nuer vice-president instead of Machar. Ezekiel Lol Gatkuoth, another Jikany Nuer from Upper Nile, also defected from IO. Member of civil society 2, July 12, 2016.

82. For example, a Nuer civilian explained how "the JCE approached Dhieu Mathok and the son of John Garang to defect from Riek Machar to Salva Kiir. Dhieu Mathok refused and one day later, he was tortured." Member of civil society 2, July 15, 2016.

83. Member of civil society 5.

84. Forty-year-old displaced man from Yei, interview with the author, June 21, 2017.

85. Member of civil society 4, interview with the author, June 14, 2017.

86. Twenty-year-old displaced woman from Gimunu, Yei county, interview with the author, June 15, 2017.

87. Fifty-five-year-old displaced man from Agoro payam, Magwi county.

88. Nineteen-year-old displaced woman from Bentiu town et al.

89. Troops came from Torit, Juba, and Lobonok. They were mostly Dinka from Bahr El Ghazal but also included some Nuer, Acholi, and Latuko soldiers. The SPLA had once again capitalized on in-group competition (just like in Unity) and co-opted Acholi soldiers, especially from Abau and Panyakwara clans, who hoped to capture land from the Acholi of Pajok. Sixty-five- and seventy-six-year-old displaced men from Pajok payam, Magwi county, July 7, 2017; aid worker 13, interview with the author, June 14, 2017.

90. Fifty-five-year-old displaced woman from Narus, Kapoeta East county, interview with the author, June 27, 2017; member of civil society 17.

91. Member of civil society 17.

92. Twenty-four-year-old displaced man from Kenyi payam, Lanya county, interview with the author, June 19, 2017. For example, the Kakwa David Lokonga from Lasu, Yei county, was an SPLA colonel appointed commissioner and then governor of Yei river state. But a former Kakwa SPLA soldier who had been rotated to Greater Upper Nile explained, "Lokonga does not coordinate attacks like Koang Biel (I know about Koang Biel). Lokonga just wants money from the Dinka—he's small minded." Former SPLA soldier 1; member of civil society 5.

93. Only an official letter allowed civilians to come out of these garrison towns, just like in Unity state. Thirty-two-year-old and seventy-seven-year-old displaced men from Pajok payam, Magwi county, interview with the author, July 7, 2017.

94. Thirty-five-year-old displaced man from Pajok village, Magwi county, interview with the author, June 27, 2017.

95. Member of civil society 1, interview with the author, June 30, 2017.

96. The SPLA also took Kaya in the summer of 2017. Observer 2; twenty-four-year-old displaced man from Kenyi payam, Lanya county; twenty-nine-year-old year old displaced man from Paiwa Sowa, Yei county, thirty-seven and forty-two-year-old displaced men from Tore payam, Yei county, twenty-year-old displaced man from Kupera payam, Yei county, twenty-three-year-old displaced man from Ngulumbi payam, Morobo county, thirty-one-year-old displaced man from Mugo payam, Yei county, and twenty-one-year-old displaced man from Manyome payam, Morobo county, interview with the author, June 29, 2017.

97. Sixty-five and seventy-six-year-old displaced men from Pajok payam, Magwi county.

98. Member of civil society 1.

99. Twenty-three-year-old displaced woman from Magalatore village, Kajo Keji county, interview with the author, June 16, 2017.

100. Seventeen-year-old displaced woman from Mongo village, Yei county, interview with the author, June 17, 2017.

101. Thirty-year-old displaced woman from Kupera village, Yei county, interview with the author, June 17, 2017.

102. The SPLA controlled Mere, Kala, Kaya, Morobo, Lanya, Kajo Keji, Nimule, the road coming to Livolo, and the road from Nadapale, Nimule, and Yei. IO controlled Pageri, Moli, Loa, Kit, and Aru junction. Six midwives.

103. Member of civil society 4.

104. Member of civil society 4.

105. Twenty-one-year-old and nineteen-year-old displaced women from Ikotos town, Ikotos county, interview with the author, June 29, 2017.

106. Seventeen-year-old displaced woman from Mongo village, Yei county; thirty-year-old displaced woman from Kupera village, Yei county; thirty-five-year-old displaced woman from Tore payam, Yei county, interview with the author, June 17, 2017.

107. Thirty-five-year-old displaced woman from Ronyi village, Yei county, June 17, 2017.

108. Two members of civil society 5, interview with the author, June 16, 2017.

109. Member of civil society 3; forty-year-old displaced man from Pigi Canal county, Jonglei, interview with the author, July 5, 2017.

110. Twenty-nine-year-old displaced man from Bereka village, Lanya county, interview with the author, June 20, 2017.

111. Its recruits were younger, paid, given new better weapons and uniforms, and higher ranks than SPLA soldiers from Division 2. Former SPLA soldier 1; forty-year-old displaced man from Pigi Canal county, Jonglei; sixty-year-old displaced man from Ikotos / IO major general, interview with the author, July 8, 2017; former SPLA soldier 1.

112. Twenty-nine-year-old displaced man from Bereka village, Lanya county, interview with the author, June 20, 2017; thirty-four-year-old displaced man from Logwili village, Lanya county, interview with the author, June 20, 2017. This would be slightly different in Magwi, Eastern Equatoria, in April 2017.

113. Thirty-five-year-old displaced woman from Ronyi village, Yei county; twenty-three-year-old displaced woman from Magalatore village, Kajo Keji county.

114. Twenty-year-old displaced woman from Ombazi village, Yei county, interview with the author, June 16, 2017.

115. Thirty-year-old displaced woman from Kayaya village, Yei county, interview with the author, June 16, 2017.

116. Thirty-year-old displaced woman from Jombu village, Yei county, interview with the author, June 17, 2017.

117. Thirty-three-year-old displaced woman from Jombu village, Yei county, interview with the author, June 17, 2017; observer 2.

118. Thirty-year-old displaced woman from Kupera village, Yei county.

119. Twenty-nine-year-old displaced man from Bereka village, Lanya county.

120. Thirty-year-old displaced man from Aweil.

121. Member of civil society 1; thirty-four-year-old displaced man from Logwili village, Lanya county; forty-year-old displaced man from Yei; IO commissioner for Kajo Keiji county; member of a civil society organization in Yei, interview with the author, July 4, 2017; forty-five-year-old displaced man from Yei town, July 6, 2017. For more on the state of Mathiang Anyoor after Malong's dismissal, see Alan Boswell, *Insecure Power and Violence: The Rise and Fall of Paul Malong and the Mathiang Anyoor* (Geneva: Small Arms Survey, Graduate Institute of International Studies, October 2019), 11–14.

122. Member of civil society 4.

123. Forty-five-year-old displaced man from Yei town, 45.

124. South Sudanese intellectual 2, interview with the author, July 11, 2017.

125. IO commissioner for Kajo Keiji county.

126. Member of civil society 3.

127. Thirty-four-year-old displaced man from Logwili village, Lanya county.

128. Member of civil society 17; twenty-nine-year-old displaced man from Paiwa Sowa, Yei county et al.

129. Six midwives. Emphasis added.

130. Seventeen-year-old displaced woman from Mongo village, Yei county.

131. Twenty-year-old displaced woman from Gimunu, Yei county.

132. Twenty-three-year-old displaced woman from Magalatore village, Kajo Keji county.

133. Seventeen-year-old displaced woman from Mongo village, Yei county.

134. Forty-year-old displaced man from Yei.

135. Thirty-year-old displaced woman from Yei town (Shilluk), interview with the author, June 19, 2017. If this Shilluk woman had been found by her Dinka attackers in Upper Nile, she would most likely not have been spared rape and/or death. On annihilating violence against the Shilluk as a group by Dinka militias and the SPLA, see Joshua Craze, *Displaced and Immiserated: The Shilluk of Upper Nile in South Sudan's Civil War, 2014–19* (Geneva: Small Arms Survey, September 2019), 52–53, 55, 67.

136. Thirty-five-year-old displaced woman from Ronyi village, Yei county.

137. Member of civil society 9, interview with the author, June 15, 2017.

138. Member of civil society 4.

139. Thirty-five-year-old displaced woman from Lomuku village, Yei county, interview with the author, June 16, 2017.

140. Translator from Mangalatore, Kajo Keji county, interview with the author, June 17, 2017; twenty-three-year-old displaced woman from Kerua village, Kajo Keji county, interview with the author, June 17, 2017; twenty-nine-year-old displaced man from Bereka village, Lanya county.

141. Thirty-year-old displaced woman from Kupera village, Yei county.

142. Thirty-five-year-old displaced woman from Lomuku village, Yei county.

143. Member of civil society 4.

144. Two members of civil society 5.

145. Two members of civil society 5.

146. Armed to their teeth, SPLA soldiers regularly shot their guns in the air in villages they occupied. They engaged the IO with tanks and weapons such as RPGs, mounted machine guns, AK47, and PKMs, and wore belts of ammunition and grenades. Twenty-four-year-old displaced man from Kenyi payam, Lanya county; twenty-three-year-old displaced woman from Ombashi village, Yei county, interview with the author, June 19, 2017.

147. Twenty-five-year-old displaced woman from Juba town.

148. Psychological aid worker, interview with the author, June 20, 2017.

149. Author observations in Imvepi Reception Center, Uganda, June 19, 2017.

150. Psychological aid worker.

151. Twenty-year-old displaced woman from Ombazi village, Yei county.

152. Twenty-year-old displaced woman from Gimunu, Yei county.

153. Thirty-five-year-old displaced woman from Tore payam, Yei county.

154. I am inspired here by Catharine A. MacKinnon: "Presumably, where humanity was found, survival did not come at a sexual price." MacKinnon, "Genocide's Sexuality," *Nomos*, Political Exclusion and Domination, 46 (2005): 324.

155. Six midwives.

156. Thirty-five-year-old displaced woman from Tore payam, Yei county.

157. Thirty-five-year-old displaced woman from Ronyi village, Yei county.

158. I base my understanding of genocidal rape on MacKinnon's work. See MacKinnon, "Genocide's Sexuality," 328–29.

159. Twenty-five-year-old displaced woman from Gimunu, Yei county, interview with the author, June 15, 2017.

160. Thirty-five-year-old displaced man from Yei, former SPLA and IO soldier.

161. Thirty-year-old displaced woman from Jombu village, Yei county, interview with the author, June 17, 2017.

162. Twenty-three-year-old displaced woman from Magalatore village, Kajo Keji county; six midwives; twenty-five-year-old displaced woman from Jigomoni village, Yei county, interview with the author, June 16, 2017.

163. Thirty-year-old displaced woman from Kupera village, Yei county.

164. Thirty-year-old displaced woman from Kupera village, Yei county; twenty-year-old displaced woman from Ombazi village, Yei county.

165. Six midwives.

166. My interpretation of killing as an act of state sovereignty draws from Achille Mbembe, "Necropolitics," *Public Culture* 15, no. 1 (Winter 2003): 11–40.

167. Thirty-year-old displaced woman from Jombu village, Yei county.

168. Member of civil society 1.

169. Eighteen-year-old displaced woman from Morsaq village, Yei county, interview with the author, June 17, 2017.

170. Thirty-year-old displaced woman from Kendila village, Morobo county, interview with the author, June 16, 2017.

171. Thirty-year-old displaced woman from Jamara village, Yei county, interview with the author, June 16, 2017.

172. Thirty-year-old displaced woman from Kendila village, Morobo county.

173. Twenty-year-old displaced woman from Gimunu, Yei county.

174. Member of civil society 9; sixty-nine-year-old displaced man from Lawaje boma, Pajok payam, Magwi county, interview with the author, July 7, 2017.

175. The argument that gang-rape reinforces group cohesion has been made in other non-genocidal contexts by Dara Kay Cohen, *Rape during Civil War* (Ithaca, NY: Cornell University Press, 2016).

176. Twenty-year-old displaced woman from Ombazi village, Yei county.

177. MacKinnon, "Genocide's Sexuality," 329.

178. Twenty-year-old displaced woman from Gimunu, Yei county.

179. Twenty-five-year-old displaced woman from Gimunu, Yei county.

180. Thirty-five-year-old displaced woman from Ronyi village, Yei county; six midwives.

181. Twenty-year-old displaced woman from Gimunu, Yei county.

182. Thirty-five-year-old displaced man from Pajok village, Magwi county.

183. Twenty-nine-year-old and twenty-seven-year-old displaced women from Kit, Magwi, interview with the author, June 27, 2017.

184. Fifty-five-year-old displaced man from Agoro payam, Magwi county; member of civil society 17.

185. Twenty-four-year-old displaced man from Kenyi payam, Lanya county.

186. Former SPLA soldier 1.

187. Thirty-three-year-old displaced woman from Kayaya village, Morobo county, interview with the author, June 19, 2017.

188. "Genocide is actually more continuous with discrimination than with war: it is a violent practice of discrimination." MacKinnon, "Genocide's Sexuality," 329.

189. This form of ethnic ranking was immutable unless members from the victim group miscued by becoming scarified too. But given the urgency of their escape, miscuing was not an option.

190. Member of civil society 5.

191. "They confiscated my documents—certificates, diplomas. When I asked why take it, the man said, 'We'll give it back to you once you return.' They took my motorbike too. They also took my passport as well." Thirty-year-old displaced male from Iwere payam, Magwi county, interview with the author, June 30, 2017.

192. Thirty-five-year-old displaced man from Pajok village, Magwi county.

193. Member of civil society 31, interview with the author, July 10, 2017.

194. Thirty-year-old displaced man from Aweil.

195. Twenty-nine-year-old displaced man from Paiwa Sowa, Yei county et al.

196. Member of civil society 17.

197. For example, in January 2015 in Mundri, Kiir called Dinka cattle herders to return to Lakes and Warrap with their cattle, but they refused. Two members of civil society 4.

198. Twenty-year-old displaced woman from Gimunu, Yei county.

199. Seventeen-year-old displaced woman from Mongo village, Yei county.

200. Twenty-three-year-old displaced woman from Ombashi village, Yei county.

201. Seventeen-year-old displaced woman from Mongo village, Yei county.

202. Twenty-five-year-old displaced woman from Juba town.

203. For example, in Lanya (Wonduruba), victims spotted mixed units containing perpetrators from the Bor Dinka, Dinka Padang, and the Dinka from Bahr El Ghazal. Thirty-six-year-old displaced man from Wonduruba payam in Lanya county; thirty-three-year-old displaced woman from Jombu village, Yei county; sixty-nine-year-old displaced man from Lawaje boma, Pajok payam, Magwi county.

204. Cattle herders included sections from Lakes but also from Bor. Thirty-four-year-old displaced man from Logwili village, Lanya county.

205. For example, the Dinka Padang civilians settled in Yei. Observer 2.

206. Thirty-four-year-old displaced man from Logwili village, Lanya county.

207. Twenty-nine-year-old displaced man from Bereka village, Lanya county.

208. Thirty-year-old displaced man from Aweil.

209. Thirty-seven-year-old displaced man from Yundu, Morobo county, interview with the author, June 29, 2017.

210. Former SPLA commander, interview with the author, August 4, 2014.

211. Member of civil society 4.

212. Member of civil society 13, interview with the author, August 9, 2014.

213. Thirty-year-old displaced man from Aweil.

214. Former high-ranking government official 1, interview with the author, July 11, 2017.

215. IO commissioner for Kajo Keiji county; six midwives.

216. Forty-five-year-old displaced man from Yei town.

217. Twenty-four-year-old displaced man from Kenyi payam, Lanya county; thirty-six-year-old displaced man from Wonduruba payam in Lanya county.

218. Thirty-six-year-old displaced man from Wonduruba payam in Lanya county.

219. Twenty-nine-year-old displaced man from Bereka village, Lanya county.

220. Twenty-three-year-old displaced woman from Magalatore village, Kajo Keji county.

221. Eighteen-year-old displaced woman from Morsaq village, Yei county.

222. Twenty-five-year-old displaced woman from Jigomoni village, Yei county.

223. See on this topic A. Dirk Moses, "Empire, Colony, Genocide: Keywords and the Philosophy of History," in *Empire, Colony, Genocide: Conquest, Occupation, and Subaltern Resistance in World History*, ed. A. Dirk Moses (New York: Berghahn Books, 2008), 3–55.

224. Twenty-nine-year-old displaced man from Bereka village, Lanya county; member of civil society 3.

225. Member of civil society 3.

226. Thirty-four-year-old displaced man from Logwili village, Lanya county; member of civil society 3.

227. Member of civil society 1.

228. Sixty-five and seventy-six-year-old displaced men from Pajok payam, Magwi county.

229. Central Equatoria had diamonds and, like Eastern Equatoria, gold, uranium, and mercury. Member of civil society 9.

230. IO commissioner for Kajo Keiji county.

ETHNIC SUPREMACY AND GENOCIDAL CONQUEST

1. Thirty-four-year-old displaced man from Wau, interview with the author, July 7, 2017.

2. Member of civil society 3, interview with the author, July 4, 2017.

3. Thirty-two-year-old displaced woman from Malakal town, interview with the author, June 21, 2017. On Dinka discourses denationalizing the Fertit in Wau dating back to the 1970s-1980s, see Sarah Vuylsteke, *Identity and Self-Determination: The Fertit Opposition in South Sudan* (Geneva: Small Arms Survey, December 2018), 5.

4. Thirty-five-year-old displaced woman from Lomuku village, Yei county, interview with the author, June 16, 2017.

5. Thirty-four-year-old displaced man from Wau.

6. Thirty-year-old displaced woman from Yei town (Shilluk), interview with the author, June 19, 2017.

7. Thirty-two-year-old displaced woman from Malakal town.

8. Thirty-two-year-old displaced woman from Malakal town.

9. Thirty-two-year-old displaced woman from Malakal town.

10. Thirty-year-old displaced woman from Yei town (Shilluk), June 19, 2017.

11. Thirty-two-year-old displaced woman from Malakal town.

12. Aid worker 14, interview with the author, December 30, 2017. On the replacement of the Shilluk population almost entirely displaced by the SPLA and affiliated Dinka militias, with Dinka settlers, see Joshua Craze, *Displaced and Immiserated: The Shilluk of Upper Nile in South Sudan's Civil War, 2014–19* (Geneva: Small Arms Survey, September 2019), 78, 82.

13. Forty-year-old displaced man from Pigi Canal county, Jonglei, interview with the author, July 5, 2017.

14. Former high-ranking government official 1, interview with the author, July 11, 2017.

15. Thirty-two-year-old displaced woman from Malakal town. On the local competition for land in Upper Nile between local Padang Dinka militias sub-contracted by the SPLA, and their conflictual relationship with Mathiang Anyoor, see Craze, *Displaced and Immiserated*, 42, 45-46, 73.

16. Two twenty-five-year-old displaced women from Bor, Jonglei, interview with the author, July 6, 2017.

Bibliography

African Rights. *Facing Genocide: The Nuba of Sudan*. London: African Rights, July 1995.
——. *Food and Power in Sudan: A Critique of Humanitarianism*. London: African Rights, 1997.
——. *Imposing Empowerment? Aid and Civil Institutions in Southern Sudan*. London: African Rights, December 1995.
African Union (AU) Commission of Inquiry on South Sudan. *Final Report of the African Union Commission of Inquiry on South Sudan*. Addis Ababa: AU Commission of Inquiry on South Sudan, October 15, 2014.
——. *Final Report of the African Union Commission of Inquiry on South Sudan—Executive Summary*. Addis Ababa: AU Commission of Inquiry on South Sudan, October 15, 2014.
Akabwai, Darlington, and Priscillar E. Ateyo. *The Scramble for Cattle, Power and Guns in Karamoja*. Boston: Feinstein International Center, December 2007.
Ali, Ali Abdel Gadir, Ibrahim A. Elbadawi, and Atta El-Batahani, "Sudan's Civil War: Why Has It Prevailed for So Long?" In *Understanding Civil War: Evidence and Analysis, Vol. 1—Africa*, edited by Nicholas Sambanis and Paul Collier, 193–219. Washington, DC: The World Bank, 2005.
American Embassy, Khartoum. "Defense White Paper Energizes SPLA Budget Process, while Expectations of USG Assistance Are Heightened by Its Completion." Wikileaks Cable: 08KHARTOUM971_a, July 2, 2008. http://wikileaks.org/plusd/cables/08KHARTOUM971_a.html.
——. "Paulino Matiep on SPLM Politics and the SPLA." Wikileaks Cable: 08KHARTOUM739_a, May 15, 2008. https://wikileaks.org/plusd/cables/08KHARTOUM739_a.html.
——. "SE Gration Meeting with SPLA Leadership." Wikileaks Cable: 09KHARTOUM508_a, April 14, 2009. http://wikileaks.org/plusd/cables/09KHARTOUM508_a.html.
——. "SPLA Defense White Paper." Wikileaks Cable: 08KHARTOUM542_a, April 8, 2008. https://wikileaks.org/plusd/cables/08KHARTOUM542_a.html.
——. "SPLA and Forces Loyal to Former Militia Leader Square Off in Juba." Wikileaks Cable: 07KHARTOUM613_a, April 19, 2007. https://wikileaks.org/plusd/cables/07KHARTOUM613_a.html.
——. "Sudan: SPLA Chief of Staff Says He Might Be Replaced." Wikileaks Cable: 07KHARTOUM470_a, March 25, 2007. https://wikileaks.org/plusd/cables/07KHARTOUM470_a.html.
Amnesty International. *South Sudan: Civil Unrest and State Repression; Human Rights Violations in Wau, Western Bahr El Ghazal State*. Amnesty International, February 2013.
——. *"We Did Not Believe We Would Survive": Killings, Rape and Looting in Juba*. Amnesty International, 2016.
Anderson, Benedict. *Imagined Communities*. 2nd ed. London: Verso, 1991.
Arjona, Ana, Nelson Kasfir, and Zachariah Mampilly. "Introduction." In *Rebel Governance in Civil War*, edited by Ana Arjona, Nelson Kasfir, and Zachariah Mampilly, 1–21. Cambridge: Cambridge University Press, 2015.

Badiey, Naseem. *The State of Post-Conflict Reconstruction: Land, Urban Development and State-Building in Juba Southern Sudan.* Woodbridge: James Currey, 2014.

Bank, Andrew. "The Politics of Mythology: The Genealogy of the Philip Myth." *Journal of Southern African Studies* 25, no. 3 (1999): 461–77.

Balcells, Laia. *Rivalry and Revenge: The Politics of Violence during Civil War.* Cambridge: Cambridge University Press, 2017.

Bayart, Jean-François. "Preface to the Second English Edition: Africa in the World; A History of Extraversion." In *The State in Africa: The Politics of the Belly,* 2nd ed. Malden, MA: Polity, 2009.

Bayart, Jean-Francois, Stephen Ellis, and Beatrice Hibou. *Criminalization of the State in Africa.* Bloomington: Indiana University Press, 2009.

Beswick, Stephanie. *Sudan's Blood Memory: The Legacy of War, Ethnicity, and Slavery in Early South Sudan.* Rochester, NY: University of Rochester Press, 2004.

Le Billon, Philippe. *Geopolitics of Resource Wars: Resource Dependence, Governance and Violence.* London: Frank Cass, 2005.

Bloch, Marc. *Feudal Society: Social Classes and Political Organisation.* 3rd ed. Vol. 2. London: Routledge, 1989.

Bloxham, Donald. "Internal Colonization, Inter-Imperial Conflict and the Armenian Genocide." In *Empire, Colony, Genocide: Conquest, Occupation and Subaltern Resistance in World History,* edited by A. Dirk Moses, 325–43. New York: Berghahn Books, 2008.

Boswell, Alan. *Insecure Power And Violence. The Rise and Fall of Paul Malong and the Mathiang Anyoor.* Geneva: Small Arms Survey, October 2019.

Bourdieu, Pierre. *Choses Dites.* Le Sens Commun. Paris: Les Éditions de Minuit, 1987.

——. *Outline of a Theory of Practice.* Cambridge, MA: Cambridge University Press, 1977.

Bourke, Joanna. *Rape: Sex, Violence, History.* London: Virago, 2007.

BRACED. *Building Climate Resilience in Fragile Contexts: Key Findings of BRACED Research in South Sudan; Improving Resilience to Climate Change in South Sudan.* BRACED, February 19, 2018.

Bradbury, Mark, Nicholas Leader, and Kate Mackintosh. *The "Agreement on Ground Rules" in South Sudan.* Humanitarian Policy Group. The Politics of Principle: The Principles of Humanitarian Action in Practice. London: Overseas Development Institute (ODI), March 2000.

Branch, Adam, and Zachariah Cherian Mampilly. "Winning the War, but Losing the Peace? The Dilemma of SPLM/A Civil Administration and the Tasks Ahead." *Journal of Modern African Studies* 43, no. 1 (March 2005): 1–20.

Breidlid, Ingrid Marie, and Michael J. Arensen. *"Anyone Who Can Carry a Gun Can Go": The Role of the White Army in the Current Conflict in South Sudan.* PRIO Paper. Oslo: Peace Research Institute Oslo (PRIO), 2014.

Breitman, Richard. "Himmler and the 'Terrible Secret' among the Executioners." *Journal of Contemporary History* 26, no. 3/4 (1991): 431–51.

Brubaker, Rogers. *Ethnicity without Groups.* Cambridge, MA: Harvard University Press, 2004.

Burr, Millard, and Robert O. Collins. *Requiem for the Sudan: War, Drought, and Disaster Relief on the Nile.* Boulder, CO: Westview Press, 1995.

Burton, John W. "Development and Cultural Genocide in the Sudan." *Journal of Modern African Studies* 29, no. 3 (September 1991): 511–20.

Buss, Doris E. "Rethinking 'Rape as a Weapon of War.'" *Feminist Legal Studies,* no. 17 (2009): 145–63.

Chabal, Patrick, and Jean-Pascal Daloz. *Africa Works: Disorder As Political Instrument.* Oxford: James Currey Publishers, 1999.

Claassen, Christopher. "Group Entitlement, Anger and Participation in Intergroup Violence." *British Journal of Political Science* 46, no. 1 (2016): 127–48.

Cohen, Dara Kay. *Rape during Civil War*. Ithaca, NY: Cornell University Press, 2016.

Collins, Robert O. *Land beyond the Rivers: The Southern Sudan 1898–1918*. 1st ed. New Haven, CT: Yale University Press, 1971.

——. *The Southern Sudan in Historical Perspective*. University of Tel Aviv: Shiloah Center for Middle Eastern and African Studies, 1975.

Comprehensive Peace Agreement between the Government of the Republic of the Sudan and the Sudan People's Liberation Movement/Sudan People's Liberation Army, January 9, 2005.

Cooper, Frederick. "The Problem of Slavery in African Studies." *Journal of African History* 20, no. 1 (1979): 103–25.

Cordaid. *Mining in South Sudan: Opportunities and Risks for Local Communities. Baseline Assessment of Small-Scale and Artisanal Gold Mining in Central and Eastern Equatoria States, South Sudan*. Cordaid, January 2016. https://www.cordaid.org/nl/wp-content/uploads/sites/2/2016/03/South_Sudan_Gold_Mining_Report-LR_1.pdf.

Coulter, Chris. *Bush Wives and Girl Soldiers: Women's Lives Through War and Peace in Sierra Leone*. Ithaca, NY: Cornell University Press, 2009.

Crawford, Kerry F. *Wartime Sexual Violence: From Silence to Condemnation of a Weapon of War*. Washington, DC: Georgetown University Press, 2017.

Craze, Joshua. *Displaced And Immiserated. The Shilluk of Upper Nile in South Sudan's Civil War, 2014–19*. Geneva: Small Arms Survey, September 2019.

——. "Unclear Lines: State and Non-State Actors in Abyei." In *The Borderlands of South Sudan. Authority and Identity in Contemporary and Historical Perspectives*, edited by Christopher Vaughan, Mareike Schomerus, and Lotje De Vries, 45–67. New York: Palgrave Macmillan, 2013.

Craze, Joshua, Jérôme Tubiana, and Claudio Gramizzi. *A State of Disunity: Conflict Dynamics in Unity State, South Sudan, 2013–15*. Geneva: Small Arms Survey, December 2016.

De Waal, Alex. *Mass Starvation: The History and Future of Famine*. Cambridge: Polity, 2018.

——. *The Real Politics of the Horn of Africa*. Cambridge: Polity, 2015.

——. "Some Comments on the Militias in the Contemporary Sudan." In *Civil War in the Sudan*, edited by M. W. Daly and Ahmad Alawad Sikainga, 142–56. London: British Academic Press, 1993.

——. "Starving out the South." In *Civil War in the Sudan*, edited by M. W. Daly and Ahmad Alawad Sikainga, 157–85. London: British Academic Press, 1993.

——. "What Actual Spending Tells Us About South Sudan's Governance." *World Peace Foundation. Reinventing Peace*. (blog), March 6, 2014. https://sites.tufts.edu/reinventingpeace/2014/03/06/what-actual-spending-tells-us-about-south-sudans-governance/.

——. "When Kleptocracy Becomes Insolvent: Brute Causes of the Civil War in South Sudan." *African Affairs* 113, no. 452 (2014): 347–69.

De Waal, Alex, and Julie Flint. *Darfur: A New History of a Long War*. 2nd ed. London/New York: Zed Books, 2008.

Debos, Marielle. *Living by the Gun in Chad: Combatants, Impunity and State Formation*. London: Zed Books, 2016.

Decker, Alicia C. *In Idi Amin's Shadow. Women, Gender and Militarism in Uganda*. Athens: Ohio University Press, 2014.

Dejung, Christof. "Dissonant Memories: National Identity, Political Power, and the Commemoration of World War Two in Switzerland." *Oral History* 35, no. 2 (Autumn 2007): 57–66.

Deng, David. *The New Frontier: A Baseline Survey of Large-Scale Land-Based Investment in Southern Sudan.* Norwegian People's Aid, March 2011. http://reliefweb.int/sites/reliefweb.int/files/resources/6F0B144DA275260B8525785C0069DB6A-Full_Report.pdf.

Deng, Francis Mading. *The Dinka of the Sudan.* New York: Holt, Rinehart and Winston, Inc., 1972.

——. *The Man Called Deng Majok: A Biography of Power, Polygyny and Change.* Lawrenceville, NJ: Red Sea Press, 2009.

——. *War of Visions: Conflict of Identities in the Sudan.* Washington, DC: Brookings Institution Press, 1995.

Diamond, Larry. "Class Formation in the Swollen African State." *Journal of Modern African Studies* 25, no. 4 (1987): 567–96.

Duany, Julia Aker. *Making Peace and Nurturing Life: A Memoir of an African Woman About a Journey of Struggle and Hope.* Bloomington, IN: 1st Books Library, 2003.

Eriksson Baaz, Maria, and Maria Stern. *Sexual Violence as a Weapon of War? Perceptions, Prescriptions, Problems in the Congo and Beyond.* London: Zed Books, 2013.

——. "Why Do Soldiers Rape? Masculinity, Violence, and Sexuality in the Armed Forces in the Congo (DRC)." *International Studies Quarterly* 53, no. 2 (June 2009): 495–518.

Fein, Helen. "Genocide by Attrition 1939–1993: The Warsaw Ghetto, Cambodia, and Sudan: Links Between Human Rights, Health, And Mass Death." *Health and Human Rights* 2, no. 2 (1997): 10–45.

Fuji, Lee Ann. *Killing Neighbors: Webs of Violence in Rwanda.* Ithaca, NY: Cornell University Press, 2009.

Global Humanitarian Assistance. *Resource Flows to Sudan: Aid to South Sudan.* Global Humanitarian Assistance, July 2011. http://devinit.org/wp-content/uploads/2011/07/gha-Sudan-aid-factsheet-2011-South-Sudan-focus1.pdf.

Global Witness. "Attack on Activist Threatens Anti-Corruption Efforts in South Sudan." Press release, July 12, 2012, http://www.globalwitness.org/library/attack-activist-threatens-anti-corruption-efforts-south-sudan.

Gonda, Sam, and William Mogga. "Loss of the Revered Cattle." In *War Wounds: Development Costs Of Conflict In Southern Sudan*, 63–82. Washington, DC: Panos Institute, 1988.

Goody, Jack. "Feudalism in Africa?" *Journal of African History* 4, no. 1 (1963): 1–18.

Graeber, David. "Turning Modes of Production Inside Out: Or, Why Capitalism Is a Transformation of Slavery." *Critique of Anthropology* 26, no. 1 (2006): 61–85.

Gurr, Ted Robert. *Why Men Rebel.* Princeton, NJ: Princeton University Press, 1970.

Guyer, Jane I. "Wealth in People, Wealth in Things—Introduction." *Journal of African History*, no. 36 (1995): 83–90.

Hale, Henry. "Explaining Ethnicity." *Comparative Political Studies* 37, no. 4 (May 2004): 458–85.

Harsch, Ernest. "Accumulators and Democrats: Challenging State Corruption in Africa." *Journal of Modern African Studies* 31, no. 1 (March 1, 1993): 31–48.

Hinton, Alexander Laban. *Why Did They Kill? Cambodia in the Shadow of Genocide.* Berkeley: University of California Press, 2005.

Holcomb, Justin S. "Southern Sudanese Chaplains: Human Rights and the Embodiment of Peace." *Other Journal* 6 (August 8, 2005), http://theotherjournal.com/2005/08/08/southern-sudanese-chaplains-human-rights-and-the-embodiment-of-peace/.

Horowitz, Donald. *Ethnic Groups in Conflict.* Berkeley: University of California Press, 1985.

Hutchinson, Sharon Elaine. *Nuer Dilemmas: Coping with Money, War, and the State.* Berkeley: University of California Press, 1996.
——. "Nuer Ethnicity Militarized." *Anthropology Today* 16, no. 3 (June 1, 2000): 6–13.
Human Rights Watch. *Civilian Devastation: Abuses by All Parties in the War in Southern Sudan.* Human Rights Watch, 1994.
——. *South Sudan's New War Abuses by Government and Opposition Forces.* Human Rights Watch, August 2014.
——. "Sudan: Government Repression Threatens Fair Elections National and Southern Officials Should End Abusive Practices." Johannesburg: Human Rights Watch, March 21, 2010, press release.
——. *Sudan: How Human Rights Abuses Caused the Disaster. Background Paper on the 1998 Famine in Bahr El Ghazal.* Human Rights Watch, July 23, 1998.
——. *Sudan, Oil, and Human Rights.* New York: Human Rights Watch, 2003.
——. *"They Are Killing Us": Abuses Against Civilians in South Sudan's Pibor County.* Human Rights Watch, September 12, 2013.
——. *"They Burned It All": Destruction of Villages, Killings, and Sexual Violence in Unity State, South Sudan.* Human Rights Watch, July 2015.
IMU OCHA SS. *5th Sudan Census 2008—Total Population Figures by County.* SS-0041. 12–29–2009: IMU OCHA SS, n.d.
Independent International Commission of Inquiry on the Syrian Arab Republic. "'They Came to Destroy': ISIS Crimes Against the Yazidis." Geneva: Independent International Commission of Inquiry on the Syrian Arab Republic, June 15, 2016.
International Criminal Tribunal for Rwanda (ICTR). "The Prosecutor vs. Jean-Paul Akayesu". Case No. ICTR-98–44-T. 1998.
International Criminal Tribunal for Rwanda (ICTR). "The Prosecutor vs. Théoneste Bagosora, Gratien Kabiligi, Aloys Ntabakuze, and Analtole Nsengiyumva". No. ICTR-98–41-T. 2008.
International Crisis Group. *The Khartoum-SPLM Agreement: Sudan's Uncertain Peace.* Africa Report. International Crisis Group, July 25, 2005.
——. *South Sudan: Jonglei—"We Have Always Been at War."* Crisis Group Africa Report. International Crisis Group, December 22, 2014.
——. *Sudan's Comprehensive Peace Agreement: Beyond the Crisis.* Africa Briefing. Policy Briefing. Nairobi/Brussels: International Crisis Group, March 13, 2008.
——. *Sudan's Comprehensive Peace Agreement: The Long Road Ahead.* International Crisis Group, March 31, 2006.
James, Wendy. *War and Survival in Sudan's Frontierlands: Voices from the Blue Nile.* Oxford: Oxford University Press, 2007.
Johnson, Douglas H. "Briefing: The Crisis In South Sudan." *African Affairs* 113, no. 451 (April 2014).
——. "Enforcing Separate Identities in the Southern Sudan: The Case of the Nilotes of the Upper Nile." In *Les ethnies ont une histoire*, edited by Gérard Prunier and Jean-Pierre Chrétien, 2nd ed., 235–45. Paris: Karthala, 2003.
——. "Evans-Pritchard, the Nuer, and the Sudan Political Service." *African Affairs* 383, no. 81 (April 1982): 231–46.
——. "Federalism in the History of South Sudan Political Thought." Rift Valley Institute Research Paper. London: Rift Valley Institute, 2014.
——. "The Fighting Nuer: Primary Sources and the Origins of a Stereotype." *Africa* 51, no. 01 (1981): 508–527.
——. "The Nuer Civil War." In *Sudanese Society in the Context of Civil War. Papers from a Seminar at the University of Copenhagen, 9–10 February 2001*, edited

by Maj-Britt Johannsen and Niels Kastfelt, 1–27. Copenhagen: University of Copenhagen North/South Priority Research Area, 2001.

——. *Nuer Prophets: A History of Prophecy from the Upper Nile in the Nineteenth and Twentieth Centuries.* Oxford: Clarendon Press, 1994.

——. "Political Ecology of Upper Nile: The Twentieth Century Expansion of the Pastoral 'Common Economy.'" In *Herders, Warriors and Traders, Pastoralism in Africa,* edited by John G. Galaty and Pierre Bonte, 89–117. Boulder, CO: Westview Press, 1991.

——. "Recruitment and Entrapment in Private Slave Armies: The Structure of the Zarä'ib in the Southern Sudan." *Slavery and Abolition* 13, no. 1 (1992): 162–73.

——. *The Root Causes of Sudan's Civil Wars.* 2nd ed. Bloomington: Indiana University Press, 2007.

——. *South Sudan: A New History for a New Nation.* Ohio Short Stories of Africa. Athens: Ohio University Press, 2016.

——. "The Structure of a Legacy: Military Slavery in Northeast Africa." *Ethnohistory,* 1989, 72–88.

——. "The Sudan People's Liberation Army and the Problem of Factionalism." In *African Guerrillas,* edited by Christopher Clapham, 53–72. Oxford: Indiana University Press, 1998.

——. "Sudanese Military Slavery from the Eighteenth to the Twentieth Century." In *Slavery and Other Forms of Unfree Labour,* edited by Léonie J. Archer, 142–56. History Workshop. London: Routledge, 1988.

——. "Twentieth-Century Civil Wars." In *The Sudan Handbook,* edited by John Ryle, Willis, Justin, Suliman Baldo, and Jok, Jok Madut, 122–32. New York: James Currey, 2011.

Johnson, Douglas H., and Gérard Prunier. "The Foundation and Expansion of the Sudan People's Liberation Army." In *Civil War in the Sudan,* edited by M. W. Daly and Ahmad Alawad Sikainga, 117–41. London: British Academic Press, 1993.

Jok, Jok Madut. "Militarism, Gender and Reproductive Suffering: The Case of Abortion in Western Dinka." *Africa* 69, no. 2 (1999): 194–212.

——. "Militarization and Gender Violence in South Sudan." In *JAAS XXXIV, 4.* Koninklijke Brill NV, Leiden, 1999.

——. *Militarization, Gender and Reproductive Health in South Sudan.* Lewiston, NY: Edwin Mellen Press, Ltd., 1998.

Jok, Jok Madut, and Sharon Elaine Hutchinson. "Sudan's Prolonged Second Civil War and the Militarization of Nuer and Dinka Ethnic Identities." *African Studies Review* 42, no. 2 (1999): 125–45.

Kalyvas, Stathis N. "Ethnic Defection in Civil War." *Comparative Political Studies* 41, no. 8 (August 2008): 1043–68.

——. *The Logic of Violence in Civil War.* New York: Cambridge University Press, 2006.

Karim, Ataul, Mark Duffield, Susanne Jaspars, Aldo Benini, Joanna Macrae, Mark Bradbury, Douglas H. Johnson, and George Larbi. *OLS—Operation Lifeline Sudan, A Review.* UNICEF, July 1996.

Kaufman, Stuart J. *Nationalist Passions.* Ithaca, NY: Cornell University Press, 2015.

Kedini, Thomas. "The Challenge to Survive." In *War Wounds: Development Costs of Conflict in Southern Sudan,* edited by Nigel Twose and Benjamin Pogrund, 29–44. Washington: Panos Institute, 1988.

Keen, David. *The Benefits of Famine: A Political Economy of Famine and Relief in Southwestern Sudan, 1983–1989.* 2nd ed. Oxford: James Currey, 2008.

——. *The Economic Functions of Violence in Civil Wars.* 1st ed. Adelphi Paper 320. Oxford: International Institute for Strategic Studies, 1998.

——. *Useful Enemies: When Waging Wars Is More Important Than Winning Them*. New Haven, CT: Yale University Press, 2012.

Kühne, Thomas. *The Rise and Fall of Comradeship: Hitler's Soldiers, Male Bonding and Mass Violence in the Twentieth Century*. Cambridge: Cambridge University Press, 2017.

Kuper, Leo. *Genocide: Its Political Use in the Twentieth Century*. New Haven: Yale University Press, 1981.

Lacher, Wolfram. *South Sudan: International State-Building and Its Limits*. SWP Research Paper. Berlin: German Institute for International and Security Affairs, February 2012.

Lako, George Tombe. *Southern Sudan: The Foundation of a War Economy*. Peter Lang Pub Inc, 1994.

Lagu, Joseph. *Sudan: Odyssey through a State: From Ruin to Hope*. Omdurman Sudan: M.O.B Center for Sudanese Studies Omdurman Ahlia University, 2006.

Large, Daniel. "The International Presence in Sudan." In *The Sudan Handbook*, edited by John Ryle et al, 272–92. Woodbridge: James Currey, 2011.

Leick, Gwendolyn. *Tombs of the Great Leaders: A Contemporary Guide*. London: Reaktion Books, 2013.

Leonardi, Cherry. *Dealing with Government in South Sudan: Histories of Chiefship, Community and State*. Woodbridge: James Currey, 2013.

——. "Paying 'Buckets of Blood' for the Land: Moral Debates over Economy, War and State in Southern Sudan." *Journal of Modern African Studies*, no. 49 (2011): 215–40.

——. "Violence, Sacrifice and Chiefship in Central Equatoria, Southern Sudan." *Africa* 77, no. 4 (2007): 535–58.

LeRiche, Matthew, and Matthew Arnold. *South Sudan: From Revolution to Independence*. London: Hurst & Company, 2012.

Levene, Mark. *Genocide in the Age of the Nation State*. Vol. 1. London: I.B. Tauris & Co. Ltd, 2005.

Levy, Kenneth, Preeti Chauhan, John F. Clarkin, Rachel H. Wasserman, and Joseph S. Reynoso. "Narcissistic Pathology: Empirical Approaches." *Psychiatric Annals* 39, no. 4 (April 2009): 203–13.

Lieberman, Benjamin. "'Ethnic Cleansing' Versus Genocide?" In *The Oxford Handbook of Genocide Studies*, edited by Donald Bloxham and A. Dirk Moses, 42–61. New York: Oxford University Press, 2010.

Littman, Rebecca. "Perpetrating Violence Increases Identification with Violent Groups: Survey Evidence from Former Combatants." *Personality and Social Psychology Bulletin* 44, no. 7 (2018): 1–13.

Littman, Rebecca, and Elizabeth Levy Paluck. "The Cycle of Violence: Understanding Individual Participation in Collective Violence." *Advances in Political Psychology* 36, suppl. 1 (2015): 79–99.

Lombard, Louisa. *State of Rebellion: Violence and Intervention in the Central African Republic*. London: Zed Books, 2016.

Lord Gleichen, Edward. *Handbook of the Sudan*. Intelligence Division, War Office of Great Britain. London: Harrison and Sons, 1898.

Lovejoy, Paul E. *Transformations in Slavery: A History of Slavery in Africa*. 1st ed. Cambridge: Cambridge University Press, 1983.

Lustick, Ian S. *Unsettled States, Disputed Lands: Britain and Ireland, France and Algeria, Israel and the West Bank-Gaza*. Ithaca, NY: Cornell University Press, 1995.

MacKinnon, Catharine A. *Are Women Human? And Other International Dialogues*. Cambridge, MA: Harvard University Press, 2007.

——. "Genocide's Sexuality." *Nomos*, Political Exclusion and Domination, 46 (2005): 313–56.

——. *Toward a Feminist Theory of the State*. Cambridge, MA: Harvard University Press, 1989.

Macklin, Audrey. "Like Water and Oil, with a Match: Militarized Commerce, Armed Conflict, and Human Security in Sudan." In *Sites of Violence. Gender and Conflict Zones.*, edited by Wenona Giles and Jennifer Hyndman, 75–116. Berkeley: University of California Press, 2004.

Madut-Arop, Arop. *Sudan's Painful Road to Peace: A Full Story of the Founding and Development of SPLM/SPLA*. Self-published, Booksurge LLC, 2005.

Makris, G. P. "Slavery, Possession and History: The Construction of the Self among Slave Descendants in the Sudan." *Africa: Journal of the International African Institute* 66, no. 2 (1996): 159–82.

Mamdani, Mahmood. *A Separate Opinion*. African Union (AU) Commission of Inquiry on South Sudan, October 20, 2014.

——. *When Victims Become Killers: Colonialism, Nativism and Genocide in Rwanda*. Princeton, NJ: Princeton University Press, 2001.

Mampilly, Zachariah Cherian. "Performing the Nation-State: Rebel Governance and Symbolic Processes." In *Rebel Governance in Civil War*, edited by Ana Arjona, Nelson Kasfir, and Zachariah Mampilly, 74–98. Cambridge: Cambridge University Press, 2015.

——. *Rebel Rulers: Insurgent Governance and Civilian Life during War*. Ithaca, NY: Cornell University Press, 2015.

Mann, Michael. *The Dark Side of Democracy: Explaining Ethnic Cleansing*. Cambridge: Cambridge University Press, 2005.

Marx, Karl. *Wage-Labor and Capital*. New York: International Publishers, 1971.

Matthäus, Jürgen. "Controlled Escalation: Himmler's Men in the Summer of 1941 and the Holocaust in the Occupied Soviet Territories." *Holocaust and Genocide Studies* 21, no. 2 (Fall 2007): 218–242.

Mauss, Marcel. *The Gift: Forms and Functions of Exchange in Archaic Societies*. Eastford, CT: Martino Fine Books, 2011.

——. "Les Origines de La Notion de Monnaie." In *Comptes-Rendus Des Séances*. Vol. 2, tome 1:14–19. Supplément à l'Anthropologie. Institut français d'anthropologie, 1914.

Mbembe, Achille. "Necropolitics." *Public Culture* 15, no. 1 (Winter 2003): 11–40.

Médecins Sans Frontières. "Retrospective Survey: South Sudanese Refugees Journey to the Uganda." Internal. Paris: Médecins Sans Frontières, May 2017.

Melson, Robert F. *Revolution and Genocide: On the Origins of the Armenian Genocide and the Holocaust*. Chicago: University of Chicago Press, 1992.

Milanovic, Branko. "The Return of 'Patrimonial Capitalism': A Review of Thomas Piketty's Capital in the Twenty-First Century." *Journal of Economic Literature* 52, no. 2 (2014): 519–34.

Morsel, Joseph. *L'Aristocratie Medievale. La domination sociale en Occident (Ve-XVe siècle)*. Histoire. Paris: Armand Colin, 2004.

Moses, A. Dirk. "Empire, Colony, Genocide: Keywords and the Philosophy of History." In *Empire, Colony, Genocide: Conquest, Occupation, and Subaltern Resistance in World History*, edited by A. Dirk Moses, 3–55. New York: Berghahn Books, 2008.

——, ed. *Genocide and Settler Society: Frontier Violence and Stolen Indigenous Children in Australian History*. New York: Berghahn Books, 2004.

——. "Raphael Lemkin, Culture, and the Concept of Genocide." In *The Oxford Handbook of Genocide Studies*, edited by Donald Bloxham and A. Dirk Moses, 19–42. New York: Oxford University Press, 2010.

Moses, A. Dirk, and Donald Bloxham. "Editor's Introduction: Changing Themes in the Study of Genocide." In *The Oxford Handbook of Genocide Studies*, 1–19. New York: Oxford University Press, 2010.

New Sudan Council of Churches. *Come Let Us Reason Together: Report of the Historic Dialogue Held between the Sudan's People Liberation Movement (SPLM) and the New Sudan Council of Churches (NSCC), Yei-Keijiko, New Sudan, 21–24 July 1997*. Nairobi: New Sudan Council of Churches, 1998.

Nyaba, Peter Adwok. *Politics of Liberation in South Sudan: An Insider's View*. Kampala: Fountain Publishers, 1997.

——. *South Sudan. Elites, Ethnicity, Endless Wars and the Stunted State*. Dar es Salaam: Mkuki Na Nyota Publishers Ltd, 2019.

——. *South Sudan: The State We Aspire To*. Cape Town: Centre for Advanced Study of African Society, 2011.

O'Balance, Edgar. *The Secret War in the Sudan, 1955–1972*. Hamden, CT: Archon Books, 1977.

Olson, Mancur. "Dictatorship, Democracy, and Development." *American Political Science Review* 87, no. 3 (September 1993): 567–76.

Patey, Luke A. "Crude Days Ahead? Oil and the Resource Curse in Sudan." *African Affairs* 109, no. 437 (October 1, 2010): 617–36.

Pendle, Naomi. "'They Are Now Community Police': Negotiating the Boundaries and Nature of the Government in South Sudan through the Identity of Militarised Cattle-Keepers." *International Journal On Minority And Group Rights*, no. 22 (2015): 410–34.

Petersen, Roger D. *Understanding Ethnic Violence Fear, Hatred, and Resentment in Twentieth-Century Eastern Europe*. Cambridge: Cambridge University Press, 2002.

Piketty, Thomas. *Capital in the Twenty-First Century*. Cambridge, MA: Belknap Press of Harvard University Press, 2014.

Pinaud, Clémence. "Are 'Griefs of More Value Than Triumphs'? Power Relations, Nation-Building and the Different Histories of Women's Wartime Contributions in Post-War South Sudan." *Journal of Northeast African Studies* 13, no. 2 (2013): 151–76.

——. "Briefing Note—The War in South Sudan." Bordeaux: Observatoire des Enjeux Politiques et Sécuritaires dans la Corne de l'Afrique, March 2015.

——. "Genocides in the Sudans." In *The Cambridge World History of Genocide*, edited by Wendy Lower, Ben Kiernan, Norman Naimark, and Scott Straus, vol. 3. Cambridge: Cambridge University Press, 2020.

——. "Military Kinship, Inc.: Patronage, Inter-Ethnic Marriages and Social Classes in South Sudan." *Review of African Political Economy*, June 2016: 243–59.

——. "South Sudan: Civil War, Predation and the Making of a Military Aristocracy." *African Affairs* 113, no. 451 (April 2014): 192–211.

——. "'We Are Trained to Be Married!' Elite Formation and Ideology in the 'Girls' Battalion' of the Sudan People's Liberation Army.'" *Journal of Eastern African Studies* 9, no. 3 (2015): 375–93.

——. "Women, Guns and Cattle: A Social History of the Second Civil War in South Sudan." Université Paris 1 Panthéon-Sorbonne, 2013.

Prunier, Gérard. *Darfour, Un Génocide Ambigu*. Paris: La Table ronde, 2005.

——. *Darfur: The Ambiguous Genocide*. Ithaca, NY: Cornell University Press, 2005.

——. "Rebel Movements and Proxy Warfare: Uganda, Sudan and the Congo (1986–99)." *African Affairs* 103, no. 412 (July 1, 2004): 359–83.

——. *The Rwanda Crisis: History of a Genocide*. London: Hurst & Company, 1995.

——. "Sudan's Regional Relations." In *Sudan Handbook*, edited by John Ryle, Justin Willis, Suliman Baldo, and Jok Madut Jok, 153–63. Woodbridge: James Currey, 2011.

Renan, Ernest. "What Is a Nation?" In *Nation and Narration*, edited by Homi K. Bhabha, 8–22. London: Routledge, 1990.

Reno, William. *Warlord Politics and African States*. Boulder, CO: Lynne Rienner Publishers, 1999.

Riehl, Volker. *Who Is Ruling in South Sudan? The Role of NGOs in Rebuilding Socio-Political Order*. Studies on Emergencies and Disaster Relief. Sweden: Nordiska Afrikainstitutet, 2001.

Robertson, Claire C., and Martin Klein. *Women and Slavery in Africa*. Madison: University of Wisconsin Press, 1983.

Rolandsen, Øystein H. "Another Civil War in South Sudan: The Failure of Guerrilla Government?" *Journal of Eastern African Studies* 9, no. 1 (January 2015): 163–74.

——. "Civil War Society?: Political Processes, Social Groups and Conflict Intensity in the Southern Sudan, 1955–2005." PhD diss., University of Oslo, 2010.

——. "A False Start: Between War and Peace in The Southern Sudan, 1956–62." *Journal of African History* 52, no. 1 (2011): 105–23.

——. *Guerrilla Government: Political Changes in the Southern Sudan during the 1990s*. Uppsala: Nordic Africa Institute, 2005.

——. "The Making of the Anya-Nya Insurgency in the Southern Sudan, 1961–64." *Journal of Eastern African Studies* 5, no. 2 (2011): 211–32.

Rolandsen, Øystein H., and M. W. Daly. *A History of South Sudan: From Slavery to Independence*. Cambridge: Cambridge University Press, 2016.

Rowe, Ian, and Laurent Banal. *Sudan: Assessment of the Disarmament and Demobilisation Process*. Khartoum: United Nations Integrated DDR Unit, November 28, 2009.

Runciman, W.G. *Relative Deprivation and Social Justice: A Study of Attitudes to Social Inequality in Twentieth-Century England*. Berkeley: University of California Press, 1966.

Safer World. *Informal Armies: Community Defence Groups in South Sudan's Civil War*. London: Safer World, February 2017.

Sanderson, Lilian Passmore, and Neville Sanderson. *Education, Religion & Politics in Southern Sudan, 1899–1964*. London: Ithaca Press, 1981.

Sardan, J. P. Olivier de. "A Moral Economy of Corruption in Africa?" *Journal of Modern African Studies* 37, no. 1 (March 1, 1999): 25–52.

Schomerus, Mareike. *Violent Legacies: Insecurity in Sudan's Central and Eastern Equatoria*. Human Security Baseline Assessment. Geneva: Small Arms Survey, June 2008.

Schweinfurth, Georg August. *The Heart of Africa. Three Years Travels and Adventures in the Unexplored Regions of Central Africa From 1868 to 1871*. 3rd ed. Vol. 1. 2 vols. London: S. Low, Marston, Searle & Rivington, 1878.

Shaller, Dominik J. "From Lemkin to Clooney: The Development and State of Genocide Studies." *Genocide Studies and Prevention: An International Journal* 6, no. 3 (2011).

Sidanius, Jim, and Felicia Pratto. *Social Dominance: An Intergroup Theory of Social Hierarchy and Oppression*. New York: Cambridge University Press, 1999.

Siegel, Mona. "'History Is the Opposite of Forgetting': The Limits of Memory and the Lessons of History in Interwar France." *Journal of Modern History* 74, no. 4 (December 2002): 770–800.

Sklar, Richard L. "The Nature of Class Domination in Africa." *Journal of Modern African Studies* 17, no. 4 (1979): 531–52.

Small Arms Survey. *Armed Groups in Sudan: The South Sudan Defence Forces in the Aftermath of the Juba Declaration*. Sudan Issue Brief. Human Security Baseline Assessment. Geneva: Small Arms Survey, October 2006.

——. *The 14-Mile Area*. Human Security Baseline Assessment. Small Arms Survey, November 3, 2014. http://www.smallarmssurveysudan.org/facts-figures/ borderdisputed-areas/14-mile-area.html.

——. *My Neighbour, My Enemy: Inter-Tribal Violence in Jonglei*. Human Security Baseline Assessment. Geneva: Small Arms Survey, Graduate Institute of International Studies, October 2012.

South Sudan Center for Census, Statistics and Evaluation, the Office of the United Nations High Commissioner for Refugees, Norwegian People's Aid, UN Population Fund, and the United Nations Entity for Gender Equality and the Empowerment of Women. *Gender-Based Violence and Protection Survey*. Juba, South Sudan: 2010.

South Sudan: Options in Crisis: Hearings Before the United States Senate Committee on Foreign Relations, 114th Cong. 2nd (2016) (Statement of Kate Almquist Knopf: "U.S. Options as South Sudan Leaders Fail the Peace").

"Stated Position of the Rebels: Background and Manifesto of the Sudan People's Liberation Movement (SPLM)." *Horn of Africa*, 1985.

Stanton, Jessica A. *Violence and Restraint in Civil War Civilian Targeting in the Shadow of International Law*. Cambridge: Cambridge University Press, 2016.

Stone, Dan. "Genocide and Memory." In *The Oxford Handbook of Genocide Studies*, edited by A. Dirk Moses and Donald Bloxham, 102–19. Oxford: Oxford University Press, 2010.

Straus, Scott. "Contested Meanings and Conflicting Imperatives: A Conceptual Analysis of Genocide." *Journal of Genocide Research* 3, no. 3 (2001): 349–75.

——. *Making and Unmaking Nations: War, Leadership and Genocide in Modern Africa*. Ithaca, NY: Cornell University Press, 2015.

——. *The Order of Genocide: Race, Power and Race in Rwanda*. Ithaca, NY: Cornell University Press, 2006.

——. *Remaking Rwanda State Building and Human Rights after Mass Violence*. Madison: University of Wisconsin Press, 2011.

Strobel, Margaret. *Muslim Women in Mombasa 1890–1975*. New Haven, CT: Yale University Press, 1979.

Tambiah, Stanley J., Mitzi Goheen, Alma Gottlieb, Jane I. Guyer, Emelie A. Olson, Charles Piot, Klaas W. Van Der Veen, and Trudeke Vuyk. "Bridewealth and Dowry Revisited: The Position of Women in Sub-Saharan Africa and North India [and Comments and Reply]." *Current Anthropology* 30, no. 4 (October 1989): 413–35.

Thomas, Edward. *South Sudan: A Slow Liberation*. London: Zed Books Ltd, 2015.

Tilly, Charles. *Coercion, Capital, and European States, AD 990–1992*. 2nd ed. Cambridge, MA: Basil Blackwell, 1992.

——. "How War Made States, and Vice Versa." In *Coercion, Capital, and European States, AD 990–1990*. Cambridge, MA: Basil Blackwell, 1990.

——. "War Making and State Making as Organized Crime." In *Bringing the State Back In*, edited by Peter Evans, Dietrich Rueschemeyer, and Theda Skocpol. Cambridge: Cambridge University Press, 1985.

Twijnstra, Rens. "On the State of Business: Trade, Entrepreneurship and Real Economic Governance in South Sudan." PhD diss., Wageningen University, 2014.

United Nations Development Program. *Factsheet: Climate Change, Food Insecurity and Resilient Livelihoods in South Sudan*. United Nations Development Program, June 28, 2017.

United Nations General Assembly. Convention On The Prevention And Punishment Of The Crime Of Genocide, 1021 § (1948). https://treaties.un.org/doc/ publication/unts/volume%2078/volume-78-i-1021-english.pdf.

United Nations Office of the Deputy Humanitarian Coordinator for South Sudan (UNOCHA). *Crisis Impacts on Households in Unity State, South Sudan, 2014–2015: Initial Results of a Survey*. Juba, South Sudan: UNOCHA, January 2016.

United Nations Security Council. *Final Report of the Panel of Experts on South Sudan Established Pursuant to Security Council Resolution 2206 (2015)*. United Nations Security Council, January 22, 2016.

United Nations Security Council. Santino Deng Wol. SSi.004. https://www.un.org/ securitycouncil/sanctions/2206/materials/summaries/individual/santino-deng-wol.

USGS & USAID. *A Climate Trend Analysis of Sudan*. Famine Early Warning Systems Network—Informing Climate Change Adaptation Series. USGS & USAID, 2011.

Utas, Mats. "West-African Warscapes: Victimcy, Girlfriending, Soldiering: Tactic Agency in a Young Woman's Social Navigation of the Liberian War Zone." *Anthropological Quarterly* 78, no. 2 (2005): 403–30.

Van Der Kolk, Bessel. *The Body Keeps The Score. Brain, Mind And Body In The Healing of Trauma*. New York: Penguin Books, 2015.

Vaughan, Christopher, Mareike Schomerus, and Lotje De Vries, eds. *The Borderlands of South Sudan: Authority and Identity in Contemporary and Historical Perspectives*. New York: Palgrave Macmillan, 2013.

Volkan, Vamık D., and J. Christopher Fowler. "Large-Group Narcissism and Political Leaders with Narcissistic Personality Organization." *Psychiatric Annals* 39, no. 4 (April 2009): 214–23.

Vuylsteke, Sarah. *Identity and Self-Determination: The Fertit Opposition in South Sudan*. Geneva: Small Arms Survey, December 2018.

Wai, Dunstan M. *The African-Arab Conflict in the Sudan*. New York: Africana Publishing Company, 1981.

Walraet, Anne. "Displacement in Post-War Southern Sudan: Survival and Accumulation within Urban Perimeters." MICROCON: A Micro Level Analysis of Violent Conflict. Brighton: Institute of Development Studies at the University of Sussex, 2011.

——. "Governance, Violence and the Struggle for Economic Regulation in South Sudan: The Case of Budi County (Eastern Equatoria)." *Afrika Focus* 21, no. 2 (2008): 53–70.

——. "South Sudan: Violence as Politics." In *Africa's Insurgents. Navigating an Evolving Landscape.*, edited by Morten Bøås and Kevin C. Dunn, 197–216. Boulder, CO: Lynne Rienner Publishers, 2017.

——. "State-Making in Southern Sudan-Kenyan Border Area." In *The Borderlands of South Sudan. Authority and Identity in Historical Perspectives.*, edited by Christopher Vaughan, Mareike Schomerus, and Lotje De Vries, 173–92. New York: Palgrave Macmillan, 2013.

——. "Violence et Géographie du Pouvoir et de l'Enrichissement dans la Zone Frontière de Chukudum (Sud Soudan)." *Politique africaine* N° 111, no. 3 (October 1, 2008): 90–109.

Weber, Max. *Economy and Society: An Outline of Interpretive Sociology*. Edited by Guenther Roth and Claus Wittich. 4th ed. Berkeley: University of California Press, 1978.

Weinstein, Jeremy M. *Inside Rebellion: The Politics of Insurgent Violence*. Cambridge: Cambridge University Press, 2007.

Weitz, Eric D. *A Century of Genocide: Utopias of Race and Nation*. Princeton, NJ: Princeton University Press, 2003.

Willems, Rens, and David Deng. "The Legacy of Kokora in South Sudan. Intersections of Truth, Justice and Reconciliation in South Sudan." Briefing paper, South Sudan Law Society, University for Peace, Pax Christi, November 2015.

Wood, Elisabeth Jean. "Variation in Sexual Violence during War." *Politics and Society* 34, no. 3 (September 2006): 307–41.

Woodward, Peter. *Sudan, 1898–1989: The Unstable State*. Boulder, CO: Lynne Rienner Publishers Inc, 1990.

Yiftachel, Oren. "'Ethnocracy': The Politics of Judaizing Israel/Palestine." *Constellations: An International Journal of Critical and Democratic Theory* 6, no. 3 (1999): 364–90.

Yongo-Bure, Benaiah. *Economic Development of Southern Sudan*. Lanham, MD: University Press of America, Inc, 2007.

——. "The Underdevelopment of the Southern Sudan since Independence." In *Civil War in the Sudan*, edited by M. W. Daly and Ahmad Alawad Sikainga, 51–77. London: British Academy Press, 1993.

Young, John. *The Fate of Sudan: The Origins and Consequences of a Flawed Peace Process*. London: Zed Books, 2012.

——. *The South Sudan Defence Forces in the Wake of the Juba Declaration*. Geneva: Small Arms Survey, November 2006.

——. *South Sudan's Civil War: Violence, Insurgency and Failed Peacemaking*. London: Zed Books Ltd, 2019.

——. *The White Army: An Introduction and Overview*. Geneva: Small Arms Survey, 2007.

Index

Milton Keynes UK
Ingram Content Group UK Ltd.
UKHW031014101024
449496UK00004B/139